D1171553

DESCUBRE 1B

Lengua y cultura del mundo hispánico

VISTA®
HIGHER LEARNING
Boston, Massachusetts

On the cover: Hand carved gourds for sale at the outdoor craft market in Otavalo, Ecuador

Publisher: José A. Blanco
Professional Development Director: Norah Lulich Jones
Editorial Development: Brian Contreras, Diego García, Sharla Zwirek
Project Management: Kayli Brownstein, Hillary Gospodarek, Sharon Inglis
Rights Management: Ashley Dos Santos, Jorgensen Fernandez, Caitlin O'Brien
Technology Production: Jamie Kostecki, Fabián Montoya, Paola Ríos Schaaf
Design: Gabriel Noreña, Andrés Vanegas
Production: Manuela Arango, Sergio Arias, Oscar Díez

© 2017 by Vista Higher Learning, Inc. All rights reserved.
No part of this work may be reproduced or distributed in any form or by any means, electronic or mechanical, including photocopying and recording, or by any information storage or retrieval system without prior written permission from Vista Higher Learning, 500 Boylston Street, Suite 620, Boston, MA 02116-3736.

Student Text ISBN: 978-1-68004-321-1
Library of Congress Control Number: 2015948650

3 4 5 6 7 8 9 TC 20 19 18

Printed in Canada.

DESCUBRE 1B

Lengua y cultura del mundo hispánico

Table of Contents

Map of the Spanish-Speaking World viii
Map of Mexico x
Map of Central America and the Caribbean xi
Map of South America xii

hola, ¿qué tal?

Lección preliminar

Nouns and articles 2
Numbers 0–30 2
Present tense of **ser** 3
Telling time 3

en la clase

Present tense of **-ar** verbs 4
Forming questions in Spanish . . 4
Present tense of **estar** 5
Numbers 31 and higher 5

Lección 5
Las vacaciones

contextos

Travel and vacation 152
Months of the year 154
Seasons and weather 154
Ordinal numbers 155

fotonovela

¡Vamos a la playa! 158
Pronunciación
Spanish **b** and **v** 161

Lección 6
¡De compras!

Clothing and shopping 190
Negotiating a price and buying 190
Colors 192
More adjectives 192

En el mercado 194
Pronunciación
The consonants **d** and **t** 197

Map of Spain xiii
Video Programs xiv
Supersite xvi
Icons xvii

Studying Spanish xviii
Getting Started xxv
Acknowledgments xxvii
Bios xxix

cultura

El español en Latinoamérica . . . 8

la familia

Descriptive adjectives 10
Possessive adjectives 10
Present tense of **-er** and **-ir** verbs 11
Present tense of **tener** and **venir** 11

los pasatiempos

Present tense of ir 12
Stem-changing verbs: **e:ie**, **o:ue** 12
Stem-changing verbs: **e:i** 13
Verbs with irregular **yo** forms 13

cultura

En detalle: Las cataratas del Iguazú 162
Perfil: Punta del Este 163

En detalle: Los mercados al aire libre 198
Perfil: Carolina Herrera 199

estructura

5.1 **Estar** with conditions and emotions 164
5.2 The present progressive 166
5.3 **Ser** and **estar** 170
5.4 Direct object nouns and pronouns 174
Recapitulación 178

6.1 **Saber** and **conocer** 200
6.2 Indirect object pronouns 202
6.3 Preterite tense of regular verbs 206
6.4 Demonstrative adjectives and pronouns 210
Recapitulación 214

adelante

Lectura: *Turismo ecológico en Puerto Rico* 180
Escritura 182
Escuchar 183
En pantalla 184
Flash cultura 185
Panorama: Puerto Rico 186

Lectura: *Corona: Real Liquidación* 216
Escritura 218
Escuchar 219
En pantalla 220
Flash cultura 221
Panorama: Cuba 222

Table of Contents

	contextos	fotonovela
Lección 7 **La rutina diaria**	Daily routine . . . . . 226 Personal hygiene . . . . . 226 Time expressions 226	**¡Necesito arreglarme!** . . . . . 230 **Pronunciación** The consonant **r** 233
Lección 8 **La comida**	Food . . . . . 262 Food descriptions . . . . . 262 Meals 264	**Una cena... romántica** . . . . . 268 **Pronunciación** **ll, ñ, c,** and **z** 271
Lección 9 **Las fiestas**	Parties and celebrations . . . . . 300 Personal relationships. . . . . 301 Stages of life 302	**El Día de Muertos** . . . . . 304 **Pronunciación** **h, j,** and **g** 307

Consulta

Apéndice A

Glossary of Grammatical Terms 332

Apéndice B

Verb Conjugation Tables 336

Vocabulario

Spanish-English Vocabulary 346

English-Spanish Vocabulary 357

cultura	estructura	adelante

En detalle: La siesta 234
Perfil: El mate 235

7.1 Reflexive verbs 236
7.2 Indefinite and negative words 240
7.3 Preterite of **ser** and **ir** . . . 244
7.4 Verbs like **gustar** 246
Recapitulación 250

Lectura: *¡Qué día!* 252
Escritura 254
Escuchar 255
En pantalla 256
Flash cultura 257
Panorama: Perú 258

En detalle: Frutas y verduras de América 272
Perfil: Ferran Adrià: arte en la cocina 273

8.1 Preterite of stem-changing verbs 274
8.2 Double object pronouns . 277
8.3 Comparisons 281
8.4 Superlatives 286
Recapitulación 288

Lectura: *Gastronomía* 290
Escritura 292
Escuchar 293
En pantalla 294
Flash cultura 295
Panorama: Guatemala. 296

En detalle: Semana Santa: vacaciones y tradición 308
Perfil: Festival de Viña del Mar 309

9.1 Irregular preterites 310
9.2 Verbs that change meaning in the preterite . 314
9.3 **¿Qué?** and **¿cuál?** 316
9.4 Pronouns after prepositions. 318
Recapitulación 320

Lectura: *Vida social* 322
Escritura 324
Escuchar 325
En pantalla 326
Flash cultura 327
Panorama: Chile. 328

References 368
Índice 380
Credits 382

The Spanish-Speaking World

OCÉANO ÁRTICO
Mar de Kara
Mar de Laptev
Mar de Barents
1. DINAMARCA
2. PAÍSES BAJOS (HOLANDA)
3. BÉLGICA
4. LUXEMBURGO
5. SUIZA
6. REPÚBLICA CHECA
7. ESLOVAQUIA
8. HUNGRÍA
9. ESLOVENIA
10. CROACIA
11. BOSNIA-HERZEGOVINA
12. SERBIA
13. MONTENEGRO
14. ALBANIA
15. MACEDONIA
16. BULGARIA
17. MALTA
Mar de Noruega
ISLANDIA
SUECIA
FINLANDIA
NORUEGA
RUSIA
ESTONIA
LETONIA
LITUANIA
Mar del Norte
REINO UNIDO
IRLANDA
POLONIA
BIELORRUSIA
ALEMANIA
UCRANIA
MOLDAVIA
FRANCIA
AUSTRIA
RUMANIA
ITALIA
Mar Negro
Mar Caspio
KAZAJISTÁN
Mar de Aral
MONGOLIA
UZBEKISTÁN
KIRGUISTÁN
GEORGIA
ARMENIA
PORTUGAL
ESPAÑA
GRECIA
TURQUÍA
TURKMENISTÁN
TAYIKISTÁN
COREA DEL NORTE
Mar de Japón
COREA DEL SUR
GIBRALTAR (R.U.)
TÚNEZ
Mar Mediterráneo
CHIPRE
LÍBANO
ISRAEL
SIRIA
AZERBAIYÁN
IRÁN
AFGANISTÁN
CHINA
JAPÓN
MARRUECOS
IRAQ
JORDANIA
KUWAIT
PAKISTÁN
NEPAL
BUTÁN
ARGELIA
LIBIA
EGIPTO
BAHRÉIN
QATAR
SAHARA OCCIDENTAL
ARABIA SAUDITA
E.A.U.
OMÁN
INDIA
MYANMAR (BIRMANIA)
TAIWÁN
OCÉANO PACÍFICO
CABO VERDE
MAURITANIA
MALÍ
NÍGER
CHAD
SUDÁN
BANGLADESH
LAOS
TAILANDIA
Mar de China Meridional
SENEGAL
ERITREA
YEMEN
Mar Arábigo
Golfo de Bengala
CAMBOYA
VIETNAM
FILIPINAS
GUAM
GAMBIA
GUINEA
BURKINA FASO
SUDÁN DEL SUR
YIBUTI
GUINEA-BISSAU
COSTA DE MARFIL
NIGERIA
REPÚBLICA CENTROAFRICANA
ETIOPÍA
SRI LANKA
BRUNÉI
SIERRA LEONA
BENÍN
CAMERÚN
SOMALIA
ISLAS MALDIVAS
MALASIA
LIBERIA
GHANA
TOGO
UGANDA
KENIA
GUINEA ECUATORIAL
GABÓN
RUANDA
BURUNDI
SINGAPUR
REPÚBLICA DEMOCRÁTICA DEL CONGO
TANZANIA
SEYCHELLES
INDONESIA
PAPÚA Y NUEVA GUINEA
REPÚBLICA DEL CONGO
CABINDA (ANGOLA)
ANGOLA
COMORES
ZAMBIA
MALAWI
TIMOR ORIENTAL
MOZAMBIQUE
OCÉANO ATLÁNTICO
NAMIBIA
ZIMBABUE
MADAGASCAR
ISLA MAURICIO
BOTSUANA
AUSTRALIA
SWAZILANDIA
SUDÁFRICA
LESOTO
OCÉANO ÍNDICO
N
O
E
S
0
1,000
2,000 millas
0
1,000
2,000 kilómetros
ANTÁRTIDA

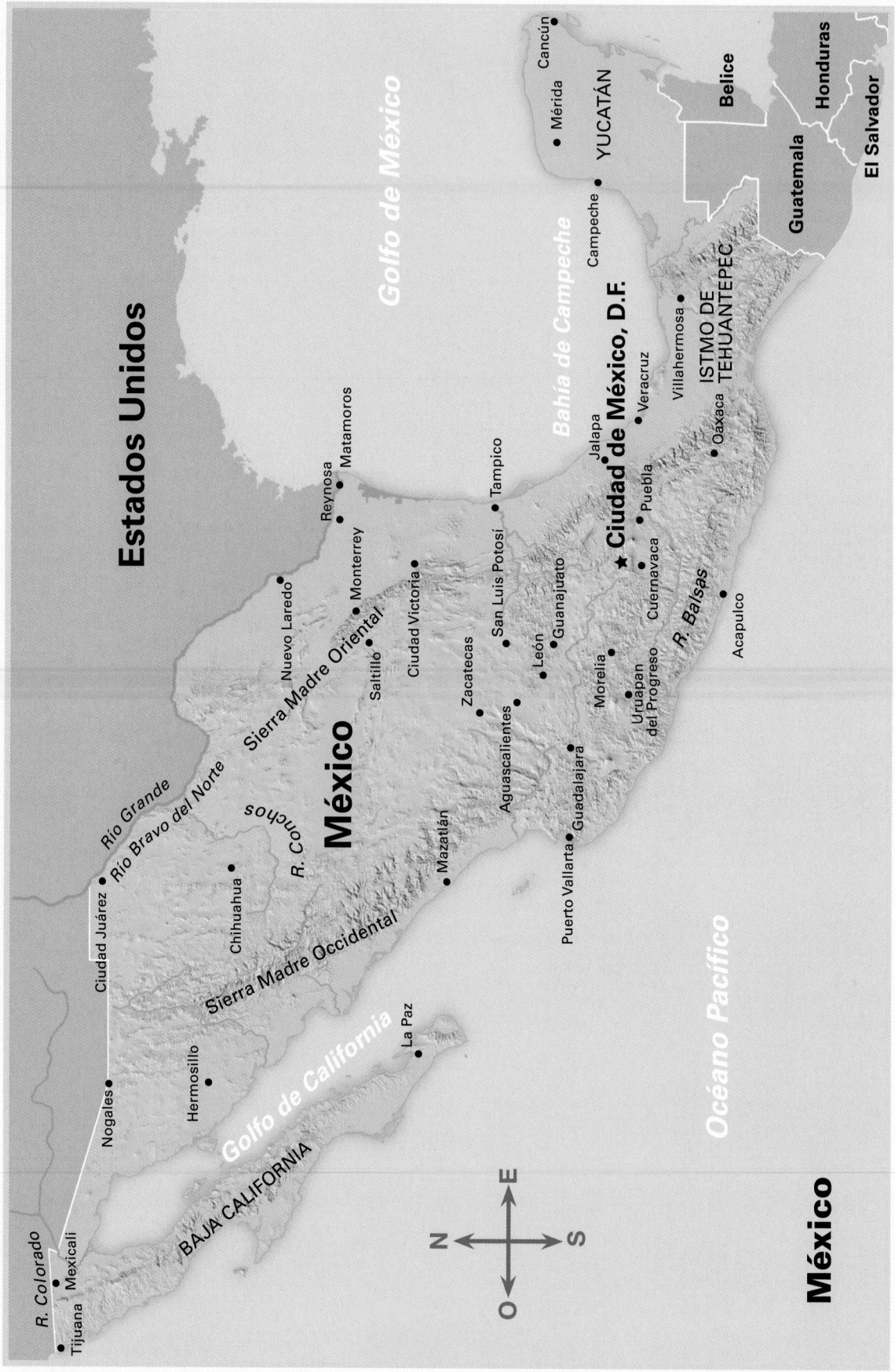
Estados Unidos
Golfo de México
Bahía de Campeche
Cancún
Mérida
YUCATÁN
Campeche
Belice
Guatemala
Honduras
El Salvador
Ciudad de México, D.F.
Jalapa
Veracruz
Villahermosa
ISTMO DE TEHUANTEPEC
Oaxaca
Puebla
Cuernavaca
Acapulco
R. Balsas
Tampico
Matamoros
Reynosa
Monterrey
Nuevo Laredo
Sierra Madre Oriental
Saltillo
Ciudad Victoria
San Luis Potosí
Guanajuato
León
Zacatecas
Aguascalientes
Morelia
Uruapan del Progreso
Guadalajara
Puerto Vallarta
Mazatlán
R. Conchos
México
Río Grande
Río Bravo del Norte
Ciudad Juárez
Chihuahua
Sierra Madre Occidental
La Paz
Hermosillo
Nogales
Golfo de California
BAJA CALIFORNIA
R. Colorado
Mexicali
Tijuana
Océano Pacífico
N
O
E
S
México

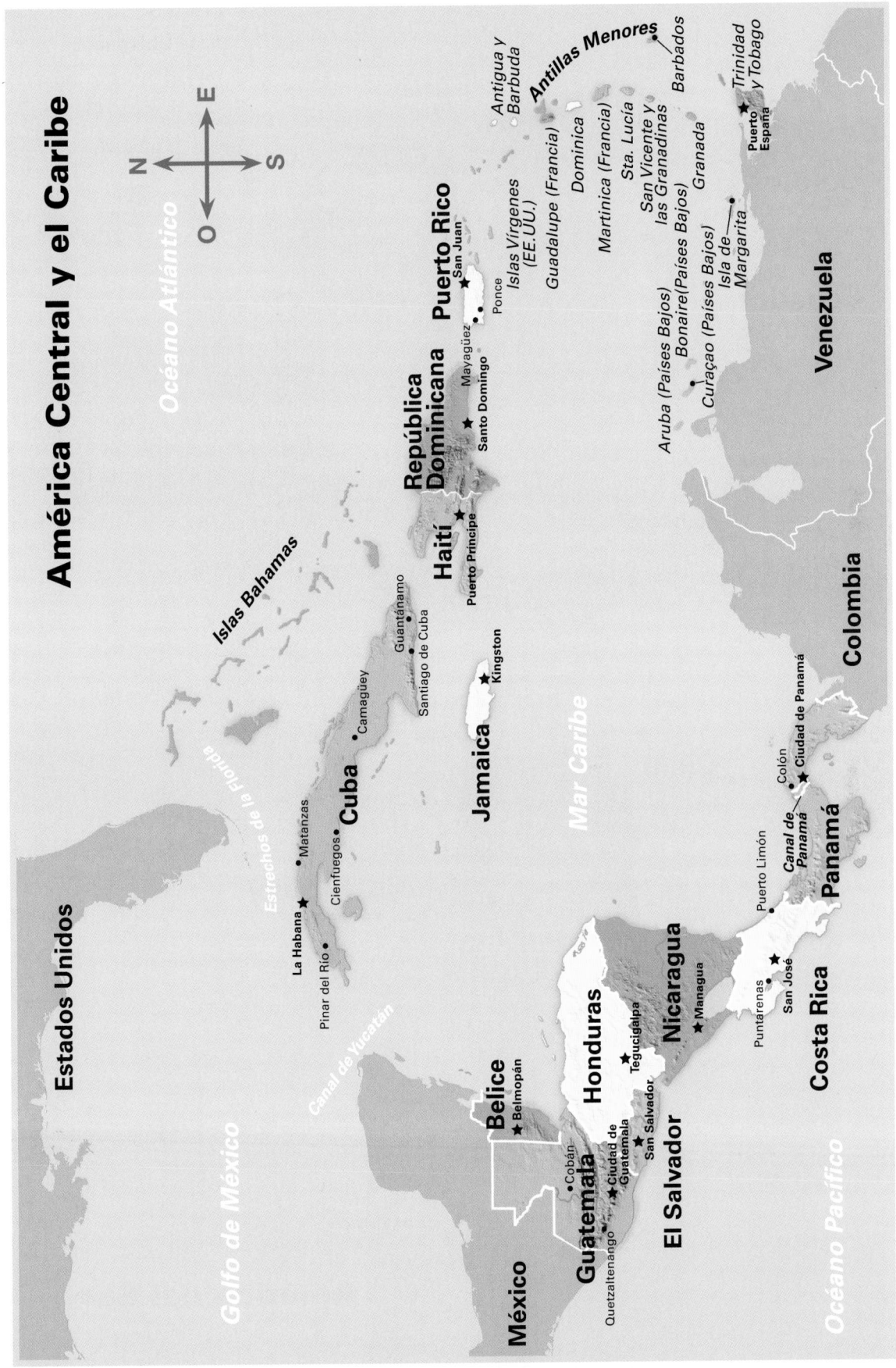
América Central y el Caribe
N
O
E
S
Océano Atlántico
Estados Unidos
Islas Bahamas
Golfo de México
Estrechos de la Florida
Canal de Yucatán
La Habana
Matanzas
Pinar del Río
Cienfuegos
Cuba
Camagüey
Guantánamo
Santiago de Cuba
Jamaica
Kingston
Haití
Puerto Príncipe
República Dominicana
Santo Domingo
Mayagüez
Puerto Rico
San Juan
Ponce
Islas Vírgenes (EE.UU.)
Antigua y Barbuda
Antillas Menores
Guadalupe (Francia)
Dominica
Martinica (Francia)
Sta. Lucía
San Vicente y las Granadinas
Barbados
Granada
Trinidad y Tobago
Puerto España
Aruba (Países Bajos)
Bonaire(Países Bajos)
Curaçao (Países Bajos)
Isla de Margarita
Venezuela
Colombia
Mar Caribe
Ciudad de Panamá
Colón
Canal de Panamá
Panamá
Puerto Limón
Puntarenas
San José
Costa Rica
Nicaragua
Managua
Honduras
Tegucigalpa
Belice
Belmopán
Cobán
Guatemala
Ciudad de Guatemala
Quetzaltenango
San Salvador
El Salvador
México
Océano Pacífico

South America

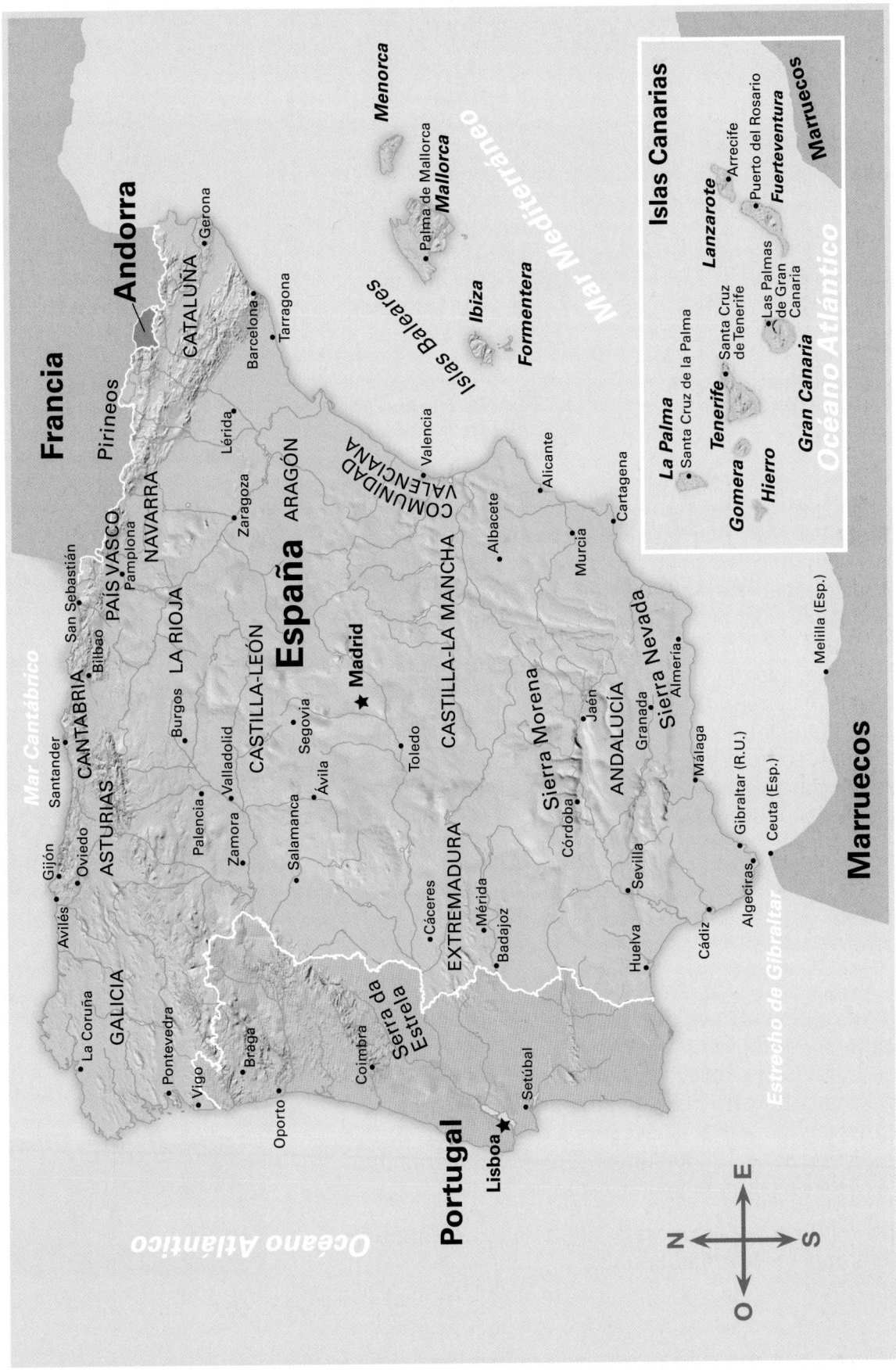
Francia
Andorra
Pirineos
Mar Cantábrico
Gijón
Santander
Oviedo
Avilés
ASTURIAS
CANTABRIA
Bilbao
San Sebastián
PAÍS VASCO
Pamplona
NAVARRA
LA RIOJA
CATALUÑA
Gerona
Barcelona
Tarragona
Lérida
Zaragoza
ARAGÓN
España
Madrid
CASTILLA-LEÓN
Burgos
Valladolid
Segovia
Ávila
Palencia
Zamora
Salamanca
CASTILLA-LA MANCHA
Toledo
Albacete
COMUNIDAD VALENCIANA
Valencia
Alicante
Murcia
Cartagena
Islas Baleares
Menorca
Palma de Mallorca
Mallorca
Ibiza
Formentera
Mar Mediterráneo
La Coruña
GALICIA
Pontevedra
Vigo
Braga
Oporto
Coimbra
Serra da Estrela
Portugal
Lisboa
Setúbal
EXTREMADURA
Cáceres
Mérida
Badajoz
Sierra Morena
Córdoba
Sevilla
Huelva
ANDALUCÍA
Jaén
Granada
Sierra Nevada
Almería
Málaga
Cádiz
Algeciras
Gibraltar (R.U.)
Ceuta (Esp.)
Melilla (Esp.)
Marruecos
Estrecho de Gibraltar
Océano Atlántico
Islas Canarias
La Palma
Santa Cruz de la Palma
Tenerife
Santa Cruz de Tenerife
Gomera
Hierro
Lanzarote
Arrecife
Puerto del Rosario
Fuerteventura
Las Palmas de Gran Canaria
Gran Canaria
Océano Atlántico
Marruecos
N
O
E
S

Fotonovela video program

The Cast

Here are the main characters you will meet in the **Fotonovela** Video:

From Mexico,
Jimena Díaz Velázquez

From Argentina,
Juan Carlos Rossi

From the U.S.,
Marissa Wagner

From Mexico,
Felipe Díaz Velázquez

From Mexico,
María Eugenia (Maru)
Castaño Ricaurte

From Spain,
Miguel Ángel
Lagasca Martínez

Fully integrated with your text, the ***Descubre*** **Fotonovela** Video is a dynamic and contemporary window into the Spanish language. The video centers around the Díaz family, whose household includes two college-aged children and a visiting student from the U.S. Over the course of an academic year, Jimena, Felipe, Marissa, and their friends explore **el D.F.** and other parts of Mexico as they make plans for their futures. Their adventures take them through some of the greatest natural and cultural treasures of the Spanish-speaking world, as well as the highs and lows of everyday life.

The **Fotonovela** section in each textbook lesson is actually an abbreviated version of the dramatic episode featured in the video. Therefore, each **Fotonovela** section can be done before you see the corresponding video episode, after it, or as a section that stands alone.

In each dramatic segment, the characters interact using the vocabulary and grammar you are studying. As the storyline unfolds, the episodes combine new vocabulary and grammar with previously taught language, exposing you to a variety of authentic accents along the way. At the end of each episode, the **Resumen** section highlights the grammar and vocabulary you are studying.

We hope you find the **Fotonovela** Video to be an engaging and useful tool for learning Spanish!

En pantalla video program

The ***Descubre*** Supersite features an authentic video clip for each lesson. Clip formats include commercials and newscasts. These clips have been carefully chosen to be comprehensible for students learning Spanish, and are accompanied by activities and vocabulary lists to facilitate understanding. More importantly, though, these clips are a fun and motivating way to improve your Spanish!

Here are the countries represented in each lesson in **En pantalla**:

Lesson 5 **Chile**
Lesson 6 **Spain**
Lesson 7 **Argentina**
Lesson 8 **Colombia**
Lesson 9 **Chile**

Flash cultura video program

In the dynamic **Flash cultura** Video, young people from all over the Spanish-speaking world share aspects of life in their countries with you. The similarities and differences among Spanish-speaking countries that come up through their adventures will challenge you to think about your own cultural practices and values. The segments provide valuable cultural insights as well as linguistic input; the episodes will introduce you to a variety of accents and vocabulary as they gradually move into Spanish.

Panorama cultural video program

The **Panorama cultural** Video is integrated with the **Panorama** section in each lesson. Each segment is 2–3 minutes long and consists of documentary footage from each of the countries featured. The images were specially chosen for interest level and visual appeal, while the all-Spanish narrations were carefully written to reflect the vocabulary and grammar covered in the textbook.

Supersite

Each section of your textbook comes with resources and activities on the ***Descubre*** Supersite. You can access them from any computer with an Internet connection. Visit vhlcentral.com to get started.

My Vocabulary Tutorials	**CONTEXTOS** Listen to audio of the **Vocabulary**, watch dynamic **Tutorials**, and practice using Flashcards.
Video: *Fotonovela*	**FOTONOVELA** Travel with Marissa to Mexico and meet her host family. Watch the **Video** again at home to see the characters use the vocabulary in a real context.
Audio	**PRONUNCIACIÓN** Improve your accent by listening to native speakers, then recording your voice and comparing it to the samples provided.
Additional Reading	**CULTURA** Explore cultural topics through the ***Conexión Internet*** activity or reading the ***Más cultura*** selection.
Tutorial	**ESTRUCTURA** Watch an animated **Tutorial**, and then answer *el profesor*'s questions to make sure you got it.
Audio: Reading Additional Reading Audio Video: TV Clip Video: *Flash cultura* Video: *Panorama cultural* Interactive Map	**ADELANTE** Listen along as the **reading** is read aloud. Read another selection related to the chapter's theme. Listen again to the audio from ***Escuchar***. Watch the **En pantalla**, **Flash cultura**, and **Panorama cultural Videos** again outside of class so that you can pause and repeat to really understand what you hear. Use the **Interactive Map** to explore the places you might want to visit.
My Vocabulary Diagnostics	**VOCABULARIO - RECAPITULACIÓN** Just what you need to get ready for the test! Review the **vocabulary** with **audio**. Practice vocabulary with Flashcards in **My Vocabulary**. Complete the Diagnostic ***Recapitulación*** to see what you might still need to study. Get additional **Remediation Activities**.

Icons

Familiarize yourself with these icons that appear throughout ***Descubre***.

Listening

The listening icon indicates that audio is available. You will see it in the lesson's **Contextos**, **Pronunciación**, **Escuchar**, and **Vocabulario** sections.

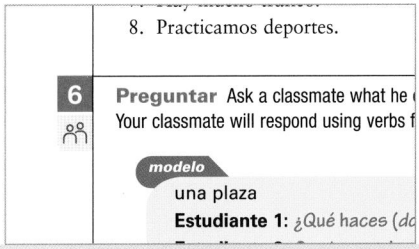

Pair Activities

Two heads indicate a pair activity.

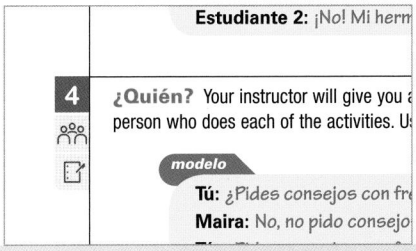

Handout

The activities marked with this icon require handouts that your teacher will give you to help you complete the activity.

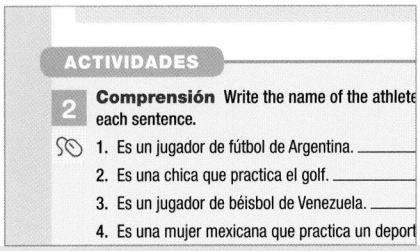

Activity Online

The mouse icon indicates when an activity is also available on the Supersite.

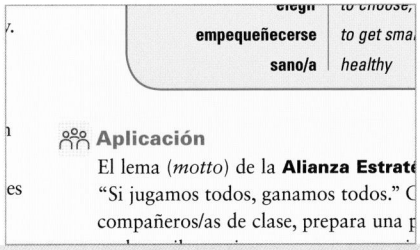

Group Activities

Three heads indicate a group activity.

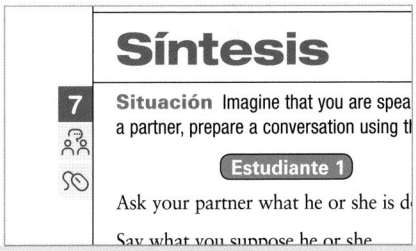

Partner Chat/Virtual Chat Activities

Two heads with a speech bubble indicate that the activity may be assigned as a Partner Chat or a Virtual Chat activity on the Supersite.

Recursos

Recursos boxes let you know exactly which print and technology ancillaries you can use to reinforce and expand on every section of the lessons in your textbook. They even include page numbers when applicable.

vText
Materials also available in the interactive online textbook

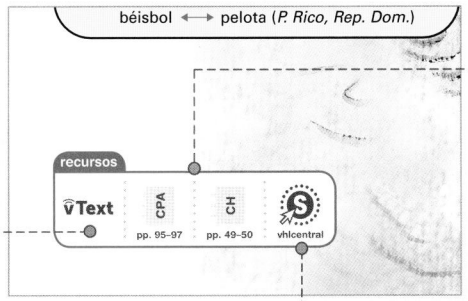

CPA Cuaderno de práctica y actividades comunicativas

CH Cuaderno para hispanohablantes

Two workbooks with additional vocabulary and grammar practice; audio activities; and pre-, during, and post-viewing activities for the video programs.

Supersite
Additional practice on the Supersite, not included in the textbook.

The Spanish-Speaking World

Spanish Speakers Outside of the U.S. and Canada

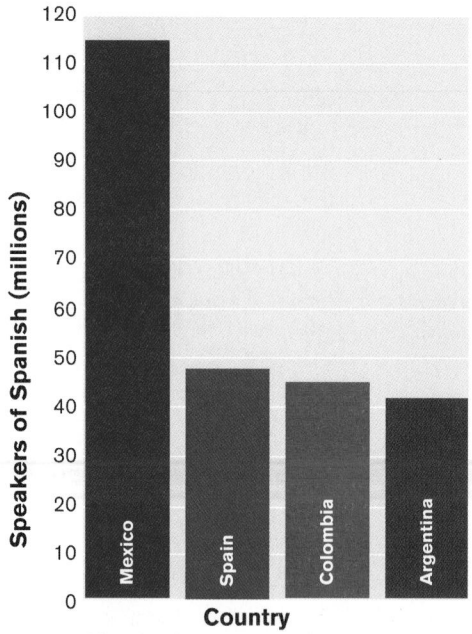

SOURCE: CIA Factbook, 2012 Estimates.

Do you know someone whose first language is Spanish? Chances are you do! More than approximately forty million people living in the U.S. speak Spanish; after English, it is the second most commonly spoken language in this country. It is the official language of twenty-two countries and an official language of the European Union and United Nations.

The Growth of Spanish

Have you ever heard of a language called Castilian? It's Spanish! The Spanish language as we know it today has its origins in a dialect called Castilian (**castellano** in Spanish). Castilian developed in the 9th century in north-central Spain, in a historic provincial region known as Old Castile. Castilian gradually spread towards the central region of New Castile, where it was adopted as the main language of commerce. By the 16th century, Spanish had become the official language of Spain and eventually, the country's role in exploration, colonization, and overseas trade led to its spread across Central and South America, North America, the Caribbean, parts of North Africa, the Canary Islands, and the Philippines.

Spanish in the United States

1500 **1600** **1700**

16th Century
Spanish is the official language of Spain.

1565
The Spanish arrive in Florida and found St. Augustine.

1610
The Spanish found Santa Fe, today's capital of New Mexico, the state with the most Spanish speakers in the U.S.

Spanish in the United States

Spanish came to North America in the 16th century with the Spanish who settled in St. Augustine, Florida. Spanish-speaking communities flourished in several parts of the continent over the next few centuries. Then, in 1848, in the aftermath of the Mexican-American War, Mexico lost almost half its land to the United States, including portions of modern-day Texas, New Mexico, Arizona, Colorado, California, Wyoming, Nevada, and Utah. Overnight, hundreds of thousands of Mexicans became citizens of the United States, bringing with them their rich history, language, and traditions.

This heritage, combined with that of the other Hispanic populations that have immigrated to the United States over the years, has led to the remarkable growth of Spanish around the country. After English, it is the most commonly spoken language in 43 states. More than 12 million people in California alone claim Spanish as their first or "home" language.

You've made a popular choice by choosing to take Spanish in school. Not only is Spanish found and heard almost everywhere in the United States, but it is the most commonly taught foreign language in classrooms throughout the country! Have you heard people speaking Spanish in your community? Chances are that you've come across an advertisement, menu, or magazine that is in Spanish. If you look around, you'll find that Spanish can be found in some pretty common places. For example, most ATMs respond to users in both English and Spanish. News agencies and television stations such as **CNN** and **Telemundo** provide Spanish-language broadcasts. When you listen to the radio or download music from the Internet, some of the most popular choices are Latino artists who perform in Spanish. Federal government agencies such as the Internal Revenue Service and the Department of State provide services in both languages. Even the White House has an official Spanish-language webpage! Learning Spanish can create opportunities within your everyday life.

1800

1848
Mexicans who choose to stay in the U.S. after the Mexican-American War become U.S. citizens.

1900

1959
After the Cuban Revolution, thousands of Cubans emigrate to the U.S.

2010

2010
Spanish is the 2nd most commonly spoken language in the U.S., with more than approximately 40 million speakers.

Why Study Spanish?

Learn an International Language

There are many reasons to learn Spanish, a language that has spread to many parts of the world and has along the way embraced words and sounds of languages as diverse as Latin, Arabic, and Nahuatl. Spanish has evolved from a medieval dialect of north-central Spain into the fourth most commonly spoken language in the world. It is the second language of choice among the majority of people in North America.

Understand the World Around You

Knowing Spanish can also open doors to communities within the United States, and it can broaden your understanding of the nation's history and geography. The very names Colorado, Montana, Nevada, and Florida are Spanish in origin. Just knowing their meanings can give you some insight into, of all things, the landscapes for which the states are renowned. Colorado means "colored red;" Montana means "mountain;" Nevada is derived from "snow-capped mountain;" and Florida means "flowered." You've already been speaking Spanish whenever you talk about some of these states!

State Name	Meaning in Spanish
Colorado	"colored red"
Florida	"flowered"
Montana	"mountain"
Nevada	"snow-capped mountain"

Connect with the World

Learning Spanish can change how you view the world. While you learn Spanish, you will also explore and learn about the origins, customs, art, music, and literature of people in close to two dozen countries. When you travel to a Spanish-speaking country, you'll be able to converse freely with the people you meet. And whether in the U.S., Canada, or abroad, you'll find that speaking to people in their native language is the best way to bridge any culture gap.

Why Study Spanish?

Explore Your Future

How many of you are already planning your future careers? Employers in today's global economy look for workers who know different languages and understand other cultures. Your knowledge of Spanish will make you a valuable candidate for careers abroad as well as in the United States or Canada. Doctors, nurses, social workers, hotel managers, journalists, businessmen, pilots, flight attendants, and many other professionals need to know Spanish or another foreign language to do their jobs well.

Expand Your Skills

Studying a foreign language can improve your ability to analyze and interpret information and help you succeed in many other subject areas. When you first begin learning Spanish, your studies will focus mainly on reading, writing, grammar, listening, and speaking skills. You'll be amazed at how the skills involved with learning how a language works can help you succeed in other areas of study. Many people who study a foreign language claim that they gained a better understanding of English. Spanish can even help you understand the origins of many English words and expand your own vocabulary in English. Knowing Spanish can also help you pick up other related languages, such as Italian, Portuguese, and French. Spanish can really open doors for learning many other skills in your school career.

How to Learn Spanish

Start with the Basics!

As with anything you want to learn, start with the basics and remember that learning takes time! The basics are vocabulary, grammar, and culture.

Vocabulary | Every new word you learn in Spanish will expand your vocabulary and ability to communicate. The more words you know, the better you can express yourself. Focus on sounds and think about ways to remember words. Use your knowledge of English and other languages to figure out the meaning of and memorize words like **conversación, teléfono, oficina, clase,** and **música**.

Grammar | Grammar helps you put your new vocabulary together. By learning the rules of grammar, you can use new words correctly and speak in complete sentences. As you learn verbs and tenses, you will be able to speak about the past, present, or future, express yourself with clarity, and be able to persuade others with your opinions. Pay attention to structures and use your knowledge of English grammar to make connections with Spanish grammar.

Culture | Culture provides you with a framework for what you may say or do. As you learn about the culture of Spanish-speaking communities, you'll improve your knowledge of Spanish. Think about a word like **salsa**, and how it connects to both food and music. Think about and explore customs observed on **Nochevieja** (New Year's Eve) or at a **fiesta de quince años** (a girl's fifteenth birthday party). Watch people greet each other or say good-bye. Listen for idioms and sayings that capture the spirit of what you want to communicate!

Teenagers celebrating at a **fiesta de quince años.**

Listen, Speak, Read, and Write

Listening | Listen for sounds and for words you can recognize. Listen for inflections and watch for key words that signal a question such as **cómo** (*how*), **dónde** (*where*), or **qué** (*what*). Get used to the sound of Spanish. Play Spanish pop songs or watch Spanish movies. Borrow books on CD from your local library, or try to visit places in your community where Spanish is spoken. Don't worry if you don't understand every single word. If you focus on key words and phrases, you'll get the main idea. The more you listen, the more you'll understand!

Speaking | Practice speaking Spanish as often as you can. As you talk, work on your pronunciation, and read aloud texts so that words and sentences flow more easily. Don't worry if you don't sound like a native speaker, or if you make some mistakes. Time and practice will help you get there. Participate actively in Spanish class. Try to speak Spanish with classmates, especially native speakers (if you know any), as often as you can.

Reading | Pick up a Spanish-language newspaper or a pamphlet on your way to school, read the lyrics of a song as you listen to it, or read books you've already read in English translated into Spanish. Use reading strategies that you know to understand the meaning of a text that looks unfamiliar. Look for cognates, or words that are related in English and Spanish, to guess the meaning of some words. Read as often as you can, and remember to read for fun!

Writing | It's easy to write in Spanish if you put your mind to it. And remember that Spanish spelling is phonetic, which means that once you learn the basic rules of how letters and sounds are related, you can probably become an expert speller in Spanish! Write for fun—make up poems or songs, write e-mails or instant messages to friends, or start a journal or blog in Spanish.

Tips for Learning Spanish

Practice, practice, practice!

Seize every opportunity you find to listen, speak, read, or write Spanish. Think of it like a sport or learning a musical instrument—the more you practice, the more you will become comfortable with the language and how it works. You'll marvel at how quickly you can begin speaking Spanish and how the world that it transports you to can change your life forever!

- Listen to Spanish radio shows. Write down words that you can't recognize or don't know and look up the meaning.
- Watch Spanish TV shows or movies. Read subtitles to help you grasp the content.
- Read Spanish-language newspapers, magazines, or blogs.
- Listen to Spanish songs that you like —anything from Shakira to a traditional mariachi melody. Sing along and concentrate on your pronunciation.

- Seek out Spanish speakers. Look for neighborhoods, markets, or cultural centers where Spanish might be spoken in your community. Greet people, ask for directions, or order from a menu at a Mexican restaurant in Spanish.
- Pursue language exchange opportunities (**intercambio cultural**) in your school or community. Try to join language clubs or cultural societies, and explore opportunities for studying abroad or hosting a student from a Spanish-speaking country in your home or school.
- Connect your learning to everyday experiences. Think about naming the ingredients of your favorite dish in Spanish. Think about the origins of Spanish place names in the U.S., like Cape Canaveral and Sacramento, or of common English words like *adobe, chocolate, mustang, tornado,* and *patio*.
- Use mnemonics, or a memorizing device, to help you remember words. Make up a saying in English to remember the order of the days of the week in Spanish (L, M, M, J, V, S, D).
- Visualize words. Try to associate words with images to help you remember meanings. For example, think of a **paella** as you learn the names of different types of seafood or meat. Imagine a national park and create mental pictures of the landscape as you learn names of animals, plants, and habitats.
- Enjoy yourself! Try to have as much fun as you can learning Spanish. Take your knowledge beyond the classroom and find ways to make the learning experience your very own.

Useful Spanish Expressions

The following expressions will be very useful in getting you started learning Spanish. You can use them in class to check your understanding or to ask and answer questions about the lessons. Read **En las instrucciones** ahead of time to help you understand direction lines in Spanish, as well as your teacher's instructions. Remember to practice your Spanish as often as you can!

En las instrucciones	*In direction lines*
Cierto o falso	*True or false*
Completa las oraciones de una manera lógica.	*Complete the sentences logically.*
Con un(a) compañero/a...	*With a classmate...*
Contesta las preguntas.	*Answer the questions.*
Corrige la información falsa.	*Correct the false information.*
Di/Digan...	*Say...*
En grupos...	*In groups...*
En parejas...	*In pairs...*
Entrevista...	*Interview...*
Forma oraciones completas.	*Create/Make complete sentences.*
Háganse preguntas.	*Ask each other questions.*
Haz el papel de...	*Play the role of...*
Haz los cambios necesarios.	*Make the necessary changes.*
Indica/Indiquen si las oraciones...	*Indicate if the sentences...*
Lee/Lean en voz alta.	*Read aloud.*
...que mejor completa...	*...that best completes...*
Toma nota...	*Take note...*
Tomen apuntes.	*Take notes.*
Túrnense...	*Take turns...*

Expresiones útiles	*Useful expressions*
¿Cómo se dice _____ en español?	*How do you say _____ in Spanish?*
¿Cómo se escribe _____?	*How do you spell _____?*
¿Comprende(n)?	*Do you understand?*
Con permiso.	*Excuse me.*
De acuerdo.	*Okay.*
De nada.	*You're welcome.*
¿De veras?	*Really?*
¿En qué página estamos?	*What page are we on?*
Enseguida.	*Right away.*
Más despacio, por favor.	*Slower, please.*
Muchas gracias.	*Thanks a lot.*
No entiendo.	*I don't understand.*
No sé.	*I don't know.*
Perdone.	*Excuse me.*
Pista	*Clue*
Por favor.	*Please.*
Por supuesto.	*Of course.*
¿Qué significa _____?	*What does _____ mean?*
Repite, por favor.	*Please repeat.*
Tengo una pregunta.	*I have a question.*
¿Tiene(n) alguna pregunta?	*Do you have questions?*
Vaya(n) a la página dos.	*Go to page 2.*

Common Names

Get started learning Spanish by using a Spanish name in class. You can choose from the lists on these pages, or you can find one yourself. How about learning the Spanish equivalent of your name? The most popular Spanish female names are Lucía, María, Paula, Sofía, and Valentina. The most popular male names in Spanish are Alejandro, Daniel, David, Mateo, and Santiago. Is your name, or that of someone you know, in the Spanish top five?

Los 5 nombres masculinos más populares	Los 5 nombres femeninos más populares
Alejandro	Lucía
Daniel	María
David	Paula
Mateo	Sofía
Santiago	Valentina

Más nombres masculinos	Más nombres femeninos
Alfonso	Alicia
Antonio (Toni)	Beatriz (Bea, Beti, Biata)
Carlos	Blanca
César	Carolina (Carol)
Diego	Claudia
Ernesto	Diana
Felipe	Emilia
Francisco (Paco)	Irene
Guillermo	Julia
Ignacio (Nacho)	Laura
Javier (Javi)	Leonor
Leonardo	Liliana
Luis	Lourdes
Manolo	Margarita (Marga)
Marcos	Marta
Oscar (Óscar)	Noelia
Rafael (Rafa)	Patricia
Sergio	Rocío
Vicente	Verónica

Acknowledgments

On behalf of its authors and editors, Vista Higher Learning expresses its sincere appreciation to the many instructors and teachers across the U.S. and Canada who contributed their ideas and suggestions. Their insights and detailed comments were invaluable to us as we created ***Descubre.***

In-depth reviewers

Patrick Brady
Tidewater Community College, VA

Christine DeGrado
Chestnut Hill College, PA

Martha L. Hughes
Georgia Southern University, GA

Aida Ramos-Sellman
Goucher College, MD

Reviewers

Kathleen Aguilar
Fort Lewis College, CO

Aleta Anderson
Grand Rapids Community College, MI

Gunnar Anderson
SUNY Potsdam, NY

Nona Anderson
Ouachita Baptist University, AR

Ken Arant
Darton College, GA

Vicki Baggia
Phillips Exeter Academy, NH

Jorge V. Bajo
Oracle Charter School, NY

Ana Basoa-McMillan
Columbia State Community College, TN

Timothy Benson
Lake Superior College, MN

Georgia Betcher
Fayetteville Technical Community College, NC

Teresa Borden
Columbia College, CA

Courtney Bradley
The Principia, MO

Vonna Breeze-Marti
Columbia College, CA

Christa Bucklin
University of Hartford, CT

Mary Cantu
South Texas College, TX

Christa Chatrnuch
University of Hartford, CT

Tina Christodouleas
SUNY Cortland, NY

Edwin Clark
SUNY Potsdam, NY

Donald Clymer
Eastern Mennonite University, VA

Ann Costanzi
Chestnut Hill College, PA

Patricia Crespo-Martin
Foothill College, CA

Miryam Criado
Hanover College, KY

Thomas Curtis
Madison Area Technical College, WI

Patricia S. Davis
Darton College, GA

Danion Doman
Truman State University, MO

Deborah Dubiner
Carnegie Mellon University, PA

Benjamin Earwicker
Northwest Nazarene University, ID

Deborah Edson
Tidewater Community College, VA

Matthew T. Fleming
Grand Rapids Community College, MI

Ruston Ford
Indian Hills Community College, IA

Marianne Franco
Modesto Junior College, CA

Elena García
Muskegon Community College, MI

María D. García
Fayetteville Technical Community College, NC

Lauren Gates
East Mississippi Community College, MS

Marta M. Gómez
Gateway Academy, MO

Danielle Gosselin
Bishop Brady High School, NH

Charlene Grant
Skidmore College, NY

Betsy Hance
Kennesaw State University, GA

Marti Hardy
Laurel School, OH

Dennis Harrod
Syracuse University, NY

Fanning Hearon
Brunswick School, CT

Richard Heath
Kirkwood Community College, IA

Óscar Hernández
South Texas College, TX

Yolanda Hernández
Community College of Southern Nevada, North Las Vegas, NV

Martha L. Hughes
Georgia Southern University, GA

Martha Ince
Cushing Academy, MA

Acknowledgments

Reviewers

Stacy Jazan
Glendale Community College, CA

María Jiménez Smith
Tarrant County College, TX

Emory Kinder
Columbia Prep School, NY

Marina Kozanova
Crafton Hills College, CA

Tamara Kunkel
Alice Lloyd College, KY

Anna Major
The Westminster Schools, GA

Armando Maldonado
Morgan Community College, CO

Molly Marostica Smith
Canterbury School of Florida, FL

Jesús G. Martínez
Fresno City College, CA

Laura Martínez
Centralia College, WA

Daniel Millis
Verde Valley School, AZ

Deborah Mistron
Middle Tennessee State University, TN

Mechteld Mitchin
Village Academy, OH

Anna Montoya
Florida Institute of Technology, FL

Robert P. Moore
Loyola Blakefield Jesuit School, MD

S. Moshir
St. Bernard High School, CA

Javier Muñoz-Basols
Trinity School, NY

William Nichols
Grand Rapids Community College, MI

Bernice Nuhfer-Halten
Southern Polytechnic State University, GA

Amanda Papanikolas
Drew School, CA

Elizabeth M. Parr
Darton College, GA

Julia E. Patiño
Dillard University, LA

Martha Pérez
Kirkwood Community College, IA

Teresa Pérez-Gamboa
University of Georgia, GA

Marion Perry
The Thacher School, CA

Molly Perry
The Thacher School, CA

Melissa Pytlak
The Canterbury School, CT

Ana F. Sache
Emporia State University, KS

Celia S. Samaniego
Cosumnes River College, CA

Virginia Sánchez-Bernardy
San Diego Mesa College, CA

Frank P. Sanfilippo
Columbia College, CA

Piedad Schor
South Kent School, CT

David Schuettler
The College of St. Scholastica, MN

Romina Self
Ankeny Christian Academy, IA

David A. Short
Indian Hills Community College, IA

Carol Snell-Feikema
South Dakota State University, SD

Matias Stebbings
Columbia Grammar & Prep School, NY

Mary Studer Shea
Napa Valley College, CA

Cathy Swain
University of Maine, Machias, ME

Cristina Szterensus
Rock Valley College, IL

John Tavernakis
College of San Mateo, CA

David E. Tipton
Circleville Bible College, OH

Larry Thornton
Trinity College School, ON

Linda Tracy
Santa Rosa Junior College, CA

Beverly Turner
Truckee Meadows Community College, OK

Christine Tyma DeGrado
Chestnut Hill College, PA

Fanny Vera de Viacava
Canterbury School, CT

Luis Viacava
Canterbury School, CT

María Villalobos-Buehner
Grand Valley State University, MI

Hector Villarreal
South Texas College, TX

Juanita Villena-Álvarez
University of South Carolina, Beaufort, SC

Marcella Anne Wendzikowski
Villa Maria College of Buffalo, NY

Doug West
Sage Hill School, CA

Paula Whittaker
Bishop Brady High School, NH

Mary Zold-Herrera
Glenbrook North High School, IL

About the Authors

José A. Blanco founded Vista Higher Learning in 1998. A native of Barranquilla, Colombia, Mr. Blanco holds degrees in Literature and Hispanic Studies from Brown University and the University of California, Santa Cruz. He has worked as a writer, editor, and translator for Houghton Mifflin and D.C. Heath and Company, and has taught Spanish at the secondary and university levels. Mr. Blanco is also the co-author of several other Vista Higher Learning programs: **Vistas, Panorama, Aventuras,** and **¡Viva!** at the introductory level; **Ventanas, Facetas**, **Enfoques, Imagina,** and **Sueña** at the intermediate level; and **Revista** at the advanced conversation level.

Philip Redwine Donley received his M.A. in Hispanic Literature from the University of Texas at Austin in 1986 and his Ph.D. in Foreign Language Education from the University of Texas at Austin in 1997. Dr. Donley taught Spanish at Austin Community College, Southwestern University, and the University of Texas at Austin. He published articles and conducted workshops about language anxiety management and the development of critical thinking skills, and was involved in research about teaching languages to the visually impaired. Dr. Donley was also the co-author of **Vistas, Aventuras,** and **Panorama**, three introductory college Spanish textbook programs published by Vista Higher Learning. Dr. Donley passed away in 2003.

About the Illustrators

Yayo, an internationally acclaimed illustrator, was born in Colombia. He has illustrated children's books, newspapers, and magazines, and has been exhibited around the world. He currently lives in Montreal, Canada.

Pere Virgili lives and works in Barcelona, Spain. His illustrations have appeared in textbooks, newspapers, and magazines throughout Spain and Europe.

Born in Caracas, Venezuela, **Hermann Mejía** studied illustration at the Instituto de Diseño de Caracas. Hermann currently lives and works in the United States.

Lección preliminar

Communicative Goals

VOICE BOARD

I will be able to:

- **Identify myself and others**
- **Talk about the time of day**
- **Discuss everyday activities**
- **Describe people and things**
- **Make plans and invitations**

¡hola, ¿qué tal?

pages 2–3
- Nouns and articles
- Numbers 0–30
- Present tense of **ser**
- Telling time

en la clase

pages 4–7
- Present tense of **-ar** verbs
- Forming questions in Spanish
- Present tense of **estar**
- Numbers 31 and higher

cultura

pages 8–9
- El español en Latinoamérica

la familia

pages 10–11
- Descriptive adjectives
- Possessive adjectives
- Present tense of **-er** and **-ir** verbs
- Present tense of **tener** and **venir**

los pasatiempos

pages 12–16
- Present tense of **ir**
- Stem-changing verbs: **e:ie, o:ue**
- Stem-changing verbs: **e:i**
  Verbs with irregular **yo** forms

1 **Completar** Complete the charts according to the models.

Masculino	Femenino
el chico	la chica
	la profesora
	la amiga
el señor	
	la pasajera
el estudiante	
	la turista
el joven	

Singular	Plural
una cosa	unas cosas
un libro	
	unas clases
una lección	
un conductor	
	unos países
	unos lápices
un problema	

2 **¿Cuántos hay?** Tell how many people and/or things there are in each drawing.

1. _____

2. _____

3. _____

4. _____

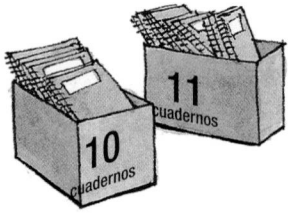

5. _____

6. _____

3 **El verbo *ser*** Complete the sentences with the correct form of the verb **ser**.

1. El diccionario _____ del profesor.
2. Nosotras _____ amigas
3. Yo _____ de Costa Rica.
4. Ustedes _____ estudiantes.
5. ¿De dónde _____ Valeria?
6. Tú _____ Ricardo, ¿no?

1.1 Nouns and articles

Gender of nouns

Nouns that refer to living things

	Masculine		Feminine
-o	el chico	-a	la chica
-or	el profesor	-ora	la profesora
-ista	el turista	-ista	la turista

Nouns that refer to non-living things

	Masculine		Feminine
-o	el libro	-a	la cosa
-ma	el programa	-ción	la lección
-s	el autobús	-dad	la nacionalidad

Plural of nouns

- For nouns ending in a vowel: add *-s*
  la cosa → las cosas
- For nouns ending in a consonant: add *-es*
  el señor → los señores
- For nouns ending in *-z*: *z* changes to *c*; add *-es*
  el lápiz → los lápices

Articles

- Articles tell the gender and number of the nouns they precede.

Definite articles (*the*)

Masculine		Feminine	
Singular	Plural	Singular	Plural
el amigo	los amigos	la palabra	las palabras

Indefinite articles (*a, an, some*)

Masculine		Feminine	
Singular	Plural	Singular	Plural
un amigo	unos amigos	una palabra	unas palabras

1.2 Numbers 0–30

0	cero	8	ocho	16	dieciséis
1	uno	9	nueve	17	diecisiete
2	dos	10	diez	18	dieciocho
3	tres	11	once	19	diecinueve
4	cuatro	12	doce	20	veinte
5	cinco	13	trece	21	veintiuno
6	seis	14	catorce	22	veintidós
7	siete	15	quince	30	treinta

- Before masculine nouns, **uno** (and all numbers ending in **-uno**) shortens to **un**; before feminine nouns, **uno** changes to **una**.

un chico	**una** chica
veinti**ún** chicos	veinti**una** chicas

- Use **hay** to express *there is/are.* Use **no hay** to express *there is/are not.*

1.3 Present tense of **ser**

- Uses of **ser**: identity, profession or occupation, origin, possession

1.4 Telling time

Es la **una.**	*It's 1:00.*
Son las **dos.**	*It's 2:00.*
Son las **tres** y diez.	*It's 3:10.*
Es la **una** y cuarto/quince.	*It's 1:15.*
Son las **siete** y media/treinta.	*It's 7:30.*
Es la **una** menos cuarto/quince.	*It's 12:45.*
Son las **once** menos veinte.	*It's 10:40.*
Es el mediodía.	*It's noon.*
Es la medianoche.	*It's midnight.*

- To ask what time it is, use **¿Qué hora es?**
- To ask at what time an event takes place, use **¿A qué hora (...)?** To state at what time an event takes place, use **a la(s)** + *time.*

4 **Conversaciones** Complete the mini-conversations by choosing the correct word for each blank.

1. —¿De quién _____ (es/hay) la maleta?
   —Es _____ (de/del) señor Rosales.
2. —¿Cuántos estudiantes _____ (eres/son) de España?
   —Dos _____ (son/soy) de España y uno _____ (cuánto/es) de México.
3. —¿_____ (Cuántos/Cuántas) pasajeros hay en el tour?
   —Hmm... hay _____ (veintiuno/veintiuna) [*21*] personas en el autobús ahora.
4. —¿_____ (De dónde/Qué) son ustedes?
   — _____ (Somos/Son) de los Estados Unidos.

5 **La hora** Write out these times in Spanish. Follow the model.

modelo
7:10 a.m.
Son las siete y diez de la mañana.

1. 6:15 p.m. _____
2. 8:40 a.m. _____
3. 1:07 p.m. _____
4. 3:22 p.m. _____
5. 11:30 a.m. _____
6. 12:55 a.m. _____
7. 4:00 p.m. _____
8. 12:00 p.m. _____

6 **Preguntas** Jot down your answers to these questions. Then, circulate around the room and try to find another student with the same answers. Ask follow-up questions. Be prepared to report back to the class.

modelo
Estudiante 1: *¿Es tu madre o padre de otro estado o país?*
Estudiante 2: *Sí, mi madre es de otro estado.*
Estudiante 1: *¿De dónde es ella?*
Estudiante 2: *Es de Michigan.*

1. ¿Es tu madre/padre de otro estado (*another state*) o país?
2. ¿A qué hora es tu programa de televisión favorito?
3. ¿Cuántas computadoras hay en tu casa?

7 **Descripción** Write a brief description of yourself and your Spanish class. Include your name, where you are from, who your Spanish teacher is and where he/she is from, what time the class is held, and how many students are in the class.

1 **Completar** Complete the sentences with the correct forms of the verbs in parentheses.

1. Los profesores _____ (explicar) las lecciones.
2. Nosotras _____ (cenar) a las ocho.
3. Tú _____ (desayunar) en la cafetería.
4. ¿_____ (Trabajar) usted los viernes?
5. Me _____ (gustar) cantar y bailar.
6. Yo no _____ (desear) tomar café ahora.
7. Los chicos _____ (dibujar) con tiza.
8. Julio y yo _____ (escuchar) música rock.
9. ¿Te _____ (gustar) las lenguas extranjeras?
10. Ustedes esperan _____ (viajar) a Perú.

2 **Gustar** Luis studies science. For each item, write what Luis would say about his preferences, according to the cue. Follow the model.

modelo

trabajar en el laboratorio ☹
No me gusta trabajar en el laboratorio.

1. las ciencias marinas ☺
2. los exámenes de física ☹
3. escuchar la radio cuando estudio ☺
4. trabajar y conversar con los profesores ☺
5. la tarea de química ☹
6. la clase de biología ☺

3 **Preguntas** Write the questions for these answers.

1. —¿_____ la profesora Castillo?
   —Enseña los martes y jueves.
2. —¿_____?
   —Los chicos descansan en la casa.
3. —¿_____ (ustedes)?
   —Deseamos cenar pizza.
4. —¿_____ (tú)?
   — Tomo cinco clases.
5. —¿_____?
   —Trabajo porque necesito dinero (*money*).
6. —¿_____ los cuadernos?
   —Son de Beatriz.
7. —¿_____ la clase de literatura?
   — Es a la una de la tarde.

2.1 Present tense of -ar verbs

▸ To conjugate most regular **-ar** verbs in the present tense, drop the **-ar** and add the appropriate endings that correspond to the different subject pronouns.

estudiar	
estudio	estudiamos
estudias	estudiáis
estudia	estudian

▸ When two verbs are used together without a change in subject, the second verb is in the infinitive. To make the sentence negative, put no before the conjugated verb.

Necesito comprar **un libro.** No **deseo viajar hoy.**

The verb *gustar*

▸ To express your likes and dislikes, use:

(no) me gusta + el/la + [*singular noun*] **No me gusta el horario.**
(no) me gustan + los/las + [*plural noun*] **Me gustan las ciencias.**

▸ To say what you like and do not like to do, use:

(no) me gusta + [*infinitive(s)*] **Me gusta leer y escribir.**

▸ To ask a classmate about likes and dislikes, use **te.**

¿Te gusta la clase?

2.2 Forming questions in Spanish

▸ There are three ways to form questions in Spanish: by raising the pitch of your voice at the end of a declarative statement; by inverting the subject and verb in a statement; or by adding tag questions (**¿verdad?** or **¿no?**) to a declarative statement.

¿Ustedes trabajan los sábados?

¿Trabajan ustedes los sábados?

Ustedes trabajan los sábados, ¿verdad?/¿no?

Interrogative words

¿Adónde?	¿Cuánto/a?	¿Por qué?
¿Cómo?	¿Cuántos/as?	¿Qué?
¿Cuál(es)?	¿De dónde?	¿Quién(es)?
¿Cuándo?	¿Dónde?	

2.3 Present tense of **estar**

estar

estoy	estamos
estás	estáis
está	están

► Uses of **estar**: location, health, well-being

Prepositions often used with estar

a la derecha de	delante de
a la izquierda de	detrás de
al lado de	en
allá	encima de
allí	entre
cerca de	lejos de
con	sin
debajo de	sobre

2.4 Numbers 31 and higher

31	treinta y uno	101	ciento uno
32	treinta y dos	200	doscientos/as
	(and so on)	500	quinientos/as
40	cuarenta	700	setecientos/as
50	cincuenta	900	novecientos/as
60	sesenta	1.000	mil
70	setenta	2.000	dos mil
80	ochenta	5.100	cinco mil cien
90	noventa	100.000	cien mil
100	cien, ciento	1.000.000	un millón (de)

► The numbers 200 through 999 agree in gender with the nouns they modify.

324 plumas **trescientas veinticuatro plumas**

4 **En la escuela** There is a substitute teacher in Clara's class today. Complete the conversation with the correct forms of **estar**.

SR. GARCÍA Buenos días. ¿Cómo (1) _____ ?
CLARA Bien, gracias. ¿Cómo (2) _____ usted?
SR. GARCÍA (3) _____ muy bien. Soy el señor García. Y tú eres Clara Rivas, ¿verdad?
CLARA Sí. Perdón, señor García, pero ¿dónde (4) _____ el señor Duque?
SR. GARCÍA (5) _____ en una conferencia, pero regresa mañana. Clara, ¿en qué parte del libro (6) _____ ustedes?
CLARA (Nosotros) (7) _____ en la lección 4.
SR. GARCÍA Y los borradores, ¿dónde (8) _____ ?
CLARA Allí, al lado de la mesa.

5 **Buscar** Imagine that you are in a school supply store and can't find various items. Ask the clerk (your partner) about the location of five items in the drawing. Then switch roles.

modelo
Estudiante 1: *¿Dónde están los diccionarios?*
Estudiante 2: *Los diccionarios están debajo de los libros de literatura.*

6 **Números** Write these numbers in Spanish.

1. 751 _____
2. 99 _____
3. 4.010 _____
4. 844 _____
5. 738.266 _____
6. 23.110.680 _____
7. 1.033 _____
8. 1.500.307 _____

7 **Un estudiante español** Complete the paragraph with the appropriate forms of the verbs in the word list. Not all the verbs will be used. Some may be used more than once.

bailar	desayunar	estar	gustar	necesitar
caminar	esperar	estudiar	hablar	tomar

Hola, soy Víctor. Soy de Madrid, España. (Yo) (1) _____ en una escuela secundaria. (2) _____ clases de ciencias, matemáticas, arte e inglés. Los días de semana, mis padres y yo (3) _____ juntos (*together*) en casa. Luego mis padres (4) _____ el autobús; sus oficinas (5) _____ lejos de la casa. Yo no (6) _____ tomar el autobús para llegar a la escuela. Afortunadamente (*Luckily*), (7) _____ cerca de mi casa. A veces (*Sometimes*) mi amigo Alberto y yo (8) _____ juntos a la escuela. (9) _____ de deportes, como el tenis o el fútbol. ¿Y tú? ¿(10) _____ en una escuela cerca de tu casa? ¿Qué clases (11) _____ ? ¿A ti te (12) _____ los deportes?

8 **Describir** With a partner, choose verbs from the list to ask and answer questions about what you see in each drawing.

buscar	dibujar	llevar
caminar	escuchar	tomar
cantar	estudiar	viajar
descansar	hablar	

modelo

enseñar, explicar, hablar
Estudiante 1: *¿Qué enseña la profesora?*
Estudiante 2: *Enseña química.*
Estudiante 1: *¿Explica la lección?*
Estudiante 2: *Sí, explica la lección.*

1.

2.

3.

4.

9 **Contestar** Answer these questions.

1. ¿Cuántas clases tomas? ¿Cuál es tu clase favorita?
2. ¿Dónde estudias, en la biblioteca o en casa? ¿Escuchas música cuando estudias?
3. ¿A qué hora llegas a la escuela? ¿A qué hora regresas a casa?
4. ¿Con quién(es) cenas normalmente? ¿Quién prepara la comida (*food*)?
5. ¿Miras mucha televisión? ¿Qué programas te gustan?
6. ¿Te gusta viajar? ¿Qué países o culturas te gustan?
7. ¿Qué música escuchan tus amigos/as y tú? ¿Bailan ustedes? ¿Cantan?
8. ¿Qué te gusta hacer los fines de semana? ¿Descansas, preparas la tarea o pasas tiempo con tu familia?

10 **Actividades** With a partner, take turns asking each other if you do these activities. Also ask follow-up questions. Jot down your partner's answers and make note of which activities you both do.

modelo

desayunar en casa
Estudiante 1: *¿Desayunas en casa?*
Estudiante 2: *Sí, desayuno en casa.*
Estudiante 1: *¿A qué hora desayunas los días de semana?*
Estudiante 2: *Desayuno a las siete de la mañana.*
Estudiante 1: *¿Con quién desayunas?*
Estudiante 2: *Desayuno con mis padres.*

bailar bien
comprar música en iTunes
estudiar geografía
mirar la televisión
practicar deportes
tomar clases aparte de la escuela
trabajar como voluntario(a)
viajar por el país
visitar museos de arte

11 **Escribir** Write an e-mail to a new friend. Introduce yourself, describe what classes you take, your studying habits, and what you do on school days and weekends. Talk about your likes and dislikes, and ask about your friend's.

modelo

Hola, Andrés:
Me llamo David y soy de Miami, Florida. Soy estudiante en una escuela secundaria. Tomo clases de historia, arte...

Practice more at vhlcentral.com.

EN DETALLE

Additional Reading

El español en Latinoamérica

As a Spanish language learner, you are on your way to being able to communicate with a vast number of people from diverse regions, backgrounds, and cultures. There are about 500 million Spanish-speakers in the world, but less than 600 years ago, Spanish was used only in the northern and central regions of the Iberian Peninsula. In 1492, the **Reyes Católicos°** unified Spain under Christian rule and the Spanish language. In that same year, they commissioned **Cristóbal Colón°** to search for a new trade route to India, on which he carried the Spanish language to the Americas.

Although Columbus initially sought to explore and establish trade routes, a principal goal of the Spaniards in the Americas quickly became conquest and evangelism—spreading the Catholic faith. The Spanish encountered millions of indigenous people who spoke a vast number of languages and dialects. The Spanish **conquistadores** used various indigenous languages to communicate their religious message, and several were preserved this way throughout colonial times. For example, **quechua** was the main means of communication in the central Andean region between the Spaniards and the indigenous population. Over time, the geographic reach of quechua continued to expand, and words from many different indigenous languages were incorporated into Spanish. **Papa°** and **jaguar°** are just two examples.

Over the following few centuries of colonial rule, descendants of the Spanish and majority **mestizo°** population perpetuated the use of Spanish. After the wars of independence, most nations opted to have Spanish as their official language. However, millions of Latin Americans continue to speak a multitude of indigenous languages, especially in rural areas. And in several Latin American countries, indigenous languages have co-official status: Bolivia (**quechua, aimará**), Ecuador (**quechua, aimará**), Paraguay (**guaraní**), and Peru (**quechua, aimará**).

Otras° lenguas indígenas

Lengua	Donde se habla	Más información
náhuatl	México	lengua de los aztecas
chibcha	(lengua extinta)	lengua dominante en Colombia y Panamá en tiempos precolombinos°
maya	Guatemala, México, Honduras	en tiempos precolombinos usan un sistema jeroglífico°
taíno	(lengua extinta)	lengua más dominante en la región del Caribe en tiempos precolombinos
mapuche	Chile	no tiene relación con otras lenguas indígenas

Reyes Católicos *the Catholic King Fernando of Aragón and Queen Isabel of Castilla* **Cristóbal Colón** *Christopher Columbus* **Papa** *Potato (from Quechua)* **jaguar** *jaguar (from Guaraní)* **mestizo** *mixed Spanish and indigenous ancestry* **Otras** *Other* **precolombinos** *pre-Columbian* **jeroglífico** *hieroglyphic*

ACTIVIDADES

1 Cierto o falso? Indicate whether each statement is **cierto** or **falso**. Correct the false statements.

1. About 500,000 people speak Spanish worldwide.
2. The Spanish **conquistadores** often communicated Catholic teachings in indigenous languages.
3. Indigenous languages did not survive the Spanish conquest.
4. **Quechua** originated in the Caribbean.
5. Many Spanish words have indigenous origins.
6. Today, indigenous languages are not widely spoken in Latin America.
7. **Aimará** is spoken in Paraguay.
8. **Taíno** and **chibcha** are extinct languages.
9. The Aztecs spoke **maya**.
10. **Mapuche** and **quechua** belong to the same linguistic family.

ASÍ SE DICE

Palabras de origen indígena

el aguacate (náhuatl)	*avocado*
la barbacoa (taíno)	*barbecue*
la cancha (quechua)	*field, court*
el chile (náhuatl)	*chili (pepper)*
el coyote (náhuatl)	*coyote*
el huracán (taíno)	*hurricane*
la maraca (guaraní)	*maraca*
la palta (quechua)	*avocado*
el puma (quechua)	*puma*

EL MUNDO HISPANO

Civilizaciones precolombinas

La civilización maya This civilization is known for its art, architecture, mathematics, and astronomy. The Mayas developed a counting system based on 20 and the concept of zero. Remains of Mayan temples, such as **Tikal** in Guatemala and **Chichén Itzá** on the Yucatan Peninsula, are now popular tourist attractions.

El imperio azteca This civilization, based in Mexico's central valley, greatly expanded its domain through military conquest and alliances. The Aztecs founded their capital, **Tenochtitlán**, in 1325; by the time the Spanish arrived in 1519, it was one of the largest cities in the world.

El imperio incaico The Incas developed an innovative agricultural system of terraces and constructed a vast network of roads with the capital, Cusco, at its center. One of the most famous legacies of the Incan Empire is the mountaintop ruins of **Machu Picchu**.

PERFIL

Día de la Independencia

During the early morning hours of September 16, 1810, a Mexican priest rang his church bell in the town of Dolores and gave a rousing call for a free, independent Mexico: **¡Viva° la Independencia! ¡Muera el mal gobierno°!** After 11 years of war, Mexico won its independence from Spain, which it commemorates on the 16th of September. Although Mexico's **Día de la Independencia** is officially September 16th, the celebrations begin the night before. Father Miguel Hidalgo's act, now known as **el Grito° de Dolores**, is reenacted every year in **zócalos°** across Mexico, accompanied by fireworks, music, and revelers dressed in the colors of the Mexican flag.

Beginning in 1811, similar movements for freedom ignited all over Central America. Finally, on September 15, 1821, Costa Rica, El Salvador, Guatemala, Honduras, and Nicaragua signed the **Acta de Independencia de Centroamérica**, thus proclaiming their autonomy from Spain. These five countries all celebrate their independence on September 15th.

Viva *Long live* Muera el mal gobierno *Down with bad government*
Grito *Shout* zócalos *plazas*

Conexión Internet

¿Qué es y qué hace la Real Academia Española?

Go to **vhlcentral.com** to find more cultural information related to this **Cultura** section.

ACTIVIDADES

2 **Comprensión** Complete these sentences.

1. Mexicans reenact _____ as part of Independence Day.
2. The capital of the _____ Empire was one of the largest cities in the world.
3. **Palta** and _____ both mean avocado.
4. Honduras and Nicaragua celebrate their independence on _____.
5. _____ is a Nahuatl word referring to an animal.

3 **Los indígenas** Have students work in pairs. Ask them to research more about one of the indigenous groups mentioned on these pages, or another pre-Columbian civilization in Latin America. Have students prepare a brief oral presentation about the group's culture, language, customs, and place in history.

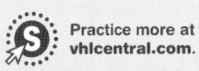

1 **Opuestos** For each adjective, give an adjective that is opposite in meaning. Keep the gender and number the same.

1. tonto
2. baja
3. gordo
4. viejos
5. simpáticas
6. bonito
7. difíciles
8. morena
9. malas
10. blanco

2 **Completar** Ernesto is talking about life at his new school. Complete the paragraph with the correct form of the adjectives from the list. Use each adjective only once. One adjective will not be used.

bueno	mismo
difícil	mucho
feo	simpático
inteligente	tonto
interesante	tres

En la escuela donde estudio tengo (1) _____ amigos: Ignacio, Carlos y Tomás. Son personas muy (2) _____; hablamos de todo. Ellos son (3) _____; reciben A en todos los exámenes. Yo no soy (4) _____, pero no tengo las (5) _____ notas. Las materias son (6) _____ y los profesores son (7) _____, pero en la clase de matemáticas hay (8) _____ tarea y la clase de química es (9) _____. Deseo tomar más clases de historia y de arte.

3 **Posesivos** Write the correct form of each possessive adjective.

1. _____ (*Your*, fam.) sobrino es muy joven.
2. _____ (*Her*) profesores son estrictos.
3. Olivia es _____ (*my*) hermana.
4. _____ (*Our*) casa es azul.
5. ¿Juliana es _____ (*your*, form.) esposa?
6. _____ (*His*) familia es pequeña.
7. Los libros viejos son de _____ (*our*) abuelos.
8. _____ (*My*) tíos son argentinos.

4 **Verbos** Complete the chart with the correct verb forms.

Infinitive	yo	nosotros/as	ustedes
	asisto		
deber		debemos	
			leen
venir			
	bebo		
describir			describen

3.1 Descriptive adjectives

Felipe es gordo, antipático y muy feo.

- Adjectives are words that describe nouns. In Spanish, adjectives agree in both gender and number with the nouns they modify.

Forms and agreement of adjectives

Masculine		Feminine	
Singular	Plural	Singular	Plural
alto	altos	alta	altas
inteligente	inteligentes	inteligente	inteligentes
trabajador	trabajadores	trabajadora	trabajadoras

- Descriptive adjectives, color words, and adjectives of nationality follow the noun:

el chico rubio, las sillas rojas, la mujer española

- Adjectives of quantity precede the noun:

muchos libros, dos turistas

Note: When placed before a singular masculine noun, these adjectives are shortened:

bueno → buen; malo → mal

un buen día, un mal hombre

When placed before a singular noun, **grande** is shortened to **gran**, and the meaning changes to *great*.

una gran escuela

3.2 Possessive adjectives

Singular		Plural	
mi	nuestro/a	mis	nuestros/as
tu	vuestro/a	tus	vuestros/as
su	su	sus	sus

- Possessive adjectives always precede the nouns they modify:

nuestros amigos, mi madre

3.3 Present tense of -er and -ir verbs

▸ To create the present-tense forms of most regular verbs, drop the infinitive ending (**-er, -ir**) and add the appropriate endings that correspond to the different subject pronouns.

comer		**escribir**	
como	comemos	escribo	escribimos
comes	coméis	escribes	escribís
come	comen	escribe	escriben

3.4 Present tense of tener and venir

tener		**venir**	
tengo	tenemos	vengo	venimos
tienes	tenéis	vienes	venís
tiene	tienen	viene	vienen

▸ **Tener** is used in many common phrases expressing feelings and age.

tener... años	*to be... years old*
tener calor	*to be hot*
tener frío	*to be cold*
tener ganas de + *inf.*	*to feel like (doing something)*
tener hambre	*to be hungry*
tener prisa	*to be in a hurry*
tener razón	*to be right*
tener sed	*to be thirsty*
tener sueño	*to be sleepy*
tener que + *inf.*	*to have to (do something)*

5 **Situaciones** Read these situations. For each one, write a logical sentence using a **tener** expression. Follow the model.

modelo

Mi primo Rubén tiene un examen mañana. Rubén tiene que estudiar.

1. Es la medianoche y escribes la tarea. Tú _____.
2. Es la hora de cenar. Yo _____.
3. Buscamos agua. Nosotros _____.
4. Son las 8:50 y José está en casa. La clase es a las 9. José _____.
5. Tus amigos y tú buscan un libro interesante. Ustedes _____.
6. Enrique dice que estamos en el año 2010. Él no _____.

6 **Oraciones** Arrange each set of words in the correct order to form a complete, logical sentence. **¡Ojo!** Remember to conjugate the verbs according to the subject.

1. las / media / venir / a / yo / escuela / a / siete / y / la
   _____
2. sus / compartir / usted / amigos / con / ¿ / ?
   _____
3. profesor / un / nosotros / buen / tener
   _____
4. interesantes / aprender / sobrinos / libros / leer / mis / a
   _____

7 **Conversación** Complete the conversation with the correct form of the appropriate verb. Then, act it out with a partner.

—Hola, Raquel. ¿Qué (1) _____ (escribir/comprender) en el teléfono?
—Hola, Simón. (2) _____ (Comer/Escribir) un mensaje de texto (*text message*) para mi amiga Inés.
—¿Inés? Ella (3) _____ (abrir/vivir) cerca del parque, ¿verdad?
—Sí, exactamente. Por las tardes ella y yo (4) _____ (correr/decidir) en el parque.
—¡Qué bien! A mí también me gusta (5) _____ (correr/leer).
—¿Ah, sí? ¿Por qué no (6) _____ (tener/venir) con nosotras? Después (7) _____ (compartir/aprender) un batido de col (*kale smoothie*) en un café.
—¿Ustedes (8) _____ (beber/creer) batidos de col? Em... no, gracias. (9) _____ (Recibir/Tener) que terminar la tarea y a las cinco (10) _____ (describir/asistir) a una lección de piano.
—Ay, Simón. De verdad (11) _____ (deber/compartir) practicar más deportes.

Practice more at vhlcentral.com.

1 **El verbo *ir*** Complete the sentences with the correct form of the verb **ir** and **a**, **al**, or **a la**.

1. Los jóvenes _____ _____ plaza.
2. ¿Ustedes _____ _____ jugar al golf?
3. Mi abuela _____ _____ iglesia.
4. Tú _____ _____ restaurante.
5. Yo _____ _____ esquiar.
6. Fernanda y yo _____ _____ cine.

2 **¿Adónde?** With a partner, take turns asking and answering questions about where these people are going and what they are going to do there.

modelo

Estudiante 1: *¿Adónde va Estela?*
Estudiante 2: *Va a la Librería Sol.*
¿Qué va a comprar allí?
Estudiante 1: *Va a comprar un libro.*

Estela

1. Álex y Miguel

2. mi amigo

3. tú

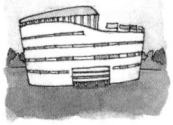
4. los estudiantes

5. la profesora Torres

6. ustedes

3 **Verbos** Complete the chart with the correct verb forms.

Infinitive	yo	nosotros/as	ellos/as
contar			
	juego		
	cierro	cerramos	
traer			traen
			siguen
oír		oímos	

4.1 Present tense of ir

ir			
yo	voy	nosotros/as	vamos
tú	vas	vosotros/as	vais
Ud./él/ella	va	Uds./ellos/ellas	van

- **Ir** is often used with the preposition **a**; if **a** is followed by the definite article **el**, they form a contraction: **a + el = al.**
- **Ir** has many everyday uses, including expressing future plans:

ir a + [*infinitivo*] = *to be going to* + [*infinitive*]
vamos a + [*infinitivo*] = *let's do something*

4.2 Stem-changing verbs e:ie, o:ue, u:ue

Los chicos empiezan a hablar del cenote.

	empezar	volver	jugar
yo	empiezo	vuelvo	juego
tú	empiezas	vuelves	juegas
Ud./él/ella	empieza	vuelve	juega
nosotros/as	empezamos	volvemos	jugamos
vosotros/as	empezáis	volvéis	jugáis
Uds./ellos/ellas	empiezan	vuelven	juegan

- Other **e:ie** verbs: **cerrar, comenzar, entender, pensar, perder, preferir, querer**
- Other **o:ue** verbs: **almorzar, contar, dormir, encontrar, mostrar, poder, recordar**

4.3 Stem-changing verbs e:i

pedir			
yo	pido	nosotros/as	pedimos
tú	pides	vosotros/as	pedís
Ud./él/ella	pide	Uds./ellos/ellas	piden

- As with other stem-changing verbs you have learned, there is no stem change in the **nosotros/as** or **vosotros/as** forms in the present tense.
- Other **e:i** verbs: **conseguir** (consigo), **decir** (digo), **repetir**, **seguir** (sigo)

4.4 Verbs with irregular yo forms

- In Spanish, several verbs have irregular **yo** forms in the present tense.

hacer	poner	salir	suponer	traer
hago	pongo	salgo	supongo	traigo

- The verbs **ver** and **oír**

ver			
yo	veo	nosotros/as	vemos
tú	ves	vosotros/as	veis
Ud./él/ella	ve	Uds./ellos/ellas	ven

oír			
yo	oigo	nosotros/as	oímos
tú	oyes	vosotros/as	oís
Ud./él/ella	oye	Uds./ellos/ellas	oyen

4 Completar Complete each sentence with the correct form of the verb.

1. Daniela _____ (mostrar) las fotos de su excursión.
2. ¿Cuándo _____ (poder) pasear tú y yo?
3. Tus clases _____ (comenzar) mañana, ¿verdad?
4. Mi familia y yo _____ (oír) música salsa en casa.
5. ¿(Tú) _____ (ver) programas de *reality* en la televisión?
6. Mateo _____ (decir) que hay un problema.
7. (Yo) _____ (suponer) que hay una solución.
8. Tus amigos y tú _____ (jugar) al fútbol los domingos.

5 El cine Complete the paragraph by choosing the appropriate verb and conjugating it in the correct form. **¡Ojo!** Not all verbs have stem changes.

Mis amigas y yo (1) _____ (repetir, ir, ver) al cine el sábado. Pilar y Lucía (2) _____ (volver, abrir, querer) ver una película romántica, pero Teresa, Elena y yo (3) _____ (preferir, traer, ir) una comedia. Entonces (*So*), este sábado nosotras (4) _____ (cerrar, llevar, pensar) comprar entradas (*tickets*) para ver una película cómica. La película (5) _____ (tener, hacer, empezar) a las ocho y (6) _____ (contar, terminar, comenzar) a las 9:45 de la noche; entonces mis amigas y yo (7) _____ (salir, creer, oír) del cine y (8) _____ (viajar, poder, nadar) ir a cenar. Aquí los restaurantes (9) _____ (cerrar, querer, vivir) tarde, más o menos a la medianoche. Normalmente (yo) (10) _____ (perder, conseguir, decidir) las entradas por Internet. Y tú, ¿cómo (11) _____ (poner, contar, comprar) las entradas del cine? ¿(12) _____ (Preferir, Comprender, Salir) películas románticas o cómicas?

6 Oraciones Arrange each set of words in the correct order to form a complete, logical sentence. **¡Ojo!** Make all necessary changes.

1. mi / clase / calculadora / yo / a / rojo / traer

_____

2. gimnasio / el / ir / a / (tú) / ¿ / ?

_____

3. en / mis / no / el / radio / la / amigos / programa / oír

_____

4. tacos / Lucas y yo / mucho / mexicano / en / restaurante / pedir / el

_____

5. excursión / el / querer / una / quién / viernes / hacer / ¿ / ?

_____

7 **Describir** In pairs, take turns describing what these people are doing, using the verbs from the list. Use each verb only once. One verb will not be used.

hacer	salir
oír	traer
perder	ver
poner	

1. Fernán

2. los aficionados

3. yo

4. nosotros

5. la señora Vargas

6. el estudiante

8 **Combinar** Combine elements from the columns to create complete sentences. Add any necessary words.

A	B	C
usted	traer	una pizza
mis amigos y yo	dormir	viajar
tú	empezar	la tarea
las clases	pedir	una siesta
ustedes	hacer	bailar merengue
los profesores	querer	¿?
mi madre	poder	

9 **Situaciones** In pairs, take turns saying where you and your friends go in these situations.

1. Cuando deseo descansar...
2. Cuando mi mejor amigo/a tiene que estudiar...
3. Si mis compañeros de clase necesitan practicar el español...
4. Si deseo hablar con mis amigos...
5. Cuando tengo dinero (*money*)...
6. Cuando mis amigos y yo tenemos hambre...
7. En mis ratos libres...
8. Cuando mis amigos desean esquiar...
9. Si estoy de vacaciones...
10. Si tengo ganas de leer...

10 **Preguntas personales** Answer these questions.

1. ¿A qué hora sales de la casa los lunes? ¿A qué hora vuelves a casa? ¿Y tus padres?
2. ¿Te gustan tus clases? ¿Qué materias prefieres? ¿Por qué?
3. ¿Haces mucha tarea? ¿Dónde prefieres estudiar?
4. ¿Pones música cuando estudias? ¿Oyes música cuando caminas a la escuela o cuando tomas el autobús? ¿Tus padres escuchan música cuando cenan?
5. Cuando no estás en la escuela, ¿qué haces? ¿Juegas deportes? ¿Juegas en la computadora? ¿Lees? ¿Escribes poemas?
6. ¿Miras la televisión? ¿Qué programas ves?
7. ¿Qué vas a hacer el fin de semana? ¿Tienes ganas de ir al cine? ¿Qué películas te gustan?

11 **La verdad** Write five sentences about yourself, using the verbs from the list or others that you know. Three of the sentences should be true and two should be false. Then, in small groups, take turns reading your statements aloud. Your classmates will try to determine which ones are true.

almorzar	hablar	jugar	salir	tener	vivir
dormir	ir	querer	ser	trabajar	¿?

12 **Encuesta** First, read through the items; under **Yo**, write **Sí** if you do the activity and **No** if you do not. Then, under the second column, place one check mark if you do the activity once a month **(una vez al mes)**, two check marks if you do it a few times a week **(varias veces a la semana)**, or three check marks if you do it every day **(todos los días)**.

	Yo	Frecuencia	Mi compañero/a	Frecuencia
1. almorzar en la cafetería	sí	✔ ✔ ✔	Lisa	✔ ✔
2. tomar café por la mañana				
3. ir a restaurantes elegantes				
4. dormir ocho horas				
5. jugar a deportes				
6. ver deportes en la televisión				
7. recordar a tus amigos/as de la infancia				
8. escuchar música				
9. salir con amigos/as				

Now circulate around the room and try to find a classmate that does each activity with the same frequency as you. When someone answers yes, write down their name and the corresponding check marks.

modelo

almorzar en la cafetería

Tú: ¿Almuerzas en la cafetería?

Lisa: Sí, almuerzo en la cafetería varias veces a la semana.

13 **Situación** Imagine that you are speaking with a member of your family or your best friend. With a partner, prepare a conversation using these cues.

Estudiante 1	Estudiante 2
Ask your partner what he or she is doing.	Tell your partner that you are watching TV.
Say what you suppose he or she is watching.	Say that you like the show _____. Ask if he or she wants to watch.
Say no, because you are going out with friends and tell where you are going.	Say you think it's a good idea, and ask what your partner and his or her friends are doing there.
Say what you are going to do, and ask your partner whether he or she wants to come along.	Say no and tell your partner what you prefer to do.

14 **Escribir** Write a journal entry about what you do and various family members do on a typical Saturday. Then talk about what you and your friends are going to do together this weekend. Use at least eight verbs from pages 12–13 to talk about your typical day and **ir a** + [*infinitive/place*] to talk about your plans.

Un sábado típico

Generalmente los sábados yo...

15 **Adivinanza** Complete the rhyme with the appropriate forms of the correct verbs from the list.

contar	poder
oír	suponer

"Si no _____ dormir
y el sueño deseas,
lo vas a conseguir
si _____ ovejas°."

ovejas *sheep*

Practice more at vhlcentral.com.

Las vacaciones

5

Communicative Goals

I will be able to:

- **Discuss and plan a vacation**
- **Describe a hotel**
- **Talk about how I feel**
- **Talk about the seasons and the weather**

VOICE BOARD

contextos

pages 152–157

- Travel and vacation
- Months of the year
- Seasons and weather
- Ordinal numbers

fotonovela

pages 158–161

Felipe plays a practical joke on Miguel and the friends take a trip to the coast. They check in to their hotel and go to the beach, where Miguel gets his revenge.

cultura

pages 162–163

- **Las cataratas del Iguazú**
- **Punta del Este**

estructura

pages 164–179

- **Estar** with conditions and emotions
- The present progressive
- **Ser** and **estar**
- Direct object nouns and pronouns
- **Recapitulación**

adelante

pages 180–187

Lectura: A hotel brochure from Puerto Rico
Escritura: A tourist brochure for a hotel
Escuchar: A weather report
En pantalla
Flash cultura
Panorama: Puerto Rico

A PRIMERA VISTA

- **¿Dónde están ellos: en la playa o en una ciudad?**
- **¿Son viejos o jóvenes?**
- **¿Toman el sol o nadan?**
- **¿Qué crees que van a hacer ahora?**

Las vacaciones

My Vocabulary Tutorials

Más vocabulario

la cama	*bed*
la habitación individual, doble	*single, double room*
el piso	*floor (of a building)*
la planta baja	*ground floor*
el campo	*countryside*
el paisaje	*landscape*
el equipaje	*luggage*
la estación de autobuses, del metro, de tren	*bus, subway, train station*
la llegada	*arrival*
el pasaje (de ida y vuelta)	*(round-trip) ticket*
la salida	*departure; exit*
la tabla de (wind)surf	*surfboard/sailboard*
acampar	*to camp*
estar de vacaciones	*to be on vacation*
hacer las maletas	*to pack (one's suitcases)*
hacer un viaje	*to take a trip*
hacer (wind)surf	*to (wind)surf*
ir de compras	*to go shopping*
ir de vacaciones	*to go on vacation*
ir en autobús (m.), auto(móvil) (m.), motocicleta (f.), taxi (m.)	*to go by bus, car, motorcycle, taxi*

Variación léxica

automóvil ⟷ coche (*Esp.*), carro (*Amér. L.*)
autobús ⟷ camión (*Méx.*), guagua (*Caribe*)
motocicleta ⟷ moto (*coloquial*)

En la agencia de viajes

En el hotel

recursos

vText | CPA pp. 1–3 | CH pp. 65–66 | vhlcentral

En el aeropuerto

En la playa

Práctica

1 **Escuchar** Indicate who would probably make each statement you hear. Each answer is used twice.

a. el agente de viajes
b. el inspector de aduanas
c. un empleado del hotel

1. _____ 4. _____
2. _____ 5. _____
3. _____ 6. _____

2 **¿Cierto o falso?** Mario and his wife, Natalia, are planning their next vacation with a travel agent. Indicate whether each statement is **cierto** or **falso** according to what you hear in the conversation.

	Cierto	Falso
1. Mario y Natalia están en Puerto Rico.	❍	❍
2. Ellos quieren hacer un viaje a Puerto Rico.	❍	❍
3. Natalia prefiere ir a una montaña.	❍	❍
4. Mario quiere pescar en Puerto Rico.	❍	❍
5. La agente de viajes va a confirmar la reservación.	❍	❍

3 **Escoger** Choose the best answer for each sentence.

1. Un huésped es una persona que _____.
   a. toma fotos b. está en un hotel c. pesca en el mar
2. Abrimos la puerta con _____.
   a. una llave b. un caballo c. una llegada
3. Enrique tiene _____ porque va a viajar a otro (*another*) país.
   a. un pasaporte b. una foto c. una llegada
4. Antes de (*Before*) ir de vacaciones, hay que _____.
   a. pescar b. ir en tren c. hacer las maletas
5. Nosotros vamos en _____ al aeropuerto.
   a. autobús b. pasaje c. viajero
6. Me gusta mucho ir al campo. El _____ es increíble.
   a. paisaje b. pasaje c. equipaje

4 **Analogías** Complete the analogies using the words below. Two words will not be used.

auto	huésped	mar	sacar
botones	llegada	pasaporte	tren

1. acampar ⟶ campo ⊜ pescar ⟶
2. agencia de viajes ⟶ agente ⊜ hotel ⟶
3. llave ⟶ habitación ⊜ pasaje ⟶
4. estudiante ⟶ libro ⊜ turista ⟶
5. aeropuerto ⟶ viajero ⊜ hotel ⟶
6. maleta ⟶ hacer ⊜ foto ⟶

Las estaciones y los meses del año

el invierno: **diciembre, enero, febrero**

la primavera: **marzo, abril, mayo**

el verano: **junio, julio, agosto**

el otoño: **septiembre, octubre, noviembre**

—¿Cuál es la fecha de hoy?	*What is today's date?*
—Es el primero de octubre.	*It's the first of October.*
—Es el dos de marzo.	*It's March 2nd.*
—Es el diez de noviembre.	*It's November 10th.*

El tiempo

—¿Qué tiempo hace?	*How's the weather?*
—Hace buen/mal tiempo.	*The weather is good/bad.*

Hace (mucho) calor.
It's (very) hot.

Hace (mucho) frío.
It's (very) cold.

Llueve. (llover o:ue)
It's raining.

Está lloviendo.
It's raining.

Nieva. (nevar e:ie)
It's snowing.

Está nevando.
It's snowing.

Más vocabulario

Está (muy) nublado.	*It's (very) cloudy.*
Hace fresco.	*It's cool.*
Hace (mucho) sol.	*It's (very) sunny.*
Hace (mucho) viento.	*It's (very) windy.*

5 **El Hotel Regis** Label the floors of the hotel.

Los números ordinales

primer *(before a masculine singular noun)*, **primero/a**	*first*
segundo/a	*second*
tercer *(before a masculine singular noun)*, **tercero/a**	*third*
cuarto/a	*fourth*
quinto/a	*fifth*
sexto/a	*sixth*
séptimo/a	*seventh*
octavo/a	*eighth*
noveno/a	*ninth*
décimo/a	*tenth*

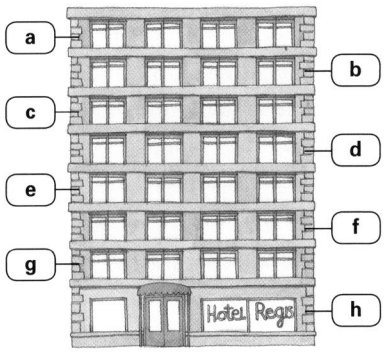

a. _____ piso
b. _____ piso
c. _____ piso
d. _____ piso
e. _____ piso
f. _____ piso
g. _____ piso
h. _____ baja

6 **Contestar** Look at the illustrations of the months and seasons on the previous page. In pairs, take turns asking each other these questions.

modelo

Estudiante 1: *¿Cuál es el primer mes de la primavera?*
Estudiante 2: *marzo*

1. ¿Cuál es el primer mes del invierno?
2. ¿Cuál es el segundo mes de la primavera?
3. ¿Cuál es el tercer mes del otoño?
4. ¿Cuál es el primer mes del año?
5. ¿Cuál es el quinto mes del año?
6. ¿Cuál es el octavo mes del año?
7. ¿Cuál es el décimo mes del año?
8. ¿Cuál es el segundo mes del verano?
9. ¿Cuál es el tercer mes del invierno?
10. ¿Cuál es el sexto mes del año?

7 **Las estaciones** Name the season that applies to the description.

1. Las clases terminan.
2. Vamos a la playa.
3. Acampamos.
4. Nieva mucho.
5. Las clases empiezan.
6. Hace mucho calor.
7. Llueve mucho.
8. Esquiamos.
9. el entrenamiento (*training*) de béisbol
10. el Día de Acción de Gracias (*Thanksgiving*)

8 **¿Cuál es la fecha?** Give the dates for these holidays.

modelo

el día de San Valentín *14 de febrero*

1. el día de San Patricio
2. el día de Halloween
3. el primer día de verano
4. el Año Nuevo
5. mi cumpleaños (*birthday*)
6. mi día de fiesta favorito

9 **Seleccionar** Paco is talking about his family and friends. Choose the word or phrase that best completes each sentence.

1. A mis padres les gusta ir a Yucatán porque (hace sol, nieva).
2. Mi primo de Kansas dice que durante (*during*) un tornado, hace mucho (sol, viento).
3. Mis amigos van a esquiar si (nieva, está nublado).
4. Tomo el sol cuando (hace calor, llueve).
5. Nosotros vamos a ver una película si hace (buen, mal) tiempo.
6. Mi hermana prefiere correr cuando (hace mucho calor, hace fresco).
7. Mis tíos van de excursión si hace (buen, mal) tiempo.
8. Mi padre no quiere jugar al golf si (hace fresco, llueve).
9. Cuando hace mucho (sol, frío) no salgo de casa y tomo chocolate caliente (*hot*).
10. Hoy mi sobrino va al parque porque (está lloviendo, hace buen tiempo).

10 **El clima** With a partner, take turns asking and answering questions about the weather and temperatures in these cities. Use the model as a guide.

modelo

Estudiante 1: ¿Qué tiempo hace hoy en Nueva York?
Estudiante 2: Hace frío y hace viento.
Estudiante 1: ¿Cuál es la temperatura máxima?
Estudiante 2: Treinta y un grados (*degrees*).
Estudiante 1: ¿Y la temperatura mínima?
Estudiante 2: Diez grados.

Nueva York	Miami	Chicago	París	Madrid	Tokio
Máx. 31°	Máx. 84°	Máx. 23°	Máx. 38°	Máx. 42°	Máx. 49°
Mín. 10°	Mín. 62°	Mín. 5°	Mín. 26°	Mín. 27°	Mín. 34°

Montreal	México D.F.	Cozumel	Caracas	Quito	Buenos Aires
Máx. 18°	Máx. 76°	Máx. 91°	Máx. 80°	Máx. 60°	Máx. 85°
Mín. 2°	Mín. 41°	Mín. 73°	Mín. 72°	Mín. 51°	Mín. 59°

NOTA CULTURAL

In most Spanish-speaking countries, temperatures are given in degrees Celsius. Use these formulas to convert between **grados centígrados** and **grados Fahrenheit**.

degrees C. × 9 ÷ 5 + 32 = degrees F.

degrees F. - 32 × 5 ÷ 9 = degrees C.

11 **Completar** Complete these sentences with your own ideas.

1. Cuando hace sol, yo...
2. Cuando llueve, mis amigos y yo...
3. Cuando hace calor, mi familia...
4. Cuando hace viento, la gente...
5. Cuando hace frío, yo...
6. Cuando hace mal tiempo, mis amigos...
7. Cuando nieva, muchas personas...
8. Cuando está nublado, mis amigos y yo...
9. Cuando hace fresco, mis padres...
10. Cuando hace buen tiempo, mis amigos...

CONSULTA

Calor and **frío** can apply to both weather and people. Use **hacer** to describe weather conditions or climate.

(**Hace frío en Santiago.** *It's cold in Santiago.*)

Use **tener** to refer to people.

(**El viajero tiene frío.** *The traveler is cold.*)

Practice more at vhlcentral.com.

Comunicación

12 **Preguntas personales** In pairs, ask each other these questions.

1. ¿Cuál es la fecha de hoy?
2. ¿Qué estación es?
3. ¿Te gusta esta estación? ¿Por qué?
4. ¿Qué estación prefieres? ¿Por qué?
5. ¿Prefieres el mar o las montañas? ¿La playa o el campo? ¿Por qué?
6. Cuando estás de vacaciones, ¿qué haces?
7. Cuando haces un viaje, ¿qué te gusta hacer y ver?
8. ¿Piensas ir de vacaciones este verano? ¿Adónde quieres ir? ¿Por qué?
9. ¿Qué deseas ver y qué lugares quieres visitar?
10. ¿Cómo te gusta viajar? ¿En avión? ¿En motocicleta...?

recursos vText CPA p. 4

13 **Encuesta** Your teacher will give you a worksheet. How does the weather affect what you do? Walk around the class and ask your classmates what they prefer or like to do in the weather conditions given. Note their responses on your worksheet. Be sure to personalize your survey by adding a few original questions to the list. Be prepared to report your findings to the class.

14 **La reservación** In pairs, imagine that one of you is a receptionist at a hotel and the other is a tourist calling to make a reservation. Read only the information that pertains to you. Then role-play the situation.

Turista

Vas a viajar a Yucatán con un amigo. Llegan a Cancún el 23 de febrero y necesitan una habitación con baño privado para cuatro noches. Ustedes quieren descansar y prefieren una habitación con vista (*view*) al mar. Averigua (*Find out*) toda la información que necesitas (el costo, cuántas camas, etc.) y decide si quieres hacer la reservación o no.

Empleado/a

Trabajas en la recepción del Hotel Oceanía en Cancún. Para el mes de febrero, sólo quedan (*remain*) dos habitaciones: una individual ($ 168/noche) en el primer piso y una doble ($ 134/noche) en el quinto piso que tiene descuento porque no hay ascensor. Todas las habitaciones tienen baño privado y vista (*view*) a la piscina.

15 **Minidrama** With two or three classmates, prepare a skit about people who are on vacation or are planning a vacation. The skit should take place in one of these locations.

- una agencia de viajes
- una casa
- un aeropuerto, una estación de tren o una estación de autobuses
- un hotel
- el campo o la playa

Síntesis

recursos vText CPA pp. 5–6

16 **Un viaje** You are planning a trip to Mexico and have many questions about your itinerary on which your partner, a travel agent, will advise you. Your teacher will give you and your partner each a sheet with different instructions for acting out the roles.

¡Vamos a la playa!

Los seis amigos hacen un viaje a la playa.

PERSONAJES

FELIPE

JUAN CARLOS

Video: *Fotonovela*

TÍA ANA MARÍA ¿Están listos para su viaje a la playa?

TODOS Sí.

TÍA ANA MARÍA Excelente... ¡A la estación de autobuses!

MARU ¿Dónde está Miguel?

FELIPE Yo lo traigo.

(*se escucha un grito de Miguel*)

FELIPE Ya está listo. Y tal vez enojado. Ahorita vamos.

EMPLEADO Bienvenidas. ¿En qué puedo servirles?

MARU Hola. Tenemos una reservación para seis personas para esta noche.

EMPLEADO ¿A nombre de quién?

JIMENA ¿Díaz? ¿López? No estoy segura.

EMPLEADO Aquí están las llaves de sus habitaciones.

MARU Gracias. Una cosa más. Mi novio y yo queremos hacer windsurf, pero no tenemos tablas.

EMPLEADO El botones las puede conseguir para ustedes.

JUAN CARLOS ¿Qué hace este libro aquí? ¿Estás estudiando en la playa?

JIMENA Sí, es que tengo un examen la próxima semana.

JUAN CARLOS Ay, Jimena. ¡No! ¿Vamos a nadar?

JIMENA Bueno, como estudiar es tan aburrido y el tiempo está tan bonito...

MARISSA

JIMENA

MARU

MIGUEL

MAITE FUENTES

ANA MARÍA

EMPLEADO

EMPLEADO No encuentro su nombre. Ah, no, ahora sí lo veo, aquí está. Díaz. Dos habitaciones en el primer piso para seis huéspedes.

FELIPE No está nada mal el hotel, ¿verdad? Limpio, cómodo... ¡Oye, Miguel! ¿Todavía estás enojado conmigo? (*a Juan Carlos*) Miguel está de mal humor. No me habla.

JUAN CARLOS ¿Todavía?

MARISSA Yo estoy un poco cansada. ¿Y tú? ¿Por qué no estás nadando?

FELIPE Es por causa de Miguel.

MARISSA Hmm, estoy confundida.

FELIPE Esta mañana. ¡Sigue enojado conmigo!

MARISSA No puede seguir enojado tanto tiempo.

recursos

vText CPA pp. 7–8 vhlcentral

Expresiones útiles

Talking with hotel personnel

¿En qué puedo servirles?
How can I help you?
Tenemos una reservación.
We have a reservation.
¿A nombre de quién?
In whose name?
¿Quizás López? ¿Tal vez Díaz?
Maybe López? Maybe Díaz?
Ahora lo veo, aquí está. Díaz.
Now I see it. Here it is. Díaz.
Dos habitaciones en el primer piso para seis huéspedes.
Two rooms on the first floor for six guests.
Aquí están las llaves.
Here are the keys.

Describing a hotel

No está nada mal el hotel.
The hotel isn't bad at all.
Todo está tan limpio y cómodo.
Everything is so clean and comfortable.
Es excelente/estupendo/fabuloso/fenomenal/increíble/magnífico/maravilloso/perfecto.
It's excellent/stupendous/fabulous/phenomenal/incredible/magnificent/marvelous/perfect.

Talking about how you feel

Yo estoy un poco cansado/a.
I am a little tired.
Estoy confundido/a. *I'm confused.*
Todavía estoy/Sigo enojado/a contigo.
I'm still angry with you.

Additional vocabulary

afuera *outside*
amable *nice; friendly*
el balde *bucket*
la crema de afeitar *shaving cream*
entonces *so, then*
es igual *it's the same*
el frente (frío) *(cold) front*
el grito *scream*
la temporada *period of time*

¿Qué pasó?

1 **Completar** Complete these sentences with the correct term from the word bank.

aburrido	la estación de autobuses	montar a caballo
el aeropuerto	habitaciones	reservación
amable	la llave	tablas de windsurf

1. Los amigos van a _____ para ir a la playa.
2. La _____ del hotel está a nombre de los Díaz.
3. Los amigos tienen dos _____ para seis personas.
4. El botones puede conseguir _____ para Maru.
5. Jimena dice que estudiar en vacaciones es muy _____.

CONSULTA

The meaning of some adjectives, such as **aburrido,** changes depending on whether they are used with **ser** or **estar.** See **Estructura 5.3,** pp. 170–171.

2 **Identificar** Identify the person who would make each statement.

EMPLEADO

MARU

TÍA ANA MARÍA

FELIPE

JUAN CARLOS

1. No lo encuentro, ¿a nombre de quién está su reservación?
2. ¿Por qué estás estudiando en la playa? ¡Mejor vamos a nadar!
3. Nuestra reservación es para seis personas en dos habitaciones.
4. El hotel es limpio y cómodo, pero estoy triste porque Miguel no me habla.
5. Suban al autobús y ¡buen viaje a la playa!

3 **Ordenar** Place these events in the correct order.

_____ a. El empleado busca la reservación.
_____ b. Marissa dice que está confundida.
_____ c. Los amigos están listos para ir a la playa.
_____ d. El empleado da (*gives*) las llaves de las habitaciones a las chicas.
_____ e. Miguel grita (*screams*).

4 **Conversar** With a partner, use these cues to create a conversation between a hotel employee and a guest in Mexico.

Huésped	Empleado/a
Say hi to the employee and ask for your reservation.	→ Tell the guest that you can't find his/her reservation.
Tell the employee that the reservation is in your name.	→ Tell him/her that you found the reservation and that it's for a double room.
Tell the employee that the hotel is very clean and orderly.	→ Say that you agree with the guest, welcome him/her, and give him/her the keys.
Ask the employee to call the bellhop to help you with your luggage.	→ Call the bellhop to help the guest with his/her luggage.

Practice more at vhlcentral.com.

Pronunciación

Audio

Spanish b and v

bueno **vóleibol** **biblioteca** **vivir**

There is no difference in pronunciation between the Spanish letters **b** and **v**. However, each letter can be pronounced two different ways, depending on which letters appear next to them.

bonito **viajar** **también** **investigar**

B and **v** are pronounced like the English hard *b* when they appear either as the first letter of a word, at the beginning of a phrase, or after **m** or **n**.

deber **novio** **abril** **cerveza**

In all other positions, **b** and **v** have a softer pronunciation, which has no equivalent in English. Unlike the hard **b**, which is produced by tightly closing the lips and stopping the flow of air, the soft **b** is produced by keeping the lips slightly open.

bola **vela** **Caribe** **declive**

In both pronunciations, there is no difference in sound between **b** and **v**. The English *v* sound, produced by friction between the upper teeth and lower lip, does not exist in Spanish. Instead, the soft **b** comes from friction between the two lips.

Verónica y su esposo cantan boleros.

When **b** or **v** begins a word, its pronunciation depends on the previous word. At the beginning of a phrase or after a word that ends in **m** or **n**, it is pronounced as a hard **b**.

Benito es de Boquerón pero vive en Victoria.

Words that begin with **b** or **v** are pronounced with a soft **b** if they appear immediately after a word that ends in a vowel or any consonant other than **m** or **n**.

Práctica Read these words aloud to practice the **b** and the **v**.

1. hablamos
2. trabajar
3. botones
4. van
5. contabilidad
6. bien
7. doble
8. novia
9. béisbol
10. nublado
11. llave
12. invierno

Oraciones Read these sentences aloud to practice the **b** and the **v**.

1. Vamos a Guaynabo en autobús.
2. Voy de vacaciones a la Isla Culebra.
3. Tengo una habitación individual en el octavo piso.
4. Víctor y Eva van por avión al Caribe.
5. La planta baja es bonita también.
6. ¿Qué vamos a ver en Bayamón?
7. Beatriz, la novia de Víctor, es de Arecibo, Puerto Rico.

Refranes Read these sayings aloud to practice the **b** and the **v**.

1 Every cloud has a silver lining.
2 An ounce of prevention equals a pound of cure.

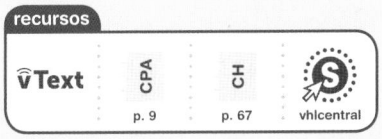

EN DETALLE

Additional Reading

Las cataratas del Iguazú

Imagine the impressive and majestic Niagara Falls, the most powerful waterfall in North America. Now, if you can, imagine a waterfall four times as wide and almost twice as tall that caused Eleanor Roosevelt to exclaim "Poor Niagara!" upon seeing it for the first time. Welcome to **las cataratas del Iguazú!**

Iguazú is located in Iguazú National Park, an area of subtropical jungle where Argentina meets Brazil. Its name comes from the indigenous Guaraní word for "great water." A UNESCO World Heritage Site, **las cataratas del Iguazú** span three kilometers and comprise 275 cascades split into two main sections by San Martín Island. Most of the falls are about 82 meters (270 feet) high. The horseshoe-shaped cataract **Garganta del Diablo** (*Devil's Throat*) has the greatest water flow and is considered to be the most impressive; it also marks the border between Argentina and Brazil.

Each country offers different views and tourist options. Most visitors opt to use the numerous catwalks that are available on both sides; however, from the Argentinean side, tourists can get very close to the falls, whereas Brazil provides more panoramic views. If you don't mind getting wet, a jet boat tour is a good choice; those looking for wildlife—such as toucans, ocelots, butterflies, and jaguars—should head for San Martín Island. Brazil boasts less conventional ways to view the falls, such as helicopter rides and rappelling, while Argentina focuses on sustainability with its **Tren Ecológico de la Selva** (*Ecological Jungle Train*), an environmentally friendly way to reach the walkways.

No matter which way you choose to enjoy the falls, you are certain to be captivated.

Más cascadas° en Latinoamérica

Nombre	País	Altura°	Datos
Salto Ángel	Venezuela	979 metros	la más alta° del mundo°
Catarata del Gocta	Perú	771 metros	descubierta° en 2006
Piedra Volada	México	453 metros	la más alta de México

cascadas *waterfalls* Altura *Height* más alta *tallest* mundo *world* descubierta *discovered*

ACTIVIDADES

1 **¿Cierto o falso?** Indicate whether these statements are **cierto** or **falso**. Correct the false statements.

1. Iguazú Falls is located on the border of Argentina and Brazil.
2. Niagara Falls is four times as wide as Iguazú Falls.
3. Iguazú Falls has a few cascades, each about 82 meters.
4. Tourists visiting Iguazú can see exotic wildlife.
5. *Iguazú* is the Guaraní word for "blue water."
6. You can access the walkways by taking the **Garganta del Diablo.**
7. It is possible for tourists to visit Iguazú Falls by air.
8. **Salto Ángel** is the tallest waterfall in the world.
9. There are no waterfalls in Mexico.
10. For the best views of Iguazú Falls, tourists should visit the Brazilian side.

ASÍ SE DICE

Viajes y turismo

el asiento del medio, del pasillo, de la ventanilla	*center, aisle, window seat*
el itinerario	*itinerary*
media pensión	*breakfast and one meal included*
el ómnibus (Perú)	**el autobús**
pensión completa	*all meals included*
el puente	*long weekend (lit., bridge)*

EL MUNDO HISPANO

Destinos populares

- **Las playas del Parque Nacional Manuel Antonio** (Costa Rica) ofrecen° la oportunidad de nadar y luego caminar por el bosque tropical°.
- **Teotihuacán** (México) Desde antes de la época° de los aztecas, aquí se celebra el equinoccio de primavera en la Pirámide del Sol.
- **Puerto Chicama** (Perú), con sus olas° de cuatro kilómetros de largo°, es un destino para surfistas expertos.
- **Tikal** (Guatemala) Aquí puedes ver las maravillas de la selva° y ruinas de la civilización maya.
- **Las playas de Rincón** (Puerto Rico) Son ideales para descansar y observar ballenas°.

ofrecen *offer* bosque tropical *rainforest* Desde antes de la época *Since before the time* olas *waves* de largo *in length* selva *jungle* ballenas *whales*

PERFIL

Punta del Este

One of South America's largest and most fashionable beach resort towns is Uruguay's **Punta del Este**, a narrow strip of land containing twenty miles of pristine beaches. Its peninsular shape gives it two very different seascapes. **La Playa Mansa**, facing the bay and therefore the more protected side, has calm waters. Here, people practice water sports like swimming, water skiing, windsurfing, and diving. **La Playa Brava**, facing east, receives the Atlantic Ocean's powerful, wave-producing winds, making it popular for surfing, body boarding, and kite surfing. Besides the beaches, posh shopping, and world-famous nightlife, **Punta** offers its 600,000 yearly visitors yacht and fishing clubs, golf courses, and excursions to observe sea lions at the **Isla de Lobos** nature reserve.

Conexión Internet

¿Cuáles son los sitios más populares para el turismo en Puerto Rico?

Go to **vhlcentral.com** to find more cultural information related to this **Cultura** section.

ACTIVIDADES

2 **Comprensión** Complete the sentences.

1. En las playas de Rincón puedes ver _____.
2. Cerca de 600.000 turistas visitan _____ cada año.
3. En el avión pides el _____ si te gusta ver el paisaje.
4. En Punta del Este, la gente prefiere nadar en la Playa _____.
5. El _____ es un medio de transporte en Perú.

3 **De vacaciones** Spring break is coming up, and your class is going on a trip abroad. Working in a small group, decide where you will go, how you will get there, and what each of you will do. Present your trip to the class.

Practice more at vhlcentral.com.

recursos

vText

CH p. 68

vhlcentral

5.1 Estar with conditions and emotions

Tutorial

ANTE TODO As you have already learned, the verb **estar** is used to talk about how you feel and to say where people, places, and things are located. **Estar** is also used with adjectives to talk about certain emotional and physical conditions.

▶ Use **estar** with adjectives to describe the physical condition of places and things.

La habitación **está** sucia.
The room is dirty.

La puerta **está** cerrada.
The door is closed.

▶ Use **estar** with adjectives to describe how people feel, both mentally and physically.

▶ **¡Atención!** Two important expressions with **estar** that you can use to talk about conditions and emotions are **estar de buen humor** (*to be in a good mood*) and **estar de mal humor** (*to be in a bad mood*).

Adjectives that describe emotions and conditions

abierto/a	*open*	**contento/a**	*happy; content*	**listo/a**	*ready*
aburrido/a	*bored*	**desordenado/a**	*disorderly*	**nervioso/a**	*nervous*
alegre	*happy; joyful*	**enamorado/a (de)**	*in love (with)*	**ocupado/a**	*busy*
avergonzado/a	*embarrassed*			**ordenado/a**	*orderly*
cansado/a	*tired*	**enojado/a**	*mad; angry*	**preocupado/a (por)**	*worried (about)*
cerrado/a	*closed*	**equivocado/a**	*wrong*		
cómodo/a	*comfortable*	**feliz**	*happy*	**seguro/a**	*sure*
confundido/a	*confused*	**limpio/a**	*clean*	**sucio/a**	*dirty*
				triste	*sad*

¡INTÉNTALO! Provide the present tense forms of **estar**, and choose which adjective best completes the sentence.

1. La biblioteca _____está_____ (cerrada / nerviosa) los domingos por la noche. *cerrada*
2. Nosotros _____ muy (ocupados / equivocados) todos los lunes.
3. Ellas _____ (alegres / confundidas) porque tienen vacaciones.
4. Javier _____ (enamorado / ordenado) de Maribel.
5. Diana _____ (enojada / limpia) con su hermano.
6. Yo _____ (nerviosa / abierta) por el viaje.
7. La habitación siempre _____ (ordenada / segura) cuando vuelven sus padres.
8. Ustedes no comprenden; _____ (equivocados / tristes).

recursos
vText
CPA pp. 10–12
CH pp. 69–70
vhlcentral

Práctica y Comunicación

1 **¿Cómo están?** Complete Martín's statements about how he and other people are feeling. In the first blank, fill in the correct form of **estar**. In the second blank, fill in the adjective that best fits the context.

AYUDA

Make sure that you have agreement between:
- Subjects and verbs in person and number
- Nouns and adjectives in gender and number

Ell**os** no est**án** enferm**os**.
They are not sick.

1. Yo _____ un poco _____ porque tengo un examen mañana.
2. Mi hermana Patricia _____ muy _____ porque mañana va a hacer una excursión al campo.
3. Mis hermanos Juan y José salen de la casa a las cinco de la mañana. Por la noche, siempre _____ muy _____.
4. Mi amigo Ramiro _____ _____; su novia se llama Adela.
5. Mi papá y sus colegas _____ muy _____ hoy. ¡Hay mucho trabajo!
6. Patricia y yo _____ un poco _____ por ellos porque trabajan mucho.
7. Mi amiga Mónica _____ un poco _____ porque sus amigos no pueden salir esta noche.
8. Esta clase no es muy interesante. ¿Tú _____ _____ también?

2 **Describir** Describe these people and places.

1. Anabela

2. Juan y Luisa

3. la habitación de Teresa

4. la habitación de César

3 **Situaciones** With a partner, use **estar** to talk about how you feel in these situations.

1. Cuando hace sol...
2. Cuando tomas un examen...
3. Cuando viajas en avión...
4. Cuando estás en la clase de español...
5. Cuando ves una película con tu actor/actriz favorito/a...

4 **En la tele** In small groups, imagine that you are a family that stars on a reality TV show. You are vacationing together, but the trip isn't going well for everyone. Write the script of a scene from the show and then act it out. Use at least six adjectives from the previous page and be creative!

modelo

Papá: ¿Por qué estás enojada, María Rosa? El hotel es muy bonito y las habitaciones están limpias.

Mamá: ¡Pero mira, Roberto! Las maletas de Elisa están abiertas y, como siempre, sus cosas están muy desordenadas.

Practice more at vhlcentral.com.

5.2 The present progressive

Tutorial

ANTE TODO Both Spanish and English use the present progressive, which consists of the present tense of the verb *to be* and the present participle of another verb (the *-ing* form in English).

Las chicas están hablando con el empleado del hotel.

¿Estás estudiando en la playa?

- Form the present progressive with the present tense of **estar** and a present participle.

FORM OF ESTAR + PRESENT PARTICIPLE		FORM OF ESTAR + PRESENT PARTICIPLE	
Estoy	**pescando.**	**Estamos**	**comiendo.**
I am	*fishing.*	*We are*	*eating.*

- The present participle of regular **-ar**, **-er**, and **-ir** verbs is formed as follows:

INFINITIVE	STEM	ENDING	PRESENT PARTICIPLE
hablar	habl-	**-ando**	habl**ando**
comer	com-	**-iendo**	com**iendo**
escribir	escrib-	**-iendo**	escrib**iendo**

- **¡Atención!** When the stem of an **-er** or **-ir** verb ends in a vowel, the present participle ends in **-yendo**.

INFINITIVE	STEM	ENDING	PRESENT PARTICIPLE
leer	le-	**-yendo**	le**yendo**
oír	o-	**-yendo**	o**yendo**
traer	tra-	**-yendo**	tra**yendo**

- **Ir**, **poder**, and **venir** have irregular present participles (**yendo**, **pudiendo**, **viniendo**). Several other verbs have irregular present participles that you will need to learn.
- **-Ir** stem-changing verbs have a stem change in the present participle.

-ir stem-changing verbs

e:ie in the present tense		e → i in the present participle
preferir	→	prefiriendo
e:i in the present tense		e → i in the present participle
conseguir	→	consiguiendo
o:ue in the present tense		o → u in the present participle
dormir	→	durmiendo

COMPARE & CONTRAST

The use of the present progressive is much more restricted in Spanish than in English. In Spanish, the present progressive is mainly used to emphasize that an action is in progress at the time of speaking.

Maru **está escuchando** música latina **ahora mismo**.
Maru is listening to Latin music right now.

Felipe y su amigo **todavía están jugando** al fútbol.
Felipe and his friend are still playing soccer.

In English, the present progressive is often used to talk about situations and actions that occur over an extended period of time or in the future. In Spanish, the simple present tense is often used instead.

Xavier **estudia** computación este semestre.
Xavier is studying computer science this semester.

Marissa **sale** mañana para los Estados Unidos.
Marissa is leaving tomorrow for the United States.

¡INTÉNTALO! Create complete sentences by putting the verbs in the present progressive.

1. mis amigos / descansar en la playa *Mis amigos están descansando en la playa.*
2. nosotros / practicar deportes _____
3. Carmen / comer en casa _____
4. nuestro equipo / ganar el partido _____
5. yo / leer el periódico _____
6. él / pensar comprar una bicicleta roja _____
7. ustedes / jugar a las cartas _____
8. José y Francisco / dormir _____
9. Marisa / leer correo electrónico _____
10. yo / preparar sándwiches _____
11. Carlos / tomar fotos _____
12. ¿dormir / tú? _____

recursos
vText
CPA pp. 13–14
CH pp. 71–72
vhlcentral

Práctica

1 **Completar** Alfredo's Spanish class is preparing to travel to Puerto Rico. Use the present progressive of the verb in parentheses to complete Alfredo's description of what everyone is doing.

1. Yo _____ (investigar) la situación política de la isla (*island*).
2. La esposa del profesor _____ (hacer) las maletas.
3. Marta y José Luis _____ (buscar) información sobre San Juan en Internet.
4. Enrique y yo _____ (leer) un correo electrónico de nuestro amigo puertorriqueño.
5. Javier _____ (aprender) mucho sobre la cultura puertorriqueña.
6. Y tú _____ (practicar) el español, ¿verdad?

2 **¿Qué están haciendo?** María and her friends are vacationing at a resort in San Juan, Puerto Rico. Complete her description of what everyone is doing right now.

CONSULTA
For more information about Puerto Rico, see **Panorama**, pp. 186–187.

1. Yo

2. Javier

3. Alejandra y Rebeca

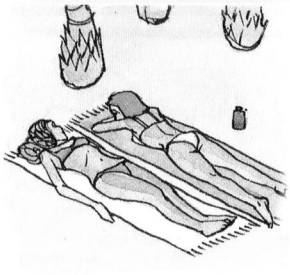
4. Celia y yo

5. Samuel

6. Lorenzo

3 **Personajes famosos** Say what these celebrities are doing right now, using the cues provided.

AYUDA
Isabel Allende: **novelas**
Rachel Ray: **televisión, negocios** (*business*)
James Cameron: **cine**
Venus y Serena Williams: **tenis**
Joey Votto: **béisbol**
Nelly Furtado: **canciones**
Dwight Howard: **baloncesto**
Las Rockettes de Nueva York: **baile**

modelo
Shakira
Shakira está cantando una canción ahora mismo.

A		B	
Isabel Allende	Nelly Furtado	bailar	hacer
Rachel Ray	Dwight Howard	cantar	jugar
James Cameron	Las Rockettes de Nueva York	correr	preparar
Venus y Serena Williams	¿?	escribir	¿?
Joey Votto	¿?	hablar	¿?

Practice more at vhlcentral.com.

Comunicación

4 **Preguntar** With a partner, take turns asking each other what you are doing at these times.

modelo

Estudiante 1: ¡Hola, Andrés! Son las ocho de la mañana. ¿Qué estás haciendo?
Estudiante 2: Estoy desayunando.

1. 5:00 a.m.
2. 9:30 a.m.
3. 11:00 a.m.
4. 12:00 p.m.
5. 2:00 p.m.
6. 5:00 p.m.
7. 9:00 p.m.
8. 11:30 p.m.

5 **Describir** Work with a partner and use the present progressive to describe what is going on in this Spanish beach scene.

NOTA CULTURAL

Nearly 60 million tourists travel to Spain every year, many of them drawn by the warm climate and beautiful coasts. Tourists wanting a beach vacation go mostly to the **Costa del Sol** or the Balearic Islands, in the Mediterranean.

6 **Conversar** Imagine that you and a classmate are each babysitting a group of children. With a partner, prepare a telephone conversation using these cues. Be creative and add further comments.

Estudiante 1	Estudiante 2
Say hello and ask what the kids are doing.	Say hello and tell your partner that two of your kids are doing their homework. Then ask what the kids at his/her house are doing.
Tell your partner that two of your kids are running and dancing in the house.	Tell your partner that one of the kids is reading.
Tell your partner that you are tired and that two of your kids are watching TV and eating pizza.	Tell your partner that one of the kids is sleeping.
Tell your partner you have to go; the kids are playing soccer in the house.	Say goodbye and good luck (**¡Buena suerte!**).

Síntesis

7 **¿Qué están haciendo?** A group of classmates is traveling to San Juan, Puerto Rico for a week-long Spanish immersion program. In order for the participants to be on time for their flight, you and your partner must locate them. Your teacher will give you each a handout to help you complete this task.

recursos
vText
CPA
pp. 15–16

5.3 Ser and estar

Tutorial

ANTE TODO

You have already learned that **ser** and **estar** both mean *to be* but are used for different purposes. These charts summarize the key differences in usage between **ser** and **estar**.

¡ATENCIÓN!

Ser de expresses not only origin (**Es de Buenos Aires.**) and possession (**Es la pluma de Jimena.**), but also what material something is made of (**La bicicleta es de metal.**).

Uses of ser

1. Nationality and place of origin	Juan Carlos **es** argentino. **Es** de Buenos Aires.
2. Profession or occupation	Adela **es** agente de viajes. Francisco **es** médico.
3. Characteristics of people and things	José y Clara **son** simpáticos. El clima de Puerto Rico **es** agradable.
4. Generalizations	¡**Es** fabuloso viajar! **Es** difícil estudiar a la una de la mañana.
5. Possession	**Es** la pluma de Jimena. **Son** las llaves del señor Díaz.
6. What something is made of	La bicicleta **es** de metal. Los pasajes **son** de papel.
7. Time and date	Hoy **es** martes. **Son** las dos. Hoy **es** el primero de julio.
8. Where or when an event takes place	El partido **es** en el estadio Santa Fe. La conferencia **es** a las siete.

Uses of estar

1. Location or spatial relationships	El aeropuerto **está** lejos de la ciudad. Tu habitación **está** en el tercer piso.
2. Health	¿Cómo **estás**? **Estoy** bien, gracias.
3. Physical states and conditions	El profesor **está** ocupado. Las ventanas **están** abiertas.
4. Emotional states	Marissa **está** feliz hoy. **Estoy** muy enojado con Maru.
5. Certain weather expressions	**Está** lloviendo. **Está** nublado.
6. Ongoing actions (progressive tenses)	**Estamos** estudiando para un examen. Ana **está** leyendo una novela.

Ser and estar with adjectives

- With many descriptive adjectives, **ser** and **estar** can both be used, but the meaning will change.

Juan **es** delgado. *Juan is thin.*	Ana **es** nerviosa. *Ana is a nervous person.*
Juan **está** más delgado hoy. *Juan looks thinner today.*	Ana **está** nerviosa por el examen. *Ana is nervous because of the exam.*

- In the examples above, the statements with **ser** are general observations about the inherent qualities of Juan and Ana. The statements with **estar** describe conditions that are variable.

- Here are some adjectives that change in meaning when used with **ser** and **estar**.

With ser	With estar
El chico **es listo**. *The boy is **smart**.*	El chico **está listo**. *The boy is **ready**.*
La profesora **es mala**. *The professor is **bad**.*	La profesora **está mala**. *The professor is **sick**.*
Jaime **es aburrido**. *Jaime is **boring**.*	Jaime **está aburrido**. *Jaime is **bored**.*
Las peras **son verdes**. *Pears are **green**.*	Las peras **están verdes**. *The pears are **not ripe**.*
El gato **es muy vivo**. *The cat is very **clever**.*	El gato **está vivo**. *The cat is **alive**.*
Iván **es un hombre seguro**. *Iván is a **confident** man.*	Iván no **está seguro**. *Iván is not **sure**.*

¡ATENCIÓN!
When referring to objects, **ser seguro/a** means *to be safe.*
El puente es seguro.
The bridge is safe.

¡INTÉNTALO! Form complete sentences by using the correct form of **ser** or **estar** and making any other necessary changes.

1. Alejandra / cansado
   Alejandra está cansada.
2. ellos / pelirrojo
   _____
3. Carmen / alto
   _____
4. yo / la clase de español
   _____
5. película / a las once
   _____
6. hoy / viernes
   _____
7. nosotras / enojado
   _____
8. Antonio / médico
   _____
9. Romeo y Julieta / enamorado
   _____
10. libros / de Ana
    _____
11. Marisa y Juan / estudiando
    _____
12. partido de baloncesto / gimnasio
    _____

recursos
vText
CPA pp. 17–19
CH pp. 73–74
vhlcentral

Práctica

1 **¿Ser o estar?** Indicate whether each adjective takes **ser** or **estar**. **¡Ojo!** Three of them can take both verbs.

	ser	estar		ser	estar
1. delgada	❍	❍	5. seguro	❍	❍
2. canadiense	❍	❍	6. enojada	❍	❍
3. enamorado	❍	❍	7. importante	❍	❍
4. lista	❍	❍	8. avergonzada	❍	❍

2 **Completar** Complete this conversation with the appropriate forms of **ser** and **estar**.

EDUARDO ¡Hola, Ceci! ¿Cómo (1)_____?
CECILIA Hola, Eduardo. Bien, gracias. ¡Qué guapo (2)_____ hoy!
EDUARDO Gracias. (3)_____ muy amable. Oye, ¿qué (4)_____ haciendo? (5)¿_____ ocupada?
CECILIA No, sólo le (6)_____ escribiendo una carta a mi prima Pilar.
EDUARDO ¿De dónde (7)_____ ella?
CECILIA Pilar (8)_____ de Ecuador. Su papá (9)_____ médico en Quito. Pero ahora Pilar y su familia (10)_____ de vacaciones en Ponce, Puerto Rico.
EDUARDO Y... ¿cómo (11)_____ Pilar?
CECILIA (12)_____ muy lista. Y también (13)_____ alta, rubia y muy bonita.

3 **En el parque** With a partner, take turns describing the people in the drawing. Your descriptions should answer the questions provided.

1. ¿Quiénes son?
2. ¿Dónde están?
3. ¿Cómo son?
4. ¿Cómo están?
5. ¿Qué están haciendo?
6. ¿Qué estación es?
7. ¿Qué tiempo hace?
8. ¿Quiénes están de vacaciones?

Practice more at vhlcentral.com.

Comunicación

4 **Describir** With a classmate, take turns describing these people. Mention where they are from, what they are like, how they are feeling, and what they are doing right now.

modelo

tu compañero/a de clase

Mi compañera de clase es de San Juan, Puerto Rico. Es muy inteligente. Está cansada pero está estudiando porque tiene un examen.

1. tu mejor (*best*) amigo/a
2. tu actor/actriz favorito/a
3. tu profesor(a) favorito/a
4. tu vecino/a
5. tus abuelos
6. tus padres

5 **Adivinar** Get together with a partner and take turns describing a celebrity using these items as a guide. Don't mention the celebrity's name. Can your partner guess who you are describing?

- descripción física
- cómo está ahora
- origen
- dónde está ahora
- qué está haciendo ahora
- profesión u ocupación

6 **En el aeropuerto** In groups of three, take turns assuming the identity of a character from this drawing. Your partners will ask you questions using **ser** and **estar** until they figure out who you are.

modelo

Estudiante 3: *¿Dónde estás?*
Estudiante 1: *Estoy cerca de la puerta.*
Estudiante 2: *¿Qué estás haciendo?*
Estudiante 1: *Estoy escuchando a otra persona.*
Estudiante 3: *¿Eres uno de los pasajeros?*
Estudiante 1: *No, soy empleado del aeropuerto.*
Estudiante 2: *¿Eres Camilo?*

NOTA CULTURAL

Luis Muñoz Marín International Airport in San Juan, Puerto Rico, is a major transportation hub of the Caribbean. It is named after Puerto Rico's first elected governor.

Síntesis

7 **Conversación** In pairs, imagine that you and your partner are two of the characters in the drawing in **Actividad 6**. After boarding, you are seated next to each other and strike up a conversation. Act out what you would say to your fellow passenger.

5.4 Direct object nouns and pronouns

SUBJECT	VERB	DIRECT OBJECT NOUN
Juan Carlos y Jimena	están tomando	fotos.
Juan Carlos and Jimena	*are taking*	*photos.*

- A direct object noun receives the action of the verb directly and generally follows the verb. In the example above, the direct object noun answers the question *What are Juan Carlos and Jimena taking?*

- When a direct object noun in Spanish is a person or a pet, it is preceded by the word **a**. This is called the personal **a**; there is no English equivalent for this construction.

  Mariela mira **a** Carlos.
  Mariela is watching Carlos.

  Mariela mira televisión.
  Mariela is watching TV.

- In the first sentence above, the personal **a** is required because the direct object is a person. In the second sentence, the personal **a** is not required because the direct object is a place, not a person.

- Direct object pronouns are words that replace direct object nouns. Like English, Spanish uses a direct object pronoun to avoid repeating a noun already mentioned.

	DIRECT OBJECT		DIRECT OBJECT PRONOUN		
Maribel hace	las maletas.	▶	Maribel	las	hace.
Felipe compra	el sombrero.		Felipe	lo	compra.
Vicky tiene	la llave.		Vicky	la	tiene.

Direct object pronouns

SINGULAR		PLURAL	
me	*me*	**nos**	*us*
te	*you*	**os**	*you* (fam.)
lo	*you*	**los**	*you* (m., form.)
	him; it		*them* (m.)
la	*you her; it*	**las**	*you* (f., form.)
			them (f.)

- In affirmative sentences, direct object pronouns generally appear before the conjugated verb. In negative sentences, the pronoun is placed between the word **no** and the verb.

Adela practica **el tenis**. Adela **lo** practica.	Gabriela no tiene **las llaves**. Gabriela **no las** tiene.
Carmen compra **los pasajes**. Carmen **los** compra.	Diego no hace **las maletas**. Diego **no las** hace.

- When the verb is an infinitive construction, such as **ir a** + [*infinitive*], the direct object pronoun can be placed before the conjugated form or attached to the infinitive.

Ellos van a escribir **unas postales**. < Ellos **las** van a escribir. / Ellos van a escribir**las**.

Lidia quiere ver **una película**. < Lidia **la** quiere ver. / Lidia quiere ver**la**.

- When the verb is in the present progressive, the direct object pronoun can be placed before the conjugated form or attached to the present participle. **¡Atención!** When a direct object pronoun is attached to the present participle, an accent mark is added to maintain the proper stress.

Gerardo está leyendo **la lección**. < Gerardo **la** está leyendo. / Gerardo está leyéndo**la**.

Toni está mirando **el partido**. < Toni **lo** está mirando. / Toni está mirándo**lo**.

¡INTÉNTALO! Choose the correct direct object pronoun for each sentence.

1. Tienes el libro de español. *c*
   a. La tienes. b. Los tienes. c. Lo tienes.
2. Voy a ver el partido de baloncesto.
   a. Voy a verlo. b. Voy a verte. c. Voy a vernos.
3. El artista quiere dibujar a Luisa con su mamá.
   a. Quiere dibujarme. b. Quiere dibujarla. c. Quiere dibujarlas.
4. Marcos busca la llave.
   a. Me busca. b. La busca. c. Las busca.
5. Rita me lleva al aeropuerto y también lleva a Tomás.
   a. Nos lleva. b. Las lleva. c. Te lleva.
6. Puedo oír a Gerardo y a Miguel.
   a. Puedo oírte. b. Puedo oírlos. c. Puedo oírlo.
7. Quieren estudiar la gramática.
   a. Quieren estudiarnos. b. Quieren estudiarlo. c. Quieren estudiarla.
8. ¿Practicas los verbos irregulares?
   a. ¿Los practicas? b. ¿Las practicas? c. ¿Lo practicas?
9. Ignacio ve la película.
   a. La ve. b. Lo ve. c. Las ve.
10. Sandra va a invitar a Mario a la excursión. También me va a invitar a mí.
    a. Los va a invitar. b. Lo va a invitar. c. Nos va a invitar.

recursos
vText
CPA pp. 20–21
CH pp. 75–76
vhlcentral

Práctica

1 **Simplificar** Señora Vega's class is planning a trip to Costa Rica. Describe their preparations by changing the direct object nouns into direct object pronouns.

modelo

La profesora Vega tiene su pasaporte.
La profesora Vega lo tiene.

1. Gustavo y Héctor confirman las reservaciones.
2. Nosotros leemos los folletos (*brochures*).
3. Ana María estudia el mapa.
4. Yo aprendo los nombres de los monumentos de San José.
5. Alicia escucha a la profesora.
6. Miguel escribe las instrucciones para ir al hotel.
7. Esteban busca el pasaje.
8. Nosotros planeamos una excursión.

¡LENGUA VIVA!

There are many Spanish words that correspond to *ticket*. **Billete** and **pasaje** usually refer to a ticket for travel, such as an airplane ticket. **Entrada** refers to a ticket to an event, such as a concert or a movie. **Boleto** can be used in either case.

2 **Vacaciones** Ramón is going to San Juan, Puerto Rico with his friends, Javier and Marcos. Express his thoughts more succinctly using direct object pronouns.

modelo

Quiero hacer una excursión.
Quiero hacerla./La quiero hacer.

1. Voy a hacer mi maleta.
2. Necesitamos llevar los pasaportes.
3. Marcos está pidiendo el folleto turístico.
4. Javier debe llamar a sus padres.
5. Ellos esperan visitar el Viejo San Juan.
6. Puedo llamar a Javier por la mañana.
7. Prefiero llevar mi cámara.
8. No queremos perder nuestras reservaciones de hotel.

NOTA CULTURAL

Since Puerto Rico is a U.S. territory, passengers traveling there from the U.S. mainland do not need passports or visas. Passengers traveling to Puerto Rico from a foreign country, however, must meet travel requirements identical to those required for travel to the U.S. mainland. Puerto Ricans are U.S. citizens and can therefore travel to the U.S. mainland without any travel documents.

3 **¿Quién?** The Garza family is preparing to go on a vacation to Puerto Rico. Based on the clues, answer the questions. Use direct object pronouns in your answers.

modelo

¿Quién hace las reservaciones para el hotel? (el Sr. Garza)
El Sr. Garza las hace.

1. ¿Quién compra los pasajes de avión? (la Sra. Garza)
2. ¿Quién tiene que hacer las maletas de los niños? (María)
3. ¿Quiénes buscan los pasaportes? (Antonio y María)
4. ¿Quién va a confirmar las reservaciones de hotel? (la Sra. Garza)
5. ¿Quién busca la cámara? (María)
6. ¿Quién compra un mapa de Puerto Rico? (Antonio)

Practice more at vhlcentral.com.

Comunicación

4 **Entrevista** Take turns asking and answering these questions with a classmate. Be sure to use direct object pronouns in your responses.

1. ¿Ves mucho la televisión?
2. ¿Cuándo vas a ver tu programa favorito?
3. ¿Quién prepara la comida (*food*) en tu casa?
4. ¿Te visita mucho tu abuelo/a?
5. ¿Visitas mucho a tus abuelos?
6. ¿Nos entienden nuestros padres a nosotros?
7. ¿Cuándo ves a tus amigos/as?
8. ¿Cuándo te llaman tus amigos/as?

5 **Los pasajeros** With a partner, take turns asking each other questions about the drawing. Use the word bank and direct object pronouns.

AYUDA

For travel-related vocabulary, see **Contextos**, pp. 152–153.

modelo

Estudiante 1: ¿Quién está leyendo el libro?
Estudiante 2: Susana lo está leyendo./Susana está leyéndolo.

buscar	confirmar	escribir	leer	tener	vender
comprar	encontrar	escuchar	llevar	traer	¿?

Síntesis

6 **Adivinanzas** In pairs, take turns describing a person, place, or thing for your partner to guess. Each of you should give at least five descriptions.

modelo

Estudiante 1: Lo uso para (*I use it to*) escribir en mi cuaderno. No es muy grande y tiene borrador. ¿Qué es?
Estudiante 2: ¿Es un lápiz?
Estudiante 1: ¡Sí!

SUBJECT Javier CONJUGATED FORM empiezo Main clause Dudan

Recapitulación

Diagnostics

Review the grammar concepts you have learned in this lesson by completing these activities.

1 **Completar** Complete the chart with the correct present participle of these verbs. 16 pts.

Infinitive	Present participle	Infinitive	Present participle
hacer		estar	
acampar		ser	
tener		vivir	
venir		estudiar	

2 **Vacaciones en París** Complete this paragraph about Julia's trip to Paris with the correct form of **ser** or **estar**. 24 pts.

Hoy (1) _____ (es/está) el 3 de julio y voy a París por tres semanas. (Yo) (2) _____ (Soy/Estoy) muy feliz porque voy a ver a mi mejor amiga. Ella (3) _____ (es/está) de Puerto Rico, pero ahora (4) _____ (es/está) viviendo en París. También (yo) (5) _____ (soy/estoy) un poco nerviosa porque (6) _____ (es/está) mi primer viaje a Francia. El vuelo (*flight*) (7) _____ (es/está) hoy por la tarde, pero ahora (8) _____ (es/está) lloviendo. Por eso (9) _____ (somos/estamos) preocupadas, porque probablemente el avión va a salir tarde. Mi equipaje ya (10) _____ (es/está) listo. (11) _____ (Es/Está) tarde y me tengo que ir. ¡Va a (12) _____ (ser/estar) un viaje fenomenal!

3 **¿Qué hacen?** Respond to these questions by indicating what people do with the items mentioned. Use direct object pronouns. 10 pts.

modelo

¿Qué hacen ellos con la película?
La ven.

1. ¿Qué haces tú con el libro de viajes? (leer) _____
2. ¿Qué hacen los turistas en la ciudad? (explorar) _____
3. ¿Qué hace el botones con el equipaje? (llevar) _____
4. ¿Qué hace la agente con las reservaciones? (confirmar) _____
5. ¿Qué hacen ustedes con los pasaportes? (mostrar) _____

RESUMEN GRAMATICAL

5.1 Estar with conditions and emotions *p. 164*

- Yo **estoy** aburrido/a, feliz, nervioso/a.
- El cuarto **está** desordenado, limpio, ordenado.
- Estos libros **están** abiertos, cerrados, sucios.

5.2 The present progressive *pp. 166–167*

- The present progressive is formed with the present tense of **estar** plus the present participle.

Forming the present participle

infinitive	stem	ending	present participle
hablar	habl-	-ando	hablando
comer	com-	-iendo	comiendo
escribir	escrib-	-iendo	escribiendo

-ir stem-changing verbs

	infinitive	present participle
e:ie	preferir	prefiriendo
e:i	conseguir	consiguiendo
o:ue	dormir	durmiendo

- Irregular present participles: **yendo (ir), pudiendo (poder), viniendo (venir)**

5.3 Ser and estar *pp. 170–171*

- Uses of **ser**: nationality, origin, profession or occupation, characteristics, generalizations, possession, what something is made of, time and date, time and place of events
- Uses of **estar**: location, health, physical states and conditions, emotional states, weather expressions, ongoing actions
- **Ser** and **estar** can both be used with many adjectives, but the meaning will change.

Juan **es** delgado. *Juan is thin.*
Juan **está** más delgado hoy. *Juan looks thinner today.*

5.4 Direct object nouns and pronouns *pp. 174–175*

Direct object pronouns

Singular		Plural	
me	lo	nos	los
te	la	os	las

In affirmative sentences:
Adela practica el tenis. → Adela lo practica.

In negative sentences: Adela **no** lo practica.

With an infinitive:
Adela lo va a practicar./Adela va a practicarlo.

With the present progressive:
Adela lo está practicando./Adela está practicándolo.

4 **Opuestos** Complete these sentences with the appropriate form of the verb **estar** and an antonym for the underlined adjective. 10 pts.

modelo

Yo estoy interesado, pero Susana *está aburrida.*

1. Las tiendas están abiertas, pero la agencia de viajes _____ _____.
2. No me gustan las habitaciones desordenadas. Incluso (*Even*) mi habitación de hotel _____ _____.
3. Nosotras estamos tristes cuando trabajamos. Hoy comienzan las vacaciones y _____ _____.
4. En esta ciudad los autobuses están sucios, pero los taxis _____ _____.
5. —El avión sale a las 5:30, ¿verdad? —No, estás confundida. Yo _____ _____ de que el avión sale a las 5:00.

5 **En la playa** Describe what these people are doing. Complete the sentences using the present progressive tense. 8 pts.

1. El señor Camacho _____.
2. Felicia _____.
3. Leo _____.
4. Nosotros _____.

6 **Antes del viaje** Write a paragraph of at least six sentences describing the time right before you go on a trip. Say how you feel and what you are doing. You can use **Actividad 2** as a model. 32 pts.

modelo

Hoy es viernes, 27 de octubre. Estoy en mi habitación...

7 **Refrán** Complete this Spanish saying by filling in the missing present participles. Refer to the translation and the drawing. 4 EXTRA points!

"Se consigue más _____ que _____."

(You can accomplish more by doing than by saying.)

recursos
vText
vhlcentral

Practice more at vhlcentral.com.

Lectura

Audio: Reading
Additional Reading

Antes de leer

Estrategia

Scanning

Scanning involves glancing over a document in search of specific information. For example, you can scan a document to identify its format, to find cognates, to locate visual clues about the document's content, or to find specific facts. Scanning allows you to learn a great deal about a text without having to read it word for word.

Examinar el texto

Scan the reading selection for cognates and write down a few of them.

1. _____ 4. _____
2. _____ 5. _____
3. _____ 6. _____

Based on the cognates you found, what do you think this document is about?

_____

Preguntas

Read these questions. Then scan the document again to look for answers.

1. What is the format of the reading selection?

   _____

2. Which place is the document about?

   _____

3. What are some of the visual cues this document provides? What do they tell you about the content of the document?

   _____

4. Who produced the document, and what do you think it is for?

   _____

recursos

vText | CH pp. 77–78 | vhlcentral

Turismo ecológico en Puerto Rico

Hotel Vistahermosa

~ Lajas, Puerto Rico ~

- 40 habitaciones individuales
- 15 habitaciones dobles
- Teléfono, TV por cable, Internet
- Aire acondicionado
- Restaurante (Bar)
- Piscina
- Área de juegos
- Cajero automático°

El hotel está situado en Playa Grande, un pequeño pueblo de pescadores del mar Caribe. Es el lugar perfecto para el viajero que viene de vacaciones. Las playas son seguras y limpias, ideales para tomar el sol, descansar, tomar fotografías y nadar. Está abierto los 365 días del año. Hay una rebaja° especial para estudiantes.

DIRECCIÓN: Playa Grande 406, Lajas, PR 00667, cerca del Parque Nacional Foresta.

Cajero automático *ATM* rebaja *discount*

Atracciones cercanas

Playa Grande ¿Busca la playa perfecta? Playa Grande es la playa que está buscando. Usted puede pescar, sacar fotos, nadar y pasear en bicicleta. Playa Grande es un paraíso para el turista que quiere practicar deportes acuáticos. El lugar es bonito e interesante y usted va a tener muchas oportunidades para descansar y disfrutar en familia.

Valle Niebla Ir de excursión, tomar café, montar a caballo, caminar, hacer picnics. Más de cien lugares para acampar.

Bahía Fosforescente Sacar fotos, salidas de noche, excursión en barco. Una maravillosa experiencia llena de luz°.

Arrecifes de Coral Sacar fotos, bucear, explorar. Es un lugar único en el Caribe.

Playa Vieja Tomar el sol, pasear en bicicleta, jugar a las cartas, escuchar música. Ideal para la familia.

Parque Nacional Foresta Sacar fotos, visitar el Museo de Arte Nativo. Reserva Mundial de la Biósfera.

Santuario de las Aves Sacar fotos, observar aves°, seguir rutas de excursión.

llena de luz *full of light* aves *birds*

Después de leer

Listas

Which amenities of Hotel Vistahermosa would most interest these potential guests? Explain your choices.

1. dos padres con un hijo de seis años y una hija de ocho años

   _____

2. un hombre y una mujer en su luna de miel (*honeymoon*)

   _____

3. una persona en un viaje de negocios (*business trip*)

   _____

Conversaciones

With a partner, take turns asking each other these questions.

1. ¿Quieres visitar el Hotel Vistahermosa? ¿Por qué?
2. Tienes tiempo de visitar sólo tres de las atracciones turísticas que están cerca del hotel. ¿Cuáles vas a visitar? ¿Por qué?
3. ¿Qué prefieres hacer en Valle Niebla? ¿En Playa Vieja? ¿En el Parque Nacional Foresta?

Situaciones

You have just arrived at Hotel Vistahermosa. Your classmate is the concierge. Use the phrases below to express your interests and ask for suggestions about where to go.

1. montar a caballo
2. bucear
3. pasear en bicicleta
4. pescar
5. observar aves

Contestar

Answer these questions.

1. ¿Quieres visitar Puerto Rico? Explica tu respuesta.

   _____

2. ¿Adónde quieres ir de vacaciones el verano que viene? Explica tu respuesta.

   _____

Practice more at vhlcentral.com.

Escritura

Estrategia

Making an outline

When we write to share information, an outline can serve to separate topics and subtopics, providing a framework for the presentation of data. Consider the following excerpt from an outline of the tourist brochure on pages 180–181.

IV. Descripción del sitio (con foto)
  A. Playa Grande
    1. Playas seguras y limpias
    2. Ideal para tomar el sol, descansar, tomar fotografías, nadar
  B. El hotel
    1. Abierto los 365 días del año
    2. Rebaja para estudiantes

Mapa de ideas

Idea maps can be used to create outlines. The major sections of an idea map correspond to the Roman numerals in an outline. The minor idea map sections correspond to the outline's capital letters, and so on. Examine the idea map that led to the outline above.

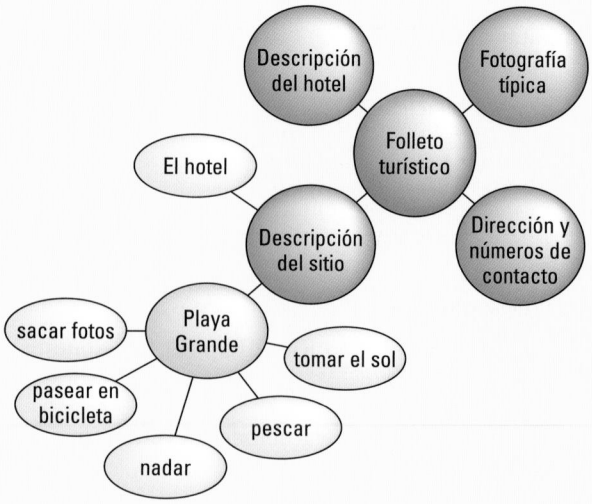

recursos

vText | CPA pp. 22–23 | CH pp. 79–80 | vhlcentral

Tema

Escribir un folleto

Write a tourist brochure for a hotel or resort you have visited. If you wish, you may write about an imaginary location. You may want to include some of this information in your brochure:

- the name of the hotel or resort
- phone and fax numbers that tourists can use to make contact
- the hotel website that tourists can consult
- an e-mail address that tourists can use to request information
- a description of the exterior of the hotel or resort
- a description of the interior of the hotel or resort, including facilities and amenities
- a description of the surrounding area, including its climate
- a listing of nearby scenic natural attractions
- a listing of nearby cultural attractions
- a listing of recreational activities that tourists can pursue in the vicinity of the hotel or resort

Escuchar

Audio

Estrategia

Listening for key words

By listening for key words or phrases, you can identify the subject and main ideas of what you hear, as well as some of the details.

To practice this strategy, you will now listen to a short paragraph. As you listen, jot down the key words that help you identify the subject of the paragraph and its main ideas.

Preparación

Based on the illustration, who do you think Hernán Jiménez is, and what is he doing? What key words might you listen for to help you understand what he is saying?

Ahora escucha

Now you are going to listen to a weather report by Hernán Jiménez. Note which phrases are correct according to the key words and phrases you hear.

Santo Domingo

1. hace sol
2. va a hacer frío
3. una mañana de mal tiempo
4. va a estar nublado
5. buena tarde para tomar el sol
6. buena mañana para la playa

San Francisco de Macorís

1. hace frío
2. hace sol
3. va a nevar
4. va a llover
5. hace calor
6. mal día para excursiones

recursos

vText vhlcentral

Comprensión

¿Cierto o falso?

Indicate whether each statement is **cierto** or **falso**, based on the weather report. Correct the false statements.

1. Según el meteorólogo, la temperatura en Santo Domingo es de 26 grados.

   _____

2. La temperatura máxima en Santo Domingo hoy va a ser de 30 grados.

   _____

3. Está lloviendo ahora en Santo Domingo.

   _____

4. En San Francisco de Macorís la temperatura mínima de hoy va a ser de 20 grados.

   _____

5. Va a llover mucho hoy en San Francisco de Macorís.

   _____

Preguntas

Answer these questions about the weather report.

1. ¿Hace viento en Santo Domingo ahora?
2. ¿Está nublado en Santo Domingo ahora?
3. ¿Está nevando ahora en San Francisco de Macorís?
4. ¿Qué tiempo hace en San Francisco de Macorís?

Practice more at vhlcentral.com.

en pantalla

Video: TV Clip

Anuncio de Santander LANPASS

Con lo que realmente nos importa°.

Preparación

Answer these questions in Spanish.

1. ¿Te gusta viajar? ¿Por qué? ¿A dónde te gusta viajar?
2. ¿Qué te gusta hacer cuando estás de vacaciones?
3. ¿Qué modo de transporte prefieres usar? ¿Por qué?

El arte de viajar

Millions of people travel on airlines every year for business and pleasure. The number of airline passengers is expected to double between 2014 and 2034 worldwide. This is true for Latin America, too, as airlines are looking at how to attract all those customers to their planes. The airline of Chile, LAN, has partnered with the international bank Santander to create the loyalty program LANPASS to encourage frequent travel on LAN. What does an airline say to travelers that captures their attention and makes their business seem like your pleasure?

importa *matters*

Vocabulario útil

arena	*sand*
cambiar	*to change*
destino	*destination*
medir	*to measure*
mismo/a	*itself*
piel	*skin*
puestas de sol	*sunsets*
recuerdos	*memories*
sentirse	*to feel*
sino	*itself*

Comprensión

Mark an X next to the phrases you hear in the ad. Irse es volver a....

_ cambiar de piel	_ trabajar	_ la oficina
_ desconectarnos	_ castillos de arena	_ sentirse vivo
_ estudiar mucho	_ destinos exóticos	_ las siestas
_ un mundo sin Internet	_ la esencia de todo	_ tiempo en familia

Conversación

Answer these questions with a classmate.

1. Según el anuncio, ¿cuáles son algunas cosas positivas de viajar?
2. ¿Cuáles de estas cosas positivas son importantes para ti? ¿Por qué?
3. Para tener experiencias positivas, ¿a dónde viajas tú? ¿A dónde viaja tu familia? ¿Y tus amigos?

Aplicación

With a classmate, prepare an ad inviting other people to travel to a special place. Explain why it is a perfect or ideal place. What evocative words and images will you use? Present your ad to the class.

Practice more at vhlcentral.com.

recursos vText vhlcentral

Video: *Flash cultura*

Between 1438 and 1533, when the vast and powerful Incan Empire was at its height, the Incas built an elaborate network of **caminos** (*trails*) that traversed the Andes Mountains and converged on the empire's capital, Cuzco. Today, hundreds of thousands of tourists come to Peru annually to walk the surviving trails and enjoy the spectacular scenery. The most popular trail, **el Camino Inca**, leads from Cuzco to **Intipunku** (*Sun Gate*), the entrance to the ancient mountain city of Machu Picchu.

Vocabulario útil

ciudadela	*citadel*
de cultivo	*farming*
el/la guía	*guide*
maravilla	*wonder*
quechua	*Quechua (indigenous Peruvian)*
sector (urbano)	*(urban) sector*

Preparación

Have you ever visited an archeological or historic site? Where? Why did you go there?

Completar

Complete these sentences. Make the necessary changes.

1. Las ruinas de Machu Picchu son una antigua _____ inca.
2. La ciudadela estaba (*was*) dividida en tres sectores: _____, religioso y de cultivo.
3. Cada año los _____ reciben a cientos (*hundreds*) de turistas de diferentes países.
4. Hoy en día, la cultura _____ está presente en las comunidades andinas (*Andean*) de Perú.

se encuentra aislada sobre *it is isolated on* siempre he querido *I have always wanted* Me encantan *I love* antiguas *ancient*

¡Vacaciones en Perú!

Machu Picchu [...] se encuentra aislada sobre° esta montaña...

... siempre he querido° venir [...] Me encantan° las civilizaciones antiguas°.

Somos una familia francesa [...] Perú es un país muy, muy bonito de verdad.

Practice more at vhlcentral.com.

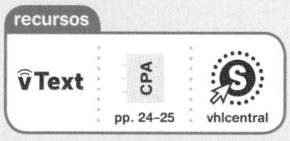

Puerto Rico

Video: *Panorama cultural*
Interactive Map

El país en cifras

- **Área:** 8.959 km^2 (3.459 millas^2), *menor° que el área de Connecticut*
- **Población:** 3.667.084

Puerto Rico es una de las islas más densamente pobladas° del mundo. Más de la mitad de la población vive en San Juan, la capital.

- **Capital:** San Juan—2.730.000
- **Ciudades principales:** Arecibo, Bayamón, Fajardo, Mayagüez, Ponce
- **Moneda:** dólar estadounidense
- **Idiomas:** español (oficial); inglés (oficial)

Aproximadamente la cuarta parte de la población puertorriqueña habla inglés, pero en las zonas turísticas este porcentaje es mucho más alto. El uso del inglés es obligatorio para documentos federales.

Bandera de Puerto Rico

Puertorriqueños célebres

- **Raúl Juliá,** actor (1940–1994)
- **Roberto Clemente,** beisbolista (1934–1972)
- **Julia de Burgos,** escritora (1914–1953)
- **Benicio del Toro,** actor y productor (1967–)
- **Rosie Pérez,** actriz y bailarina (1964–)
- **José Rivera,** dramaturgo y guionista (1955–)

Faro en Arecibo

Playa en San Juan

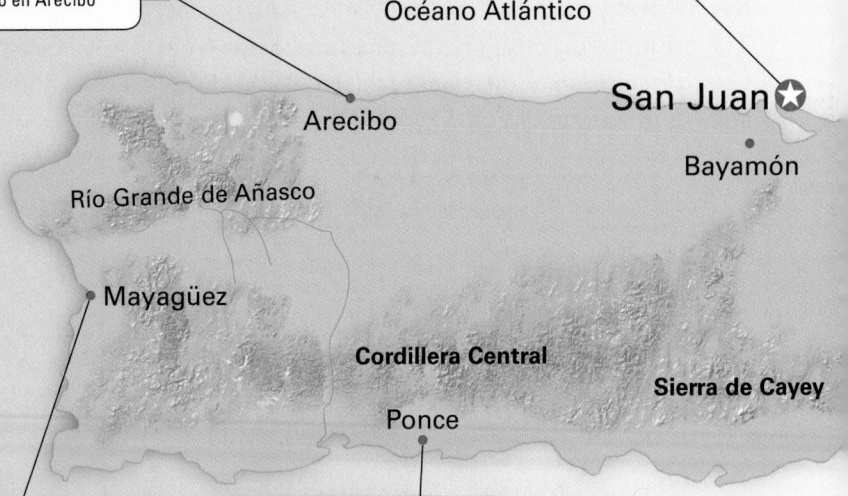

Clausura de los Juegos Centroamericanos y del Caribe en Mayagüez

Iglesia en Ponce

recursos
vText | CPA pp. 26–29 | vhlcentral

menor *less* pobladas *populated* río subterráneo *underground river* más largo *longest* cuevas *caves* bóveda *vault* fortaleza *fort* caber *fit*

¡Increíble pero cierto!

El río Camuy es el tercer río subterráneo° más largo° del mundo y tiene el sistema de cuevas° más grande del hemisferio occidental.
La Cueva de los Tres Pueblos es una gigantesca bóveda°, tan grande que toda la fortaleza° del Morro puede caber° en su interior.

Lugares • El Morro

El Morro es una fortaleza que se construyó para proteger° la bahía° de San Juan desde principios del siglo° XVI hasta principios del siglo XX. Hoy día muchos turistas visitan este lugar, convertido en un museo. Es el sitio más fotografiado de Puerto Rico. La arquitectura de la fortaleza es impresionante. Tiene misteriosos túneles, oscuras mazmorras° y vistas fabulosas de la bahía.

Artes • Salsa

La salsa, un estilo musical de origen puertorriqueño y cubano, nació° en el barrio latino de la ciudad de Nueva York. Dos de los músicos de salsa más famosos son Tito Puente y Willie Colón, los dos de Nueva York. Las estrellas° de la salsa en Puerto Rico son Felipe Rodríguez y Héctor Lavoe. Hoy en día, Puerto Rico es el centro internacional de este estilo musical. El Gran Combo de Puerto Rico es una de las orquestas de salsa más famosas del mundo°.

Ciencias • El Observatorio de Arecibo

El Observatorio de Arecibo tiene uno de los radiotelescopios más grandes del mundo. Gracias a este telescopio, los científicos° pueden estudiar las propiedades de la Tierra°, la Luna° y otros cuerpos celestes. También pueden analizar fenómenos celestiales como los quasares y pulsares, y detectar emisiones de radio de otras galaxias, en busca de inteligencia extraterrestre.

Historia • Relación con los Estados Unidos

Puerto Rico pasó a ser° parte de los Estados Unidos después de° la guerra° de 1898 y se hizo° un estado libre asociado en 1952. Los puertorriqueños, ciudadanos° estadounidenses desde° 1917, tienen representación política en el Congreso, pero no votan en las elecciones presidenciales y no pagan impuestos° federales. Hay un debate entre los puertorriqueños: ¿debe la isla seguir como estado libre asociado, hacerse un estado como los otros° o volverse° independiente?

¿Qué aprendiste? Responde a cada pregunta con una oración completa.

1. ¿Cuál es la moneda de Puerto Rico?
2. ¿Qué idiomas se hablan (*are spoken*) en Puerto Rico?
3. ¿Cuál es el sitio más fotografiado de Puerto Rico?
4. ¿Qué es el Gran Combo?
5. ¿Qué hacen los científicos en el Observatorio de Arecibo?

Conexión Internet Investiga estos temas en **vhlcentral.com**.

1. Describe a dos puertorriqueños famosos. ¿Cómo son? ¿Qué hacen? ¿Dónde viven? ¿Por qué son célebres?
2. Busca información sobre lugares en los que se puede hacer ecoturismo en Puerto Rico. Luego presenta un informe a la clase.

Practice more at **vhlcentral.com**.

proteger *protect* bahía *bay* siglo *century* mazmorras *dungeons* nació *was born* estrellas *stars* mundo *world* científicos *scientists* Tierra *Earth* Luna *Moon* pasó a ser *became* después de *after* guerra *war* se hizo *became* ciudadanos *citizens* desde *since* pagan impuestos *pay taxes* otros *others* volverse *to become*

Los viajes y las vacaciones

acampar	*to camp*
confirmar una reservación	*to confirm a reservation*
estar de vacaciones (*f. pl.*)	*to be on vacation*
hacer las maletas	*to pack (one's suitcases)*
hacer un viaje	*to take a trip*
hacer (wind)surf	*to (wind)surf*
ir de compras (*f. pl.*)	*to go shopping*
ir de vacaciones	*to go on vacation*
ir en autobús (*m.*), auto(móvil) (*m.*), avión (*m.*), barco (*m.*), moto(cicleta) (*f.*), taxi (*m.*)	*to go by bus, car, plane, boat, motorcycle, taxi*
jugar a las cartas	*to play cards*
montar a caballo (*m.*)	*to ride a horse*
pescar	*to fish*
sacar/tomar fotos (*f. pl.*)	*to take photos*
el/la agente de viajes	*travel agent*
el/la inspector(a) de aduanas	*customs inspector*
el/la viajero/a	*traveler*
el aeropuerto	*airport*
la agencia de viajes	*travel agency*
el campo	*countryside*
el equipaje	*luggage*
la estación de autobuses, del metro, de tren	*bus, subway, train station*
la llegada	*arrival*
el mar	*sea*
el paisaje	*landscape*
el pasaje (de ida y vuelta)	*(round-trip) ticket*
el pasaporte	*passport*
la playa	*beach*
la salida	*departure; exit*
la tabla de (wind)surf	*surfboard/sailboard*

El hotel

el ascensor	*elevator*
el/la botones	*bellhop*
la cama	*bed*
el/la empleado/a	*employee*
la habitación individual, doble	*single, double room*
el hotel	*hotel*
el/la huésped	*guest*
la llave	*key*
el piso	*floor (of a building)*
la planta baja	*ground floor*

Adjetivos

abierto/a	*open*
aburrido/a	*bored; boring*
alegre	*happy; joyful*
amable	*nice; friendly*
avergonzado/a	*embarrassed*
cansado/a	*tired*
cerrado/a	*closed*
cómodo/a	*comfortable*
confundido/a	*confused*
contento/a	*happy; content*
desordenado/a	*disorderly*
enamorado/a (de)	*in love (with)*
enojado/a	*mad; angry*
equivocado/a	*wrong*
feliz	*happy*
limpio/a	*clean*
listo/a	*ready; smart*
nervioso/a	*nervous*
ocupado/a	*busy*
ordenado/a	*orderly*
preocupado/a (por)	*worried (about)*
seguro/a	*sure; safe*
sucio/a	*dirty*
triste	*sad*

Los números ordinales

primer, primero/a	*first*
segundo/a	*second*
tercer, tercero/a	*third*
cuarto/a	*fourth*
quinto/a	*fifth*
sexto/a	*sixth*
séptimo/a	*seventh*
octavo/a	*eighth*
noveno/a	*ninth*
décimo/a	*tenth*

Palabras adicionales

ahora mismo	*right now*
el año	*year*
¿Cuál es la fecha (de hoy)?	*What is the date (today)?*
de buen/mal humor	*in a good/bad mood*
la estación	*season*
el mes	*month*
todavía	*yet; still*

Seasons, months, and dates	*See page 154.*
Weather expressions	*See page 154.*
Direct object pronouns	*See page 174.*
Expresiones útiles	*See page 159.*

¡De compras!

6

Communicative Goals

I will be able to:

- **Talk about and describe clothing**
- **Express preferences in a store**
- **Negotiate and pay for items I buy**

VOICE BOARD

A PRIMERA VISTA

- **¿Está comprando algo la chica?**
- **¿Crees que busca una maleta o una blusa?**
- **¿Está contenta o enojada?**
- **¿Cómo es ella?**

contextos

pages 190–193

- Clothing and shopping
- Negotiating a price and buying
- Colors
- More adjectives

fotonovela

pages 194–197

The friends are back in Mérida, where they go to the market to do some shopping. Who will get the best deal?

cultura

pages 198–199

- Open-air markets
- Carolina Herrera

estructura

pages 200–215

- **Saber** and **conocer**
- Indirect object pronouns
- Preterite tense of regular verbs
- Demonstrative adjectives and pronouns
- **Recapitulación**

adelante

pages 216–223

Lectura: An advertisement for a store sale
Escritura: A report for the school newspaper
Escuchar: A conversation about clothes
En pantalla
Flash cultura
Panorama: Cuba

¡De compras!

My Vocabulary Tutorials

Más vocabulario

el abrigo	*coat*
los calcetines (el calcetín)	*sock(s)*
el cinturón	*belt*
las gafas (de sol)	*(sun)glasses*
los guantes	*gloves*
el impermeable	*raincoat*
la ropa	*clothing; clothes*
la ropa interior	*underwear*
las sandalias	*sandals*
el traje	*suit*
el vestido	*dress*
los zapatos de tenis	*sneakers*
el regalo	*gift*
el almacén	*department store*
el centro comercial	*shopping mall*
el mercado (al aire libre)	*(open-air) market*
el precio (fijo)	*(fixed; set) price*
la rebaja	*sale*
la tienda	*shop; store*
costar (o:ue)	*to cost*
gastar	*to spend (money)*
pagar	*to pay*
regatear	*to bargain*
vender	*to sell*
hacer juego (con)	*to match (with)*
llevar	*to wear; to take*
usar	*to wear; to use*

Variación léxica

calcetines ⟷	medias (*Amér. L.*)
cinturón ⟷	correa (*Col., Venez.*)
gafas/lentes ⟷	espejuelos (*Cuba, P.R.*), anteojos (*Arg., Chile*)
zapatos de tenis ⟷	zapatillas de deporte (*Esp.*), zapatillas (*Arg., Perú*)

recursos
vText
CPA pp. 31–33
CH pp. 81–82
vhlcentral

Práctica

1 **Escuchar** Listen to Juanita and Vicente talk about what they're packing for their vacations. Indicate who is packing each item. If both are packing an item, write both names. If neither is packing an item, write an **X**.

1. abrigo _____
2. zapatos de tenis _____
3. impermeable _____
4. chaqueta _____
5. sandalias _____
6. bluejeans _____
7. gafas de sol _____
8. camisetas _____
9. traje de baño _____
10. botas _____
11. pantalones cortos _____
12. suéter _____

2 **¿Lógico o ilógico?** Listen to Guillermo and Ana talk about vacation destinations. Indicate whether each statement is **lógico** or **ilógico**.

1. _____
2. _____
3. _____
4. _____

3 **Completar** Anita is talking about going shopping. Complete each sentence with the correct word(s), adding definite or indefinite articles when necessary.

caja	medias	tarjeta de crédito
centro comercial	par	traje de baño
dependientas	ropa	vendedores

1. Hoy voy a ir de compras al _____.
2. Voy a ir a la tienda de ropa para mujeres. Siempre hay muchas rebajas y las _____ son muy simpáticas.
3. Necesito comprar _____ de zapatos.
4. Y tengo que comprar _____ porque el sábado voy a la playa con mis amigos.
5. También voy a comprar unas _____ para mi mamá.
6. Voy a pagar todo (*everything*) en _____.
7. Pero hoy no tengo dinero. Voy a tener que usar mi _____.
8. Mañana voy al mercado al aire libre. Me gusta regatear con los _____.

4 **Escoger** Choose the item in each group that does not belong.

1. almacén • centro comercial • mercado • sombrero
2. camisa • camiseta • blusa • botas
3. jeans • bolsa • falda • pantalones
4. abrigo • suéter • corbata • chaqueta
5. mercado • tienda • almacén • cartera
6. pagar • llevar • hacer juego (con) • usar
7. botas • sandalias • zapatos • traje
8. vender • regatear • ropa interior • gastar

Los colores

anaranjado/a **gris** **marrón, café** **morado/a** **rosado/a**

Adjetivos

barato/a **corto/a** **largo/a** **caro/a**

¡LENGUA VIVA!

The names of colors vary throughout the Spanish-speaking world. For example, in some countries, **anaranjado/a** may be referred to as **naranja**, **morado/a** as **púrpura**, and **rojo/a** as **colorado/a**.

Other terms that will prove helpful include **claro** (*light*) and **oscuro** (*dark*): **café claro, café oscuro.**

Más adjetivos

bueno/a	*good*
cada	*each*
elegante	*elegant*
hermoso/a	*beautiful*
loco/a	*crazy*
nuevo/a	*new*
otro/a	*other; another*
pobre	*poor*
rico/a	*rich*

5 **Contrastes** Complete each phrase with the opposite of the underlined word.

1. una corbata <u>barata</u> • unas camisas...
2. unas vendedoras <u>malas</u> • unos dependientes...
3. un vestido <u>corto</u> • una falda...
4. un hombre muy <u>pobre</u> • una mujer muy...
5. una cartera <u>nueva</u> • un cinturón...
6. unos trajes <u>hermosos</u> • unos jeans...
7. un impermeable <u>caro</u> • unos suéteres...
8. unos calcetines <u>blancos</u> • unas medias...

CONSULTA

Like other adjectives you have seen, colors must agree in gender and number with the nouns they modify. Ex: **las camisas grises, el vestido anaranjado.**

6 **Preguntas** Answer these questions with a classmate.

1. ¿De qué color es la rosa de Texas?
2. ¿De qué color es la bandera (*flag*) de Canadá?
3. ¿De qué color es la casa donde vive el presidente de los EE.UU.?
4. ¿De qué color es el océano Atlántico?
5. ¿De qué color es la nieve?
6. ¿De qué color es el café?
7. ¿De qué color es el dólar de los EE.UU.?
8. ¿De qué color son los elefantes (*elephants*)?

Practice more at vhlcentral.com.

Comunicación

7 **Las maletas** With a classmate, answer these questions about the drawings.

1. ¿Qué ropa hay al lado de la maleta de Carmela?
2. ¿Qué hay en la maleta?
3. ¿De qué color son las sandalias?
4. ¿Adónde va Carmela?
5. ¿Qué tiempo va a hacer?
6. ¿Qué hay al lado de la maleta de Pepe?
7. ¿Qué hay en la maleta?
8. ¿De qué color es el suéter?
9. ¿Qué va a hacer Pepe en Bariloche?
10. ¿Qué tiempo va a hacer?

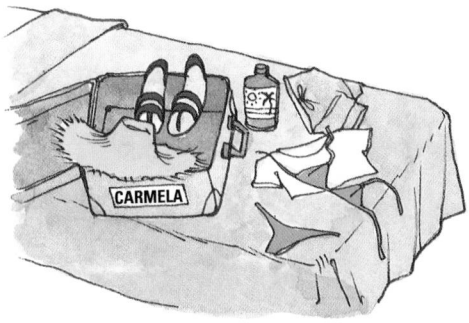

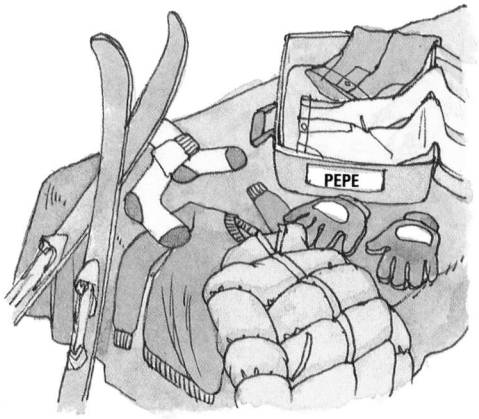

CONSULTA

To review weather, see **Lección 5, Contextos,** p. 154.

NOTA CULTURAL

Bariloche is a popular resort for skiing in South America. Located in Argentina's Patagonia region, the town is also known for its chocolate factories and its beautiful lakes, mountains, and forests.

8 **El viaje** Get together with two classmates and imagine that the three of you are going on vacation. Pick a destination and then draw three suitcases. Write what clothing each of you is taking. Present your lists to the class, answering these questions.

- ¿Adónde van?
- ¿Qué tiempo va a hacer allí?
- ¿Qué van a hacer allí?
- ¿Qué hay en sus maletas?
- ¿De qué color es la ropa que llevan?

9 **Preferencias** Take turns asking and answering these questions with a classmate.

1. ¿Adónde vas a comprar ropa? ¿Por qué?
2. ¿Qué tipo de ropa prefieres? ¿Por qué?
3. ¿Cuáles son tus colores favoritos?
4. En tu opinión, ¿es importante comprar ropa nueva frecuentemente? ¿Por qué?
5. Y tu familia, ¿gasta mucho dinero en ropa cada mes? ¿Buscan rebajas tus padres?
6. ¿Regatea tu familia cuando compra ropa? ¿Usan tus padres tarjetas de crédito?

En el mercado

Los chicos van de compras al mercado. ¿Quién hizo la mejor compra?

PERSONAJES FELIPE JUAN CARLOS

Video: *Fotonovela*

MARISSA Oigan, vamos al mercado.

JUAN CARLOS ¡Sí! Los chicos en un equipo y las chicas en otro.

FELIPE Tenemos dos horas para ir de compras.

MARU Y don Guillermo decide quién gana.

JIMENA Esta falda azul es muy elegante.

MARISSA ¡Sí! Además, este color está de moda.

MARU Éste rojo es de algodón.

MARISSA ¿Me das aquella blusa rosada? Me parece que hace juego con esta falda, ¿no? ¿No tienen otras tallas?

JIMENA Sí, aquí. ¿Qué talla usas?

MARISSA Uso talla 4.

JIMENA La encontré. ¡Qué ropa más bonita!

VENDEDOR Son 530 por las tres bolsas. Pero como ustedes son tan bonitas, son 500 pesos.

MARU Señor, no somos turistas ricas. Somos estudiantes pobres.

VENDEDOR Bueno, son 480 pesos.

JUAN CARLOS Miren, mi nueva camisa. Elegante, ¿verdad?

FELIPE A ver, Juan Carlos... te queda bien.

MARU ¿Qué compraste?

MIGUEL Sólo esto.

MARU ¡Qué bonitos aretes! Gracias, mi amor.

MARISSA

JIMENA

MARU

MIGUEL

DON GUILLERMO

VENDEDORA

VENDEDOR

(*En otra parte del mercado*)

FELIPE Juan Carlos compró una camisa de muy buena calidad.

MIGUEL (*a la vendedora*) ¿Puedo ver ésos, por favor?

VENDEDORA Sí, señor. Le doy un muy buen precio.

(*Las chicas encuentran unas bolsas.*)

VENDEDOR Ésta de rayas cuesta 190 pesos, ésta 120 pesos y ésta 220 pesos.

JUAN CARLOS Y ustedes, ¿qué compraron?

JIMENA Bolsas.

MARU Acabamos de comprar tres bolsas por sólo 480 pesos. ¡Una ganga!

FELIPE Don Guillermo, usted tiene que decidir quién gana. ¿Los chicos o las chicas?

DON GUILLERMO El ganador es... Miguel. ¡Porque no compró nada para él, sino para su novia!

recursos

vText | CPA pp. 34–35 | vhlcentral

Expresiones útiles

Talking about clothing

¡Qué ropa más bonita!
What nice clothing!
Esta falda azul es muy elegante.
This blue skirt is very elegant.
Está de moda.
It's in style.
Éste rojo es de algodón/lana.
This red one is cotton/wool.
Ésta de rayas/lunares/cuadros es de seda.
This striped / polka-dotted / plaid one is silk.
Es de muy buena calidad.
It's very good quality.
¿Qué talla usas/llevas?
What size do you wear?
Uso/Llevo talla 4.
I wear a size 4.
¿Qué número calza?
What size shoe do you wear?
Yo calzo siete.
I wear a size seven.

Negotiating a price

¿Cuánto cuesta?
How much does it cost?
Demasiado caro/a.
Too expensive.
Es una ganga.
It's a bargain.

Saying what you bought

¿Qué compraste?/¿Qué compró usted?
What did you buy?
Sólo compré esto.
I only bought this.
¡Qué bonitos aretes!
What beautiful earrings!
Y ustedes, ¿qué compraron?
And you guys, what did you buy?

Additional vocabulary

híjole *wow*

¿Qué pasó?

1 **¿Cierto o falso?** Indicate whether each sentence is **cierto** or **falso**. Correct the false statements.

	Cierto	Falso
1. Jimena dice que la falda azul no es elegante.	❍	❍
2. Juan Carlos compra una camisa.	❍	❍
3. Marissa dice que el azul es un color que está de moda.	❍	❍
4. Miguel compra unas sandalias para Maru.	❍	❍

2 **Identificar** Provide the first initial of the person who would make each statement.

___ 1. ¿Te gusta cómo se me ven mis nuevos aretes?
___ 2. Juan Carlos compró una camisa de muy buena calidad.
___ 3. No podemos pagar 500, señor, eso es muy caro.
___ 4. Aquí tienen ropa de muchas tallas.
___ 5. Esta falda me gusta mucho, el color azul es muy elegante.
___ 6. Hay que darnos prisa, sólo tenemos dos horas para ir de compras.

MARU

FELIPE

JIMENA

3 **Completar** Answer the questions using the information in the **Fotonovela**.

1. ¿Qué talla usa Marissa?
2. Normalmente (*normally*), ¿cuánto cuestan las tres bolsas?
3. ¿Cuál es el precio que pagan las tres amigas por las bolsas?
4. ¿Qué dice Juan Carlos sobre su nueva camisa?
5. ¿Quién ganó al hacer las compras? ¿Por qué?

AYUDA

When discussing prices, it's important to keep in mind singular and plural forms of verbs.

La **camisa cuesta** diez dólares.

Las **botas cuestan** sesenta dólares.

El **precio** de las botas **es** sesenta dólares.

Los **precios** de la ropa **son** altos.

4 **Conversar** With a partner, role-play a conversation between a customer and a salesperson in an open-air market. Use these expressions and also look at **Expresiones útiles** on the previous page.

¿Qué desea?	Estoy buscando...	Prefiero el/la rojo/a.
What would you like?	*I'm looking for...*	*I prefer the red one.*

Cliente/a	Vendedor(a)
Say good afternoon.	Greet the customer and ask what he/she would like.
Explain that you are looking for a particular item of clothing.	Show him/her some items and ask what he/she prefers.
Discuss colors and sizes.	Discuss colors and sizes.
Ask for the price and begin bargaining.	Tell him/her a price. Negotiate a price.
Settle on a price and purchase the item.	Accept a price and say thank you.

Practice more at vhlcentral.com.

Pronunciación

Audio

The consonants d and t

¿Dónde? vender nadar verdad

Like **b** and **v**, the Spanish **d** can also have a hard sound or a soft sound, depending on which letters appear next to it.

Don dinero tienda falda

At the beginning of a phrase and after **n** or **l**, the letter **d** is pronounced with a hard sound. This sound is similar to the English *d* in *dog*, but a little softer and duller. The tongue should touch the back of the upper teeth, not the roof of the mouth.

medias verde vestido huésped

In all other positions, **d** has a soft sound. It is similar to the English *th* in *there*, but a little softer.

Don Diego no tiene el diccionario.

When **d** begins a word, its pronunciation depends on the previous word. At the beginning of a phrase or after a word that ends in **n** or **l**, it is pronounced as a hard **d**.

Doña Dolores es de la capital.

Words that begin with **d** are pronounced with a soft **d** if they appear immediately after a word that ends in a vowel or any consonant other than **n** or **l**.

traje pantalones tarjeta tienda

When pronouncing the Spanish **t**, the tongue should touch the back of the upper teeth, not the roof of the mouth. Unlike the English *t*, no air is expelled from the mouth.

Práctica Read these phrases aloud to practice the **d** and the **t**.

1. Hasta pronto.
2. De nada.
3. Mucho gusto.
4. Lo siento.
5. No hay de qué.
6. ¿De dónde es usted?
7. ¡Todos a bordo!
8. No puedo.
9. Es estupendo.
10. No tengo computadora.
11. ¿Cuándo vienen?
12. Son las tres y media.

Oraciones Read these sentences aloud to practice the **d** and the **t**.

1. Don Teodoro tiene una tienda en un almacén en La Habana.
2. Don Teodoro vende muchos trajes, vestidos y zapatos todos los días.
3. Un día un turista, Federico Machado, entra en la tienda para comprar un par de botas.
4. Federico regatea con don Teodoro y compra las botas y también un par de sandalias.

Refranes Read these sayings aloud to practice the **d** and the **t**.

1 Variety is the spice of life.
2 You can't make a silk purse out of a sow's ear.

recursos

vText | CPA p. 36 | CH p. 83 | vhlcentral

EN DETALLE

Additional Reading

Los mercados al aire libre

Mercados al aire libre are an integral part of commerce and culture in the Spanish-speaking world. Whether they take place daily or weekly, these markets are an important forum where tourists, locals, and vendors interact. People come to the marketplace to shop, socialize, taste local foods, and watch street performers. Wandering from one **puesto** (*stand*) to the next, one can browse for fresh fruits and vegetables, clothing, music and movies, and **artesanías** (*crafts*). Some markets offer a mix of products, while others specialize in food, fashion, or used merchandise, such as antiques and books.

When shoppers see an item they like, they can bargain with the vendor. Friendly bargaining is an expected ritual and may result in a significantly lower price. When selling food, vendors may give the customer a little extra of what they purchase; this free addition is known as **la ñapa**.

Many open-air markets are also tourist attractions. The market in Otavalo, Ecuador, is world-famous and has taken place every Saturday since pre-Incan times. This market is well-known for the colorful textiles woven by the **otavaleños**, the indigenous people of the area. One can also find leather goods and wood carvings from nearby towns. Another popular market is **El Rastro**, held every Sunday in Madrid, Spain. Sellers set up **puestos** along the streets to display their wares, which range from local artwork and antiques to inexpensive clothing and electronics.

Mercado de Otavalo

Otros mercados famosos

Mercado	Lugar	Productos
Feria Artesanal de Recoleta	Buenos Aires, Argentina	artesanías
Mercado Central	Santiago, Chile	mariscos°, pescado°, frutas, verduras°
Tianguis Cultural del Chopo	Ciudad de México, México	ropa, música, revistas, libros, arte, artesanías
El mercado de Chichicastenango	Chichicastenango, Guatemala	frutas y verduras, flores°, cerámica, textiles

mariscos *seafood* pescado *fish* verduras *vegetables* flores *flowers*

ACTIVIDADES

1 **¿Cierto o falso?** Indicate whether these statements are **cierto** or **falso**. Correct the false statements.

1. Generally, open-air markets specialize in one type of goods.
2. Bargaining is commonplace at outdoor markets.
3. Only new goods can be found at open-air markets.
4. A Spaniard in search of antiques could search at **El Rastro**.
5. If you are in Guatemala and want to buy ceramics, you can go to Chichicastenango.
6. A **ñapa** is a tax on open-air market goods.
7. The **otavaleños** weave colorful textiles to sell on Saturdays.
8. Santiago's **Mercado Central** is known for books and music.

Practice more at vhlcentral.com.

ASÍ SE DICE

La ropa

la chamarra (Méx.)	**la chaqueta**
de manga corta/larga	*short/long-sleeved*
los mahones (P. Rico); el pantalón de mezclilla (Méx.); los tejanos (Esp.); los vaqueros (Arg., Cuba, Esp., Uru.)	**los bluejeans**
la marca	*brand*
la playera (Méx.); la remera (Arg.)	**la camiseta**

EL MUNDO HISPANO

Diseñadores de moda

- **Adolfo Domínguez** (España) Su ropa tiene un estilo minimalista y práctico. Usa telas° naturales y cómodas en sus diseños.
- **Silvia Tcherassi** (Colombia) Los colores vivos y las líneas asimétricas de sus vestidos y trajes muestran influencias tropicales.

- **Óscar de la Renta** (República Dominicana) Diseñaba ropa opulenta para la mujer clásica.
- **Narciso Rodríguez** (EE.UU.) En sus diseños delicados y finos predominan los colores blanco y negro. Hizo° el vestido de boda° de Carolyn Bessette Kennedy. También diseñó varios vestidos para Michelle Obama.

telas *fabrics* Hizo *He made* de boda *wedding*

PERFIL

Carolina Herrera

In 1980, at the urging of some friends, **Carolina Herrera** created a fashion collection as a "test." The Venezuelan designer received such a favorable response that within one year she moved her family from Caracas to New York City and created her own label, Carolina Herrera, Ltd.

"I love elegance and intricacy, but whether it is in a piece of clothing or a fragrance, the intricacy must appear as simplicity," Herrera once stated. She quickly found that many sophisticated women agreed; from the start, her sleek and glamorous designs have been in constant demand. Over the years, Herrera has grown her brand into a veritable fashion empire that encompasses her fashion and bridal collections, cosmetics, perfume, and accessories that are sold around the globe.

Conexión Internet

¿Qué marcas de ropa son populares en el mundo hispano?

Go to **vhlcentral.com** to find more cultural information related to this **Cultura** section.

ACTIVIDADES

2 **Comprensión** Complete these sentences.

1. Adolfo Domínguez usa telas _____ y _____ en su ropa.
2. Si hace fresco en el D.F., puedes llevar una _____.
3. La diseñadora _____ hace ropa, perfumes y más.
4. La ropa de _____ muestra influencias tropicales.
5. Los _____ son una ropa casual en Puerto Rico.

3 **Mi ropa favorita** Write a brief description of your favorite article of clothing. Mention what store it is from, the brand, colors, fabric, style, and any other information. Then get together with a small group, collect the descriptions, and take turns reading them aloud at random. Can the rest of the group guess whose favorite piece of clothing is being described?

recursos

vText

CH p. 84

vhlcentral

6.1 Saber and conocer

Tutorial

ANTE TODO Spanish has two verbs that mean *to know*: **saber** and **conocer**. They cannot be used interchangeably. Note the irregular **yo** forms.

The verbs saber and conocer

		saber *(to know)*	conocer *(to know)*
SINGULAR FORMS	yo	**sé**	**conozco**
	tú	**sabes**	**conoces**
	Ud./él/ella	**sabe**	**conoce**
PLURAL FORMS	nosotros/as	**sabemos**	**conocemos**
	vosotros/as	**sabéis**	**conocéis**
	Uds./ellos/ellas	**saben**	**conocen**

- **Saber** means *to know a fact or piece(s) of information* or *to know how to do something.*

  No **sé** tu número de teléfono.
  I don't know your telephone number.

  Mi hermana **sabe** hablar francés.
  My sister knows how to speak French.

- **Conocer** means *to know* or *be familiar/acquainted* with a person, place, or thing.

  ¿**Conoces** la ciudad de Nueva York?
  Do you know New York City?

  No **conozco** a tu amigo Esteban.
  I don't know your friend Esteban.

- When the direct object of **conocer** is a person or pet, the personal **a** is used.

  ¿Conoces La Habana? *but* ¿Conoces **a** Celia Cruz?
  Do you know Havana? *Do you know Celia Cruz?*

- **¡Atención! Parecer** (*to seem*) and **ofrecer** (*to offer*) are conjugated like **conocer**.

- **¡Atención! Conducir** (*to drive*) and **traducir** (*to translate*) also have an irregular **yo** form, but since they are **-ir** verbs, they are conjugated differently from **conocer**.

conducir → **conduzco, conduces, conduce, conducimos, conducís, conducen**
traducir → **traduzco, traduces, traduce, traducimos, traducís, traducen**

NOTA CULTURAL
Cuban singer **Celia Cruz** (1925–2003), known as the "Queen of Salsa," recorded many albums over her long career. Adored by her fans, she was famous for her colorful and lively on-stage performances.

¡INTÉNTALO! Provide the appropriate forms of these verbs.

saber

1. José no *sabe* la hora.
2. Sara y yo _____ jugar al tenis.
3. ¿Por qué no _____ tú estos verbos?
4. Mis padres _____ hablar japonés.
5. Yo _____ a qué hora es la clase.
6. Usted no _____ dónde vivo.
7. Mi hermano no _____ nadar.
8. Nosotros _____ muchas cosas.

conocer

1. Usted y yo *conocemos* bien Miami.
2. ¿Tú _____ a mi amigo Manuel?
3. Sergio y Taydé _____ mi pueblo.
4. Emiliano _____ a mis padres.
5. Yo _____ muy bien el centro.
6. ¿Ustedes _____ la tienda Gigante?
7. Nosotras _____ una playa hermosa.
8. ¿Usted _____ a mi profesora?

recursos
vText
CPA pp. 37–38
CH pp. 85–86
vhlcentral

Práctica y Comunicación

1 **Completar** Indicate the correct verb for each sentence.

1. Mis hermanos (conocen/saben) conducir, pero yo no (sé/conozco).
2. —¿(Conocen/Saben) ustedes dónde está el estadio? —No, no (conocemos/sabemos).
3. —¿(Conoces/Sabes) a Lady Gaga? —Bueno, (sé/conozco) quién es, pero no la (conozco/sé).
4. Mi profesora (sabe/conoce) Cuba y también (conoce/sabe) bailar salsa.

2 **Combinar** Combine elements from each column to create sentences.

A	B	C
Shakira	(no) conocer	Jimmy Fallon
los Yankees	(no) saber	cantar y bailar
el primer ministro de Canadá		La Habana Vieja
mis amigos y yo		muchas personas importantes
tú		hablar dos lenguas extranjeras
		jugar al béisbol

3 **Preguntas** In pairs, ask each other these questions. Answer with complete sentences.

1. ¿Conoces a un(a) cantante famoso/a? ¿Te gusta cómo canta?
2. En tu familia, ¿quién sabe cantar bien? ¿Tu opinión es objetiva?
3. Tus padres, ¿conducen bien o mal? ¿Y tus hermanos mayores?
4. Si una persona no conduce muy bien, ¿le ofreces crítica constructiva?
5. ¿Cómo parece estar el/la profesor(a) hoy? ¿Y tus compañeros de clase?

4 **Entrevista** Jot down three things you know how to do, three people you know, and three places you are familiar with. Then, in a small group, find out what you have in common.

modelo

Estudiante 1: *¿Conocen ustedes a David Lomas?*
Estudiante 2: *Sí, conozco a David. Vivimos en el mismo barrio (neighborhood).*
Estudiante 3: *No, no lo conozco. ¿Cómo es?*

5 **Anuncio** In groups, read the ad and answer these questions.

1. Busquen ejemplos de los verbos **saber** y **conocer**.
2. ¿Qué saben del Centro Comercial Málaga?
3. ¿Qué pueden hacer en el Centro Comercial Málaga?
4. ¿Conocen otros centros comerciales similares? ¿Cómo se llaman? ¿Dónde están?
5. ¿Conocen un centro comercial en otro país? ¿Cómo es?

Practice more at vhlcentral.com.

6.2 Indirect object pronouns

Tutorial

ANTE TODO

In **Lección 5**, you learned that a direct object receives the action of the verb directly. In contrast, an indirect object receives the action of the verb indirectly.

SUBJECT	I.O. PRONOUN	VERB	DIRECT OBJECT	INDIRECT OBJECT
Roberto	**le**	presta	cien pesos	**a Luisa**.
Roberto		*lends*	*100 pesos*	*to Luisa.*

An indirect object is a noun or pronoun that answers the question *to whom* or *for whom* an action is done. In the preceding example, the indirect object answers this question: **¿A quién le presta Roberto cien pesos?** *To whom does Roberto lend 100 pesos?*

Indirect object pronouns

Singular forms		Plural forms	
me	(to, for) *me*	**nos**	(to, for) *us*
te	(to, for) *you* (fam.)	**os**	(to, for) *you* (fam.)
le	(to, for) *you* (form.) (to, for) *him; her*	**les**	(to, for) *you* (form.) (to, for) *them*

▶ **¡Atención!** The forms of indirect object pronouns for the first and second persons (**me, te, nos, os**) are the same as the direct object pronouns. Indirect object pronouns agree in number with the corresponding nouns, but not in gender.

Using indirect object pronouns

▶ Spanish speakers commonly use both an indirect object pronoun and the noun to which it refers in the same sentence. This is done to emphasize and clarify to whom the pronoun refers.

I.O. PRONOUN	INDIRECT OBJECT	I.O. PRONOUN	INDIRECT OBJECT
Ella **le** vende la ropa	**a Elena**.	**Les** prestamos el dinero	**a Inés y a Álex**.

▶ Indirect object pronouns are also used without the indirect object noun when the person for whom the action is being done is known.

Ana **le** presta la falda **a Elena**.
Ana lends her skirt to Elena.

También **le** presta unos jeans.
She also lends her a pair of jeans.

- Indirect object pronouns are usually placed before the conjugated form of the verb. In negative sentences the pronoun is placed between **no** and the conjugated verb.

Martín **me** compra un regalo. *Martín is buying me a gift.*	Eva **no me** escribe cartas. *Eva doesn't write me letters.*

- When a conjugated verb is followed by an infinitive or the present progressive, the indirect object pronoun may be placed before the conjugated verb or attached to the infinitive or present participle. **¡Atención!** When an indirect object pronoun is attached to a present participle, an accent mark is added to maintain the proper stress.

Él no quiere **pagarte**./ Él no **te** quiere pagar. *He does not want to pay you.*	Él está **escribiéndole** una postal a ella./ Él **le** está escribiendo una postal a ella. *He is writing a postcard to her.*

- Because the indirect object pronouns **le** and **les** have multiple meanings, Spanish speakers often clarify to whom the pronouns refer with the preposition **a** + [*pronoun*] or **a** + [*noun*].

UNCLARIFIED STATEMENTS	CLARIFIED STATEMENTS
Yo **le** compro un abrigo.	Yo **le** compro un abrigo **a usted/él/ella**.
Ella **le** describe un libro.	Ella **le** describe un libro **a Juan**.
UNCLARIFIED STATEMENTS	**CLARIFIED STATEMENTS**
Él **les** vende unos sombreros.	Él **les** vende unos sombreros **a ustedes/ellos/ellas**.
Ellos **les** hablan muy claro.	Ellos **les** hablan muy claro **a los clientes**.

- The irregular verbs **dar** (*to give*) and **decir** (*to say; to tell*) are often used with indirect object pronouns.

The verbs dar and decir

Singular forms	dar	decir	Plural forms	dar	decir
yo	**doy**	**digo**	nosotros/as	**damos**	**decimos**
tú	**das**	**dices**	vosotros/as	**dais**	**decís**
Ud./él/ella	**da**	**dice**	Uds./ellos/ellas	**dan**	**dicen**

Me dan una fiesta cada año. *They give (throw) me a party every year.*	**Te digo** la verdad. *I'm telling you the truth.*
Voy a **darle** consejos. *I'm going to give her advice.*	No **les digo** mentiras a mis padres. *I don't tell lies to my parents.*

¡INTÉNTALO! Use the cues in parentheses to provide the correct indirect object pronoun for each sentence.

1. Juan ___le___ quiere dar un regalo. (*to Elena*)
2. María _____ prepara un café. (*for us*)
3. Beatriz y Felipe _____ escriben desde (*from*) Cuba. (*to me*)
4. Marta y yo _____ compramos unos guantes. (*for them*)
5. Los vendedores _____ venden ropa. (*to you, fam. sing.*)
6. La dependienta _____ muestra los guantes. (*to us*)

recursos
vText
CPA pp. 39–41
CH pp. 87–88
vhlcentral

Práctica

1 **Completar** Fill in the blanks with the correct pronouns to complete Mónica's description of her family's gift giving.

1. Juan y yo _____ damos una blusa a nuestra hermana Gisela.
2. Mi tía _____ da a nosotros una mesa para la casa.
3. Gisela _____ da dos corbatas a su novio.
4. A mi mamá yo _____ doy un par de guantes negros.
5. A mi profesora _____ doy dos libros de José Martí.
6. Juan _____ da un regalo a mis padres.
7. Mis padres _____ dan un traje nuevo a mí.
8. Y a ti, yo _____ doy un regalo también. ¿Quieres verlo?

NOTA CULTURAL

Cuban writer and patriot **José Martí** (1853–1895) was born in **La Habana Vieja**, the old colonial center of Havana.

2 **En La Habana** Describe what happens on Pascual's trip to Cuba based on the cues provided.

1. ellos / cantar / canción / (mí)

2. él / comprar / libros / (sus hijos) / Plaza de Armas

3. yo / preparar el almuerzo (*lunch*) / (ti)

4. él / explicar cómo llegar / (conductor)

5. mi novia / sacar / foto / (nosotros)

6. el guía (*guide*) / mostrar / catedral de San Cristóbal / (ustedes)

3 **Combinar** Use an item from each column and an indirect object pronoun to create logical sentences.

modelo

Mis padres les dan regalos a mis primos.

A	B	C	D
yo	comprar	mensajes electrónicos	mí
el dependiente	dar	corbata	ustedes
el profesor Arce	decir	dinero en efectivo	clienta
la vendedora	escribir	tarea	novia
mis padres	explicar	problemas	primos
tú	pagar	regalos	ti
nosotros/as	prestar	ropa	nosotros
¿?	vender	¿?	¿?

Practice more at vhlcentral.com.

Comunicación

4 **Entrevista** In pairs, take turns asking and answering for whom you do these activities. Use the model as a guide.

cantar	escribir mensajes electrónicos
comprar ropa	mostrar fotos de un viaje
dar una fiesta	pedir dinero
decir mentiras	preparar comida (*food*) mexicana

modelo

escribir mensajes electrónicos

Estudiante 1: *¿A quién le escribes mensajes electrónicos?*

Estudiante 2: *Le escribo mensajes electrónicos a mi hermano.*

5 **¡Somos ricos!** You and your classmates just received a large sum of money. Now you want to spend money on your loved ones. In groups of three, discuss what each person is buying for family and friends.

modelo

Estudiante 1: *Quiero comprarle un vestido de Carolina Herrera a mi madre.*

Estudiante 2: *Y yo voy a darles un automóvil nuevo a mis padres.*

Estudiante 3: *Voy a comprarles una casa a mis padres, pero a mis amigos no les voy a dar nada.*

6 **Entrevista** Use these questions to interview a classmate.

1. ¿Qué tiendas, almacenes o centros comerciales prefieres?
2. ¿A quién le compras regalos cuando hay rebajas?
3. ¿A quién le prestas dinero cuando lo necesita?
4. Quiero ir de compras. ¿Cuánto dinero me puedes prestar?
5. ¿Te dan tus padres su tarjeta de crédito cuando vas de compras?

Síntesis

7 **Minidrama** In groups of three, take turns playing the roles of two shoppers and a clerk in a clothing store. The shoppers should talk about the articles of clothing they want and for whom they are buying them. The clerk should recommend several items based on the shoppers' descriptions. Use these expressions and also look at **Expresiones útiles** on page 195.

Me queda grande/pequeño. *It's big/small on me.*	**¿Está en rebaja?** *Is it on sale?*
¿Tiene otro color? *Do you have another color?*	**También estoy buscando...** *I'm also looking for...*

6.3 Preterite tense of regular verbs

Tutorial

ANTE TODO In order to talk about events in the past, Spanish uses two simple tenses: the preterite and the imperfect. In this lesson, you will learn how to form the preterite tense, which is used to express actions or states completed in the past.

Preterite of regular -ar, -er, and -ir verbs

		-ar verbs **comprar**	-er verbs **vender**	-ir verbs **escribir**
SINGULAR FORMS	yo	compr**é** *I bought*	vend**í** *I sold*	escrib**í** *I wrote*
	tú	compr**aste**	vend**iste**	escrib**iste**
	Ud./él/ella	compr**ó**	vend**ió**	escrib**ió**
PLURAL FORMS	nosotros/as	compr**amos**	vend**imos**	escrib**imos**
	vosotros/as	compr**asteis**	vend**isteis**	escrib**isteis**
	Uds./ellos/ellas	compr**aron**	vend**ieron**	escrib**ieron**

- **¡Atención!** The **yo** and **Ud./él/ella** forms of all three conjugations have written accents on the last syllable to show that it is stressed.
- As the chart shows, the endings for regular **-er** and **-ir** verbs are identical in the preterite.

- Note that the **nosotros/as** forms of regular **-ar** and **-ir** verbs in the preterite are identical to the present tense forms. Context will help you determine which tense is being used.

En invierno **compramos** ropa.
In the winter, we buy clothing.

Anoche **compramos** unos zapatos.
Last night we bought some shoes.

- **-Ar** and **-er** verbs that have a stem change in the present tense are regular in the preterite. They do *not* have a stem change.

	PRESENT	PRETERITE
cerrar (e:ie)	La tienda **cierra** a las seis.	La tienda **cerró** a las seis.
volver (o:ue)	Carlitos **vuelve** tarde.	Carlitos **volvió** tarde.
jugar (u:ue)	Él **juega** al fútbol.	Él **jugó** al fútbol.

- **¡Atención!** **-Ir** verbs that have a stem change in the present tense also have a stem change in the preterite.

CONSULTA
There are a few high-frequency irregular verbs in the preterite. You will learn more about them in **Estructura 9.1**, p. 310.

CONSULTA
You will learn about the preterite of **-ir** stem-changing verbs in **Estructura 8.1**, p. 274.

- Verbs that end in **-car**, **-gar**, and **-zar** have a spelling change in the first person singular (**yo** form) in the preterite.

bus**car**	▶	bus**c-**	▶	**qu-**	▶	yo bus**qué**
lle**gar**		lle**g-**		**gu-**		yo lle**gué**
empe**zar**		empe**z-**		**c-**		yo empe**cé**

- Except for the **yo** form, all other forms of **-car**, **-gar**, and **-zar** verbs are regular in the preterite.
- Three other verbs—**creer**, **leer**, and **oír**—have spelling changes in the preterite. The **i** of the verb endings of **creer**, **leer**, and **oír** carries an accent in the **yo**, **tú**, **nosotros/as**, and **vosotros/as** forms, and changes to **y** in the **Ud./él/ella** and **Uds./ellos/ellas** forms.

creer	▶	cre-	▶	cre**í**, cre**í**ste, cre**y**ó, cre**í**mos, cre**í**steis, cre**y**eron
leer		le-		le**í**, le**í**ste, le**y**ó, le**í**mos, le**í**steis, le**y**eron
oír		o-		o**í**, o**í**ste, o**y**ó, o**í**mos, o**í**steis, o**y**eron

- **Ver** is regular in the preterite, but none of its forms has an accent.

ver ⟶ vi, viste, vio, vimos, visteis, vieron

Words commonly used with the preterite

anoche	*last night*	**pasado/a (*adj.*)**	*last; past*
anteayer	*the day before yesterday*	**el año pasado**	*last year*
ayer	*yesterday*	**la semana pasada**	*last week*
de repente	*suddenly*	**una vez**	*once; one time*
desde... hasta...	*from... until...*	**dos veces**	*twice; two times*
		ya	*already*

Ayer llegué a Santiago de Cuba.
Yesterday I arrived in Santiago de Cuba.

Anoche oí un ruido extraño.
Last night I heard a strange noise.

- **Acabar de** + [*infinitive*] is used to say that something has just occurred. Note that **acabar** is in the present tense in this construction.

Acabo de comprar una falda.
I just bought a skirt.

Acabas de ir de compras.
You just went shopping.

recursos
vText
CPA pp. 42–44
CH pp. 89–92
vhlcentral

¡INTÉNTALO! Provide the appropriate preterite forms of the verbs.

	comer	**salir**	**comenzar**	**leer**
1. ellas	comieron	salieron	comenzaron	leyeron
2. tú	_____	_____	_____	_____
3. usted	_____	_____	_____	_____
4. nosotros	_____	_____	_____	_____
5. yo	_____	_____	_____	_____

Práctica

1 **Completar** Andrea is talking about what happened last weekend. Complete each sentence by choosing the correct verb and putting it in the preterite.

1. El viernes a las cuatro de la tarde, la profesora Mora _____ (asistir, costar, usar) a una reunión (*meeting*) de profesores.
2. El sábado por la mañana, yo _____ (llegar, bucear, llevar) a la tienda con mis amigos.
3. Mis amigos y yo _____ (comprar, regatear, gastar) dos o tres cosas.
4. Yo _____ (costar, comprar, escribir) unos pantalones negros y mi amigo Mateo _____ (gastar, pasear, comprar) una camisa azul.
5. Después, nosotros _____ (llevar, vivir, comer) cerca de un mercado.
6. A las tres, Pepe _____ (hablar, pasear, nadar) con su novia por teléfono.
7. El sábado por la tarde, mi mamá _____ (escribir, beber, vivir) una carta.
8. El domingo mi tía _____ (decidir, salir, escribir) comprarme un traje.
9. A las cuatro de la tarde, mi tía _____ (beber, salir, encontrar) el traje y después nosotras _____ (acabar, ver, salir) una película.

2 **Preguntas** Imagine that you have a pesky friend who keeps asking you questions. Respond that you already did or have just done what he/she asks. Make sure you and your partner take turns playing the role of the pesky friend and responding to his/her questions.

modelo

leer la lección

Estudiante 1: ¿Leíste la lección?

Estudiante 2: Sí, ya la leí./Sí, acabo de leerla.

1. escribir el mensaje electrónico
2. lavar (*to wash*) la ropa
3. oír las noticias (*news*)
4. comprar pantalones cortos
5. practicar los verbos
6. leer el artículo
7. empezar la composición
8. ver la nueva película de Almodóvar

3 **¿Cuándo?** Use the time expressions from the word bank to talk about when you and others did the activities listed.

anoche	anteayer	el mes pasado	una vez
ayer	la semana pasada	el año pasado	dos veces

1. mi mejor amigo/a: llegar tarde a clase
2. mi hermano/a mayor: salir con un(a) chico/a guapo/a
3. mis padres: ver una película
4. yo: llevar un traje/vestido
5. el presidente/primer ministro de mi país: no escuchar a la gente
6. mis amigos y yo: comer en un restaurante
7. ¿?: comprar algo (*something*) bueno, bonito y barato

Practice more at vhlcentral.com.

Comunicación

4 **Ayer** Jot down at what time you did these activities yesterday. Then get together with a classmate and find out at what time he or she did these activities. Be prepared to share your findings with the class.

1. desayunar
2. empezar la primera clase
3. almorzar
4. ver a un(a) amigo/a
5. salir de clase
6. volver a casa

5 **Las vacaciones** Imagine that you took these photos on a vacation. Get together with a partner and use the pictures to tell him or her about your trip.

recursos
vText
CPA
pp. 45–46

6 **El fin de semana** Your teacher will give you and your partner different incomplete charts about what four employees at **Almacén Gigante** did last weekend. After you fill out the chart based on each other's information, you will fill out the final column about your partner.

Síntesis

7 **Conversación** With a partner, have a conversation about what you did last week, using verbs from the word bank. Don't forget to include school activities, shopping, and pastimes.

acampar	comprar	hablar	tomar
asistir	correr	jugar	trabajar
bailar	escribir	leer	vender
buscar	estudiar	oír	ver
comer	gastar	pagar	viajar

6.4 Demonstrative adjectives and pronouns

Demonstrative adjectives

ANTE TODO

In Spanish, as in English, demonstrative adjectives are words that "demonstrate" or "point out" nouns. Demonstrative adjectives precede the nouns they modify and, like other Spanish adjectives you have studied, agree with them in gender and number. Observe these examples and then study the chart below.

esta camisa
this shirt

ese vendedor
that salesman

aquellos zapatos
those shoes (over there)

Demonstrative adjectives

Singular		Plural		
MASCULINE	FEMININE	MASCULINE	FEMININE	
este	**esta**	**estos**	**estas**	*this; these*
ese	**esa**	**esos**	**esas**	*that; those*
aquel	**aquella**	**aquellos**	**aquellas**	*that; those (over there)*

- There are three sets of demonstrative adjectives. To determine which one to use, you must establish the relationship between the speaker and the thing(s) being pointed out.
- The demonstrative adjectives **este**, **esta**, **estos**, and **estas** are used to point out things that are close to the speaker and the listener.

- The demonstrative adjectives **ese**, **esa**, **esos**, and **esas** are used to point out things that are not close in space and time to the speaker. They may, however, be close to the listener.

▶ The demonstrative adjectives **aquel**, **aquella**, **aquellos**, and **aquellas** are used to point out things that are far away from the speaker and the listener.

Demonstrative pronouns

▶ Demonstrative pronouns are identical to their corresponding demonstrative adjectives, with the exception that they carry an accent mark on the stressed vowel.

Demonstrative pronouns

Singular		Plural	
MASCULINE	FEMININE	MASCULINE	FEMININE
éste	**ésta**	**éstos**	**éstas**
ése	**ésa**	**ésos**	**ésas**
aquél	**aquélla**	**aquéllos**	**aquéllas**

—¿Quieres comprar **este suéter**?
Do you want to buy this sweater?

—No, no quiero **éste**. Quiero **ése**.
No, I don't want this one. I want that one.

—¿Vas a leer **estas revistas**?
Are you going to read these magazines?

—Sí, voy a leer **éstas**. También voy a leer **aquéllas**.
Yes, I'm going to read these. I'll also read those (over there).

▶ **¡Atención!** Like demonstrative adjectives, demonstrative pronouns agree in gender and number with the corresponding noun.

Este libro es de Pablito. **Éstos** son de Juana.

▶ There are three neuter demonstrative pronouns: **esto**, **eso**, and **aquello**. These forms refer to unidentified or unspecified things, situations, ideas, and concepts. They do not change in gender or number and never carry an accent mark.

—¿Qué es **esto**?
What's this?

—**Eso** es interesante.
That's interesting.

—**Aquello** es bonito.
That's pretty.

¡INTÉNTALO! Provide the correct form of the demonstrative adjective for these nouns.

1. la falda / este esta falda
2. los estudiantes / este _____
3. los países / aquel _____
4. la ventana / ese _____
5. los periodistas / ese _____
6. el chico / aquel _____
7. las sandalias / este _____
8. las chicas / aquel _____

recursos
vText
CPA pp. 47–50
CH pp. 93–94
vhlcentral

Práctica

1 **Cambiar** Make the singular sentences plural and the plural sentences singular.

modelo

Estas camisas son blancas.
Esta camisa es blanca.

1. Aquellos sombreros son muy elegantes.
2. Ese abrigo es muy caro.
3. Estos cinturones son hermosos.
4. Esos precios son muy buenos.
5. Estas faldas son muy cortas.
6. ¿Quieres ir a aquel almacén?
7. Esas blusas son baratas.
8. Esta corbata hace juego con mi traje.

2 **Completar** Here are some things people might say while shopping. Complete the sentences with the correct demonstrative pronouns.

1. No me gustan esos zapatos. Voy a comprar _____. (*these*)
2. ¿Vas a comprar ese traje o _____? (*this one*)
3. Esta guayabera es bonita, pero prefiero _____. (*that one*)
4. Estas corbatas rojas son muy bonitas, pero _____ son fabulosas. (*those*)
5. Estos cinturones cuestan demasiado. Prefiero _____. (*those over there*)
6. ¿Te gustan esas botas o _____? (*these*)
7. Esa bolsa roja es bonita, pero prefiero _____. (*that one over there*)
8. No voy a comprar estas botas; voy a comprar _____. (*those over there*)
9. ¿Prefieres estos pantalones o _____? (*those*)
10. Me gusta este vestido, pero voy a comprar _____. (*that one*)
11. Me gusta ese almacén, pero _____ es mejor (*better*). (*that one over there*)
12. Esa blusa es bonita, pero cuesta demasiado. Voy a comprar _____. (*this one*)

NOTA CULTURAL

The **guayabera** is a men's shirt typically worn in some parts of the Caribbean. Never tucked in, it is casual wear, but variations exist for more formal occasions, such as weddings, parties, or the office.

3 **Describir** With your partner, look for two items in the classroom that are one of these colors: **amarillo, azul, blanco, marrón, negro, verde, rojo.** Take turns pointing them out to each other, first using demonstrative adjectives, and then demonstrative pronouns.

modelo

azul
Estudiante 1: *Esta silla es azul. Aquella mochila es azul.*
Estudiante 2: *Ésta es azul. Aquélla es azul.*

Now use demonstrative adjectives and pronouns to discuss the colors of your classmates' clothing. One of you can ask a question about an article of clothing, using the wrong color. Your partner will correct you and point out that color somewhere else in the room.

modelo

Estudiante 1: *¿Esa camisa es negra?*
Estudiante 2: *No, ésa es azul. Aquélla es negra.*

Practice more at vhlcentral.com.

Comunicación

4 **Conversación** With a classmate, use demonstrative adjectives and pronouns to ask each other questions about the people around you. Use expressions from the word bank and/or your own ideas.

¿A qué hora...?	¿Cuántos años tiene(n)...?
¿Cómo es/son...?	¿De dónde es/son...?
¿Cómo se llama...?	¿De quién es/son...?
¿Cuándo...?	¿Qué clases toma(n)...?

modelo

Estudiante 1: *¿Cómo se llama esa chica?*
Estudiante 2: *Se llama Rebeca.*
Estudiante 1: *¿A qué hora llegó aquel chico a la clase?*
Estudiante 2: *A las nueve.*

5 **En una tienda** Imagine that you and a classmate are in Madrid shopping at Zara. Study the floor plan, then have a conversation about your surroundings. Use demonstrative adjectives and pronouns.

NOTA CULTURAL

Zara is an international clothing company based in Spain. Its innovative processes take a product from the design room to the store shelves in less than one month. This means that the merchandise is constantly changing to keep up with the latest trends.

modelo

Estudiante 1: *Me gusta este suéter azul.*
Estudiante 2: *Yo prefiero aquella chaqueta.*

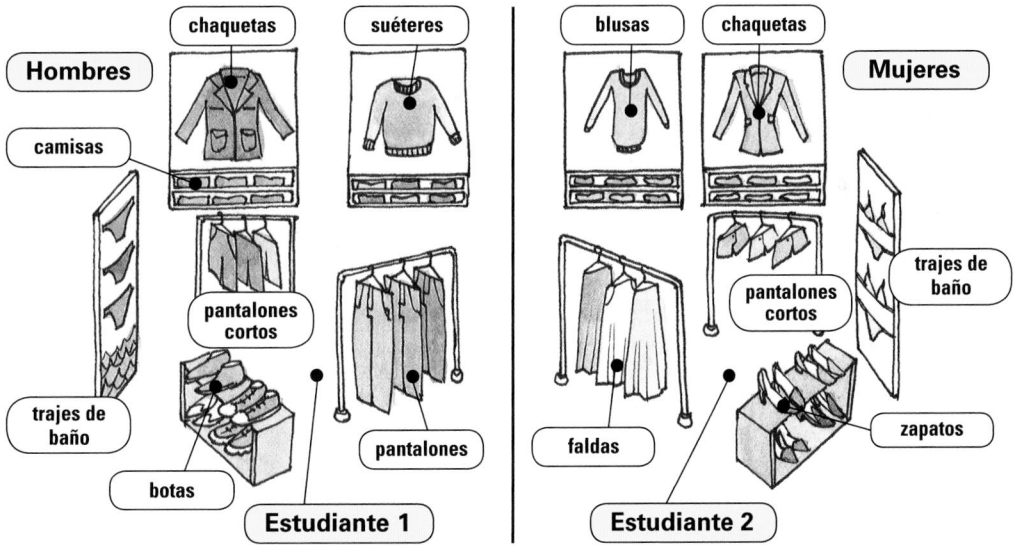

Síntesis

recursos
vText
CPA
pp. 51–52

6 **Diferencias** Your teacher will give you and a partner each a drawing of a store. They are almost identical, but not quite. Use demonstrative adjectives and pronouns to find seven differences.

modelo

Estudiante 1: *Aquellas gafas de sol son feas, ¿verdad?*
Estudiante 2: *No. Aquellas gafas de sol son hermosas.*

SUBJECT Javier CONJUGATED FORM empiezo Main clause Dudan

Recapitulación

Diagnostics

Review the grammar concepts you have learned in this lesson by completing these activities.

1 **Completar** Complete the chart with the correct preterite or infinitive form of the verbs. 30 pts.

Infinitive	yo	ella	ellos
			tomaron
		abrió	
comprender			
	leí		
pagar			

2 **En la tienda** Look at the drawing and complete the conversation with demonstrative adjectives and pronouns. 14 pts.

CLIENTE Buenos días, señorita. Deseo comprar (1) _____ corbata.

VENDEDORA Muy bien, señor. ¿No le interesa mirar (2) _____ trajes que están allá? Hay unos que hacen juego con la corbata.

CLIENTE (3) _____ de allá son de lana, ¿no? Prefiero ver (4) _____ traje marrón que está detrás de usted.

VENDEDORA Estupendo. Como puede ver, es de seda. Cuesta ciento ochenta dólares.

CLIENTE Ah... eh... no, creo que sólo voy a comprar la corbata, gracias.

VENDEDORA Bueno... si busca algo más económico, hay rebaja en (5) _____ sombreros. Cuestan sólo treinta dólares.

CLIENTE ¡Magnífico! Me gusta (6) _____, el blanco que está hasta arriba (*at the top*). Y quiero pagar todo con (7) _____ tarjeta.

VENDEDORA Sí, señor. Ahora mismo le traigo el sombrero.

RESUMEN GRAMATICAL

6.1 Saber and conocer *p. 200*

saber	conocer
sé	conozco
sabes	conoces
sabe	conoce
sabemos	conocemos
sabéis	conocéis
saben	conocen

- **saber** = to know facts/how to do something
- **conocer** = to know a person, place, or thing

6.2 Indirect object pronouns *pp. 202–203*

Indirect object pronouns

Singular	Plural
me	nos
te	os
le	les

- **dar** = doy, das, da, damos, dais, dan
- **decir (e:i)** = digo, dices, dice, decimos, decís, dicen

6.3 Preterite tense of regular verbs *pp. 206–207*

comprar	vender	escribir
compré	vendí	escribí
compraste	vendiste	escribiste
compró	vendió	escribió
compramos	vendimos	escribimos
comprasteis	vendisteis	escribisteis
compraron	vendieron	escribieron

Verbs with spelling changes in the preterite

- **-car:** buscar → yo busqué
- **-gar:** llegar → yo llegué
- **-zar:** empezar → yo empecé
- **creer:** creí, creíste, creyó, creímos, creísteis, creyeron
- **leer:** leí, leíste, leyó, leímos, leísteis, leyeron
- **oír:** oí, oíste, oyó, oímos, oísteis, oyeron
- **ver:** vi, viste, vio, vimos, visteis, vieron

3 **¿Saber o conocer?** Complete each dialogue with the correct form of **saber** or **conocer**. 20 pts.

1. —¿Qué _____ hacer tú?
   —(Yo) _____ jugar al fútbol.
2. —¿_____ tú esta tienda de ropa?
   —No, (yo) no la _____. ¿Es buena?
3. —¿Tus padres no _____ a tu profesor?
   —No, ¡ellos no _____ quién es!
4. —Mi hermanastro todavía no me _____ bien.
   —Y tú, ¿lo quieres _____ a él?
5. —¿_____ ustedes dónde está el mercado?
   —No, nosotros no _____ bien esta ciudad.

4 **Oraciones** Form complete sentences using the information provided. Use indirect object pronouns and the present tense of the verbs. 10 pts.

1. Javier / prestar / el abrigo / a Maripili
   _____
2. nosotros / vender / ropa / a los clientes
   _____
3. el vendedor / traer / las camisetas / a mis amigos y a mí
   _____
4. yo / querer dar / consejos (*advice*) / a ti
   _____
5. ¿tú / ir a comprar / un regalo / a mí?
   _____

5 **Mi última compra** Write a short paragraph describing the last time you went shopping. Use at least four verbs in the preterite tense. 26 pts.

modelo

El viernes pasado, busqué unos zapatos en el centro comercial...

6 **Refranes** Write the missing words to complete the proverbs. 4 EXTRA points!

"A la cama no te irás° sin _____ (conocer/saber) una cosa más."
(*You learn something new every day.*)

"A todos _____ (les/te) llega su momento de gloria°."
(*Every dog has its day.*)

no te irás *you will not go* gloria *glory*

6.4 Demonstrative adjectives and pronouns *pp. 210–211*

Demonstrative adjectives

Singular		Plural	
Masc.	Fem.	Masc.	Fem.
este	esta	estos	estas
ese	esa	esos	esas
aquel	aquella	aquellos	aquellas

Demonstrative pronouns

Singular		Plural	
Masc.	Fem.	Masc.	Fem.
éste	ésta	éstos	éstas
ése	ésa	ésos	ésas
aquél	aquélla	aquéllos	aquéllas

Lectura

Audio: Reading
Additional Reading

Antes de leer

Estrategia

Skimming

Skimming involves quickly reading through a document to absorb its general meaning. This allows you to understand the main ideas without having to read word for word. When you skim a text, you might want to look at its title and subtitles. You might also want to read the first sentence of each paragraph.

Examinar el texto

Look at the format of the reading selection. How is it organized? What does the organization of the document tell you about its content?

Buscar cognados

Scan the reading selection to locate at least five cognates. Based on the cognates, what do you think the reading selection is about?

1. _____ 4. _____
2. _____ 5. _____
3. _____

The reading selection is about _____.

Impresiones generales

Now skim the reading selection to understand its general meaning. Jot down your impressions. What new information did you learn about the document by skimming it? Based on all the information you now have, answer these questions in Spanish.

1. Who created this document?
2. What is its purpose?
3. Who is its intended audience?

recursos

vText | CH pp. 95–96 | vhlcentral

Corona

¡Corona tiene las ofertas más locas del verano!

La tienda más elegante de la ciudad con precios increíbles

Carteras
ELEGANCIA
Colores anaranjado, blanco, rosado y amarillo
Ahora: 15.000 pesos
50% de rebaja

Sandalias de playa
GINO
Números del 35 al 38
A sólo 12.000 pesos
50% de descuento

Faldas largas
ROPA BONITA
Algodón. De distintos colores
Talla mediana
Precio especial: 8.000 pesos

Blusas de seda
BAMBÚ
De cuadros y de lunares
Ahora: 21.000 pesos
40% de rebaja

Vestido de algodón
PANAMÁ
Colores blanco, azul y verde
Ahora: 18.000 pesos
30% de rebaja

Accesorios
BELLEZA
Cinturones, gafas de sol, sombreros, medias
Diversos estilos
Todos con un 40% de rebaja

Lunes a sábado de 9 a 21 horas.
Domingo de 10 a 14 horas.

¡Grandes rebajas!

Real° Liquidación°

¡La rebaja está de moda en Corona!

y con la tarjeta de crédito más conveniente del mercado.

Chaquetas
CASINO
Microfibra. Colores negro, café y gris
Tallas: P, M, G, XG
Ahora: 22.500 pesos

Zapatos
COLOR
Italianos y franceses
Números del 40 al 45
A sólo 20.000 pesos

Pantalones
OCÉANO
Colores negro, gris y café
Ahora: 11.500 pesos
30% de rebaja

Ropa interior
ATLÁNTICO
Tallas: P, M, G
Colores blanco, negro y gris
40% de rebaja

Traje inglés
GALES
Modelos originales
Ahora: 105.000 pesos
30% de rebaja

Accesorios
GUAPO
Gafas de sol, corbatas, cinturones, calcetines
Diversos estilos
Todos con un 40% de rebaja

Real *Royal* Liquidación *Clearance sale*

Por la compra de 40.000 pesos, puede llevar un regalo gratis.

- Un hermoso cinturón de mujer
- Un par de calcetines
- Una corbata de seda
- Una bolsa para la playa
- Una mochila
- Unas medias

Después de leer

Completar

Complete this paragraph about the reading selection with the correct forms of the words from the word bank.

almacén	hacer juego	tarjeta de crédito
caro	increíble	tienda
dinero	pantalones	verano
falda	rebaja	zapato

En este anuncio, el _____ Corona anuncia la liquidación de _____ con grandes _____. Con muy poco _____ usted puede conseguir ropa fina y elegante. Si no tiene dinero en efectivo, puede utilizar su _____ y pagar luego. Para el hombre de gustos refinados, hay _____ importados de París y Roma. La señora elegante puede encontrar blusas de seda que _____ con todo tipo de _____ o _____. Los precios de esta liquidación son realmente _____.

¿Cierto o falso?

Indicate whether each statement is **cierto** or **falso**. Correct the false statements.

1. Hay sandalias de playa.
2. Las corbatas tienen una rebaja del 30%.
3. El almacén Corona tiene un departamento de zapatos.
4. Normalmente las sandalias cuestan 22.000 pesos.
5. Cuando gastas 30.000 pesos en la tienda, llevas un regalo gratis.
6. Tienen carteras amarillas.

Preguntas

In pairs, take turns asking and answering these questions.

1. Imagina que vas a ir a la tienda Corona. ¿Qué departamentos vas a visitar? ¿El departamento de ropa para mujeres, el departamento de ropa para hombres...?
2. ¿Qué vas a buscar en Corona?
3. ¿Hay tiendas similares a la tienda Corona en tu pueblo o ciudad? ¿Cómo se llaman? ¿Tienen muchas gangas?

Practice more at vhlcentral.com.

Escritura

Estrategia

How to report an interview

There are several ways to prepare a written report about an interview. For example, you can transcribe the interview verbatim, you can simply summarize it, or you can summarize it but quote the speakers occasionally. In any event, the report should begin with an interesting title and a brief introduction, which may include the five Ws (*what, where, when, who, why*) and the H (*how*) of the interview. The report should end with an interesting conclusion. Note that when you transcribe dialogue in Spanish, you should pay careful attention to format and punctuation.

Writing dialogue in Spanish

- If you need to transcribe an interview verbatim, you can use speakers' names to indicate a change of speaker.

CARMELA ¿Qué compraste? ¿Encontraste muchas gangas?

ROBERTO Sí, muchas. Compré un suéter, una camisa y dos corbatas. Y tú, ¿qué compraste?

CARMELA Una blusa y una falda muy bonitas. ¿Cuánto costó tu camisa?

ROBERTO Sólo diez dólares. ¿Cuánto costó tu blusa?

CARMELA Veinte dólares.

- You can also use a dash (*raya*) to mark the beginning of each speaker's words.

—¿Qué compraste?
—Un suéter y una camisa muy bonitos. Y tú, ¿encontraste muchas gangas?
—Sí... compré dos blusas, tres camisetas y un par de zapatos.
—¡A ver!

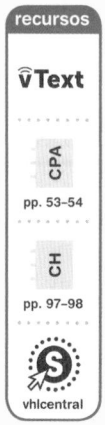

Tema

Escribe un informe

Write a report for the school newspaper about an interview you conducted with a student about his or her shopping habits and clothing preferences. First, brainstorm a list of interview questions. Then conduct the interview using the questions below as a guide, but feel free to ask other questions as they occur to you.

Examples of questions:

- ¿Cuándo vas de compras?
- ¿Adónde vas de compras?
- ¿Con quién vas de compras?
- ¿Qué tiendas, almacenes o centros comerciales prefieres?
- ¿Compras ropa de catálogos o por Internet?
- ¿Prefieres comprar ropa cara o barata? ¿Por qué? ¿Te gusta buscar gangas?
- ¿Qué ropa llevas cuando vas a clase?
- ¿Qué ropa llevas cuando sales con tus amigos/as?
- ¿Qué ropa llevas cuando practicas un deporte?
- ¿Cuáles son tus colores favoritos? ¿Compras mucha ropa de esos colores?
- ¿Les das ropa a tu familia o a tus amigos/as?

Escuchar

Audio

Estrategia

Listening for linguistic cues

You can enhance your listening comprehension by listening for specific linguistic cues. For example, if you listen for the endings of conjugated verbs, or for familiar constructions, such as **acabar de** + [*infinitive*] or **ir a** + [*infinitive*], you can find out whether an event already took place, is taking place now, or will take place in the future. Verb endings also give clues about who is participating in the action.

To practice listening for linguistic cues, you will now listen to four sentences. As you listen, note whether each sentence refers to a past, present, or future action. Also jot down the subject of each sentence.

Preparación

Based on the photograph, what do you think Marisol has recently done? What do you think Marisol and Alicia are talking about? What else can you guess about their conversation from the visual clues in the photograph?

Ahora escucha

Now you are going to hear Marisol and Alicia's conversation. Make a list of the clothing items that each person mentions. Then put a check mark after the item if the person actually purchased it.

Marisol	Alicia
1. _____	1. _____
2. _____	2. _____
3. _____	3. _____
4. _____	4. _____

recursos

vText vhlcentral

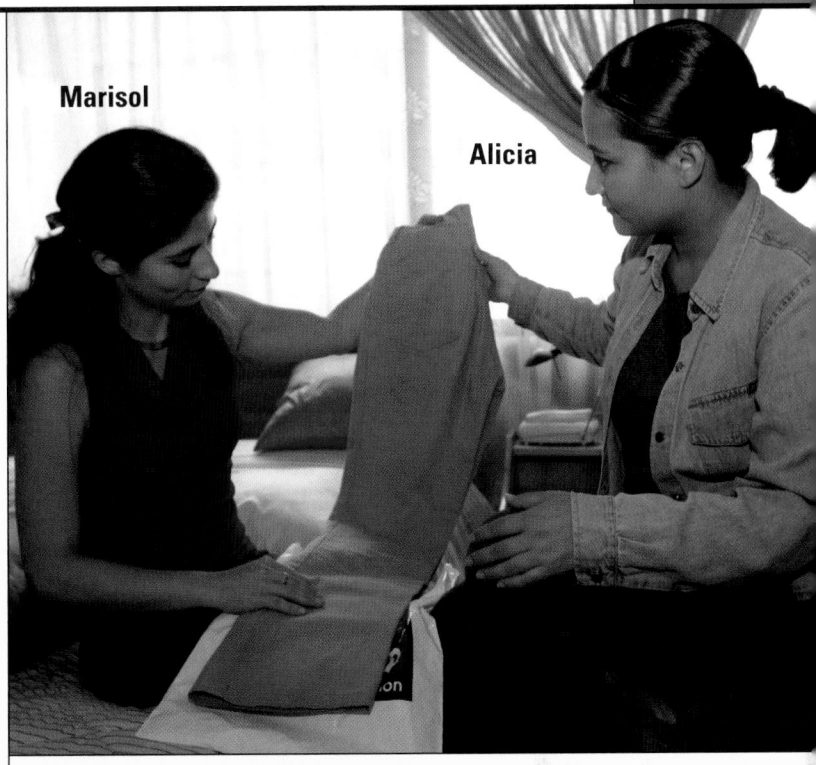

Comprensión

¿Cierto o falso?

Indicate whether each statement is **cierto** or **falso**. Then correct the false statements.

1. Marisol y Alicia acaban de ir de compras juntas (*together*).
2. Marisol va a comprar unos pantalones y una blusa mañana.
3. Marisol compró una blusa de cuadros.
4. Alicia compró unos zapatos nuevos hoy.
5. Alicia y Marisol van a ir al café.
6. Marisol gastó todo el dinero de la semana en ropa nueva.

Preguntas

Discuss the following questions with a classmate. Be sure to explain your answers.

1. ¿Crees que Alicia y Marisol son buenas amigas? ¿Por qué?
2. ¿Cuál de las dos estudiantes es más ahorradora (*frugal*)? ¿Por qué?
3. ¿Crees que a Alicia le gusta la ropa que Marisol compró?
4. ¿Crees que la moda es importante para Alicia? ¿Para Marisol? ¿Por qué?
5. ¿Es importante para ti estar a la moda? ¿Por qué?

Practice more at vhlcentral.com.

en pantalla

Video: TV Clip

Anuncio de tiendas Galerías

Presentamos la moda para el próximo° curso.

Preparación

Answer these questions in Spanish.

1. ¿Qué ropa llevas normalmente cuando vienes a la escuela? ¿Y los fines de semana?
2. ¿Cómo es tu ropa favorita? Describe los dos o tres artículos que más te gustan.

¿Uniformes o no?

This TV clip from Spain has special historical impact for its viewers. In Spain, during Francisco Franco's dictatorship (1939–1975), students in public schools were required to wear uniforms. After the fall of Franco's regime and the establishment of democracy, educational authorities rejected this former policy and decided it should no longer be obligatory to wear uniforms in public schools. Today, only some private schools in Spain enforce the use of uniforms; even Catholic schools do not have anything more than a basic dress code.

próximo *next*

Vocabulario útil

anchas	*loose-fitting*
carteras	*book bags (Spain)*
chándals	*tracksuits (Spain)*
lavables	*washable*
resiste	*withstands*
tanto como	*as much as*
trencas	*duffel coats (Spain)*
vaqueros	*jeans (Spain)*

Comprensión

Check off each word that you hear in the ad.

____ 1. camisetas	____ 5. chaquetas
____ 2. hijos	____ 6. clientas
____ 3. zapatos	____ 7. lana
____ 4. algodón	____ 8. precio

Conversación

Answer these questions with a classmate.

1. ¿Qué tipo de ropa expresa bien tu personalidad? ¿Por qué?
2. ¿Los estudiantes de tu escuela llevan uniforme? ¿Por qué?
3. ¿En tu opinión, cómo debe ser un buen uniforme para los estudiantes? ¿Y cómo no debe ser un uniforme?

Aplicación

As a class, make a list of special groups that usually wear uniforms. Identify the work or special service offered by each group. Then, with two or three classmates, draw the uniform of one of the groups and present it to the class.

Practice more at vhlcentral.com.

recursos vText vhlcentral

Video: *Flash cultura*

In the Spanish-speaking world, most city dwellers shop at large supermarkets and little stores that specialize in just one item, such as a butcher shop (**carnicería**), vegetable market (**verdulería**), perfume shop (**perfumería**), or hat shop (**sombrerería**). In small towns where supermarkets are less common, many people rely exclusively on specialty shops. This requires shopping more frequently—often every day or every other day for perishable items—but also means that the foods they consume are fresher and the goods are usually locally produced. Each neighborhood generally has its own shops, so people don't have to walk far to find fresh bread (at a **panadería**) for the midday meal.

Vocabulario útil

colones (pl.)	*currency from Costa Rica*
¿Cuánto vale?	**¿Cuánto cuesta?**
descuento	*discount*
disculpe	*excuse me*
¿Dónde queda...?	*Where is... located?*
los helados	*ice cream*
el regateo	*bargaining*

Preparación

Have you ever been to an open-air market? What did you buy? Have you ever negotiated a price? What did you say?

Comprensión

Select the option that best summarizes this episode.

a. Randy Cruz va al mercado al aire libre para comprar papayas. Luego va al Mercado Central. Él les pregunta a varios clientes qué compran, prueba (*he tastes*) platos típicos y busca la heladería.

b. Randy Cruz va al mercado al aire libre para comprar papayas y pedir un descuento. Luego va al Mercado Central para preguntarles a los clientes qué compran en los mercados.

Comprar en los mercados

Trescientos colones.

... pero me hace un buen descuento.

¿Qué compran en el Mercado Central?

Practice more at vhlcentral.com.

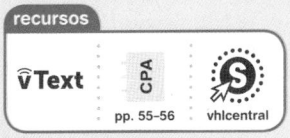

Cuba

Video: *Panorama cultural*
Interactive Map

El país en cifras

- **Área:** 110.860 km^2 (42.803 millas^2), *aproximadamente el área de Pensilvania*
- **Población:** 11.061.886
- **Capital:** La Habana—2.116.000

La Habana Vieja fue declarada° Patrimonio° Cultural de la Humanidad por la UNESCO en 1982. Este distrito es uno de los lugares más fascinantes de Cuba. En La Plaza de Armas, se puede visitar el majestuoso Palacio de Capitanes Generales, que ahora es un museo. En la calle° Obispo, frecuentada por el autor Ernest Hemingway, hay hermosos cafés, clubes nocturnos y tiendas elegantes.

- **Ciudades principales:** Santiago de Cuba; Camagüey; Holguín; Guantánamo
- **Moneda:** peso cubano
- **Idiomas:** español (oficial)

Bandera de Cuba

Cubanos célebres

- **Carlos Finlay,** doctor y científico (1833–1915)
- **José Martí,** político y poeta (1853–1895)
- **Fidel Castro,** ex presidente, ex comandante en jefe° de las fuerzas armadas (1926–)
- **Zoé Valdés,** escritora (1959–)
- **Ibrahim Ferrer,** músico (1927–2005)
- **Carlos Acosta,** bailarín (1973–)

fue declarada *was declared* Patrimonio *Heritage* calle *street* comandante en jefe *commander in chief* liviano *light* colibrí abeja *bee hummingbird* ave *bird* mundo *world* miden *measure* pesan *weigh*

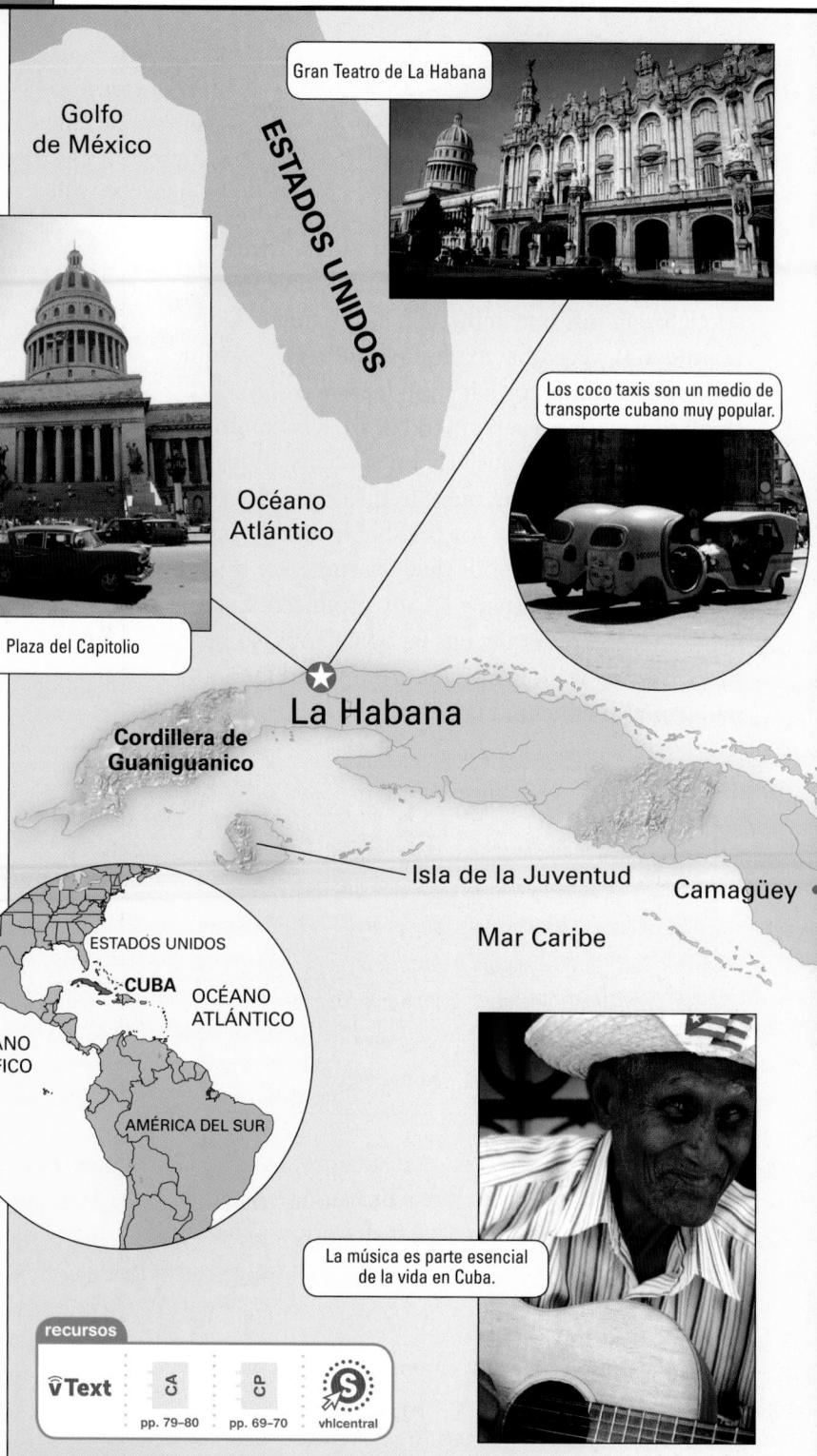

recursos
vText | CA pp. 79–80 | CP pp. 69–70 | vhlcentral

¡Increíble pero cierto!

Pequeño y liviano°, el colibrí abeja° de Cuba es una de las más de 320 especies de colibrí y es también el ave° más pequeña del mundo°. Menores que muchos insectos, estas aves minúsculas miden° 5 centímetros y pesan° sólo 1,95 gramos.

Baile • Ballet Nacional de Cuba

La bailarina Alicia Alonso fundó el Ballet Nacional de Cuba en 1948, después de° convertirse en una estrella° internacional en el Ballet de Nueva York y en Broadway. El Ballet Nacional de Cuba es famoso en todo el mundo por su creatividad y perfección técnica.

Economía • La caña de azúcar y el tabaco

La caña de azúcar° es el producto agrícola° que más se cultiva en la isla y su exportación es muy importante para la economía del país. El tabaco, que se usa para fabricar los famosos puros° cubanos, es otro cultivo° de mucha importancia.

Gente • Población

La población cubana tiene raíces° muy heterogéneas. La inmigración a la isla fue determinante° desde la colonia hasta mediados° del siglo° XX. Los cubanos de hoy son descendientes de africanos, europeos, chinos y antillanos, entre otros.

Música • Buena Vista Social Club

En 1997 nace° el fenómeno musical conocido como *Buena Vista Social Club*. Este proyecto reúne° a un grupo de importantes músicos de Cuba, la mayoría ya mayores, con una larga trayectoria interpretando canciones clásicas del son° cubano. Ese mismo año ganaron un *Grammy*. Hoy en día estos músicos son conocidos en todo el mundo, y personas de todas las edades bailan al ritmo° de su música.

¿Qué aprendiste? Responde a las preguntas con una oración completa.

1. ¿Qué autor está asociado con La Habana Vieja?
2. ¿Por qué es famoso el Ballet Nacional de Cuba?
3. ¿Cuáles son los dos cultivos más importantes para la economía cubana?
4. ¿Qué fabrican los cubanos con la planta del tabaco?
5. ¿De dónde son muchos de los inmigrantes que llegaron a Cuba?
6. ¿En qué año ganó un *Grammy* el disco *Buena Vista Social Club*?

Conexión Internet Investiga estos temas en **vhlcentral.com.**

1. Busca información sobre un(a) cubano/a célebre. ¿Por qué es célebre? ¿Qué hace? ¿Todavía vive en Cuba?
2. Busca información sobre una de las ciudades principales de Cuba. ¿Qué atracciones hay en esta ciudad?

Practice more at **vhlcentral.com.**

después de *after* estrella *star* caña de azúcar *sugar cane* agrícola *farming* puros *cigars* cultivo *crop* raíces *roots* determinante *deciding* mediados *halfway through* siglo *century* nace *is born* reúne *gets together* son *Cuban musical genre* ritmo *rhythm*

La ropa

el abrigo	*coat*
los (blue)jeans	*jeans*
la blusa	*blouse*
la bolsa	*purse; bag*
la bota	*boot*
los calcetines (el calcetín)	*sock(s)*
la camisa	*shirt*
la camiseta	*t-shirt*
la cartera	*wallet*
la chaqueta	*jacket*
el cinturón	*belt*
la corbata	*tie*
la falda	*skirt*
las gafas (de sol)	*(sun)glasses*
los guantes	*gloves*
el impermeable	*raincoat*
las medias	*pantyhose; stockings*
los pantalones	*pants*
los pantalones cortos	*shorts*
la ropa	*clothing; clothes*
la ropa interior	*underwear*
las sandalias	*sandals*
el sombrero	*hat*
el suéter	*sweater*
el traje	*suit*
el traje de baño	*bathing suit*
el vestido	*dress*
los zapatos de tenis	*sneakers*

Verbos

conducir	*to drive*
conocer	*to know; to be acquainted with*
dar	*to give*
ofrecer	*to offer*
parecer	*to seem*
saber	*to know; to know how*
traducir	*to translate*

Ir de compras

el almacén	*department store*
la caja	*cash register*
el centro comercial	*shopping mall*
el/la cliente/a	*customer*
el/la dependiente/a	*clerk*
el dinero	*money*
(en) efectivo	*cash*
el mercado (al aire libre)	*(open-air) market*
un par (de zapatos)	*a pair (of shoes)*
el precio (fijo)	*(fixed; set) price*
la rebaja	*sale*
el regalo	*gift*
la tarjeta de crédito	*credit card*
la tienda	*shop; store*
el/la vendedor(a)	*salesperson*
costar (o:ue)	*to cost*
gastar	*to spend (money)*
hacer juego (con)	*to match (with)*
llevar	*to wear; to take*
pagar	*to pay*
regatear	*to bargain*
usar	*to wear; to use*
vender	*to sell*

Adjetivos

barato/a	*cheap*
bueno/a	*good*
cada	*each*
caro/a	*expensive*
corto/a	*short (in length)*
elegante	*elegant*
hermoso/a	*beautiful*
largo/a	*long*
loco/a	*crazy*
nuevo/a	*new*
otro/a	*other; another*
pobre	*poor*
rico/a	*rich*

My Vocabulary

Los colores

el color	*color*
anaranjado/a	*orange*
gris	*gray*
marrón, café	*brown*
morado/a	*purple*
rosado/a	*pink*

Palabras adicionales

acabar de (+ *inf.*)	*to have just done something*
anoche	*last night*
anteayer	*the day before yesterday*
ayer	*yesterday*
de repente	*suddenly*
desde	*from*
dos veces	*twice; two times*
hasta	*until*
pasado/a (*adj.*)	*last; past*
el año pasado	*last year*
la semana pasada	*last week*
prestar	*to lend; to loan*
una vez	*once; one time*
ya	*already*

Indirect object pronouns	*See page 202.*
Demonstrative adjectives and pronouns	*See page 210.*
Expresiones útiles	*See page 195.*

La rutina diaria

7

Communicative Goals

I will be able to:

- **Describe my daily routine**
- **Talk about personal hygiene**
- **Reassure someone**

VOICE BOARD

contextos

pages 226–229

- Daily routine
- Personal hygiene
- Time expressions

fotonovela

pages 230–233

Marisa, Felipe, and Jimena all compete for space in front of the mirror as they get ready to go out on Friday night.

cultura

pages 234–235

- **La siesta**
- **El mate**

estructura

pages 236–251

- Reflexive verbs
- Indefinite and negative words
- Preterite of **ser** and **ir**
- Verbs like **gustar**
- **Recapitulación**

adelante

pages 252–259

Lectura: An e-mail from Guillermo
Escritura: A daily routine
Escuchar: An interview with a famous actor
En pantalla
Flash cultura
Panorama: Perú

A PRIMERA VISTA

- **¿Está él en casa o en una tienda?**
- **¿Está contento o enojado?**
- **¿Cómo es él?**
- **¿Qué colores hay en la foto?**

La rutina diaria

My Vocabulary Tutorials

Más vocabulario

el baño, el cuarto de baño	*bathroom*
el inodoro	*toilet*
el jabón	*soap*
el despertador	*alarm clock*
el maquillaje	*makeup*
la rutina diaria	*daily routine*
bañarse	*to bathe; to take a bath*
cepillarse el pelo	*to brush one's hair*
dormirse (o:ue)	*to go to sleep; to fall asleep*
lavarse la cara	*to wash one's face*
levantarse	*to get up*
maquillarse	*to put on makeup*
antes (de)	*before*
después	*afterwards; then*
después (de)	*after*
durante	*during*
entonces	*then*
luego	*then*
más tarde	*later on*
por la mañana	*in the morning*
por la noche	*at night*
por la tarde	*in the afternoon; in the evening*
por último	*finally*

Variación léxica

afeitarse	⟷	rasurarse *(Méx., Amér. C.)*
ducha	⟷	regadera *(Col., Méx., Venez.)*
ducharse	⟷	bañarse *(Amér. L.)*
pantuflas	⟷	chancletas *(Méx., Col.)*; zapatillas *(Esp.)*

En la habitación por la mañana

En el baño por la mañana

recursos

vText | CPA pp. 63–65 | CH pp. 99–100 | vhlcentral

En la habitación por la noche

En el baño por la noche

Práctica

1 **Escuchar** Escucha las oraciones e indica si cada oración es **cierta** o **falsa**, según el dibujo.

1. _____
2. _____
3. _____
4. _____
5. _____
6. _____
7. _____
8. _____
9. _____
10. _____

2 **Ordenar** Escucha la rutina diaria de Marta. Después ordena los verbos según lo que escuchaste.

___ a. almorzar
___ b. ducharse
___ c. peinarse
___ d. ver la televisión
___ e. desayunar
___ f. dormirse
___ g. despertarse
___ h. estudiar en la biblioteca

3 **Seleccionar** Selecciona la palabra que no está relacionada con cada grupo.

1. lavabo • toalla • despertador • jabón _____
2. manos • antes de • después de • por último _____
3. acostarse • jabón • despertarse • dormirse _____
4. espejo • lavabo • despertador • entonces _____
5. dormirse • toalla • vestirse • levantarse _____
6. pelo • cara • manos • inodoro _____
7. espejo • champú • jabón • pasta de dientes _____
8. maquillarse • vestirse • peinarse • dientes _____
9. baño • dormirse • despertador • acostarse _____
10. ducharse • luego • bañarse • lavarse _____

4 **Identificar** Con un(a) compañero/a, identifica las cosas que cada persona necesita. Sigue el modelo.

modelo

Jorge / lavarse la cara
Estudiante 1: *¿Qué necesita Jorge para lavarse la cara?*
Estudiante 2: *Necesita jabón y una toalla.*

1. Mariana / maquillarse
2. Gerardo / despertarse
3. Celia / bañarse
4. Gabriel / ducharse
5. Roberto / afeitarse
6. Sonia / lavarse el pelo
7. Vanesa / lavarse las manos
8. Manuel / vestirse

5 **La rutina de Andrés** Ordena esta rutina de una manera lógica.

a. Se afeita después de cepillarse los dientes. _____
b. Se acuesta a las once y media de la noche. _____
c. Por último, se duerme. _____
d. Después de afeitarse, sale para las clases. _____
e. Asiste a todas sus clases y vuelve a su casa. _____
f. Andrés se despierta a las seis y media de la mañana. _____
g. Después de volver a casa, come un poco. Luego estudia en su habitación. _____
h. Se viste y entonces se cepilla los dientes. _____
i. Se cepilla los dientes antes de acostarse. _____
j. Se ducha antes de vestirse. _____

6 **La rutina diaria** Con un(a) compañero/a, mira los dibujos y describe lo que hacen Juan y Ana.

1.

2.

3.

4.

5.

6.

7.

8.

Practice more at vhlcentral.com.

Comunicación

7 **La farmacia** Lee el anuncio y responde a las preguntas con un(a) compañero/a.

LA FARMACIA NUEVO SOL tiene todo lo que necesitas para la vida diaria.

Esta semana tenemos grandes rebajas.

Con poco dinero puedes comprar lo que necesitas para el cuarto de baño ideal.

Para los hombres ofrecemos...
Excelentes cremas de afeitar de Guapo y Máximo

Para las mujeres ofrecemos...
Nuevo maquillaje de Marisol y jabones de baño Ilusiones y Belleza

Y para todos tenemos los mejores jabones, pastas de dientes y cepillos de dientes.

¡Visita **LA FARMACIA NUEVO SOL!**
Tenemos los mejores precios. Visita nuestra tienda muy cerca de tu casa.

1. ¿Qué tipo de tienda es?
2. ¿Qué productos ofrecen para las mujeres?
3. ¿Qué productos ofrecen para los hombres?
4. Haz (*Make*) una lista de los verbos que asocias con los productos del anuncio.
5. ¿Dónde compras tus productos de higiene?
6. ¿Tienes una tienda favorita? ¿Cuál es?

8 **Rutinas diarias** Trabajen en parejas para describir la rutina diaria de dos o tres de estas personas. Pueden usar palabras de la lista.

antes (de)	entonces	primero
después (de)	luego	tarde
durante el día	por último	temprano

- un(a) maestro/a
- un(a) turista
- un hombre o una mujer de negocios (*businessman/woman*)
- un vigilante nocturno (*night watchman*)
- un(a) jubilado/a (*retired person*)
- el presidente/primer ministro de tu país
- un niño de cuatro años
- Daniel Espinosa

NOTA CULTURAL

Daniel Espinosa (México, 1961) es un famoso diseñador de joyería (*jewelry*). Su trabajo es vanguardista (*avant-garde*), arriesgado (*daring*) e innovador. Su material favorito es la plata (*silver*). Entre sus clientes están Salma Hayek, Nelly Furtado, Eva Longoria, Gwyneth Paltrow, Shakira y Daisy Fuentes.

¡Necesito arreglarme!

Es viernes por la tarde y Marissa, Jimena y Felipe se preparan para salir.

PERSONAJES

MARISSA

JIMENA

Video: *Fotonovela*

MARISSA ¿Hola? ¿Está ocupado?

JIMENA Sí. Me estoy lavando la cara.

MARISSA Necesito usar el baño.

MARISSA Tengo que terminar de arreglarme. Voy al cine esta noche.

JIMENA Yo también tengo que salir. ¿Te importa si me maquillo primero? Me voy a encontrar con mi amiga Elena en una hora.

JIMENA ¡Felipe! ¿Qué estás haciendo?

FELIPE Me estoy afeitando. ¿Hay algún problema?

JIMENA ¡Siempre haces lo mismo!

FELIPE Pues, yo no vi a nadie aquí.

MARISSA Tú ganas. ¿Adónde vas a ir esta noche, Felipe?

FELIPE Juan Carlos y yo vamos a ir a un café en el centro. Siempre hay música en vivo. (*Sale.*) Me siento guapísimo. Todavía me falta cambiarme la camisa.

MARISSA ¿Adónde vas esta noche?

JIMENA A la biblioteca.

MARISSA ¡Es viernes! ¡Nadie debe estudiar los viernes! Voy a ver una película de Pedro Almodóvar con unas amigas.

MARISSA ¿Por qué no vienen tú y Elena al cine con nosotras? Después, podemos ir a ese café y molestar a Felipe.

FELIPE

4

5

JIMENA ¿Por qué no te afeitaste por la mañana?

FELIPE Porque cada vez que quiero usar el baño, una de ustedes está aquí. O bañándose o maquillándose.

JIMENA No te preocupes, Marissa. Llegaste primero. Entonces, te arreglas el pelo y después me maquillo.

FELIPE ¿Y yo? Tengo crema de afeitar en la cara. No me voy a ir. Estoy aquí y aquí me quedo.

9

10

JIMENA No sé.

MARISSA ¿Cuándo fue la última vez que viste a Juan Carlos?

JIMENA Cuando fuimos a Mérida.

MARISSA A ti te gusta ese chico.

JIMENA No tengo idea de qué estás hablando. Si no te importa, nos vemos en el cine.

recursos

vText | CPA pp. 66–67 | vhlcentral

Expresiones útiles

Talking about getting ready

Necesito arreglarme.
I need to get ready.
Me estoy lavando la cara.
I'm washing my face.
¿Te importa si me maquillo primero?
Is it OK with you if I put on my makeup first?
Tú te arreglas el pelo y después yo me maquillo.
You fix your hair and then I'll put on my makeup.
Todavía me falta cambiarme la camisa.
I still have to change my shirt.

Reassuring someone

Tranquilo/a.
Relax.
No te preocupes.
Don't worry.

Talking about past actions

¿Cuándo fue la última vez que viste a Juan Carlos?
When was the last time you saw Juan Carlos?
Cuando fuimos a Mérida.
When we went to Mérida.

Talking about likes and dislikes

Me fascinan las películas de Almodóvar.
I love Almodóvar's movies.
Me encanta la música en vivo.
I love live music.
Me molesta compartir el baño.
It bothers me to share the bathroom.

Additional vocabulary

encontrarse con *to meet up with*
molestar *to bother*
nadie *no one*

¿Qué pasó?

1 **¿Cierto o falso?** Indica si lo que dicen estas oraciones es **cierto** o **falso.** Corrige las oraciones falsas.

1. Marissa va a ver una película de Pedro Almodóvar con unas amigas.
2. Jimena se va a encontrar con Elena en dos horas.
3. Felipe se siente muy feo después de afeitarse.
4. Jimena quiere maquillarse.
5. Marissa quiere ir al café para molestar a Juan Carlos.

2 **Identificar** Identifica quién puede decir estas oraciones. Puedes usar cada nombre más de una vez.

1. No puedo usar el baño porque siempre están aquí, o bañándose o maquillándose. _____
2. Quiero arreglarme el pelo porque voy al cine esta noche. _____
3. Hoy voy a ir a la biblioteca. _____
4. ¡Necesito arreglarme! _____
5. Te gusta Juan Carlos. _____
6. ¿Por qué quieres afeitarte cuando estamos en el baño? _____

MARISSA

FELIPE

JIMENA

3 **Ordenar** Ordena correctamente los planes que tiene Marissa.

____ a. Voy al café.
____ b. Me arreglo el pelo.
____ c. Molesto a Felipe.
____ d. Me encuentro con unas amigas.
____ e. Entro al baño.
____ f. Voy al cine.

4 **En el baño** Trabajen en parejas para representar los papeles de dos compañeros/as de cuarto que deben usar el baño al mismo tiempo para hacer su rutina diaria. Usen las instrucciones como guía.

Estudiante 1	Estudiante 2
Di (*Say*) que quieres arreglarte porque vas a ir al cine.	Di (*Say*) que necesitas arreglarte porque te vas a encontrar con tus amigos/as.
Pregunta si puedes secarte (*dry*) el pelo.	Responde que no porque necesitas lavarte la cara.
Di que puede lavarse la cara, pero que después necesitas secarte el pelo.	Di que puede secarse el pelo, pero que después necesitas peinarte.

Practice more at vhlcentral.com.

Pronunciación

Audio

The consonant r

ropa **rutina** **rico** **Ramón**

In Spanish, **r** has a strong trilled sound at the beginning of a word. No English words have a trill, but English speakers often produce a trill when they imitate the sound of a motor.

gustar **durante** **primero** **crema**

In any other position, **r** has a weak sound similar to the English *tt* in *better* or the English *dd* in *ladder*. In contrast to English, the tongue touches the roof of the mouth behind the teeth.

pizarra **corro** **marrón** **aburrido**

The letter combination **rr**, which only appears between vowels, always has a strong trilled sound.

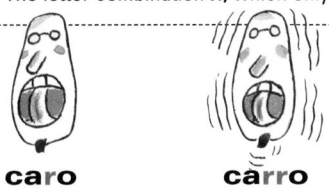

caro **carro** **pero** **perro**

Between vowels, the difference between the strong trilled **rr** and the weak **r** is very important, as a mispronunciation could lead to confusion between two different words.

Práctica Lee las palabras en voz alta, prestando (*paying*) atención a la pronunciación de la **r** y la **rr**.

1. Perú
2. Rosa
3. borrador
4. madre
5. comprar
6. favor
7. rubio
8. reloj
9. Arequipa
10. tarde
11. cerrar
12. despertador

Oraciones Lee las oraciones en voz alta, prestando atención a la pronunciación de la **r** y la **rr**.

1. Ramón Robles Ruiz es programador. Su esposa Rosaura es artista.
2. A Rosaura Robles le encanta regatear en el mercado.
3. Ramón nunca regatea... le aburre regatear.
4. Rosaura siempre compra cosas baratas.
5. Ramón no es rico, pero prefiere comprar cosas muy caras.
6. ¡El martes Ramón compró un carro nuevo!

Refranes Lee en voz alta los refranes, prestando atención a la **r** y a la **rr**.

1 A dog's bark is worse than its bite.
2 Rome wasn't built in a day.

recursos

vText | CPA p. 68 | CH p. 101 | vhlcentral

EN DETALLE

Additional Reading

La siesta

¿Sientes cansancio° después de comer?

¿Te cuesta° volver al trabajo° o a clase después del almuerzo? Estas sensaciones son normales. A muchas personas les gusta relajarse° después de almorzar. Este momento de descanso es **la siesta.** La siesta es popular en los países hispanos y viene de una antigua costumbre° del área del Mediterráneo. La palabra *siesta* viene del latín, es una forma corta de decir "sexta hora". La sexta hora del día es después del mediodía, el momento de más calor. Debido al° calor y al cansancio, los habitantes de España, Italia, Grecia y Portugal tienen la costumbre de dormir la siesta desde hace° más de° dos mil años. Los españoles y los portugueses llevaron la costumbre a los países americanos.

Aunque° hoy día esta costumbre está desapareciendo° en las grandes ciudades, la siesta todavía es importante en la cultura hispana. En pueblos pequeños, por ejemplo, muchas oficinas° y tiendas tienen la costumbre de cerrar por dos o tres horas después del mediodía. Los empleados van a su casa, almuerzan con sus familias, duermen la siesta o hacen actividades, como ir al gimnasio, y luego regresan al trabajo entre las 2:30 y las 4:30 de la tarde.

Los estudios científicos explican que una siesta corta después de almorzar ayuda° a trabajar más y mejor° durante la tarde. Pero ¡cuidado! Esta siesta debe durar° sólo entre veinte y cuarenta minutos. Si dormimos más, entramos en la fase de sueño profundo y es difícil despertarse.

Hoy, algunas empresas° de los EE.UU., Canadá, Japón, Inglaterra y Alemania tienen salas° especiales donde los empleados pueden dormir la siesta.

¿Dónde duermen la siesta?

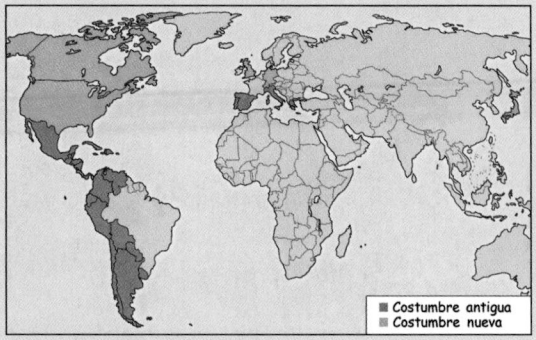

En los lugares donde la siesta es una costumbre antigua, las personas la duermen en su casa. En los países donde la siesta es una costumbre nueva, la gente duerme en sus lugares de trabajo o en centros de siesta.

Sientes cansancio *Do you feel tired* **Te cuesta** *Is it hard for you* **trabajo** *work* **relajarse** *to relax* **antigua costumbre** *old custom* **Debido al** *Because (of)* **desde hace** *for* **más de** *more than* **Aunque** *Although* **está desapareciendo** *is disappearing* **oficinas** *offices* **ayuda** *helps* **mejor** *better* **durar** *last* **algunas empresas** *some businesses* **salas** *rooms*

ACTIVIDADES

1 ¿Cierto o falso? **Indica si lo que dicen las oraciones es cierto o falso. Corrige la información falsa.**

1. La costumbre de la siesta empezó en Asia.
2. La palabra siesta está relacionada con la sexta hora del día.
3. Los españoles y los portugueses llevaron la costumbre de la siesta a Latinoamérica.
4. La siesta ayuda a trabajar más y mejor durante la tarde.
5. Los horarios de trabajo de las grandes ciudades hispanas son los mismos que los pueblos pequeños.
6. Una siesta larga siempre es mejor que una siesta corta.
7. En los Estados Unidos, los empleados de algunas empresas pueden dormir la siesta en el trabajo.
8. Es fácil despertar de un sueño profundo.

ASÍ SE DICE

El cuidado personal

el aseo; el excusado; el servicio; el váter (Esp.)	**el baño**
el cortaúñas	*nail clippers*
el desodorante	*deodorant*
el enjuague bucal	*mouthwash*
el hilo dental/ la seda dental	*dental floss*
la máquina de afeitar/ de rasurar (Méx.)	*electric razor*

EL MUNDO HISPANO

Costumbres especiales

- **México y El Salvador** Los vendedores pasan por las calles anunciando a gritos° su mercancía°: tanques de gas y flores° en México; pan y tortillas en El Salvador.
- **Costa Rica** Para encontrar las direcciones°, los costarricenses usan referencias a anécdotas, lugares o características geográficas. Por ejemplo: *200 metros norte de la iglesia Católica, frente al° supermercado Mi Mega.*
- **Argentina** En Tigre, una ciudad junto al Río° de la Plata, la gente usa barcos particulares°, barcos colectivos y barcos-taxi para ir de una isla a otra. Todas las mañanas, un barco colectivo recoge° a los niños y los lleva a la escuela.

gritos *shouts* mercancía *merchandise* flores *flowers* direcciones *addresses* frente al *opposite* río *river* particulares *private* recoge *picks up*

PERFIL

El mate

El mate es una parte muy importante de la rutina diaria en muchos países. Es una bebida° muy similar al té que se consume en Argentina, Uruguay y Paraguay. Tradicionalmente se bebe caliente° con una *bombilla*° y en un recipiente° que también se llama *mate*. Por ser amarga, algunos le agregan° azúcar para suavizar su sabor°. El mate se puede tomar a cualquier° hora y en cualquier lugar, aunque en Argentina las personas prefieren sentarse en círculo e ir pasando el mate de mano en mano mientras° conversan. Los uruguayos, por otra parte, acostumbran llevar el agua° caliente para el mate en un termo° bajo el brazo° y lo beben mientras caminan. Si ves a una persona con un termo bajo el brazo y un mate en la mano, ¡es casi seguro que es de Uruguay!

bebida *drink* caliente *hot* bombilla *straw (in Argentina)* recipiente *container* amarga *bitter* agregan *add* suavizar su sabor *soften its flavor* cualquier *any* mientras *while* agua *water* termo *thermos* bajo el brazo *under their arm*

Conexión Internet

¿Qué costumbres son populares en los países hispanos?

Go to **vhlcentral.com** to find more cultural information related to this **Cultura** section.

ACTIVIDADES

2 **Comprensión** Completa las oraciones.

1. Uso _____ para limpiar (*to clean*) entre los dientes.
2. En _____ las personas compran pan y tortillas a los vendedores que pasan por la calle.
3. El _____ es una bebida similar al té.
4. Los uruguayos beben mate mientras _____.

3 **¿Qué costumbres tienes?** Escribe cuatro oraciones sobre una costumbre que compartes con tus amigos o con tu familia (por ejemplo: ir al cine, ir a eventos deportivos, leer, comer juntos, etc.). Explica qué haces, cuándo lo haces y con quién.

Practice more at vhlcentral.com.

recursos

vText

CH p. 102

vhlcentral

7.1 Reflexive verbs

Tutorial

ANTE TODO A reflexive verb is used to indicate that the subject does something to or for himself or herself. In other words, it "reflects" the action of the verb back to the subject. Reflexive verbs always use reflexive pronouns.

SUBJECT	REFLEXIVE VERB
Joaquín	**se ducha** por la mañana.

The verb **lavarse** (*to wash oneself*)

SINGULAR FORMS	yo	**me lavo**	*I wash (myself)*
	tú	**te lavas**	*you wash (yourself)*
	Ud.	**se lava**	*you wash (yourself)*
	él/ella	**se lava**	*he/she washes (himself/herself)*
PLURAL FORMS	nosotros/as	**nos lavamos**	*we wash (ourselves)*
	vosotros/as	**os laváis**	*you wash (yourselves)*
	Uds.	**se lavan**	*you wash (yourselves)*
	ellos/ellas	**se lavan**	*they wash (themselves)*

AYUDA

Except for **se**, reflexive pronouns have the same forms as direct and indirect object pronouns.

•••

Se is used for both singular and plural subjects—there is no individual plural form:
Pablo **se** lava.
Ellos **se** lavan.

- The pronoun **se** attached to an infinitive identifies the verb as reflexive: **lavarse.**
- When a reflexive verb is conjugated, the reflexive pronoun agrees with the subject.

Me afeito. **Te despiertas** a las siete.

- Like object pronouns, reflexive pronouns generally appear before a conjugated verb. With infinitives and present participles, they may be placed before the conjugated verb or attached to the infinitive or present participle.

Ellos **se** van a vestir.
Ellos van a vestir**se**.
They are going to get dressed.

Nos estamos lavando las manos.
Estamos lavándo**nos** las manos.
We are washing our hands.

- **¡Atención!** When a reflexive pronoun is attached to a present participle, an accent mark is added to maintain the original stress.

bañando ⟶ bañ**á**ndo**se** durmiendo ⟶ durmi**é**ndo**se**

Common reflexive verbs

acordarse (de) (o:ue)	*to remember*	**llamarse**	*to be called; to be named*
acostarse (o:ue)	*to go to bed*		
afeitarse	*to shave*	**maquillarse**	*to put on makeup*
bañarse	*to bathe; to take a bath*	**peinarse**	*to comb one's hair*
cepillarse	*to brush*	**ponerse**	*to put on*
despertarse (e:ie)	*to wake up*	**ponerse (+ *adj.*)**	*to become (+ adj.)*
dormirse (o:ue)	*to go to sleep; to fall asleep*	**preocuparse (por)**	*to worry (about)*
		probarse (o:ue)	*to try on*
ducharse	*to shower; to take a shower*	**quedarse**	*to stay; to remain*
		quitarse	*to take off*
enojarse (con)	*to get angry (with)*	**secarse**	*to dry (oneself)*
irse	*to go away; to leave*	**sentarse** (e:ie)	*to sit down*
lavarse	*to wash (oneself)*	**sentirse** (e:ie)	*to feel*
levantarse	*to get up*	**vestirse** (e:i)	*to get dressed*

AYUDA

You have already learned several adjectives that can be used with **ponerse** when it means *to become*:

alegre, cómodo/a, contento/a, elegante, guapo/a, nervioso/a, rojo/a, and **triste**.

COMPARE & CONTRAST

Unlike English, a number of verbs in Spanish can be reflexive or non-reflexive. If the verb acts upon the subject, the reflexive form is used. If the verb acts upon something other than the subject, the non-reflexive form is used. Compare these sentences.

Lola **lava** los platos.

Patricia **se lava** la cara.

As the preceding sentences show, reflexive verbs sometimes have different meanings than their non-reflexive counterparts. For example, **lavar** means *to wash,* while **lavarse** means *to wash oneself, to wash up.*

▶ **¡Atención!** Parts of the body or clothing are generally not referred to with possessives, but with articles.

La niña se quitó **un** zapato.

Necesito cepillarme **los** dientes.

recursos

vText

CPA pp. 69–71

CH pp. 103–104

vhlcentral

¡INTÉNTALO! Indica el presente de estos verbos reflexivos.

despertarse

1. Mis hermanos *se despiertan* tarde.
2. Tú _____ tarde.
3. Nosotros _____ tarde.
4. Benito _____ tarde.
5. Yo _____ tarde.

ponerse

1. Él *se pone* una chaqueta.
2. Yo _____ una chaqueta.
3. Usted _____ una chaqueta.
4. Nosotras _____ una chaqueta.
5. Las niñas _____ una chaqueta.

Práctica

1 **Nuestra rutina** La familia de Blanca sigue la misma rutina todos los días. Según Blanca, ¿qué hacen ellos?

modelo

mamá / despertarse a las 5:00

Mamá se despierta a las cinco.

1. Roberto y yo / levantarse a las 7:00
2. papá / ducharse primero y / luego afeitarse
3. yo / lavarse la cara y / vestirse antes de tomar café
4. mamá / peinarse y / luego maquillarse
5. todos (nosotros) / sentarse a la mesa para comer
6. Roberto / cepillarse los dientes después de comer
7. yo / ponerse el abrigo antes de salir
8. nosotros / irse

NOTA CULTURAL

Como en los EE.UU., **tomar café** en el desayuno es muy común en los países hispanos.

En muchas familias, incluso los niños toman café con leche (*milk*) en el desayuno antes de ir a la escuela.

El café en los países hispanos generalmente es más fuerte que en los EE.UU., y el descafeinado no es muy popular.

2 **La fiesta elegante** Selecciona el verbo apropiado y completa las oraciones con la forma correcta.

1. Tú _____ (lavar / lavarse) el auto antes de ir a la fiesta.
2. Nosotros _____ (bañar / bañarse) antes de ir a la fiesta.
3. Para llegar a tiempo, Raúl y Marta _____ (acostar / acostarse) a los niños antes de salir.
4. Cecilia _____ (maquillar / maquillarse) antes de salir.
5. Mis amigos siempre _____ (vestir / vestirse) con ropa muy elegante.
6. Julia y Ana _____ (poner / ponerse) los vestidos nuevos.
7. Usted _____ (ir / irse) a llegar antes que (*before*) los demás invitados, ¿no?
8. En general, _____ (afeitar / afeitarse) yo mismo, pero hoy es un día especial y el barbero (*barber*) me _____ (afeitar / afeitarse). ¡Será una fiesta inolvidable!

¡LENGUA VIVA!

In Spain, a car is called **un coche**, while in many parts of Latin America it is known as **un carro**. Although you will be understood using either of these terms, using **auto (automóvil)** will always avoid any confusion.

3 **Describir** Mira los dibujos y describe lo que estas personas hacen.

1. el joven

2. Carmen

3. Juan

4. los pasajeros

5. Estrella

6. Toni

Practice more at vhlcentral.com.

Comunicación

4 **Preguntas personales** En parejas, túrnense para hacerse estas preguntas.

1. ¿A qué hora te levantas durante la semana?
2. ¿A qué hora te levantas los fines de semana?
3. ¿Prefieres levantarte tarde o temprano? ¿Por qué?
4. ¿Te enojas frecuentemente con tus amigos?
5. ¿Te preocupas fácilmente? ¿Qué te preocupa?
6. ¿Qué te pone contento/a?
7. ¿Qué haces cuando te sientes triste?
8. ¿Y cuando te sientes alegre?
9. ¿Te acuestas tarde o temprano durante la semana?
10. ¿A qué hora te acuestas los fines de semana?

5 **Charadas** En grupos, jueguen a las charadas. Cada persona debe pensar en dos oraciones con verbos reflexivos. La primera persona que adivina la charada dramatiza la siguiente.

6 **Debate** En grupos, discutan este tema: ¿Quiénes necesitan más tiempo para arreglarse (*to get ready*) antes de salir, los hombres o las mujeres? Hagan una lista de las razones (*reasons*) que tienen para defender sus ideas e informen a la clase.

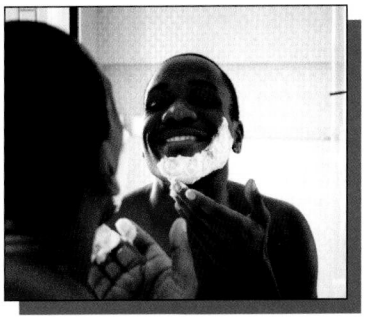

7 **La coartada** Hoy se cometió un crimen entre las 7 y las 11 de la mañana. En parejas, imaginen que uno de ustedes es un sospechoso y el otro un policía investigador. El policía le pregunta al sospechoso qué hace habitualmente a esas horas y el sospechoso responde. Luego, el policía presenta las respuestas del sospechoso ante el jurado (la clase) y entre todos deciden si es culpable o no.

Síntesis

recursos
vText
CPA
pp. 72–73

8 **La familia ocupada** Tú y tu compañero/a asisten a un programa de verano en Lima, Perú. Viven con la familia Ramos. Tu profesor(a) te va a dar la rutina incompleta que la familia sigue en las mañanas. Trabaja con tu compañero/a para completarla.

modelo

Estudiante 1: *¿Qué hace el señor Ramos a las seis y cuarto?*
Estudiante 2: *El señor Ramos se levanta.*

7.2 Indefinite and negative words

Tutorial

ANTE TODO Indefinite words refer to people and things that are not specific, for example, *someone* or *something*. In Spanish, indefinite words have corresponding negative words, which are opposite in meaning.

Indefinite and negative words

Indefinite words		Negative words	
algo	*something; anything*	**nada**	*nothing; not anything*
alguien	*someone; somebody; anyone*	**nadie**	*no one; nobody; not anyone*
alguno/a(s), algún	*some; any*	**ninguno/a, ningún**	*no; none; not any*
o... o	*either... or*	**ni... ni**	*neither... nor*
siempre	*always*	**nunca, jamás**	*never, not ever*
también	*also; too*	**tampoco**	*neither; not either*

- There are two ways to form negative sentences in Spanish. You can place the negative word before the verb, or you can place **no** before the verb and the negative word after.

Nadie se levanta temprano.
No one gets up early.

No se levanta nadie temprano.
No one gets up early.

Ellos **nunca gritan**.
They never shout.

Ellos **no gritan nunca**.
They never shout.

- Because they refer to people, **alguien** and **nadie** are often used with the personal **a**. The personal **a** is also used before **alguno/a**, **algunos/as**, and **ninguno/a** when these words refer to people and they are the direct object of the verb.

—Perdón, señor, ¿busca usted **a alguien**?
—No, gracias, señorita, no busco **a nadie**.

—Tomás, ¿buscas **a alguno** de tus hermanos?
—No, mamá, no busco **a ninguno**.

- **¡Atención!** Before a masculine singular noun, **alguno** and **ninguno** are shortened to **algún** and **ningún**.

—¿Tienen ustedes **algún** amigo peruano?

—No, no tenemos **ningún** amigo peruano.

AYUDA

Alguno/a, algunos/as are not always used in the same way English uses *some* or *any*. Often, **algún** is used where *a* would be used in English.

¿Tienes algún libro que hable de los incas?
*Do you have **a** book that talks about the Incas?*

Note that **ninguno/a** is rarely used in the plural.

—¿Visitaste algunos museos?
—No, no visité ninguno.

COMPARE & CONTRAST

In English, it is incorrect to use more than one negative word in a sentence. In Spanish, however, sentences frequently contain two or more negative words. Compare these Spanish and English sentences.

Nunca le escribo a **nadie**.
I never write to anyone.

No me preocupo **nunca** por **nada**.
I do not ever worry about anything.

As the preceding sentences show, once an English sentence contains one negative word (for example, *not* or *never*), no other negative word may be used. Instead, indefinite (or affirmative) words are used. In Spanish, however, once a sentence is negative, no other affirmative (that is, indefinite) word may be used. Instead, all indefinite ideas must be expressed in the negative.

▶ **Pero** is used to mean *but*. The meaning of **sino** is *but rather* or *on the contrary*. It is used when the first part of the sentence is negative and the second part contradicts it.

Los estudiantes no se acuestan temprano **sino** tarde.
The students don't go to bed early, but rather late.

María no habla francés **sino** español.
María doesn't speak French, but rather Spanish.

Esas gafas son caras, **pero** bonitas.
Those glasses are expensive, but pretty.

José es inteligente, **pero** no saca buenas notas.
José is intelligent but doesn't get good grades.

¡INTÉNTALO! Cambia las oraciones para que sean negativas.

1. Siempre se viste bien.
   Nunca se viste bien.
   No se viste bien nunca.
2. Alguien se ducha.
   _____ se ducha.
   _____ se ducha _____.
3. Ellas van también.
   Ellas _____ van.
   Ellas _____ van _____.
4. Alguien se pone nervioso.
   _____ se pone nervioso.
   _____ se pone nervioso _____.
5. Tú siempre te lavas las manos.
   Tú _____ te lavas las manos.
   Tú ____ te lavas las manos _____.
6. Voy a traer algo.
   _____ voy a traer _____.
7. Juan se afeita también.
   Juan _____ se afeita.
   Juan _____ se afeita _____.
8. Mis amigos viven en una residencia o en casa.
   Mis amigos _____ viven _____ en una residencia _____ en casa.
9. La profesora hace algo en su escritorio.
   La profesora _____ hace _____ en su escritorio.
10. Tú y yo vamos al mercado.
    _____ tú _____ yo vamos al mercado.
11. Tienen un espejo en su casa.
    _____ tienen _____ espejo en su casa.
12. Algunos niños se ponen los abrigos.
    _____ niño se pone el abrigo.

recursos
vText
CPA pp. 74–76
CH pp. 105–106
vhlcentral

Práctica

1 **¿Pero o sino?** Forma oraciones sobre estas personas usando **pero** o **sino**.

modelo

muchos estudiantes comen en la cafetería / algunos de ellos quieren salir a comer a un restaurante local.

Muchos estudiantes comen en la cafetería, pero algunos de ellos quieren salir a comer a un restaurante local.

1. Marcos nunca se despierta temprano / siempre llega puntual a clase
2. Lisa y Katarina no se acuestan temprano / muy tarde
3. Alfonso es inteligente / algunas veces es antipático
4. los directores de la escuela no son ecuatorianos / peruanos
5. no nos acordamos de comprar champú / compramos jabón
6. Emilia no es estudiante / profesora
7. no quiero levantarme / tengo que ir a clase
8. Miguel no se afeita por la mañana / por la noche

2 **Completar** Completa esta conversación entre dos hermanos. Usa expresiones negativas en tus respuestas. Luego, dramatiza la conversación con un(a) compañero/a.

AURELIO Ana María, ¿encontraste algún regalo para Eliana?

ANA MARÍA (1)_____

AURELIO ¿Viste a alguna amiga en el centro comercial?

ANA MARÍA (2)_____

AURELIO ¿Me llamó alguien?

ANA MARÍA (3)_____

AURELIO ¿Quieres ir al teatro o al cine esta noche?

ANA MARÍA (4)_____

AURELIO ¿No quieres salir a comer?

ANA MARÍA (5)_____

AURELIO ¿Hay algo interesante en la televisión esta noche?

ANA MARÍA (6)_____

AURELIO ¿Tienes algún problema?

ANA MARÍA (7)_____

Practice more at vhlcentral.com.

Comunicación

3 **Opiniones** Completa estas oraciones de una manera lógica. Luego, compara tus respuestas con las de un(a) compañero/a.

1. Mi habitación es _____, pero _____.
2. Por la noche me gusta _____, pero _____.
3. Un(a) profesor(a) ideal no es _____, sino _____.
4. Mis amigos son _____, pero _____.

4 **¿Qué hay?** En parejas, háganse preguntas sobre qué hay en su ciudad o pueblo: tiendas interesantes, almacenes, cines, librerías baratas, una biblioteca, una plaza central, playa, cafés, museos, una estación de tren. Sigan el modelo.

modelo

Estudiante 1: ¿Hay algunas tiendas interesantes?
Estudiante 2: Sí, hay una/algunas. Está(n) detrás del estadio.
Estudiante 1: ¿Hay algún museo?
Estudiante 2: No, no hay ninguno.

5 **Quejas** En parejas, hagan una lista de cinco quejas (*complaints*) comunes que tienen los estudiantes. Usen expresiones negativas.

modelo
Nadie me entiende.

Ahora hagan una lista de cinco quejas que los padres tienen de sus hijos.

modelo
Nunca hacen sus camas.

6 **Anuncios** En parejas, lean el anuncio y contesten las preguntas.

1. ¿Es el anuncio positivo o negativo? ¿Por qué?
2. ¿Qué palabras indefinidas hay?
3. Escriban el texto del anuncio cambiando todo por expresiones negativas.

Ahora preparen su propio (*own*) anuncio usando expresiones afirmativas y negativas.

Síntesis

7 **Encuesta** Tu profesor(a) te va a dar una hoja de actividades para hacer una encuesta. Circula por la clase y pídeles a tus compañeros/as que comparen las actividades que hacen durante la semana con las que hacen durante los fines de semana. Escribe las respuestas.

recursos
vText
CPA
p. 77

7.3 Preterite of ser and ir

Tutorial

ANTE TODO

In **Lección 6**, you learned how to form the preterite tense of regular **-ar**, **-er**, and **-ir** verbs. The following chart contains the preterite forms of **ser** (*to be*) and **ir** (*to go*). Since these forms are irregular, you will need to memorize them.

Preterite of ser and ir

		ser *(to be)*	**ir** *(to go)*
SINGULAR FORMS	yo	**fui**	**fui**
	tú	**fuiste**	**fuiste**
	Ud./él/ella	**fue**	**fue**
PLURAL FORMS	nosotros/as	**fuimos**	**fuimos**
	vosotros/as	**fuisteis**	**fuisteis**
	Uds./ellos/ellas	**fueron**	**fueron**

AYUDA

Note that, whereas regular **-er** and **-ir** verbs have accent marks in the **yo** and **Ud./él/ella** forms of the preterite, **ser** and **ir** do not.

▶ Since the preterite forms of **ser** and **ir** are identical, context clarifies which of the two verbs is being used.

Él **fue** a comprar champú y jabón.
He went to buy shampoo and soap.

¿Cómo **fue** la película anoche?
How was the movie last night?

¡INTÉNTALO! Completa las oraciones usando el pretérito de **ser** e **ir**.

ir

1. Los viajeros fueron a Perú.
2. Patricia _____ a Cuzco.
3. Tú _____ a Iquitos.
4. Gregorio y yo _____ a Lima.
5. Yo _____ a Trujillo.
6. Ustedes _____ a Arequipa.
7. Mi padre _____ a Lima.
8. Nosotras _____ a Cuzco.
9. Él _____ a Machu Picchu.
10. Usted _____ a Nazca.

ser

1. Usted fue muy amable.
2. Yo _____ muy cordial.
3. Ellos _____ simpáticos.
4. Nosotros _____ muy tontos.
5. Ella _____ antipática.
6. Tú _____ muy generoso.
7. Ustedes _____ cordiales.
8. La gente _____ amable.
9. Tomás y yo _____ muy felices.
10. Los profesores _____ buenos.

recursos
vText
CPA pp. 78–79
CH pp. 107–108
vhlcentral

Práctica y Comunicación

NOTA CULTURAL

La ciudad peruana de **El Callao**, fundada en 1537, fue por muchos años el puerto (*port*) más activo de la costa del Pacífico en Suramérica. En el siglo XVIII, una fortaleza fue construida (*built*) allí para proteger (*protect*) la ciudad de los ataques de piratas y bucaneros.

1 **Completar** Completa estas conversaciones con la forma correcta del pretérito de **ser** o **ir**. Indica el infinitivo de cada forma verbal.

Conversación 1

		ser	ir
RAÚL	¿Adónde (1)_____ ustedes de vacaciones?	❍	❍
PILAR	(2)_____ a Perú.	❍	❍
RAÚL	¿Cómo (3)_____ el viaje?	❍	❍
▶ **PILAR**	¡(4)_____ estupendo! Machu Picchu y El Callao son increíbles.	❍	❍
RAÚL	¿(5)_____ caro el viaje?	❍	❍
PILAR	No, el precio (6)_____ muy bajo. Sólo costó tres mil dólares.	❍	❍

Conversación 2

ISABEL	Tina y Vicente (7)_____ novios, ¿no?	❍	❍
LUCÍA	Sí, pero ahora no. Anoche Tina (8)_____ a comer con Gregorio	❍	❍
	y la semana pasada ellos (9)_____ al partido de fútbol.	❍	❍
ISABEL	¿Ah sí? Javier y yo (10)_____ al partido y no los vimos.	❍	❍

2 **Descripciones** Forma oraciones con estos elementos. Usa el pretérito.

A	B	C	D
yo	(no) ir	a un restaurante	ayer
tú	(no) ser	en autobús	anoche
mi compañero/a		estudiante	anteayer
nosotros		muy simpático/a	la semana pasada
mis amigos		a la playa	el año pasado
ustedes		dependiente/a en una tienda	

3 **Preguntas** En parejas, túrnense para hacerse estas preguntas.

1. ¿Cuándo fuiste al cine por última vez? ¿Con quién fuiste?
2. ¿Fuiste en auto, en autobús o en metro? ¿Cómo fue el viaje?
3. ¿Cómo fue la película?
4. ¿Fue una película de terror, de acción o un drama?
5. ¿Fue una de las mejores películas que viste? ¿Por qué?
6. ¿Fueron buenos los actores o no? ¿Cuál fue el mejor?
7. ¿Adónde fuiste/fueron después?
8. ¿Fue una buena idea ir al cine?
9. ¿Fuiste feliz ese día?

4 **El viaje** En parejas, escriban un diálogo de un(a) viajero/a hablando con el/la agente de viajes sobre un viaje que hizo recientemente. Usen el pretérito de **ser** e **ir**.

modelo

Agente: *¿Cómo fue el viaje?*
Viajero: *El viaje fue maravilloso/horrible...*

Practice more at vhlcentral.com.

7.4 Verbs like gustar

Tutorial

ANTE TODO You have learned how to express preferences with **gustar**. You will now learn more about the verb **gustar** and other similar verbs. Observe these examples.

Me gusta ese champú.

ENGLISH EQUIVALENT
I like that shampoo.
LITERAL MEANING
That shampoo is pleasing to me.

¿**Te gustaron** las clases?

ENGLISH EQUIVALENT
Did you like the classes?
LITERAL MEANING
Were the classes pleasing to you?

- As the examples show, constructions with **gustar** do not have a direct equivalent in English. The literal meaning of this construction is *to be pleasing to* (*someone*), and it requires the use of an indirect object pronoun.

INDIRECT OBJECT PRONOUN	VERB	SUBJECT	SUBJECT	VERB	DIRECT OBJECT
Me	**gusta**	ese champú.	*I*	*like*	*that shampoo.*

- In the diagram above, observe how in the Spanish sentence the object being liked (**ese champú**) is really the subject of the sentence. The person who likes the object, in turn, is an indirect object because it answers the question: *To whom is the shampoo pleasing?*

- Other verbs in Spanish are used in the same way as **gustar**. Here is a list of the most common ones.

Verbs like gustar

aburrir	*to bore*	**importar**	*to be important to; to matter*
encantar	*to like very much; to love* (inanimate objects)	**interesar**	*to be interesting to; to interest*
faltar	*to lack; to need*	**molestar**	*to bother; to annoy*
fascinar	*to fascinate; to like very much*	**quedar**	*to be left over; to fit* (clothing)

¡ATENCIÓN!

Faltar expresses what is lacking or missing.
Me falta una página. *I'm missing one page.*

Quedar expresses how much of something is left.
Nos quedan tres pesos. *We have three pesos left.*

• • •

Quedar also means *to fit.* It can be used to tell how something looks (on someone).
Estos zapatos me quedan bien. *These shoes fit me well.*
Esa camisa te queda muy bien. *That shirt looks good on you.*

- The most commonly used forms of **gustar** and similar verbs are the third person (singular and plural). When the object or person being liked is singular, the singular form (**gusta**) is used. When two or more objects or persons are being liked, the plural form (**gustan**) is used. Observe the following diagram:

- To express what someone likes or does not like to do, use an appropriate verb followed by an infinitive. The singular form is used even if there is more than one infinitive.

Nos molesta comer a las nueve.
It bothers us to eat at nine o'clock.

Les encanta bailar y **cantar** en las fiestas.
They love to dance and sing at parties.

AYUDA

Note that the **a** must be repeated if there is more than one person.
A Armando y **a Carmen** les molesta levantarse temprano.

- As you have already learned, the construction **a** + [*pronoun*] (**a mí, a ti, a usted, a él,** etc.) is used to clarify or to emphasize who is pleased, bored, etc. The construction **a** + [*noun*] can also be used before the indirect object pronoun to clarify or to emphasize who is pleased.

A los turistas les gustó mucho Machu Picchu.
The tourists liked Machu Picchu a lot.

A ti te gusta cenar en casa, pero **a mí** me aburre.
You like eating dinner at home, but I get bored.

- **¡Atención! Mí** (*me*) has an accent mark to distinguish it from the possessive adjective **mi** (*my*).

¡INTÉNTALO! Indica el pronombre de objeto indirecto y la forma del tiempo presente adecuados en cada oración.

fascinar

1. A él le fascina viajar.
2. A mí _____ bailar.
3. A nosotras _____ cantar.
4. A ustedes _____ leer.
5. A ti _____ correr y patinar.
6. A ellos _____ los aviones.
7. A mis padres _____ caminar.
8. A usted _____ jugar al tenis.
9. A mi esposo y a mí _____ dormir.
10. A Alberto _____ dibujar y pintar.
11. A todos _____ opinar.
12. A Pili _____ los sombreros.

aburrir

1. A ellos les aburren los deportes.
2. A ti _____ las películas.
3. A usted _____ los viajes.
4. A mí _____ las revistas.
5. A Jorge y a Luis _____ los perros.
6. A nosotros _____ las vacaciones.
7. A ustedes _____ el béisbol.
8. A Marcela _____ los libros.
9. A mis amigos _____ los museos.
10. A ella _____ el ciclismo.
11. A Omar _____ ir de compras.
12. A ti y a mí _____ el baile.

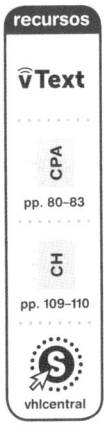

Práctica

1 **Completar** Completa las oraciones con todos los elementos necesarios.

1. _____ Adela _____ (encantar) la música de Tito "El Bambino".
2. A _____ me _____ (interesar) la música de otros países.
3. A mis amigos _____ (encantar) las canciones (*songs*) de Calle 13.
4. A Juan y _____ Rafael no les _____ (molestar) la música alta (*loud*).
5. _____ nosotros _____ (fascinar) los grupos de pop latino.
6. _____ señor Ruiz _____ (interesar) más la música clásica.
7. A _____ me _____ (aburrir) la música clásica.
8. ¿A _____ te _____ (faltar) dinero para el concierto de Carlos Santana?
9. No. Ya compré el boleto y _____ (quedar) cinco dólares.
10. ¿Cuánto dinero te _____ (quedar) a _____?

NOTA CULTURAL

Hoy día, la música latina es popular en los EE.UU. gracias a artistas como **Shakira**, de nacionalidad colombiana, y **Tito "El Bambino"**, puertorriqueño. Otros artistas, como **Carlos Santana** y **Gloria Estefan**, difundieron (*spread*) la música latina en los años 60, 70, 80 y 90.

2 **Describir** Mira los dibujos y describe lo que está pasando. Usa los verbos de la lista.

aburrir	**faltar**	**molestar**
encantar	**interesar**	**quedar**

1. a Ramón

2. a nosotros

3. a ti

4. a Sara

3 **Gustos** Forma oraciones con los elementos de las columnas.

modelo

A ti te interesan las ruinas de Machu Picchu.

A	B	C
yo	aburrir	despertarse temprano
tú	encantar	mirarse en el espejo
mi mejor amigo/a	faltar	la música rock
mis amigos y yo	fascinar	las pantuflas rosadas
Bart y Homero Simpson	interesar	la pasta de dientes con menta (*mint*)
Shakira	molestar	las ruinas de Machu Picchu
Antonio Banderas		los zapatos caros

Practice more at vhlcentral.com.

Comunicación

4 **Preguntas** En parejas, túrnense para hacer y contestar estas preguntas.

1. ¿Te gusta levantarte temprano o tarde? ¿Por qué?
2. ¿Te gusta acostarte temprano o tarde? ¿Y a tus hermanos/as?
3. ¿Te gusta dormir la siesta?
4. A tu familia, ¿le encanta acampar o prefiere quedarse en un hotel cuando va de vacaciones?
5. ¿Qué te gusta hacer en el verano?
6. ¿Qué te fascina de esta escuela? ¿Qué te molesta?
7. ¿Te interesan más las ciencias o las humanidades? ¿Por qué?
8. ¿Qué cosas te aburren?

5 **Completar** Trabajen en parejas. Túrnense para completar estas frases de una manera lógica.

1. A mi perro (*dog*) le fascina(n)...
2. A mi mejor (*best*) amigo/a no le interesa(n)...
3. A mis padres les importa(n)...
4. A nosotros nos molesta(n)...
5. A mis hermanos les aburre(n)...
6. A mi compañero/a de clase le aburre(n)...
7. A los turistas les interesa(n)...
8. A los jugadores profesionales les encanta(n)...
9. A nuestro/a profesor(a) le molesta(n)...
10. A mí me importa(n)...

recursos
vText
CPA
pp. 84–85

6 **La residencia** Tú y tu compañero/a de clase son los directores de una residencia estudiantil en Perú. Su profesor(a) les va a dar a cada uno de ustedes las descripciones de cinco estudiantes. Con la información tienen que escoger quiénes van a ser compañeros de cuarto. Después, completen la lista.

Síntesis

7 **Situación** Trabajen en parejas para representar los papeles de un(a) cliente/a y un(a) dependiente/a en una tienda de ropa. Usen las instrucciones como guía.

Dependiente/a	Cliente/a
Saluda al/a la cliente/a y pregúntale en qué le puedes servir.	Saluda al/a la dependiente/a y dile (*tell him/her*) qué quieres comprar y qué colores prefieres.
Pregúntale si le interesan los estilos modernos y empieza a mostrarle la ropa.	Explícale que los estilos modernos te interesan. Escoge las cosas que te interesan.
Habla de los gustos del/de la cliente/a.	Habla de la ropa (me queda(n) bien/mal, me encanta(n)...).
Da opiniones favorables al/a la cliente/a (las botas te quedan fantásticas...).	Decide cuáles son las cosas que te gustan y qué vas a comprar.

SUBJECT Javier CONJUGATED FORM empiezo Main clause Dudan

Recapitulación

Diagnostics

Completa estas actividades para repasar los conceptos de gramática que aprendiste en esta lección.

1 Completar Completa la tabla con la forma correcta de los verbos. 24 pts.

yo	tú	nosotros	ellas
me levanto			
	te afeitas		
		nos vestimos	
			se secan

2 Hoy y ayer Cambia los verbos del presente al pretérito. 10 pts.

1. Vamos de compras hoy. _____ de compras hoy.
2. Por último, voy al supermercado. Por último, _____ al supermercado.
3. Lalo es el primero en levantarse. Lalo _____ el primero en levantarse.
4. ¿Vas a tu habitación? ¿_____ a tu habitación?
5. Ustedes son profesores. Ustedes _____ profesores.

3 Reflexivos Completa cada conversación con la forma correcta del presente del verbo reflexivo. 22 pts.

TOMÁS Yo siempre (1) _____ (bañarse) antes de (2) _____ (acostarse). Esto me relaja porque no (3) _____ (dormirse) fácilmente. Y así puedo (4) _____ (levantarse) más tarde. Y tú, ¿cuándo (5) _____ (ducharse)?

LETI Pues por la mañana, para poder (6) _____ (despertarse).

DAVID ¿Cómo (7) _____ (sentirse) Pepa hoy?

MARÍA Todavía está enojada.

DAVID ¿De verdad? Ella nunca (8) _____ (enojarse) con nadie.

BETO ¿(Nosotros) (9) _____ (Irse) de esta tienda? Estoy cansado.

SARA Pero antes vamos a (10) _____ (probarse) estos sombreros. Si quieres, después (nosotros) (11) _____ (sentarse) un rato.

RESUMEN GRAMATICAL

7.1 Reflexive verbs *pp. 236–237*

lavarse	
me lavo	nos lavamos
te lavas	os laváis
se lava	se lavan

7.2 Indefinite and negative words *pp. 240–241*

Indefinite words	Negative words
algo	nada
alguien	nadie
alguno/a(s), algún	ninguno/a, ningún
o... o	ni... ni
siempre	nunca, jamás
también	tampoco

7.3 Preterite of ser and ir *p. 244*

► The preterite of **ser** and **ir** are identical. Context will determine the meaning.

ser and ir	
fui	fuimos
fuiste	fuisteis
fue	fueron

7.4 Verbs like gustar *pp. 246–247*

aburrir	importar
encantar	interesar
faltar	molestar
fascinar	quedar

me, te, le, nos, os, les

SINGULAR: encanta / interesó → la película / el concierto

PLURAL: importan / fascinaron → las vacaciones / los museos

► Use the construction **a** + [*noun/pronoun*] to clarify the person in question.

A mí me encanta ver películas, ¿y **a ti**?

4 **Conversaciones** Completa cada conversación de manera lógica con palabras de la lista. No tienes que usar todas las palabras. 18 pts.

algo	nada	ningún	siempre
alguien	nadie	nunca	también
algún	ni... ni	o... o	tampoco

1. —¿Tienes _____ plan para esta noche?
   —No, prefiero quedarme en casa. Hoy no quiero ver a _____.
   —Yo _____ me quedo. Estoy muy cansado.
2. —¿Puedo entrar? ¿Hay _____ en el cuarto de baño?
   —Sí. ¡Un momento! Ahora mismo salgo.
3. —¿Puedes prestarme _____ para peinarme? No encuentro _____ mi cepillo (*brush*) _____ mi peine (*comb*).
   —Lo siento, yo _____ encuentro los míos (*mine*).
4. —¿Me prestas tu maquillaje?
   —Lo siento, no tengo. _____ me maquillo.

5 **Oraciones** Forma oraciones completas con los elementos dados (*given*). Usa el presente de los verbos. 8 pts.

1. David y Juan / molestar / levantarse temprano
2. Lucía / encantar / las películas de terror
3. todos (nosotros) / importar / la educación
4. tú / aburrir / ver / la televisión

6 **Rutinas** Escribe seis oraciones que describan las rutinas de dos personas que conoces. 18 pts.

modelo

Mi tía se despierta temprano, pero mi primo...

7 **Adivinanza** Completa la adivinanza con las palabras que faltan y adivina la respuesta. ¡4 puntos EXTRA!

"Cuanto más° _____ (*it dries you*),
más se moja°".
¿Qué es? _____

Cuanto más *The more* se moja *it gets wet*

recursos
vText
vhlcentral

Practice more at vhlcentral.com.

Lectura

Audio: Reading
Additional Reading

Antes de leer

Estrategia

Predicting content from the title

Prediction is an invaluable strategy in reading for comprehension. For example, we can usually predict the content of a newspaper article from its headline. We often decide whether to read the article based on its headline. Predicting content from the title will help you increase your reading comprehension in Spanish.

Examinar el texto

Lee el título de la lectura y haz tres predicciones sobre el contenido. Escribe tus predicciones en una hoja de papel.

Compartir

Comparte tus ideas con un(a) compañero/a de clase.

Cognados

Haz una lista de seis cognados que encuentres en la lectura.

1. _____
2. _____
3. _____
4. _____
5. _____
6. _____

¿Qué te dicen los cognados sobre el tema de la lectura?

recursos

vText | CH pp. 111–112 | vhlcentral

Mensaje

Anterior | Siguiente | Responder | Reenviar

De	Guillermo Zamora
Para	Lupe; Marcos; Sandra; Jorge
Asunto	¡Qué día!

Hola, chicos:

La semana pasada me di cuenta° de que necesito organizar mejor° mi rutina... pero especialmente debo prepararme mejor para los exámenes. Me falta disciplina, me molesta no tener control de mi tiempo y nunca deseo repetir los eventos de la semana pasada.

El miércoles pasé todo el día y toda la noche estudiando para el examen de biología del jueves por la mañana. Me aburre la biología y no empecé a estudiar hasta el día antes del examen. El jueves a las 8, después de no dormir en toda la noche, fui exhausto al examen. Fue difícil, pero afortunadamente° me acordé de todo el material. Esa noche me acosté temprano y dormí mucho.

Me desperté a las 7, y fue extraño° ver a mi compañero de cuarto, Andrés, preparándose para ir a dormir. Como° siempre se enferma°, tiene problemas para dormir y no hablamos mucho, no le comenté nada. Fui al baño a cepillarme los dientes para ir a clase. ¿Y Andrés? Él se acostó. "Debe estar enfermo°, ¡otra vez!", pensé.

Marcar Imprimir Redactar Bandeja entrada

Enviar

Mi clase es a las 8, y fue necesario hacer las cosas rápido. Todo empezó a ir mal... eso pasa siempre cuando uno tiene prisa. Cuando busqué mis cosas para el baño, no las encontré. Entonces me duché sin jabón, me cepillé los dientes sin cepillo de dientes y me peiné con las manos. Tampoco encontré ropa limpia y usé la sucia. Rápido, tomé mis libros. ¿Y Andrés? Roncando°... ¡a las 7:50!

Cuando salí corriendo para la clase, la prisa no me permitió ver el campus desierto. Cuando llegué a la clase, no vi a nadie. No vi al profesor ni a los estudiantes. Por último miré mi reloj, y vi la hora. Las 8 en punto... ¡de la noche!

¡Dormí 24 horas!

Guillermo

me di cuenta *I realized* mejor *better* afortunadamente *fortunately* extraño *strange* Como *Since* se enferma *he gets sick* enfermo *sick* Roncando *Snoring*

Después de leer

Seleccionar

Selecciona la respuesta correcta.

1. ¿Quién es el/la narrador(a)?
   a. Andrés
   b. una profesora
   c. Guillermo
2. ¿Qué le molesta al narrador?
   a. Le molestan los exámenes de biología.
   b. Le molesta no tener control de su tiempo.
   c. Le molesta mucho organizar su rutina.
3. ¿Por qué está exhausto?
   a. Porque fue a una fiesta la noche anterior.
   b. Porque no le gusta la biología.
   c. Porque pasó la noche anterior estudiando.
4. ¿Por qué no hay nadie en clase?
   a. Porque es de noche.
   b. Porque todos están de vacaciones.
   c. Porque el profesor canceló la clase.
5. ¿Cómo es la relación de Guillermo y Andrés?
   a. Son buenos amigos.
   b. No hablan mucho.
   c. Tienen una buena relación.

Ordenar

Ordena los sucesos de la narración. Utiliza los números del 1 al 9.

a. Toma el examen de biología. ____
b. No encuentra sus cosas para el baño. ____
c. Andrés se duerme. ____
d. Pasa todo el día y toda la noche estudiando para un examen. ____
e. Se ducha sin jabón. ____
f. Se acuesta temprano. ____
g. Vuelve a su cuarto después de las 8 de la noche. ____
h. Se despierta a las 7 y su hermano se prepara para dormir. ____
i. Va a clase y no hay nadie. ____

Contestar

Contesta estas preguntas.

1. ¿Cómo es tu rutina diaria? ¿Muy organizada?
2. ¿Estudias mucho? ¿Cuándo empiezas a estudiar para los exámenes?
3. Para comunicarte con tus amigos/as, ¿prefieres el teléfono o el correo electrónico? ¿Por qué?

Practice more at vhlcentral.com.

Escritura

Estrategia

Sequencing events

Paying strict attention to sequencing in a narrative will ensure that your writing flows logically from one part to the next.

Every composition should have an introduction, a body, and a conclusion. The introduction presents the subject, the setting, the situation, and the people involved. The main part, or the body, describes the events and people's reactions to these events. The conclusion brings the narrative to a close.

Adverbs and adverbial phrases are sometimes used as transitions between the introduction, the body, and the conclusion. Here is a list of commonly used adverbs in Spanish:

Adverbios

además; también	*in addition; also*
al principio; en un principio	*at first*
antes (de)	*before*
después	*then*
después (de)	*after*
entonces; luego	*then*
más tarde	*later on*
primero	*first*
pronto	*soon*
por fin; finalmente	*finally*
al final	*finally*

Tema

Escribe tu rutina

Imagina tu rutina diaria en uno de estos lugares:

- una isla desierta
- el Polo Norte
- un crucero° transatlántico
- un desierto

Escribe una composición en la que describes tu rutina diaria en uno de estos lugares o en algún otro lugar interesante que imagines°. Mientras planeas tu composición, considera cómo cambian algunos de los elementos más básicos de tu rutina diaria en el lugar que escogiste°. Por ejemplo, ¿dónde te acuestas en el Polo Norte? ¿Cómo te duchas en el desierto?

Usa el presente de los verbos reflexivos que conoces e incluye algunos de los adverbios de esta página para organizar la secuencia de tus actividades. Piensa también en la información que debes incluir en cada sección de la narración. Por ejemplo, en la introducción puedes hacer una descripción del lugar y de las personas que están allí, y en la conclusión puedes dar tus opiniones acerca del° lugar y de tu vida diaria allí.

recursos

vText | CPA pp. 86–87 | CH pp. 113–114 | vhlcentral

crucero *cruise ship* que imagines *that you dream up* escogiste *you chose*
acerca del *about the*

Escuchar

Audio

Estrategia

Using background information

Once you discern the topic of a conversation, take a minute to think about what you already know about the subject. Using this background information will help you guess the meaning of unknown words or linguistic structures.

To help you practice this strategy, you will now listen to a short paragraph. Jot down the subject of the paragraph, and then use your knowledge of the subject to listen for and write down the paragraph's main points.

Preparación

Según la foto, ¿dónde están Carolina y Julián? Piensa en lo que sabes de este tipo de situación. ¿De qué van a hablar?

Ahora escucha

Ahora escucha la entrevista entre Carolina y Julián, teniendo en cuenta (*taking into account*) lo que sabes sobre este tipo de situación. Elige la información que completa correctamente cada oración.

1. Julián es _____.
   a. político
   b. deportista profesional
   c. artista de cine
2. El público de Julián quiere saber de _____.
   a. sus películas
   b. su vida
   c. su novia
3. Julián habla de _____.
   a. sus viajes y sus rutinas
   b. sus parientes y amigos
   c. sus comidas favoritas
4. Julián _____.
   a. se levanta y se acuesta a diferentes horas todos los días
   b. tiene una rutina diaria
   c. no quiere hablar de su vida

Comprensión

¿Cierto o falso?

Indica si las oraciones son **ciertas** o **falsas** según la información que Julián da en la entrevista.

1. Es difícil despertarme; generalmente duermo hasta las diez.
2. Pienso que mi vida no es más interesante que las vidas de ustedes.
3. Me gusta tener tiempo para pensar y meditar.
4. Nunca hago mucho ejercicio; no soy una persona activa.
5. Me fascinan las actividades tranquilas, como escribir y escuchar música clásica.
6. Los viajes me parecen aburridos.

Preguntas

1. ¿Qué tiene Julián en común con otras personas de su misma profesión?
2. ¿Te parece que Julián siempre fue rico? ¿Por qué?
3. ¿Qué piensas de Julián como persona?

Practice more at vhlcentral.com.

recursos vText vhlcentral

en pantalla

Video: TV Clip

Anuncio de Asepxia

Me levanté con una invasión de granos.

Preparación

Contesta las preguntas en español.

¿Qué ocasiones especiales celebran los adolescentes en tu país? ¿Cómo se preparan para esas fiestas? ¿A quiénes invitan? ¿Qué ropa llevan?

La fiesta de quince años

La fiesta de quince años se celebra en algunos países de Latinoamérica cuando las chicas cumplen° quince años. Los quince años representan la transición de niña a mujer. Los orígenes de esta ceremonia son mayas y aztecas, pero también tiene influencias del catolicismo. La celebración varía según el país, pero es común en todas la importancia del vestido de la quinceañera°, la elaboración de las invitaciones, el baile de la quinceañera con su padre y con otros familiares° y, por último, el banquete para los invitados°.

cumplen *turn* quinceañera *young woman celebrating her fifteenth birthday*
familiares *family members* invitados *guests*

Vocabulario útil

cubren	*cover*
granos	*zits, pimples*
hice	*I did*
peor	*worse*
tapar	*to cover*
tenía	*I had*

Comprensión

Escoge la opción correcta para completar cada oración.

1. La chica se levantó ___ el día de las fotos.
   a. con granos b. muy tarde
2. Después de levantarse, la chica ___.
   a. se bañó b. se maquilló
3. Para las fotos, la chica tapó los granos con ___.
   a. la flora y la fauna b. maquillaje Asepxia
4. Ahora la chica ___.
   a. tiene muchos granos b. usa maquillaje Asepxia

Conversación

Contesta estas preguntas con un(a) compañero/a.

¿Cuál fue la última fiesta a la que fuiste? ¿Qué fue lo que más te gustó? ¿Te aburrió algo? ¿Cómo te preparaste para la fiesta? ¿Cuánto tiempo necesitaste para prepararte?

Aplicación

Con un grupo de compañeros/as, creen un anuncio para vender un producto de uso diario, como el champú o la pasta de dientes. En su anuncio, muestren cómo el producto les puede ayudar a las personas a solucionar algún problema de su rutina diaria. Presenten el anuncio a la clase.

Practice more at vhlcentral.com.

recursos vText vhlcentral

Video: *Flash cultura*

En este episodio de *Flash cultura* vas a conocer unos entremeses° españoles llamados **tapas**. Hay varias teorías sobre el origen de su nombre. Una dice que viene de la costumbre antigua° de **tapar**° los vasos de vino para evitar° que insectos o polvo entren en° ellos. Otra teoría cuenta que el rey Alfonso X debía° beber un poco de vino por indicación médica y decidió acompañarlo° con algunos bocados° para tapar los efectos del alcohol. Cuando estuvo° mejor, ordenó que siempre en Castilla se sirviera° algo de comer con las bebidas° alcohólicas.

Vocabulario útil

económicas	*inexpensive*
montaditos	*bread slices with assorted toppings*
pagar propinas	*to tip*
tapar el hambre	*to take the edge off (lit. putting the lid on one's hunger)*

Preparación

En el área donde vives, ¿qué hacen las personas normalmente después del trabajo (*work*)? ¿Van a sus casas? ¿Salen con amigos? ¿Comen?

Ordenar

Ordena estos sucesos de manera lógica.

____ a. El empleado cuenta los palillos (*counts the toothpicks*) de los montaditos que Mari Carmen comió.

____ b. Mari Carmen va al barrio de la Ribera.

____ c. Un hombre en un bar explica cuándo sale a tomar tapas.

____ d. Un hombre explica la tradición de los montaditos o pinchos.

____ e. Carmen le pregunta a la chica si los montaditos son buenos para la salud.

entremeses *appetizers* antigua *ancient* tapar *cover* evitar *avoid* entren en *get in* debía *should* acompañarlo *accompany it* bocados *snacks* estuvo *he was* se sirviera *they should serve* bebidas *drinks* sueles *do you tend*

Tapas para todos los días

Estamos en la Plaza Cataluña, el puro centro de Barcelona.

—¿Cuándo sueles° venir a tomar tapas?
—Generalmente después del trabajo.

Éstos son los montaditos, o también llamados pinchos. ¿Te gustan?

Practice more at vhlcentral.com.

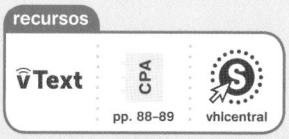

Perú

Video: *Panorama cultural*
Interactive Map

El país en cifras

- **Área:** 1.285.220 km^2 (496.224 millas^2), *un poco menos que el área de Alaska*
- **Población:** 30.147.000
- **Capital:** Lima—8.769.000
- **Ciudades principales:** Arequipa—778.000, Trujillo, Chiclayo, Callao, Iquitos

Iquitos es un puerto muy importante en el río Amazonas. Desde Iquitos se envían° muchos productos a otros lugares, incluyendo goma°, nueces°, madera°, arroz°, café y tabaco. Iquitos es también un destino popular para los ecoturistas que visitan la selva°.

- **Moneda:** nuevo sol
- **Idiomas:** español (oficial); quechua, aimara y otras lenguas indígenas (oficiales en los territorios donde se usan)

Bandera de Perú

Peruanos célebres

- **Clorinda Matto de Turner,** escritora (1854–1909)
- **César Vallejo,** poeta (1892–1938)
- **Javier Pérez de Cuéllar,** diplomático (1920–)
- **Juan Diego Flórez,** cantante de ópera (1973–)
- **Mario Vargas Llosa,** escritor (1936–)

Mario Vargas Llosa, Premio Nobel de Literatura 2010

se envían *are shipped* goma *rubber* nueces *nuts* madera *timber* arroz *rice* selva *jungle* Hace más de *More than... ago* grabó *engraved* tamaño *size*

Bailando marinera norteña en Trujillo

Calle en la ciudad de Iquitos

Pasaje Santa Rosa de Lima

Mercado indígena en Cuzco

recursos
vText
CPA pp. 90–93
vhlcentral

¡Increíble pero cierto!

Hace más de° dos mil años la civilización nazca de Perú grabó° más de dos mil kilómetros de líneas en el desierto. Los dibujos sólo son descifrables desde el aire. Uno de ellos es un cóndor del tamaño° de un estadio. Las Líneas de Nazca son uno de los grandes misterios de la humanidad.

Lugares • Lima

Lima es una ciudad moderna y antigua° a la vez°. La Iglesia de San Francisco es notable por su arquitectura barroca colonial. También son fascinantes las exhibiciones sobre los incas en el Museo Oro del Perú y en el Museo Nacional de Antropología y Arqueología. Barranco, el barrio° bohemio de la ciudad, es famoso por su ambiente cultural y sus bares y restaurantes.

BRASIL

Historia • Machu Picchu

A 80 kilómetros al noroeste de Cuzco está Machu Picchu, una ciudad antigua del Imperio inca. Está a una altitud de 2.350 metros (7.710 pies), entre dos cimas° de los Andes. Cuando los españoles llegaron a Perú y recorrieron la región, nunca encontraron Machu Picchu. En 1911, el arqueólogo estadounidense Hiram Bingham la redescubrió. Todavía no se sabe ni cómo se construyó° una ciudad a esa altura, ni por qué los incas la abandonaron. Sin embargo°, esta ciudad situada en desniveles° naturales es el ejemplo más conocido de la arquitectura inca.

Artes • La música andina

Machu Picchu aún no existía° cuando se originó la música cautivadora° de las culturas indígenas de los Andes. Los ritmos actuales° de la música andina tienen influencias españolas y africanas. Varios tipos de flauta°, entre ellos la quena y la zampoña, caracterizan esta música. En las décadas de los 60 y los 70 se popularizó un movimiento para preservar la música andina, y hasta° Simon y Garfunkel incorporaron a su repertorio la canción *El cóndor pasa*.

Economía • Llamas y alpacas

Perú se conoce por sus llamas, alpacas, guanacos y vicuñas, todos ellos animales mamíferos° parientes del camello. Estos animales todavía tienen una enorme importancia en la economía del país. Dan lana para exportar a otros países y para hacer ropa, mantas°, bolsas y otros artículos artesanales. La llama se usa también para la carga y el transporte.

BOLIVIA

¿Qué aprendiste? Responde a cada pregunta con una oración completa.

1. ¿Qué productos envía Iquitos a otros lugares?
2. ¿Cuáles son las lenguas oficiales de Perú?
3. ¿Por qué es notable la Iglesia de San Francisco en Lima?
4. ¿Qué información sobre Machu Picchu no se sabe todavía?
5. ¿Qué son la quena y la zampoña?
6. ¿Qué hacen los peruanos con la lana de sus llamas y alpacas?

Conexión Internet Investiga estos temas en **vhlcentral.com.**

1. Investiga la cultura incaica. ¿Cuáles son algunos de los aspectos interesantes de su cultura?
2. Busca información sobre dos artistas, escritores o músicos peruanos y presenta un breve informe a tu clase.

Practice more at **vhlcentral.com.**

antigua *old* a la vez *at the same time* barrio *neighborhood* cimas *summits* se construyó *was built* Sin embargo *However* desniveles *uneven pieces of land* aún no existía *didn't exist yet* cautivadora *captivating* actuales *present-day* flauta *flute* hasta *even* mamíferos *mammalian* mantas *blankets*

Los verbos reflexivos

acordarse (de) (o:ue)	*to remember*
acostarse (o:ue)	*to go to bed*
afeitarse	*to shave*
bañarse	*to bathe; to take a bath*
cepillarse el pelo	*to brush one's hair*
cepillarse los dientes	*to brush one's teeth*
despertarse (e:ie)	*to wake up*
dormirse (o:ue)	*to go to sleep; to fall asleep*
ducharse	*to shower; to take a shower*
enojarse (con)	*to get angry (with)*
irse	*to go away; to leave*
lavarse la cara	*to wash one's face*
lavarse las manos	*to wash one's hands*
levantarse	*to get up*
llamarse	*to be called; to be named*
maquillarse	*to put on makeup*
peinarse	*to comb one's hair*
ponerse	*to put on*
ponerse (+ *adj.*)	*to become (+ adj.)*
preocuparse (por)	*to worry (about)*
probarse (o:ue)	*to try on*
quedarse	*to stay; to remain*
quitarse	*to take off*
secarse	*to dry oneself*
sentarse (e:ie)	*to sit down*
sentirse (e:ie)	*to feel*
vestirse (e:i)	*to get dressed*

Palabras de secuencia

antes (de)	*before*
después	*afterwards; then*
después (de)	*after*
durante	*during*
entonces	*then*
luego	*then*
más tarde	*later on*
por último	*finally*

Palabras indefinidas y negativas

algo	*something; anything*
alguien	*someone; somebody; anyone*
alguno/a(s), algún	*some; any*
jamás	*never; not ever*
nada	*nothing; not anything*
nadie	*no one; nobody; not anyone*
ni... ni	*neither... nor*
ninguno/a, ningún	*no; none; not any*
nunca	*never; not ever*
o... o	*either... or*
siempre	*always*
también	*also; too*
tampoco	*neither; not either*

En el baño

el baño, el cuarto de baño	*bathroom*
el champú	*shampoo*
la crema de afeitar	*shaving cream*
la ducha	*shower*
el espejo	*mirror*
el inodoro	*toilet*
el jabón	*soap*
el lavabo	*sink*
el maquillaje	*makeup*
la pasta de dientes	*toothpaste*
la toalla	*towel*

Verbos similares a gustar

aburrir	*to bore*
encantar	*to like very much; to love (inanimate objects)*
faltar	*to lack; to need*
fascinar	*to fascinate; to like very much*
importar	*to be important to; to matter*
interesar	*to be interesting to; to interest*
molestar	*to bother; to annoy*
quedar	*to be left over; to fit (clothing)*

Palabras adicionales

el despertador	*alarm clock*
las pantuflas	*slippers*
la rutina diaria	*daily routine*
por la mañana	*in the morning*
por la noche	*at night*
por la tarde	*in the afternoon; in the evening*

Expresiones útiles	*See page 231.*

La comida

8

Communicative Goals

I will be able to:

- **Order food in a restaurant**
- **Talk about and describe food**

VOICE BOARD

A PRIMERA VISTA

- **¿Dónde están ellos?**
- **¿Qué hacen?**
- **¿Es parte de su rutina diaria?**
- **¿Qué colores hay en la foto?**

contextos

pages 262–267

- Food
- Food descriptions
- Meals

fotonovela

pages 268–271

Miguel and Maru are at one of Mexico City's best restaurants enjoying a romantic dinner... until Felipe and Juan Carlos show up.

cultura

pages 272–273

- Fruits and vegetables from the Americas
- Ferran Adrià

estructura

pages 274–289

- Preterite of stem-changing verbs
- Double object pronouns
- Comparisons
- Superlatives
- **Recapitulación**

adelante

pages 290–297

Lectura: A menu and restaurant review
Escritura: A restaurant review
Escuchar: A conversation at a restaurant
En pantalla
Flash cultura
Panorama: Guatemala

La comida

My Vocabulary Tutorials

Más vocabulario

el/la camarero/a	*waiter/waitress*
la comida	*food; meal*
el/la dueño/a	*owner; landlord*
los entremeses	*hors d'oeuvres; appetizers*
el menú	*menu*
el plato (principal)	*(main) dish*
la sección de (no) fumar	*(non) smoking section*
el agua (mineral)	*(mineral) water*
la bebida	*drink*
la cerveza	*beer*
la leche	*milk*
el refresco	*soft drink; soda*
el ajo	*garlic*
las arvejas	*peas*
los cereales	*cereal; grains*
los frijoles	*beans*
el melocotón	*peach*
el pollo (asado)	*(roast) chicken*
el queso	*cheese*
el sándwich	*sandwich*
el yogur	*yogurt*
el aceite	*oil*
la margarina	*margarine*
la mayonesa	*mayonnaise*
el vinagre	*vinegar*
delicioso/a	*delicious*
sabroso/a	*tasty; delicious*
saber (a)	*to taste (like)*

Variación léxica

camarones ⟷ gambas (*Esp.*)
camarero ⟷ mesero (*Amér. L.*), mesonero (*Ven.*), mozo (*Arg., Chile, Urug., Perú*)
refresco ⟷ gaseosa (*Amér. C., Amér. S.*)

recursos

vText | CPA pp. 95–97 | CH pp. 115–116 | vhlcentral

¡LENGUA VIVA!

You learned the verb **saber** in **Lección 6**. This verb is also used to describe food.

Use **saber** + [*adjective*] to explain how something *tastes*.

Ex: **Este plato sabe dulce/rico/amargo.**

(*This dish tastes sweet/delicious/bitter.*)

Use **saber** + **a** to say what something *tastes like*.

Ex: **Sabe a ajo.**

(*It tastes like garlic.*)

Estas langostas no saben a nada.

(*These lobsters don't taste like anything./ These lobsters don't have any flavor.*)

Práctica

1 **Escuchar** Indica si las oraciones que vas a escuchar son **ciertas** o **falsas**, según el dibujo. Después, corrige las falsas.

1. _____
2. _____
3. _____
4. _____
5. _____
6. _____
7. _____
8. _____
9. _____
10. _____

2 **Seleccionar** Paulino y Pilar van a cenar a un restaurante. Escucha la conversación y selecciona la respuesta que mejor completa cada oración.

1. Paulino le pide el _____ (menú / plato) al camarero.
2. El plato del día es (atún / salmón) _____.
3. Pilar ordena _____ (leche / agua mineral) para beber.
4. Paulino quiere un refresco de _____ (naranja / limón).
5. Paulino hoy prefiere _____ (el salmón / la chuleta).
6. Dicen que la carne en ese restaurante es muy _____ (sabrosa / mala).
7. Pilar come salmón con _____ (zanahorias / champiñones).

3 **Identificar** Identifica la palabra que no está relacionada con cada grupo.

1. champiñón • cebolla • banana • zanahoria
2. camarones • ajo • atún • salmón
3. aceite • leche • refresco • agua mineral
4. jamón • chuleta de cerdo • vinagre • carne de res
5. cerveza • lechuga • arvejas • frijoles
6. carne • pescado • mariscos • camarero
7. pollo • naranja • limón • melocotón
8. maíz • queso • tomate • champiñón

4 **Completar** Completa las oraciones con las palabras más lógicas.

1. ¡Me gusta mucho este plato! Sabe _____.
   a. mal b. delicioso c. antipático
2. Camarero, ¿puedo ver el _____, por favor?
   a. aceite b. maíz c. menú
3. Carlos y yo bebemos siempre agua _____.
   a. cómoda b. mineral c. principal
4. El plato del día es _____.
   a. pollo asado b. mayonesa c. ajo
5. Margarita es vegetariana. Ella come _____.
   a. frijoles b. chuletas c. jamón
6. Mi hermana le da _____ a su niña.
   a. ajo b. vinagre c. yogur

el desayuno

NOTA CULTURAL

En Guatemala, un desayuno típico incluye huevos, frijoles, fruta, tortillas, jugo y café.

Otros desayunos populares son:

madalenas (*muffins*) España

pan dulce (*assorted breads/pastries*) México

champurradas (*sugar cookies*) Guatemala

gallo pinto (*fried rice and beans*) Costa Rica

perico (*scrambled eggs with peppers and onions*) Venezuela

el almuerzo

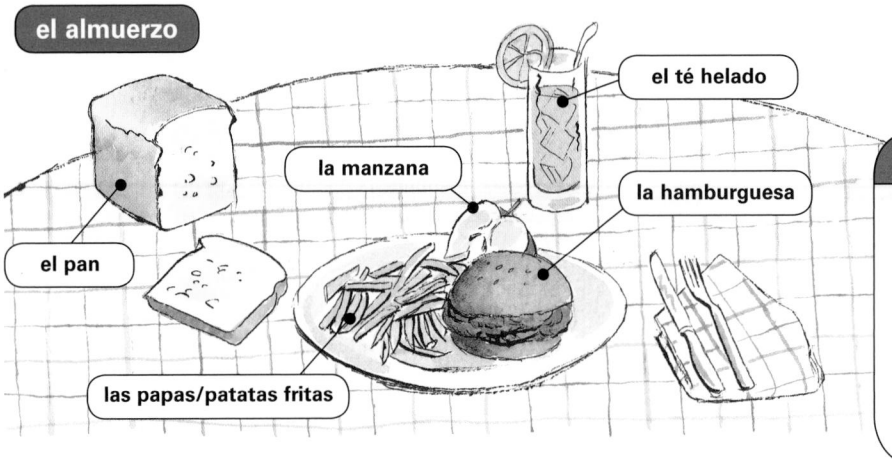

Más vocabulario

escoger	*to choose*
merendar (e:ie)	*to snack*
probar (o:ue)	*to taste; to try*
recomendar (e:ie)	*to recommend*
servir (e:i)	*to serve*
el té	*tea*
el vino blanco	*white wine*

la cena

5 **Completar** Trabaja con un(a) compañero/a de clase para relacionar cada producto con el grupo alimenticio (*food group*) correcto.

modelo

La carne es del grupo uno.

el aceite	las bananas	los cereales	la leche
el arroz	el café	los espárragos	el pescado
el azúcar	la carne	los frijoles	el vino

1. _____ y el queso son del grupo cuatro.
2. _____ son del grupo ocho.
3. _____ y el pollo son del grupo tres.
4. _____ es del grupo cinco.
5. _____ es del grupo dos.
6. Las manzanas y _____ son del grupo siete.
7. _____ es del grupo seis.
8. _____ son del grupo diez.
9. _____ y los tomates son del grupo nueve.
10. El pan y _____ son del grupo diez.

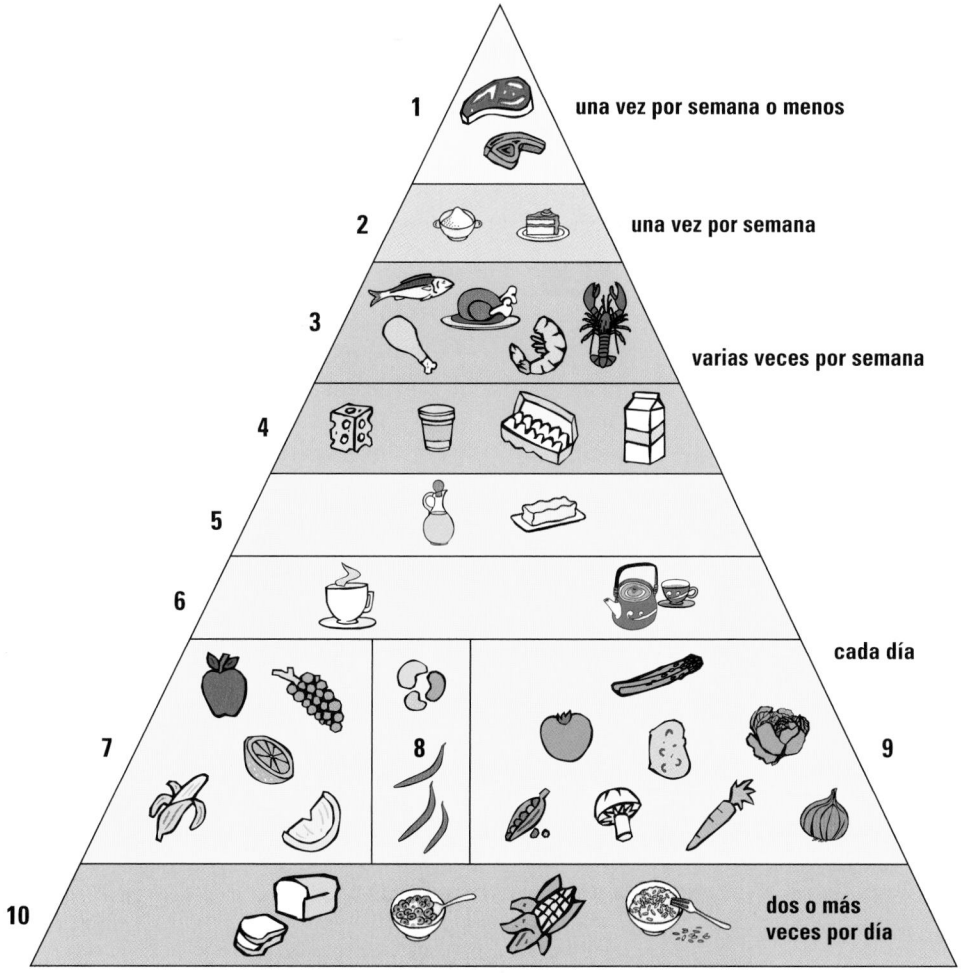

La Pirámide Alimenticia Latinoamericana

6 **¿Cierto o falso?** Consulta la Pirámide Alimenticia Latinoamericana de la página 265 e indica si lo que dice cada oración es **cierto** o **falso**. Si la oración es falsa, escribe las comidas que sí están en el grupo indicado.

modelo

El queso está en el grupo diez.

Falso. En ese grupo están el maíz, el pan, los cereales y el arroz.

1. La manzana, la banana, el limón y las arvejas están en el grupo siete.
2. En el grupo cuatro están los huevos, la leche y el aceite.
3. El azúcar está en el grupo dos.
4. En el grupo diez están el pan, el arroz y el maíz.
5. El pollo está en el grupo uno.
6. En el grupo nueve están la lechuga, el tomate, las arvejas, la naranja, la papa, los espárragos y la cebolla.
7. El café y el té están en el mismo grupo.
8. En el grupo cinco está el arroz.
9. El pescado, el yogur y el bistec están en el grupo tres.

7 **Combinar** Combina palabras de cada columna, en cualquier (*any*) orden, para formar nueve oraciones lógicas sobre las comidas. Añade otras palabras si es necesario.

modelo

La camarera nos sirve la ensalada.

A	B	C
el/la camarero/a	almorzar	la sección de no fumar
el/la dueño/a	escoger	el desayuno
mi familia	gustar	la ensalada
mi novio/a	merendar	las uvas
mis amigos y yo	pedir	el restaurante
mis padres	preferir	el jugo de naranja
mi hermano/a	probar	el refresco
el/la médico/a	recomendar	el plato
yo	servir	el arroz

NOTA CULTURAL

El arroz es un alimento básico en el Caribe, Centroamérica y México, entre otros países. Aparece frecuentemente como acompañamiento del plato principal y muchas veces se sirve con frijoles. Un plato muy popular en varios países es **el arroz con pollo** *(chicken and rice casserole).*

8 **Un menú** En parejas, usen la Pirámide Alimenticia Latinoamericana de la página 265 para crear un menú para una cena especial. Incluyan alimentos de los diez grupos para los entremeses, los platos principales y las bebidas. Luego presenten el menú a la clase.

modelo

La cena especial que vamos a preparar es deliciosa. Primero, hay dos entremeses: ensalada César y sopa de langosta. El plato principal es salmón con salsa de ajo y espárragos. También vamos a servir arroz...

Practice more at vhlcentral.com.

Comunicación

9 **Conversación** En parejas, túrnense para hacerse estas preguntas.

1. ¿Meriendas mucho durante el día? ¿Qué comes? ¿A qué hora?
2. ¿Qué te gusta cenar?
3. ¿A qué hora, dónde y con quién almuerzas?
4. ¿Cuáles son las comidas más (*most*) típicas de tu almuerzo?
5. ¿Desayunas? ¿Qué comes y bebes por la mañana?
6. ¿Qué comida te gusta más? ¿Qué comida no conoces y quieres probar?
7. ¿Comes cada día alimentos de los diferentes grupos de la pirámide alimenticia? ¿Cuáles son los alimentos y bebidas más frecuentes en tu dieta?
8. ¿Qué comida recomiendas a tus amigos? ¿Por qué?
9. ¿Eres vegetariano/a? ¿Crees que ser vegetariano/a es una buena idea? ¿Por qué?
10. ¿Te gusta cocinar (*to cook*)? ¿Qué comidas preparas para tus amigos? ¿Para tu familia?

10 **Describir** Con dos compañeros/as de clase, describe las dos fotos, contestando estas preguntas.

- ¿Quiénes están en las fotos?
- ¿Dónde están?
- ¿Qué hora es?
- ¿Qué comen y qué beben?

recursos
vText
CPA
pp. 98–99
vhlcentral

11 **Crucigrama** Tu profesor(a) les va a dar a ti y a tu compañero/a un crucigrama (*crossword puzzle*) incompleto. Tú tienes las palabras que necesita tu compañero/a y él/ella tiene las palabras que tú necesitas. Tienen que darse pistas (*clues*) para completarlo. No pueden decir la palabra; deben utilizar definiciones, ejemplos y frases.

modelo

6 vertical: Es un condimento que normalmente viene con la sal.
2 horizontal: Es una fruta amarilla.

Una cena... romántica

Maru y Miguel quieren tener una cena romántica, pero les espera una sorpresa.

PERSONAJES **MARU** **MIGUEL**

Video: *Fotonovela*

MARU No sé qué pedir. ¿Qué me recomiendas?

MIGUEL No estoy seguro. Las chuletas de cerdo se ven muy buenas.

MARU ¿Vas a pedirlas?

MIGUEL No sé.

MIGUEL ¡Qué bonitos! ¿Quién te los dio?

MARU Me los compró un chico muy guapo e inteligente.

MIGUEL ¿Es tan guapo como yo?

MARU Sí, como tú, guapísimo.

(*El camarero llega a la mesa.*)

CAMARERO ¿Les gustaría saber nuestras especialidades del día?

MARU Sí, por favor.

CAMARERO Para el entremés, tenemos ceviche de camarón. De plato principal ofrecemos bistec con verduras a la plancha.

(*en otra parte del restaurante*)

JUAN CARLOS Disculpe. ¿Qué me puede contar del pollo? ¿Dónde lo consiguió el chef?

CAMARERO ¡Oiga! ¿Qué está haciendo?

FELIPE Los espárragos están sabrosísimos esta noche. Usted pidió el pollo, señor. Estos champiñones saben a mantequilla.

GERENTE ¿Qué pasa aquí, Esteban?

CAMARERO Lo siento, señor. Me quitaron la comida.

GERENTE (*a Felipe*) Señor, ¿quién es usted? ¿Qué cree que está haciendo?

CAMARERO

JUAN CARLOS

FELIPE

GERENTE

MARU Voy a probar el jamón.

CAMARERO Perfecto. ¿Y para usted, caballero?

MIGUEL Pollo asado con champiñones y papas, por favor.

CAMARERO Excelente.

MIGUEL Por nosotros.

MARU Dos años.

JUAN CARLOS Felipe y yo les servimos la comida a nuestros amigos. Pero desafortunadamente, salió todo mal.

FELIPE Soy el peor camarero del mundo. ¡Lo siento! Nosotros vamos a pagar la comida.

JUAN CARLOS ¿Nosotros?

FELIPE Todo esto fue idea tuya, Juan Carlos.

JUAN CARLOS ¿Mi idea? ¡Felipe! (*al gerente*) Señor, él es más responsable que yo.

GERENTE Tú y tú, vamos.

recursos

vText CPA pp. 100–101 vhlcentral

Expresiones útiles

Ordering food

¿Qué me recomiendas?
What do you recommend?
Las chuletas de cerdo se ven muy buenas.
The pork chops look good.
¿Les gustaría saber nuestras especialidades del día?
Would you like to hear our specials?
Para el entremés, tenemos ceviche de camarón.
For an appetizer, we have shrimp ceviche.
De plato principal ofrecemos bistec con verduras a la plancha.
For a main course, we have beef with grilled vegetables.
Voy a probar el jamón.
I am going to try the ham.

Describing people and things

¡Qué bonitos! ¿Quién te los dio?
How pretty! Who gave them to you?
Me los compró un chico muy guapo e inteligente.
A really handsome, intelligent guy bought them for me.
¿Es tan guapo como yo?
Is he as handsome as I am?
Sí, como tú, guapísimo.
Yes, like you, gorgeous.
Soy el peor camarero del mundo.
I am the worst waiter in the world.
Él es más responsable que yo.
He is more responsible than I am.

Additional vocabulary

el/la gerente *manager*
caballero *gentleman, sir*

¿Qué pasó?

1 **Escoger** Escoge la respuesta que completa mejor cada oración.

1. Miguel lleva a Maru a un restaurante para _____.
   a. almorzar b. desayunar c. cenar
2. El camarero les ofrece _____ como plato principal.
   a. ceviche de camarón b. bistec con verduras a la plancha
   c. pescado, arroz y ensalada
3. Miguel va a pedir _____.
   a. pollo asado con champiñones y papas
   b. langosta al horno c. pescado con verduras a la mantequilla
4. Felipe les lleva la comida a sus amigos y prueba _____.
   a. el jamón y los vinos b. el atún y la lechuga
   c. los espárragos y los champiñones

NOTA CULTURAL

El **ceviche** es un plato típico de varios países hispanos como México, Perú y Costa Rica. En México, se prepara con pescado o mariscos frescos, jugo de limón, tomate, cebolla, chile y cilantro. Se puede comer como plato principal, pero también como entremés o merienda. Casi siempre se sirve con tostadas (*fried tortillas*) o galletas saladas (*crackers*).

2 **Identificar** Indica quién puede decir estas oraciones.

1. ¡Qué desastre! Soy un camarero muy malo.
2. Les recomiendo el bistec con verduras a la plancha.
3. Tal vez escoja las chuletas de cerdo, creo que son muy sabrosas.
4. ¿Qué pasa aquí?
5. Dígame las especialidades del día, por favor.
6. No fue mi idea. Felipe es más responsable que yo.

FELIPE

MARU

JUAN CARLOS

CAMARERO

MIGUEL

GERENTE

3 **Preguntas** Contesta estas preguntas sobre la **Fotonovela**.

1. ¿Por qué fueron Maru y Miguel a un restaurante?
2. ¿Qué entremés es una de las especialidades del día?
3. ¿Qué pidió Maru?
4. ¿Quiénes van a pagar la cuenta?

4 **En el restaurante**

1. Prepara con un(a) compañero/a una conversación en la que le preguntas si conoce algún buen restaurante en tu comunidad. Tu compañero/a responde que él/ella sí conoce un restaurante que sirve una comida deliciosa. Lo/La invitas a cenar y tu compañero/a acepta. Determinan la hora para verse en el restaurante.
2. Trabaja con un(a) compañero/a para representar los papeles de un(a) cliente/a y un(a) camarero/a en un restaurante. El/La camarero/a te pregunta qué te puede servir y tú preguntas cuál es la especialidad de la casa. El/La camarero/a te dice cuál es la especialidad y te recomienda algunos platos del menú. Tú pides entremeses, un plato principal y escoges una bebida. El/La camarero/a te sirve la comida y tú le das las gracias.

CONSULTA

To review indefinite words like **algún,** see **Estructura 7.2,** p. 240.

Pronunciación

Audio

ll, ñ, c, and z

pollo **llave** **ella** **cebolla**

Most Spanish speakers pronounce **ll** like the *y* in *yes*.

mañana **señor** **baño** **niña**

The letter ***ñ*** is pronounced much like the *ny* in *canyon*.

café **colombiano** **cuando** **rico**

Before **a**, **o**, or **u**, the Spanish **c** is pronounced like the *c* in *car*.

cereales **delicioso** **conducir** **conocer**

Before **e** or **i**, the Spanish **c** is pronounced like the *s* in *sit*. (In parts of Spain, **c** before **e** or **i** is pronounced like the *th* in *think*.)

zeta **zanahoria** **almuerzo** **cerveza**

The Spanish **z** is pronounced like the *s* in *sit*. (In parts of Spain, **z** is pronounced like the *th* in *think*.)

Práctica Lee las palabras en voz alta.

1. mantequilla
2. cuñada
3. aceite
4. manzana
5. español
6. cepillo
7. zapato
8. azúcar
9. quince
10. compañera
11. almorzar
12. calle

Oraciones Lee las oraciones en voz alta.

1. Mi compañero de cuarto se llama Toño Núñez. Su familia es de la ciudad de Guatemala y de Quetzaltenango.
2. Dice que la comida de su mamá es deliciosa, especialmente su pollo al champiñón y sus tortillas de maíz.
3. Creo que Toño tiene razón porque hoy cené en su casa y quiero volver mañana para cenar allí otra vez.

Refranes Lee los refranes en voz alta.

1 *Looks can be deceiving.*
2 *A full belly makes a happy heart.*

recursos
vText CPA p. 102 CH p. 117 vhlcentral

EN DETALLE

Additional Reading

Frutas y verduras de América

Imagínate una pizza sin salsa° de tomate o una hamburguesa sin papas fritas. Ahora piensa que quieres ver una película, pero las palomitas de maíz° y el chocolate no existen. ¡Qué mundo° tan insípido°! Muchas de las comidas más populares del mundo tienen ingredientes esenciales que son originarios del continente llamado Nuevo Mundo. Estas frutas y verduras no fueron introducidas en Europa sino hasta° el siglo° XVI.

El tomate, por ejemplo, era° usado como planta ornamental cuando llegó por primera vez a Europa porque pensaron que era venenoso°. El maíz, por su parte, era ya la base de la comida de muchos países latinoamericanos muchos siglos antes de la llegada de los españoles.

La papa fue un alimento° básico para los incas. Incluso consiguieron deshidratarla para almacenarla° por largos períodos de tiempo. El cacao (planta con la que se hace el chocolate) fue muy importante para los aztecas y los mayas. Ellos usaban sus semillas° como moneda° y como ingrediente de diversas salsas. También las molían° para preparar una bebida, mezclándolas° con agua ¡y con chile!

El aguacate°, la guayaba°, la papaya, la piña y el maracuyá (o fruta de la pasión) son otros ejemplos de frutas originarias de América que son hoy día conocidas en todo el mundo.

Mole

¿En qué alimentos encontramos estas frutas y verduras?

Tomate: pizza, ketchup, salsa de tomate, sopa de tomate

Maíz: palomitas de maíz, tamales, tortillas, arepas (Colombia y Venezuela), pan

Papa: papas fritas, frituras de papa°, puré de papas°, sopa de papas, tortilla de patatas (España)

Cacao: mole (México), chocolatinas°, cereales, helados°, tartas°

Aguacate: guacamole (México), coctel de camarones, sopa de aguacate, nachos, enchiladas hondureñas

salsa *sauce* **palomitas de maíz** *popcorn* **mundo** *world* **insípido** *flavorless* **hasta** *until* **siglo** *century* **era** *was* **venenoso** *poisonous* **alimento** *food* **almacenarla** *to store it* **semillas** *seeds* **moneda** *currency* **las molían** *they used to grind them* **mezclándolas** *mixing them* **aguacate** *avocado* **guayaba** *guava* **frituras de papa** *chips* **puré de papas** *mashed potatoes* **chocolatinas** *chocolate bars* **helados** *ice cream* **tartas** *cakes*

ACTIVIDADES

1 **¿Cierto o falso?** Indica si lo que dicen las oraciones es **cierto** o **falso**. Corrige la información falsa.

1. El tomate se introdujo a Europa como planta ornamental.
2. Los incas sólo consiguieron almacenar las papas por poco tiempo.
3. Los aztecas y los mayas usaron las papas como moneda.
4. El maíz era una comida poco popular en Latinoamérica.
5. El aguacate era el alimento básico de los incas.
6. En México se hace una salsa con chocolate.
7. El aguacate, la guayaba, la papaya, la piña y el maracuyá son originarios de América.
8. Las arepas se hacen con cacao.
9. El aguacate es un ingrediente del cóctel de camarones.
10. En España hacen una tortilla con papas.

ASÍ SE DICE

Viajes y turismo

el banano (Col.), el cambur (Ven.), el guineo (Nic.), el plátano (Amér. L., Esp.)	la banana
el choclo (Amér. S.), el elote (Méx.), el jojoto (Ven.), la mazorca (Esp.)	*corncob*
las caraotas (Ven.), los porotos (Amér. S.), las habichuelas (P. R.)	los frijoles
el durazno (Méx.)	el melocotón
el jitomate (Méx.)	el tomate

EL MUNDO HISPANO

Algunos platos típicos

- **Ceviche peruano:** Es un plato de pescado crudo° que se marina° en jugo de limón, con sal, pimienta, cebolla y ají°. Se sirve con lechuga, maíz, camote° y papa amarilla.
- **Gazpacho andaluz:** Es una sopa fría típica del sur de España. Se hace con verduras crudas y molidas°: tomate, ají, pepino° y ajo. También lleva pan, sal, aceite y vinagre.
- **Sancocho colombiano:** Es una sopa de pollo, pescado o carne con plátano, maíz, zanahoria, yuca, papas, cebolla, cilantro y ajo. Se sirve con arroz blanco.

crudo *raw* se marina *gets marinated* ají *pepper* camote *sweet potato* molidas *mashed* pepino *cucumber*

PERFIL

Ferran Adrià: arte en la cocina°

¿Qué haces si un amigo te invita a comer croquetas líquidas o paella de *Kellogg's*? ¿Piensas que es una broma°? ¡Cuidado! Puedes estar perdiendo la oportunidad de probar los platos de uno de los chefs más innovadores del mundo°: **Ferran Adrià.**

Este artista de la cocina basa su éxito° en la creatividad y en la química. Adrià modifica combinaciones de ingredientes y juega con contrastes de gustos y sensaciones: frío-caliente, crudo-cocido°, dulce°-salado°... A partir de nuevas técnicas, altera la textura de los alimentos sin alterar su sabor°. Sus platos sorprendentes° y divertidos atraen a muchos nuevos chefs a su academia de cocina experimental. Quizás un día compraremos° en el supermercado té esférico°, carne líquida y espuma° de tomate.

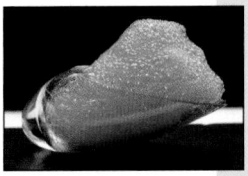

Aire de zanahorias

cocina *kitchen* broma *joke* mundo *world* éxito *success* cocido *cooked* dulce *sweet* salado *savory* sabor *taste* sorprendentes *surprising* compraremos *we will buy* esférico *spheric* espuma *foam*

Conexión Internet

¿Qué platos comen los hispanos en los Estados Unidos?

Go to **vhlcentral.com** to find more cultural information related to this **Cultura** section.

ACTIVIDADES

2 Comprensión Empareja cada palabra con su definición.

1. fruta amarilla
2. sopa típica de Colombia
3. ingrediente del ceviche
4. chef español

a. gazpacho
b. Ferran Adrià
c. sancocho
d. guineo
e. pescado

3 ¿Qué plato especial hay en tu región? Escribe cuatro oraciones sobre un plato típico de tu región. Explica los ingredientes que contiene y cómo se sirve.

Practice more at **vhlcentral.com.**

recursos

vText

CH p. 118

vhlcentral

8.1 Preterite of stem-changing verbs

Tutorial

ANTE TODO As you learned in **Lección 6**, **-ar** and **-er** stem-changing verbs have no stem change in the preterite. **-Ir** stem-changing verbs, however, do have a stem change. Study the following chart and observe where the stem changes occur.

CONSULTA

There are a few high-frequency irregular verbs in the preterite. You will learn more about them in **Estructura 9.1**, p. 310.

Preterite of -ir stem-changing verbs

		servir *(to serve)*	**dormir** *(to sleep)*
SINGULAR FORMS	yo	serví	dormí
	tú	serviste	dormiste
	Ud./él/ella	**si**rvió	d**u**rmió
PLURAL FORMS	nosotros/as	servimos	dormimos
	vosotros/as	servisteis	dormisteis
	Uds./ellos/ellas	**si**rvieron	d**u**rmieron

▶ Stem-changing **-ir** verbs, in the preterite only, have a stem change in the third-person singular and plural forms. The stem change consists of either **e** to **i** or **o** to **u**.

(e → i) pedir: p**i**dió, p**i**dieron (o → u) morir (*to die*): m**u**rió, m**u**rieron

¡INTÉNTALO! Cambia cada infinitivo al pretérito.

1. Yo *serví, dormí, pedí...*. (servir, dormir, pedir, preferir, repetir, seguir)
2. Usted _____. (morir, conseguir, pedir, sentirse, servir, vestirse)
3. Tú _____. (conseguir, servir, morir, pedir, dormir, repetir)
4. Ellas _____. (repetir, dormir, seguir, preferir, morir, servir)
5. Nosotros _____. (seguir, preferir, servir, vestirse, pedir, dormirse)
6. Ustedes _____. (sentirse, vestirse, conseguir, pedir, repetir, dormirse)
7. Él _____. (dormir, morir, preferir, repetir, seguir, pedir)

recursos
vText
CPA pp. 103–105
CH pp. 119–120
vhlcentral

Práctica

1 **Completar** Completa estas oraciones para describir lo que pasó anoche en el restaurante El Famoso.

1. Paula y Humberto Suárez llegaron al restaurante El Famoso a las ocho y _____ (seguir) al camarero a una mesa en la sección de no fumar.
2. El señor Suárez _____ (pedir) una chuleta de cerdo.
3. La señora Suárez _____ (preferir) probar los camarones.
4. De tomar, los dos _____ (pedir) vino tinto.
5. El camarero _____ (repetir) el pedido (*the order*) para confirmarlo.
6. La comida tardó mucho (*took a long time*) en llegar y los señores Suárez _____ (dormirse) esperando la comida.
7. A las nueve y media el camarero les _____ (servir) la comida.
8. Después de comer la chuleta, el señor Suárez _____ (sentirse) muy mal.
9. Pobre señor Suárez... ¿por qué no _____ (pedir) los camarones?

2 **El camarero loco** En el restaurante La Hermosa trabaja un camarero muy loco que siempre comete muchos errores. Indica lo que los clientes pidieron y lo que el camarero les sirvió.

modelo

Armando / papas fritas

Armando pidió papas fritas, pero el camarero le sirvió maíz.

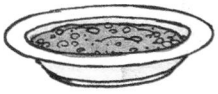

1. nosotros / jugo de naranja
2. Beatriz / queso
3. tú / arroz

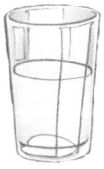

4. Elena y Alejandro / atún
5. usted / refresco
6. yo / hamburguesa

Practice more at vhlcentral.com.

Comunicación

3 **El almuerzo** Trabajen en parejas. Túrnense para completar las oraciones de César de una manera lógica.

modelo

Mi abuelo se despertó temprano, pero yo...
Mi abuelo se despertó temprano, pero yo me desperté tarde.

1. Yo llegué al restaurante a tiempo, pero mis amigos...
2. Beatriz pidió la ensalada de frutas, pero yo...
3. Yolanda les recomendó el bistec, pero Eva y Paco...
4. Nosotros preferimos las papas fritas, pero Yolanda...
5. El camarero sirvió la carne, pero yo...
6. Beatriz y yo pedimos café, pero Yolanda y Paco...
7. Eva se sintió enferma, pero Paco y yo...
8. Nosotros repetimos postre (*dessert*), pero Eva...
9. Ellos salieron tarde, pero yo...
10. Yo me dormí temprano, pero mi hermano...

¡LENGUA VIVA!

In Spanish, the verb **repetir** is used to express *to have a second helping (of something)*.

Cuando mi mamá prepara sopa de champiñones, yo siempre repito.
When my mom makes mushroom soup, I always have a second helping.

4 **Entrevista** Trabajen en parejas y túrnense para entrevistar a su compañero/a.

1. ¿Te acostaste tarde o temprano anoche? ¿A qué hora te dormiste? ¿Dormiste bien?
2. ¿A qué hora te despertaste esta mañana? Y, ¿a qué hora te levantaste?
3. ¿A qué hora vas a acostarte esta noche?
4. ¿Qué almorzaste ayer? ¿Quién te sirvió el almuerzo?
5. ¿Qué cenaste ayer?
6. ¿Cenaste en un restaurante recientemente? ¿Con quién(es)?
7. ¿Qué pediste en el restaurante? ¿Qué pidieron los demás?
8. ¿Se durmió alguien en alguna de tus clases la semana pasada? ¿En qué clase?

Síntesis

5 **Describir** En grupos, estudien la foto y las preguntas. Luego, describan la primera (¿y la última?) cita de César y Libertad.

CONSULTA

To review words commonly associated with the preterite, such as **anoche**, see **Estructura 6.3**, p. 207.

- ¿Adónde salieron a cenar?
- ¿Qué pidieron?
- ¿Les gustó la comida?
- ¿Quién prefirió una comida vegetariana? ¿Por qué?
- ¿Cómo se vistieron?
- ¿De qué hablaron? ¿Les gustó la conversación?
- ¿Van a volver a verse? ¿Por qué?

8.2 Double object pronouns

ANTE TODO

In **Lecciones 5** and **6**, you learned that direct and indirect object pronouns replace nouns and that they often refer to nouns that have already been referenced. You will now learn how to use direct and indirect object pronouns together. Observe the following diagram.

Indirect Object Pronouns			Direct Object Pronouns	
me	nos	+	lo	los
te	os		la	las
le (se)	les (se)			

▶ When direct and indirect object pronouns are used together, the indirect object pronoun always precedes the direct object pronoun.

I.O. D.O.
La camarera **me** muestra **el menú**. → DOUBLE OBJECT PRONOUNS: La camarera **me lo** muestra.
The waitress shows me the menu. → *The waitress shows it to me.*

I.O. D.O.
Nos sirven **los platos**. → DOUBLE OBJECT PRONOUNS: **Nos los** sirven.
They serve us the dishes. → *They serve them to us.*

I.O. D.O.
Maribel **te** pidió **una hamburguesa**. → DOUBLE OBJECT PRONOUNS: Maribel **te la** pidió.
Maribel ordered a hamburger for you. → *Maribel ordered it for you.*

▶ In Spanish, two pronouns that begin with the letter **l** cannot be used together. Therefore, the indirect object pronouns **le** and **les** always change to **se** when they are used with **lo, los, la,** and **las.**

I.O. D.O.
Le escribí **la carta**. → DOUBLE OBJECT PRONOUNS: **Se la** escribí.
I wrote him the letter. → *I wrote it to him.*

I.O. D.O.
Les sirvió **los sándwiches**. → DOUBLE OBJECT PRONOUNS: **Se los** sirvió.
He served them the sandwiches. → *He served them to them.*

- Because **se** has multiple meanings, Spanish speakers often clarify to whom the pronoun refers by adding **a usted, a él, a ella, a ustedes, a ellos,** or **a ellas.**

¿El sombrero? Carlos **se** lo vendió **a ella.**
The hat? Carlos sold it to her.

¿Las verduras? Ellos **se** las compran **a usted.**
The vegetables? They are buying them for you.

- Double object pronouns are placed before a conjugated verb. With infinitives and present participles, they may be placed before the conjugated verb or attached to the end of the infinitive or present participle.

DOUBLE OBJECT PRONOUNS
Te lo voy a mostrar.

DOUBLE OBJECT PRONOUNS
Voy a mostrár**telo**.

DOUBLE OBJECT PRONOUNS
Nos las están comprando.

DOUBLE OBJECT PRONOUNS
Están comprándo**noslas**.

Mi abuelo **me lo** está leyendo.
Mi abuelo está leyéndo**melo**.

El camarero **se los** va a servir.
El camarero va a servír**selos**.

- As you can see above, when double object pronouns are attached to an infinitive or a present participle, an accent mark is added to maintain the original stress.

¡INTÉNTALO! Escribe el pronombre de objeto directo o indirecto que falta en cada oración.

Objeto directo

1. ¿La ensalada? El camarero nos ___la___ sirvió.
2. ¿El salmón? La dueña me _____ recomienda.
3. ¿La comida? Voy a prepararte_____.
4. ¿Las bebidas? Estamos pidiéndose_____.
5. ¿Los refrescos? Te _____ puedo traer ahora.
6. ¿Los platos de arroz? Van a servírnos_____ después.

Objeto indirecto

1. —¿Puedes traerme tu plato? —No, no ___te___ lo puedo traer.
2. —¿Quieres mostrarle la carta? —Sí, voy a mostrár_____la ahora.
3. —¿Les serviste la carne? —No, no _____ la serví.
4. —¿Vas a leerle el menú? —No, no _____ lo voy a leer.
5. —¿Me recomiendas la langosta? —Sí, _____ la recomiendo.
6. —¿Cuándo vas a prepararnos la cena? —_____ la voy a preparar en una hora.

recursos
vText
CPA pp. 106–108
CH pp. 121–122
vhlcentral

Práctica

1 **Responder** Imagínate que trabajas de camarero/a en un restaurante. Responde a los pedidos (*requests*) de estos clientes usando pronombres.

modelo

Sra. Gómez: Una ensalada, por favor.
Sí, señora. Enseguida (Right away) se la traigo.

AYUDA

Here are some other useful expressions:
ahora mismo
right now
inmediatamente
immediately
¡A la orden!
At your service!
¡Ya voy!
I'm on my way!

1. Sres. López: La mantequilla, por favor.
2. Srta. Rivas: Los camarones, por favor.
3. Sra. Lugones: El pollo asado, por favor.
4. Tus compañeros/as de clase: Café, por favor.
5. Tu profesor(a) de español: Papas fritas, por favor.
6. Dra. González: La chuleta de cerdo, por favor.
7. Tu padre: Los champiñones, por favor.
8. Dr. Torres: La cuenta (*check*), por favor.

2 **¿Quién?** La señora Cevallos está planeando una cena. Se pregunta cómo va a resolver ciertas situaciones. En parejas, túrnense para decir lo que ella está pensando. Cambien los sustantivos subrayados por pronombres de objeto directo y hagan los otros cambios necesarios.

modelo

¡No tengo carne! ¿Quién va a traerme la carne del supermercado? (mi esposo)
Mi esposo va a traérmela./Mi esposo me la va a traer.

1. ¡Las invitaciones! ¿Quién les manda las invitaciones a los invitados (*guests*)? (mi hija)
2. No tengo tiempo de ir a la tienda. ¿Quién me puede comprar el vinagre? (mi hijo)
3. ¡Ay! No tengo suficientes platos (*plates*). ¿Quién puede prestarme los platos que necesito? (mi mamá)
4. Nos falta mantequilla. ¿Quién nos trae la mantequilla? (mi cuñada)
5. ¡Los entremeses! ¿Quién está preparándonos los entremeses? (Silvia y Renata)
6. No hay suficientes sillas. ¿Quién nos trae las sillas que faltan? (Héctor y Lorena)
7. No tengo tiempo de pedirle el aceite a Mónica. ¿Quién puede pedirle el aceite? (mi hijo)
8. ¿Quién va a servirles la cena a los invitados? (mis hijos)
9. Quiero poner buena música de fondo (*background*). ¿Quién me va a recomendar la música? (mi esposo)
10. ¡Los postres! ¿Quién va a preparar los postres para los invitados? (Sra. Villalba)

Practice more at vhlcentral.com.

Comunicación

3 **Contestar** Trabajen en parejas. Túrnense para hacer preguntas, usando las palabras interrogativas **¿Quién?** o **¿Cuándo?**, y para responderlas. Sigan el modelo.

modelo

nos enseña español

Estudiante 1: *¿Quién nos enseña español?*

Estudiante 2: *La profesora Camacho nos lo enseña.*

1. te puede explicar la tarea cuando no la entiendes
2. les vende el almuerzo a los estudiantes
3. vas a comprarme boletos para un concierto
4. te escribe mensajes de texto
5. nos prepara los entremeses
6. me vas a prestar tu computadora
7. te compró esa bebida
8. nos va a recomendar el menú de la cafetería
9. le enseñó español al/a la profesor(a)
10. me vas a mostrar tu casa o apartamento

4 **Preguntas** En parejas, túrnense para hacerse estas preguntas.

modelo

Estudiante 1: *¿Les prestas tu computadora a tus amigos?*

Estudiante 2: *No, no se la presto a mis amigos porque no son muy responsables.*

1. ¿Me prestas tu chaqueta? ¿Ya le prestaste tu chaqueta a otro/a amigo/a?
2. ¿Quién te presta dinero cuando lo necesitas?
3. ¿Les prestas dinero a tus amigos? ¿Por qué?
4. ¿Nos compras el almuerzo a mí y a los otros compañeros de clase?
5. ¿Les mandas correo electrónico a tus amigos? ¿Y a tu familia?
6. ¿Les das regalos a tus amigos? ¿Cuándo?
7. ¿Quién te va a preparar la cena esta noche?
8. ¿Quién te va a preparar el desayuno mañana?

Síntesis

5 **Regalos de Navidad** Tu profesor(a) les va a dar a ti y a un(a) compañero/a una parte de la lista de los regalos de Navidad (*Christmas*) que Berta pidió y los regalos que sus parientes le compraron. Conversen para completar sus listas.

modelo

Estudiante 1: *¿Qué le pidió Berta a su mamá?*

Estudiante 2: *Le pidió una computadora. ¿Se la compró?*

Estudiante 1: *Sí, se la compró.*

8.3 Comparisons

Tutorial

ANTE TODO Both Spanish and English use comparisons to indicate which of two people or things has a lesser, equal, or greater degree of a quality.

Comparisons

menos interesante	**más grande**	**tan sabroso como**
less interesting	*bigger*	*as delicious as*

Comparisons of inequality

- Comparisons of inequality are formed by placing **más** (*more*) or **menos** (*less*) before adjectives, adverbs, and nouns and **que** (*than*) after them.

más/menos + [*adjective* / *adverb* / *noun*] + **que**

- **¡Atención!** Note that while English has a comparative form for short adjectives (*tall**er***), such forms do not exist in Spanish (**más** alto).

adjectives

Los bistecs son **más caros que** el pollo.
Steaks are more expensive than chicken.

Estas uvas son **menos ricas que** esa pera.
These grapes are less tasty than that pear.

adverbs

Me acuesto **más tarde que** tú.
I go to bed later than you (do).

Luis se despierta **menos temprano que** yo.
Luis wakes up less early than I (do).

nouns

Juan prepara **más platos que** José.
Juan prepares more dishes than José (does).

Susana come **menos carne que** Enrique.
Susana eats less meat than Enrique (does).

- When the comparison involves a numerical expression, **de** is used before the number instead of **que**.

Hay más **de** cincuenta naranjas.
There are more than fifty oranges.

Llego en menos **de** diez minutos.
I'll be there in less than ten minutes.

- With verbs, this construction is used to make comparisons of inequality.

[*verb*] + **más/menos que**

Mis hermanos **comen más que** yo.
My brothers eat more than I (do).

Arturo **duerme menos que** su padre.
Arturo sleeps less than his father (does).

Comparisons of equality

- This construction is used to make comparisons of equality.

tan + [*adjective* / *adverb*] + **como**

tanto/a(s) + [*singular noun* / *plural noun*] + **como**

- **¡Atención!** Note that unlike **tan**, **tanto** acts as an adjective and therefore agrees in number and gender with the noun it modifies.

Estas uvas son **tan ricas como** aquéllas.
These grapes are as tasty as those ones (are).

Yo probé **tantos platos como** él.
I tried as many dishes as he did.

- **Tan** and **tanto** can also be used for emphasis, rather than to compare, with these meanings: **tan** *so*, **tanto** *so much*, **tantos/as** *so many*.

¡Tu almuerzo es **tan** grande!
Your lunch is so big!

¡Comes **tantas** manzanas!
You eat so many apples!

¡Comes **tanto**!
You eat so much!

¡Preparan **tantos** platos!
They prepare so many dishes!

- Comparisons of equality with verbs are formed by placing **tanto como** after the verb. Note that in this construction **tanto** does not change in number or gender.

[*verb*] + **tanto como**

Tú viajas **tanto como** mi tía.
You travel as much as my aunt (does).

Ellos hablan **tanto como** mis hermanas.
They talk as much as my sisters.

Comemos **tanto como** ustedes.
We eat as much as you (do).

No estudio **tanto como** Felipe.
I don't study as much as Felipe (does).

Irregular comparisons

- Some adjectives have irregular comparative forms.

Irregular comparative forms

Adjective		Comparative form	
bueno/a	*good*	**mejor**	*better*
malo/a	*bad*	**peor**	*worse*
grande	*big, grown, adult*	**mayor**	*bigger, older*
pequeño/a	*small*	**menor**	*smaller*
joven	*young*	**menor**	*younger*
viejo/a	*old*	**mayor**	*older*

- When **grande** and **pequeño/a** refer to age, the irregular comparative forms, **mayor** and **menor**, are used. However, when these adjectives refer to size, the regular forms, **más grande** and **más pequeño/a**, are used.

Yo soy **menor** que tú.
I'm younger than you.

Pedí un plato **más pequeño**.
I ordered a smaller dish.

Nuestro hijo es **mayor** que el hijo de los Andrade.
Our son is older than the Andrades' son.

El plato de Isabel es **más grande** que ése.
Isabel's dish is bigger than that one.

- The adverbs **bien** and **mal** have the same irregular comparative forms as the adjectives **bueno/a** and **malo/a**.

Julio nada **mejor** que los otros chicos.
Julio swims better than the other boys.

Ellas cantan **peor** que las otras chicas.
They sing worse than the other girls.

recursos
vText
CPA pp. 111–113
CH pp. 123–124
vhlcentral

¡INTÉNTALO! Escribe el equivalente de las palabras en inglés.

1. Ernesto mira más televisión ___que___ (*than*) Alberto.
2. Tú eres _____ (*less*) simpático que Federico.
3. La camarera sirve _____ (*as much*) carne como pescado.
4. Conozco _____ (*more*) restaurantes que tú.
5. No estudio _____ (*as much as*) tú.
6. ¿Sabes jugar al tenis tan bien _____ (*as*) tu hermana?
7. ¿Puedes beber _____ (*as many*) refrescos como yo?
8. Mis amigos parecen _____ (*as*) simpáticos como ustedes.

Práctica

1 **Escoger** Escoge la palabra correcta para comparar a dos hermanas muy diferentes. Haz los cambios necesarios.

1. Lucila es más alta y más bonita _____ Tita. (de, más, menos, que)
2. Tita es más delgada porque come _____ verduras que su hermana. (de, más, menos, que)
3. Lucila es más _____ que Tita porque es alegre. (listo, simpático, bajo)
4. A Tita le gusta comer en casa. Va a _____ restaurantes que su hermana. (más, menos, que) Es tímida, pero activa. Hace _____ ejercicio (*exercise*) que su hermana. (más, tanto, menos) Todos los días toma más _____ cinco vasos (*glasses*) de agua mineral. (que, tan, de)
5. Lucila come muchas papas fritas y se preocupa _____ que Tita por comer frutas. (de, más, menos) ¡Son _____ diferentes! Pero se llevan (*they get along*) muy bien. (como, tan, tanto)

2 **Emparejar** Compara a Mario y a Luis, los novios de Lucila y Tita, completando las oraciones de la columna A con las palabras o frases de la columna B.

A	B
1. Mario es _____ como Luis.	tantas
2. Mario viaja tanto _____ Luis.	diferencia
3. Luis toma _____ clases de cocina (*cooking*) como Mario.	tan interesante
4. Luis habla _____ tan bien como Mario.	amigos extranjeros
5. Mario tiene tantos _____ como Luis.	como
6. ¡Qué casualidad (*coincidence*)! Mario y Luis también son hermanos, pero no hay tanta _____ entre ellos como entre Lucila y Tita.	francés

3 **Oraciones** Combina elementos de las columnas A, B y C para hacer comparaciones. Escribe oraciones completas.

modelo

George Clooney tiene tantos autos como el presidente de los EE.UU.
Emma Stone es menor que George Clooney.

A	B	C
la comida japonesa	costar	la gente de Montreal
el fútbol	saber	la música *country*
George Clooney	ser	el brócoli
el pollo	tener	el presidente de los EE.UU.
la gente de Vancouver	¿?	la comida italiana
la primera dama (*lady*) de los EE.UU.		el hockey
las escuelas privadas		Emma Stone
las espinacas		las escuelas públicas
la música rap		la carne de res

Practice more at vhlcentral.com.

Comunicación

4 **Intercambiar** En parejas, hagan comparaciones sobre diferentes cosas. Pueden usar las sugerencias de la lista u otras ideas.

AYUDA

You can use these adjectives in your comparisons:
bonito/a
caro/a
elegante
interesante
inteligente

modelo

Estudiante 1: Los pollos de *Pollitos del Corral* son muy ricos.
Estudiante 2: Pues yo creo que los pollos de *Rostipollos* son tan buenos como los pollos de *Pollitos del Corral.*
Estudiante 1: Mmm... no tienen tanta mantequilla como los pollos de *Pollitos del Corral.* Tienes razón. Son muy sabrosos.

restaurantes en tu ciudad/pueblo
cafés en tu comunidad
tiendas en tu ciudad/pueblo

periódicos en tu ciudad/pueblo
revistas favoritas
libros favoritos

comidas favoritas
los profesores
las clases que toman

5 **Conversar** En grupos, túrnense para hacer comparaciones entre ustedes mismos (*yourselves*) y una persona de cada categoría de la lista.

- una persona de tu familia
- un(a) amigo/a especial
- una persona famosa

Síntesis

6 **La familia López** En grupos, túrnense para hablar de Sara, Sabrina, Cristina, Ricardo y David y hacer comparaciones entre ellos.

modelo

Estudiante 1: Sara es tan alta como Sabrina.
Estudiante 2: Sí, pero David es más alto que ellas.
Estudiante 3: En mi opinión, él es guapo también.

8.4 Superlatives

Tutorial

ANTE TODO Both English and Spanish use superlatives to express the highest or lowest degree of a quality.

el/la mejor	**el/la peor**	**el/la más alto/a**
the best	*the worst*	*the tallest*

- This construction is used to form superlatives. Note that the noun is always preceded by a definite article and that **de** is equivalent to the English *in* or *of*.

el/la/los/las + [*noun*] + **más/menos** + [*adjective*] + **de**

- The noun can be omitted if the person, place, or thing referred to is clear.

¿El restaurante Las Delicias?
Es **el más elegante** de la ciudad.
The restaurant Las Delicias?
It's the most elegant (one) in the city.

Recomiendo el pollo asado.
Es **el más sabroso** del menú.
I recommend the roast chicken.
It's the most delicious on the menu.

- Here are some irregular superlative forms.

Irregular superlatives

Adjective		Superlative form	
bueno/a	*good*	**el/la mejor**	*(the) best*
malo/a	*bad*	**el/la peor**	*(the) worst*
grande	*big, grown, adult*	**el/la mayor**	*(the) biggest (the) oldest*
pequeño/a	*small*	**el/la menor**	*(the) smallest*
joven	*young*	**el/la menor**	*(the) youngest*
viejo/a	*old*	**el/la mayor**	*(the) oldest*

- The absolute superlative is equivalent to *extremely, super,* or *very*. To form the absolute superlative of most adjectives and adverbs, drop the final vowel, if there is one, and add **-ísimo/a(s)**.

malo → mal- → malísimo
¡El bistec está **malísimo**!

mucho → much- → muchísimo
Comes **muchísimo**.

- Note these spelling changes.

rico → riquísimo **largo → larguísimo** **feliz → felicísimo**
fácil → facilísimo **joven → jovencísimo** **trabajador → trabajadorcísimo**

¡ATENCIÓN!
While **más** alone means *more*, after **el, la, los,** or **las**, it means *most*. Likewise, **menos** can mean *less* or *least*.
Es **el café más rico del** país.
It's the most delicious coffee in the country.
Es **el menú menos caro de** todos éstos.
It is the least expensive menu of all of these.

CONSULTA
The rule you learned in **Estructura 8.3** (p. 283) regarding the use of **mayor/menor** with age, but not with size, is also true with superlative forms.

¡INTÉNTALO! Escribe el equivalente de las palabras en inglés.

1. Marisa es la más inteligente (*the most intelligent*) de todas.
2. Ricardo y Tomás son _____ (*the least boring*) de la fiesta.
3. Miguel y Antonio son _____ (*the worst*) estudiantes de la clase.
4. Mi profesor de biología es _____ (*the oldest*) de la escuela.

recursos
vText
CPA pp. 114–116
CH pp. 125–126
vhlcentral

Práctica y Comunicación

1 **El más...** Responde a las preguntas afirmativamente. Usa las palabras entre paréntesis.

modelo

El cuarto está sucísimo, ¿no? (casa)
Sí, es el más sucio de la casa.

1. El almacén Velasco es buenísimo, ¿no? (centro comercial)
2. La silla de tu madre es comodísima, ¿no? (casa)
3. Ángela y Julia están nerviosísimas por el examen, ¿no? (clase)
4. Jorge es jovencísimo, ¿no? (mis amigos)

recursos vText CPA p. 117

2 **Completar** Tu profesor(a) te va a dar una hoja de actividades con descripciones de José Valenzuela Carranza y Ana Orozco Hoffman. Completa las oraciones con las palabras de la lista.

altísima	del	mayor	peor
atlética	guapísimo	mejor	periodista
bajo	la	menor	trabajadorcísimo
de	más	Orozco	Valenzuela

1. José tiene 22 años; es el _____ y el más _____ de su familia. Es _____ y _____. Es el mejor _____ de la ciudad y el _____ jugador de baloncesto.
2. Ana es la más _____ y _____ mejor jugadora de baloncesto del estado. Es la _____ de sus hermanos (tiene 28 años) y es _____. Estudió la profesión _____ difícil _____ todas: medicina.
3. Jorge es el _____ jugador de videojuegos de su familia.
4. Mauricio es el menor de la familia _____.
5. El abuelo es el _____ de todos los miembros de la familia Valenzuela.
6. Fifí es la perra más antipática _____ mundo.

3 **Superlativos** Trabajen en parejas para hacer comparaciones. Usen superlativos.

modelo

Angelina Jolie, Bill Gates, Jimmy Carter
Estudiante 1: *Bill Gates es el más rico de los tres.*
Estudiante 2: *Sí, ¡es riquísimo! Y Jimmy Carter es el mayor de los tres.*

1. Guatemala, Argentina, España
2. Jaguar, Prius, Smart
3. la comida mexicana, la comida francesa, la comida árabe
4. Amy Adams, Meryl Streep, Ellen Page
5. Ciudad de México, Buenos Aires, Nueva York
6. *Don Quijote de la Mancha, Cien años de soledad, Como agua para chocolate*
7. el fútbol americano, el golf, el béisbol
8. las películas románticas, las películas de acción, las películas cómicas

Practice more at vhlcentral.com.

SUBJECT Javier CONJUGATED FORM empiezo Main clause Dudan

Recapitulación

Diagnostics

Completa estas actividades para repasar los conceptos de gramática que aprendiste en esta lección.

1 **Completar** Completa la tabla con la forma correcta del pretérito. 18 pts.

Infinitive	yo	usted	ellos
dormir			
servir			
vestirse			

2 **La cena** Completa la conversación con el pretérito de los verbos. 14 pts.

PAULA ¡Hola, Daniel! ¿Qué tal el fin de semana?

DANIEL Muy bien. Marta y yo (1) _____ (conseguir) hacer muchas cosas, pero lo mejor fue la cena del sábado.

PAULA Ah, ¿sí? ¿Adónde fueron?

DANIEL Al restaurante Vistahermosa. Es elegante, así que (nosotros) (2) _____ (vestirse) bien.

PAULA Y ¿qué platos (3) _____ (pedir, ustedes)?

DANIEL Yo (4) _____ (pedir) camarones y Marta (5) _____ (preferir) el pollo. Y al final, el camarero nos (6) _____ (servir) flan.

PAULA ¡Qué rico!

DANIEL Sí. Pero después de la cena Marta no (7) _____ (sentirse) bien.

3 **Camareros** Genaro y Úrsula son camareros en un restaurante. Usa pronombres para completar la conversación que tienen con su jefe. 8 pts.

JEFE Úrsula, ¿le ofreciste agua fría al cliente de la mesa 22?

ÚRSULA Sí, (1) _____ de inmediato.

JEFE Genaro, ¿los clientes de la mesa 5 te pidieron ensaladas?

GENARO Sí, (2) _____.

ÚRSULA Genaro, ¿recuerdas si ya me mostraste los vinos nuevos?

GENARO Sí, ya (3) _____.

JEFE Genaro, ¿van a pagarte la cuenta (*bill*) los clientes de la mesa 5?

GENARO Sí, (4) _____ ahora mismo.

RESUMEN GRAMATICAL

8.1 Preterite of stem-changing verbs *p. 274*

servir	dormir
serví	dormí
serviste	dormiste
sirvió	durmió
servimos	dormimos
servisteis	dormisteis
sirvieron	durmieron

8.2 Double object pronouns *pp. 277–278*

Indirect Object Pronouns: **me, te, le (se), nos, os, les (se)**

Direct Object Pronouns: **lo, la, los, las**

Le escribí la carta. → Se la escribí.

Nos van a servir los platos. → Nos los van a servir./ Van a servírnoslos.

8.3 Comparisons *pp. 281–283*

Comparisons of inequality

más/menos +	*adj., adv., n.*	**+ que**
verb + **más/menos + que**		

Comparisons of equality

tan +	*adj., adv.*	**+ como**
tanto/a(s) +	*noun*	**+ como**
verb + **tanto como**		

Irregular comparative forms

bueno/a	**mejor**
malo/a	**peor**
grande	**mayor**
pequeño/a	**menor**
joven	**menor**
viejo/a	**mayor**

8.4 Superlatives *p. 286*

el/la/ los/las +	*noun*	+ más/ menos +	*adjective*	+ de

▸ Irregular superlatives follow the same pattern as irregular comparatives.

4 **El menú** Observa el menú y sus características. Completa las oraciones basándote en los elementos dados. Usa comparativos y superlativos. **14 pts.**

Ensaladas	*Precio*	*Calorías*
Ensalada de tomates	$9.00	170
Ensalada de mariscos	$12.99	325
Ensalada de zanahorias	$9.00	200
Platos principales		
Pollo con champiñones	$13.00	495
Cerdo con papas	$10.50	725
Atún con esparrágos	$18.95	495

1. ensalada de mariscos / otras ensaladas / costar
   La ensalada de mariscos _____ las otras ensaladas.
2. pollo con champiñones / cerdo con papas / calorías
   El pollo con champiñones tiene _____ el cerdo con papas.
3. atún con espárragos / pollo con champiñones / calorías
   El atún con espárragos tiene _____ el pollo con champiñones.
4. ensalada de tomates / ensalada de zanahorias / caro
   La ensalada de tomates es _____ la ensalada de zanahorias.
5. cerdo con papas / platos principales / caro
   El cerdo con papas es _____ los platos principales.
6. ensalada de zanahorias / ensalada de tomates / costar
   La ensalada de zanahorias _____ la ensalada de tomates.
7. ensalada de mariscos / ensaladas / caro
   La ensalada de mariscos es _____ las ensaladas.

5 **Dos restaurantes** ¿Cuál es el mejor restaurante que conoces? ¿Y el peor? Escribe un párrafo de por lo menos (*at least*) seis oraciones donde expliques por qué piensas así. Puedes hablar de la calidad de la comida, el ambiente, los precios, el servicio, etc. **46 pts.**

6 **Adivinanza** Completa la adivinanza y adivina la respuesta. **¡4 puntos EXTRA!**

"En el campo yo nací°,
mis hermanos son
los _____ (*garlic, pl.*),
y aquél que llora° por mí
me está partiendo°
en pedazos°".
¿Quién soy? _____

nací *was born* llora *cries* partiendo *cutting* pedazos *pieces*

Lectura

Audio: Reading
Additional Reading

Antes de leer

Estrategia

Reading for the main idea

As you know, you can learn a great deal about a reading selection by looking at the format and looking for cognates, titles, and subtitles. You can skim to get the gist of the reading selection and scan it for specific information. Reading for the main idea is another useful strategy; it involves locating the topic sentences of each paragraph to determine the author's purpose for writing a particular piece. Topic sentences can provide clues about the content of each paragraph, as well as the general organization of the reading. Your choice of which reading strategies to use will depend on the style and format of each reading selection.

Examinar el texto

En esta sección tenemos dos textos diferentes. ¿Qué estrategias puedes usar para leer la crítica culinaria°? ¿Cuáles son las apropiadas para familiarizarte con el menú? Utiliza las estrategias más eficaces° para cada texto. ¿Qué tienen en común? ¿Qué tipo de comida sirven en el restaurante?

Identificar la idea principal

Lee la primera oración de cada párrafo de la crítica culinaria del restaurante **La feria del maíz.** Apunta° el tema principal de cada párrafo. Luego lee todo el primer párrafo. ¿Crees que el restaurante le gustó al autor de la crítica culinaria? ¿Por qué? Ahora lee la crítica entera. En tu opinión, ¿cuál es la idea principal de la crítica? ¿Por qué la escribió el autor? Compara tus opiniones con las de un(a) compañero/a.

crítica culinaria *restaurant review* eficaces *effective* Apunta *Jot down*

recursos

vText CH pp. 127–128 vhlcentral

MENÚ

Entremeses

Tortilla servida con
• Ajiaceite (chile, aceite) • Ajicomino (chile, comino)

Pan tostado servido con
• Queso frito a la pimienta • Salsa de ajo y mayonesa

Sopas

• Tomate • Cebolla • Verduras • Pollo y huevo
• Carne de res • Mariscos

Entradas

Tomaticán
(tomate, papas, maíz, chile, arvejas y zanahorias)

Tamales
(maíz, azúcar, ajo, cebolla)

Frijoles enchilados
(frijoles negros, carne de cerdo o de res, arroz, chile)

Chilaquil
(tortilla de maíz, queso, hierbas y chile)

Tacos
(tortillas, pollo, verduras y salsa)

Cóctel de mariscos
(camarones, langosta, vinagre, sal, pimienta, aceite)

Postres°

• Plátanos caribeños • Cóctel de frutas al ron°
• Uvate (uvas, azúcar de caña y ron) • Flan napolitano
• Helado° de piña y naranja • Pastel° de yogur

Después de leer

Preguntas

En parejas, contesten estas preguntas sobre la crítica culinaria de **La feria del maíz.**

1. ¿Quién es el dueño y chef de **La feria del maíz**?
2. ¿Qué tipo de comida se sirve en el restaurante?
3. ¿Cuál es el problema con el servicio?
4. ¿Cómo es el ambiente del restaurante?
5. ¿Qué comidas probó el autor?
6. ¿Quieren ir ustedes al restaurante **La feria del maíz**? ¿Por qué?

23F

Gastronomía

Por Eduardo Fernández

La feria del maíz

Sobresaliente°. En el nuevo restaurante **La feria del maíz** va a encontrar la perfecta combinación entre la comida tradicional y el encanto° de la vieja ciudad de Antigua. Ernesto Sandoval, antiguo jefe de cocina° del famoso restaurante **El fogón**, está teniendo mucho éxito° en su nueva aventura culinaria.

El gerente°, el experimentado José Sierra, controla a la perfección la calidad del servicio. El camarero que me atendió esa noche fue muy amable en todo momento. Sólo hay que comentar que, debido al éxito inmediato de **La feria del maíz**, se necesitan más camareros para atender a los clientes de una forma más eficaz. En esta ocasión, el mesero se tomó unos veinte minutos en traerme la bebida.

La feria del maíz
13 calle 4-41 Zona 1
La Antigua, Guatemala
2329912

lunes a sábado
10:30am-11:30pm
domingo 10:00am-10:00pm

Comida 🍴🍴🍴🍴🍴
Servicio 🍴🍴🍴
Ambiente 🍴🍴🍴🍴
Precio 🍴🍴🍴

Afortunadamente, no me importó mucho la espera entre plato y plato, pues el ambiente es tan agradable que me sentí como en casa. El restaurante mantiene el estilo colonial de Antigua. Por dentro°, es elegante y rústico a la vez. Cuando el tiempo lo permite, se puede comer también en el patio, donde hay muchas flores.

El servicio de camareros y el ambiente agradable del local pasan a un segundo plano cuando llega la comida, de una calidad extraordinaria. Las tortillas de casa se sirven con un ajiaceite delicioso. La sopa de mariscos es excelente y los tamales, pues, tengo que confesar que son mejores que los de mi abuelita. También recomiendo los tacos de pollo, servidos con un mole buenísimo. De postre, don Ernesto me preparó su especialidad, unos plátanos caribeños sabrosísimos.

Los precios pueden parecer altos° para una comida tradicional, pero la calidad de los productos con que se cocinan los platos y el exquisito ambiente de **La feria del maíz** garantizan° una experiencia inolvidable°.

Bebidas

- Cerveza negra
- Chilate (bebida de maíz, chile y cacao)
- Jugos de fruta
- Agua mineral
- Té helado
- Vino tinto/blanco
- Ron

Postres *Desserts* ron *rum* Helado *Ice cream* Pastel *Cake* Sobresaliente *Outstanding* encanto *charm* jefe de cocina *head chef* éxito *success* gerente *manager* Por dentro *Inside* altos *high* garantizan *guarantee* inolvidable *unforgettable*

Un(a) guía turístico/a

Tú eres un(a) guía turístico/a en Guatemala. Estás en el restaurante **La feria del maíz** con un grupo de turistas norteamericanos. Ellos no hablan español y quieren pedir de comer, pero necesitan tu ayuda. Lee nuevamente el menú e indica qué error comete cada turista.

1. La señora Johnson es diabética y no puede comer azúcar. Pide sopa de verduras y tamales. No pide nada de postre.
2. Los señores Petit son vegetarianos y piden sopa de tomate, frijoles enchilados y plátanos caribeños.
3. El señor Smith, que es alérgico al chocolate, pide tortilla servida con ajiaceite, chilaquil y chilate para beber.
4. La adorable hija del señor Smith tiene sólo cuatro años y le gustan mucho las verduras y las frutas naturales. Su papá le pide tomaticán y un cóctel de frutas.
5. La señorita Jackson está a dieta y pide uvate, flan napolitano y helado.

Practice more at vhlcentral.com.

Escritura

Estrategia

Expressing and supporting opinions

Written reviews are just one of the many kinds of writing which require you to state your opinions. In order to convince your reader to take your opinions seriously, it is important to support them as thoroughly as possible. Details, facts, examples, and other forms of evidence are necessary. In a restaurant review, for example, it is not enough just to rate the food, service, and atmosphere. Readers will want details about the dishes you ordered, the kind of service you received, and the type of atmosphere you encountered. If you were writing a concert or album review, what kinds of details might your readers expect to find?

It is easier to include details that support your opinions if you plan ahead. Before going to a place or event that you are planning to review, write a list of questions that your readers might ask. Decide which aspects of the experience you are going to rate and list the details that will help you decide upon a rating. You can then organize these lists into a questionnaire and a rating sheet. Bring these forms with you to help you make your opinions and to remind you of the kinds of information you need to gather in order to support those opinions. Later, these forms will help you organize your review into logical categories. They can also provide the details and other evidence you need to convince your readers of your opinions.

recursos
vText
CPA pp. 118–119
CH pp. 129–130
vhlcentral

Tema

Escribir una crítica

Escribe una crítica culinaria° sobre un restaurante local para el periódico de la escuela. Clasifica el restaurante, dándole de una a cinco estrellas°, y anota tus recomendaciones para futuros clientes del restaurante. Incluye tus opiniones acerca de°:

- La comida
  ¿Qué tipo de comida es? ¿Qué tipo de ingredientes usan?
  ¿Es de buena calidad? ¿Cuál es el mejor plato? ¿Y el peor?
  ¿Quién es el/la chef?
- El servicio
  ¿Es necesario esperar mucho para conseguir una mesa?
  ¿Tienen los camareros un buen conocimiento del menú?
  ¿Atienden° a los clientes con rapidez° y cortesía?
- El ambiente
  ¿Cómo es la decoración del restaurante?
  ¿Es el ambiente informal o elegante?
  ¿Hay música o algún tipo de entretenimiento°?
  ¿Hay un balcón? ¿Un patio?
- Información práctica
  ¿Cómo son los precios?
  ¿Se aceptan tarjetas de crédito?
  ¿Cuál es la dirección° y el número de teléfono?
  ¿Quién es el/la dueño/a? ¿El/La gerente?

crítica culinaria *restaurant review* estrellas *stars* acerca de *about* Atienden *They take care of* rapidez *speed* entretenimiento *entertainment* dirección *address*

Escuchar

Audio

Estrategia

Jotting down notes as you listen

Jotting down notes while you listen to a conversation in Spanish can help you keep track of the important points or details. It will help you to focus actively on comprehension rather than on remembering what you have heard.

To practice this strategy, you will now listen to a paragraph. Jot down the main points you hear.

Preparación

Mira la foto. ¿Dónde están estas personas y qué hacen? ¿Sobre qué crees que están hablando?

Ahora escucha

Rosa y Roberto están en un restaurante. Escucha la conversación entre ellos y la camarera y toma nota de cuáles son los especiales del día, qué pidieron y qué bebidas se mencionan.

Especiales del día

Entremeses

_____

Plato principal

_____

_____

_____

¿Qué pidieron?

Roberto

_____

Rosa

_____

Bebidas

_____

_____

recursos

vText vhlcentral

Comprensión

Seleccionar

Usa tus notas para seleccionar la opción correcta para completar cada oración.

1. Dos de los mejores platos del restaurante son _____.
   a. los entremeses del día y el cerdo
   b. el salmón y el arroz con pollo
   c. la carne y el arroz con pollo
2. La camarera _____.
   a. los lleva a su mesa, les muestra el menú y les sirve el postre
   b. les habla de los especiales del día, les recomienda unos platos y ellos deciden qué van a comer
   c. les lleva unas bebidas, les recomienda unos platos y les sirve pan
3. Roberto va a comer _____ Rosa.
   a. tantos platos como
   b. más platos que
   c. menos platos que

Preguntas

En grupos de tres o cuatro, respondan a las preguntas: ¿Conocen los platos que Rosa y Roberto pidieron? ¿Conocen platos con los mismos ingredientes? ¿En qué son diferentes o similares? ¿Cuál les gusta más? ¿Por qué?

Practice more at vhlcentral.com.

en pantalla

Video: TV Clip

Anuncio de Sopas Roa

Me voy de esta casa.

Preparación

Contesta las preguntas en español.

1. ¿Normalmente qué comes para el desayuno? ¿Y qué comes para el almuerzo y la cena?
2. ¿Qué comen usualmente los niños? ¿En qué se diferencian las comidas de los niños y las de los adultos? ¿Por qué?

La sopa

La sopa es un plato muy importante en las cocinas° del mundo hispano. Se pueden tomar° frías, como el famoso gazpacho español, a base de tomate y otras verduras y servida totalmente líquida. La mayoría se sirven calientes, como el pozole de México, un plato precolombino preparado con nixtamal°, cerdo, chiles y otras especias°. Otra sopa de origen indígena es la changua, de la región andina central de Colombia. Aunque° las sopas normalmente forman parte del almuerzo, la changua siempre se toma en el desayuno: se hace con agua, leche, huevo y cilantro.

cocinas *cuisines* tomar *to eat (soup)* nixtamal *hominy* especias *spices*
Aunque *Although*

Vocabulario útil

bajar	*to descend*
la escalera	*staircase*
lo que yo quiera	*whatever I want*
sabor marinero	*seafood flavor*

Comprensión

Ordena cronológicamente estas oraciones.

_____ a. El niño abre la puerta.
_____ b. El niño decide almorzar.
_____ c. El niño baja la escalera con una maleta.
_____ d. El niño se va a lavar las manos.
_____ e. La madre dice que la sopa está servida.

Conversación

Contesta estas preguntas con un(a) compañero/a. ¿Con qué frecuencia comes sopa? ¿Cuál es tu sopa favorita? ¿Quién la prepara o dónde la compras? ¿Qué ingredientes tiene? ¿Con qué se sirve? ¿Cómo la prefieres, caliente o fría? ¿La tomas en el almuerzo o en la cena? ¿En invierno o en verano?

Aplicación

Escoge una de tus recetas (*recipes*) favoritas para compartir con un grupo de compañeros/as. Explica al grupo por qué escogiste esta receta (¿Es tradicional en tu familia? ¿La encontraste al viajar o al leer algo interesante?) y cuáles son los ingredientes que te gustan. Prepara un póster o una presentación digital de tu receta: dale un título a la receta, identifica e ilustra los ingredientes, y escribe un párrafo para explicar por qué compartes esta receta con el grupo.

Practice more at vhlcentral.com.

recursos vText vhlcentral

Video: *Flash cultura*

Los países hispanos tienen una producción muy abundante de frutas y verduras. Por eso, en los hogares° hispanos se cocina° con productos frescos° más que con alimentos° que vienen en latas° o frascos°. Las salsas mexicanas, el gazpacho español y el sancocho colombiano, por ejemplo, deben prepararse con ingredientes frescos para que mantengan° su sabor° auténtico. Actualmente, en los Estados Unidos está creciendo el interés en cocinar con productos frescos y orgánicos. Cada vez hay más mercados° donde los agricultores° pueden vender sus frutas y verduras directamente° al público. En este episodio de *Flash cultura* vas a ver algunos ingredientes típicos de la comida hispana.

Vocabulario útil

blanda	*soft*
cocinar	*to cook*
dura	*hard*
¿Está lista para ordenar?	*Are you ready to order?*
el plato	*dish (in a meal)*
pruébala	*try it, taste it*
las ventas	*sales*

Preparación

¿Probaste alguna vez comida latina? ¿La compraste en un supermercado o fuiste a un restaurante? ¿Qué plato(s) probaste? ¿Te gustó?

¿Cierto o falso?

Indica si cada oración es **cierta** o **falsa**.

1. En Los Ángeles hay comida de países latinoamericanos y de España.
2. Leticia explica que la tortilla del taco americano es blanda y la del taco mexicano es dura.
3. Las ventas de salsa son bajas en los Estados Unidos.
4. Leticia fue a un restaurante ecuatoriano.
5. Leticia probó Inca Kola en un supermercado.

hogares *homes* se cocina *they cook* frescos *fresh* alimentos *foods* latas *cans* frascos *jars* para que mantengan *so that they keep* sabor *flavor* mercados *markets* agricultores *farmers* directamente *directly* mostrará *will show*

La comida latina

La mejor comida latina no sólo se encuentra en los grandes restaurantes.

Marta nos mostrará° algunos de los platos de la comida mexicana.

... hay más lugares donde podemos comprar productos hispanos.

Practice more at **vhlcentral.com.**

recursos

vText CPA pp. 120–121 vhlcentral

Guatemala

Video: *Panorama cultural*
Interactive Map

El país en cifras

- **Área:** 108.890 km² (42.042 millas²), *un poco más pequeño que Tennessee*
- **Población:** 14.647.000
- **Capital:** Ciudad de Guatemala—1.075.000
- **Ciudades principales:** Quetzaltenango, Escuintla, Mazatenango, Puerto Barrios
- **Moneda:** quetzal
- **Idiomas:** español (oficial), lenguas mayas, xinca, garífuna

El español es la lengua de un 60 por ciento° de la población; el otro 40 por ciento tiene como lengua materna el xinca, el garífuna o, en su mayoría°, una de las lenguas mayas (cakchiquel, quiché y kekchícomo, entre otras). Una palabra que las lenguas mayas tienen en común es ixim, *que significa "maíz", un cultivo° de mucha importancia en estas culturas.*

Bandera de Guatemala

Guatemaltecos célebres

- **Carlos Mérida,** pintor (1891–1984)
- **Miguel Ángel Asturias,** escritor (1899–1974)
- **Margarita Carrera,** poeta y ensayista (1929–)
- **Rigoberta Menchú Tum,** activista (1959–), Premio Nobel de la Paz° en 1992
- **Jaime Viñals Massanet,** montañista (1966–)

por ciento *percent* en su mayoría *most of them* cultivo *crop*
Paz *Peace* telas *fabrics* tinte *dye* aplastados *crushed*
hace... destiñan *keeps the colors from running*

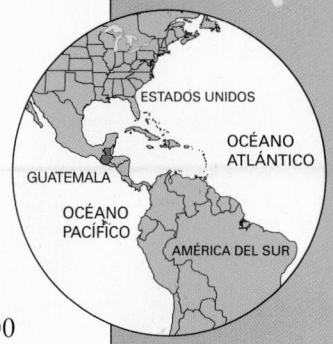

Palacio Nacional de la Cultura en la Ciudad de Guatemala

Mujeres indígenas preparando tortillas

MÉXICO
Sierra de Lacandón
Río Usumacinta
Lago Petén Itzá
Río de la Pasión
BELICE
Lago de Izabal
Sierra de las Minas
Quetzaltenango
Sierra Madre
Río Motagua
Lago de Atitlán
Guatemala
Mazatenango
Antigua Guatemala
Escuintla
EL SALVADOR
Océano Pacífico

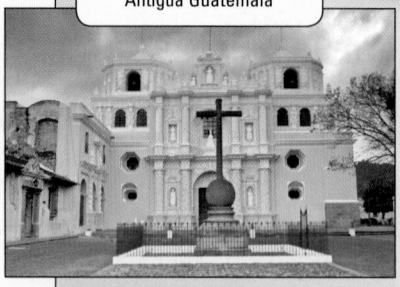

Iglesia de la Merced en Antigua Guatemala

recursos
vText CPA pp. 122–125 vhlcentral

¡Increíble pero cierto!

¿Qué "ingrediente" secreto se encuentra en las telas° tradicionales de Guatemala? ¡El mosquito! El excepcional tinte° de estas telas es producto de una combinación de flores y de mosquitos aplastados°. El insecto hace que los colores no se destiñan°. Quizás es por esto que los artesanos representan la figura del mosquito en muchas de sus telas.

Ciudades • Antigua Guatemala

Antigua Guatemala fue fundada en 1543. Fue una capital de gran importancia hasta 1773, cuando un terremoto° la destruyó. Sin embargo, conserva el carácter original de su arquitectura y hoy es uno de los centros turísticos del país. Su celebración de la Semana Santa° es, para muchas personas, la más importante del hemisferio.

Naturaleza • El quetzal

El quetzal simbolizó la libertad para los antiguos° mayas porque creían° que este pájaro° no podía° vivir en cautiverio°. Hoy el quetzal es el símbolo nacional. El pájaro da su nombre a la moneda nacional y aparece también en los billetes° del país. Desafortunadamente, está en peligro° de extinción. Para su protección, el gobierno mantiene una reserva ecológica especial.

Historia • Los mayas

Desde 1500 a.C. hasta 900 d.C., los mayas habitaron gran parte de lo que ahora es Guatemala. Su civilización fue muy avanzada. Los mayas fueron arquitectos y constructores de pirámides, templos y observatorios. También descubrieron° y usaron el cero antes que los europeos, e inventaron un calendario complejo° y preciso.

Artesanía • La ropa tradicional

La ropa tradicional de los guatemaltecos se llama *huipil* y muestra el amor° de la cultura maya por la naturaleza. Ellos se inspiran en las flores°, plantas y animales para crear sus diseños° de colores vivos° y formas geométricas. El diseño y los colores de cada *huipil* indican el pueblo de origen y a veces también el sexo y la edad° de la persona que lo lleva.

¿Qué aprendiste? Responde a cada pregunta con una oración completa.

1. ¿Qué significa la palabra *ixim*?
2. ¿Quién es Rigoberta Menchú?
3. ¿Qué pájaro representa a Guatemala?
4. ¿Qué simbolizó el quetzal para los mayas?
5. ¿Cuál es la moneda nacional de Guatemala?
6. ¿De qué fueron arquitectos los mayas?
7. ¿Qué celebración de la Antigua Guatemala es la más importante del hemisferio para muchas personas?
8. ¿Qué descubrieron los mayas antes que los europeos?
9. ¿Qué muestra la ropa tradicional de los guatemaltecos?
10. ¿Qué indica un *huipil* con su diseño y sus colores?

Conexión Internet Investiga estos temas en **vhlcentral.com.**

1. Busca información sobre Rigoberta Menchú. ¿De dónde es? ¿Qué libros publicó? ¿Por qué es famosa?
2. Estudia un sitio arqueológico de Guatemala para aprender más sobre los mayas y prepara un breve informe para tu clase.

Practice more at vhlcentral.com.

terremoto *earthquake* Semana Santa *Holy Week* antiguos *ancient* creían *they believed* pájaro *bird* no podía *couldn't* cautiverio *captivity* los billetes *bills* peligro *danger* descubrieron *they discovered* complejo *complex* amor *love* flores *flowers* diseños *designs* vivos *bright* edad *age*

Las comidas

el/la camarero/a	*waiter/waitress*
la comida	*food; meal*
el/la dueño/a	*owner; landlord*
el menú	*menu*
la sección de (no) fumar	*(non) smoking section*
el almuerzo	*lunch*
la cena	*dinner*
el desayuno	*breakfast*
los entremeses	*hors d'oeuvres; appetizers*
el plato (principal)	*(main) dish*
delicioso/a	*delicious*
rico/a	*tasty; delicious*
sabroso/a	*tasty; delicious*

Las frutas

la banana	*banana*
las frutas	*fruits*
el limón	*lemon*
la manzana	*apple*
el melocotón	*peach*
la naranja	*orange*
la pera	*pear*
la uva	*grape*

Las verduras

las arvejas	*peas*
la cebolla	*onion*
el champiñón	*mushroom*
la ensalada	*salad*
los espárragos	*asparagus*
los frijoles	*beans*
la lechuga	*lettuce*
el maíz	*corn*
las papas/patatas (fritas)	*(fried) potatoes; French fries*
el tomate	*tomato*
las verduras	*vegetables*
la zanahoria	*carrot*

La carne y el pescado

el atún	*tuna*
el bistec	*steak*
los camarones	*shrimp*
la carne	*meat*
la carne de res	*beef*
la chuleta (de cerdo)	*(pork) chop*
la hamburguesa	*hamburger*
el jamón	*ham*
la langosta	*lobster*
los mariscos	*shellfish*
el pavo	*turkey*
el pescado	*fish*
el pollo (asado)	*(roast) chicken*
la salchicha	*sausage*
el salmón	*salmon*

Otras comidas

el aceite	*oil*
el ajo	*garlic*
el arroz	*rice*
el azúcar	*sugar*
los cereales	*cereal; grains*
el huevo	*egg*
la mantequilla	*butter*
la margarina	*margarine*
la mayonesa	*mayonnaise*
el pan (tostado)	*(toasted) bread*
la pimienta	*black pepper*
el queso	*cheese*
la sal	*salt*
el sándwich	*sandwich*
la sopa	*soup*
el vinagre	*vinegar*
el yogur	*yogurt*

Las bebidas

el agua (mineral)	*(mineral) water*
la bebida	*drink*
el café	*coffee*
la cerveza	*beer*
el jugo (de fruta)	*(fruit) juice*
la leche	*milk*
el refresco	*soft drink; soda*
el té (helado)	*(iced) tea*
el vino (blanco/tinto)	*(white/red) wine*

Verbos

escoger	*to choose*
merendar (e:ie)	*to snack*
morir (o:ue)	*to die*
pedir (e:i)	*to order (food)*
probar (o:ue)	*to taste; to try*
recomendar (e:ie)	*to recommend*
saber (a)	*to taste (like)*
servir (e:i)	*to serve*

Las comparaciones

como	*like; as*
más de *(+ number)*	*more than*
más... que	*more... than*
menos de *(+ number)*	*fewer than*
menos... que	*less... than*
tan... como	*as... as*
tantos/as... como	*as many... as*
tanto... como	*as much... as*
el/la mayor	*the oldest*
el/la mejor	*the best*
el/la menor	*the youngest*
el/la peor	*the worst*
mejor	*better*
peor	*worse*

Expresiones útiles	*See page 269.*

recursos
vText
CPA p. 116
vhlcentral

Las fiestas

9

Communicative Goals

VOICE BOARD

I will be able to:

- **Express congratulations**
- **Express gratitude**
- **Ask for and pay the bill at a restaurant**

A PRIMERA VISTA

- **¿Cuál crees que es la relación entre las dos personas de la foto?**
- **¿Qué están haciendo? ¿Por qué?**
- **¿Cómo se sienten, alegres o tristes?**
- **¿Qué llevan puesto? ¿De qué color es su ropa?**

contextos

pages 300–303

- Parties and celebrations
- Personal relationships
- Stages of life

fotonovela

pages 304–307

The Díaz family gets ready for their annual **Día de Muertos** celebration. The whole family participates in the preparations, and even friends are invited to the main event.

cultura

pages 308–309

- **Semana Santa** celebrations
- The International Music Festival in **Viña del Mar**

estructura

pages 310–321

- Irregular preterites
- Verbs that change meaning in the preterite
- **¿Qué?** and **¿cuál?**
- Pronouns after prepositions
- **Recapitulación**

adelante

pages 322–329

Lectura: The society section of a newspaper
Escritura: An essay about celebrations
Escuchar: A conversation about an anniversary party
En pantalla
Flash cultura
Panorama: Chile

Las fiestas

My Vocabulary Tutorials

Más vocabulario

la alegría	*happiness*
la amistad	*friendship*
el amor	*love*
el beso	*kiss*
la sorpresa	*surprise*
el aniversario (de bodas)	*(wedding) anniversary*
la boda	*wedding*
el cumpleaños	*birthday*
el día de fiesta	*holiday*
el divorcio	*divorce*
el matrimonio	*marriage*
la Navidad	*Christmas*
la quinceañera	*young woman celebrating her fifteenth birthday*
el/la recién casado/a	*newlywed*
cambiar (de)	*to change*
celebrar	*to celebrate*
divertirse (e:ie)	*to have fun*
graduarse (de/en)	*to graduate (from/in)*
invitar	*to invite*
jubilarse	*to retire (from work)*
nacer	*to be born*
odiar	*to hate*
pasarlo bien/mal	*to have a good/bad time*
reírse (e:i)	*to laugh*
relajarse	*to relax*
sonreír (e:i)	*to smile*
sorprender	*to surprise*
juntos/as	*together*

Variación léxica

pastel ⟷ torta (*Arg., Col., Venez.*)
comprometerse ⟷ prometerse (*Esp.*)

recursos

vText | CPA pp. 127–129 | CH pp. 131–132 | vhlcentral

la pareja
el pastel de chocolate
la botella de vino
el flan de caramelo
las galletas
los postres
el champán
los dulces

Relaciones personales

casarse (con)	*to get married (to)*
comprometerse (con)	*to get engaged (to)*
divorciarse (de)	*to get divorced (from)*
enamorarse (de)	*to fall in love (with)*
llevarse bien/mal (con)	*to get along well/ badly (with)*
romper (con)	*to break up (with)*
salir (con)	*to go out (with); to date*
separarse (de)	*to separate (from)*
tener una cita	*to have a date; to have an appointment*

Práctica

1 **Escuchar** Escucha la conversación e indica si las oraciones son **ciertas** o **falsas**.

1. A Silvia no le gusta mucho el chocolate.
2. Silvia sabe que sus amigos le van a hacer una fiesta.
3. Los amigos de Silvia le compraron un pastel de chocolate.
4. Los amigos brindan por Silvia con refrescos.
5. Silvia y sus amigos van a comer helado.
6. Los amigos de Silvia le van a servir flan y galletas.

2 **Ordenar** Escucha la narración y ordena las oraciones de acuerdo con los eventos de la vida de Beatriz.

____ a. Beatriz se compromete con Roberto.
____ b. Beatriz se gradúa.
____ c. Beatriz sale con Emilio.
____ d. Sus padres le hacen una gran fiesta.
____ e. La pareja se casa.
____ f. Beatriz nace en Montevideo.

3 **Emparejar** Indica la letra de la frase que mejor completa cada oración.

a. **cambió de**	d. **nos divertimos**	g. **se llevan bien**
b. **lo pasaron mal**	e. **se casaron**	h. **sonrió**
c. **nació**	f. **se jubiló**	i. **tenemos una cita**

1. María y sus compañeras de clase ____. Son buenas amigas.
2. Pablo y yo ____ en la fiesta. Bailamos y comimos mucho.
3. Manuel y Felipe ____ en el cine. La película fue muy mala.
4. ¡Tengo una nueva sobrina! Ella ____ ayer por la mañana.
5. Mi madre ____ profesión. Ahora es artista.
6. Mi padre ____ el año pasado. Ahora no trabaja.
7. Jorge y yo ____ esta noche. Vamos a ir a un restaurante muy elegante.
8. Jaime y Laura ____ el septiembre pasado. La boda fue maravillosa.

4 **Definiciones** En parejas, definan las palabras y escriban una oración para cada ejemplo.

modelo

romper (con) una pareja termina la relación
Marta rompió con su novio.

1. regalar
2. helado
3. pareja
4. invitado
5. casarse
6. pasarlo bien
7. sorpresa
8. amistad

Las etapas de la vida de Sergio

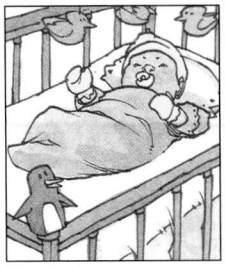
el nacimiento

la niñez

la adolescencia

la juventud

la madurez

la vejez

Más vocabulario

la edad	*age*
el estado civil	*marital status*
las etapas de la vida	*the stages of life*
la muerte	*death*
casado/a	*married*
divorciado/a	*divorced*
separado/a	*separated*
soltero/a	*single*
viudo/a	*widower/widow*

5 **Las etapas de la vida** Identifica las etapas de la vida que se describen en estas oraciones.

1. Mi abuela se jubiló y se mudó (*moved*) a Viña del Mar.
2. Mi padre trabaja para una compañía grande en Santiago.
3. ¿Viste a mi nuevo sobrino en el hospital? Es precioso y ¡tan pequeño!
4. Mi abuelo murió este año.
5. Mi hermana celebró su fiesta de quince años.
6. Mi hermana pequeña juega con muñecas (*dolls*).

NOTA CULTURAL

Viña del Mar es una ciudad en la costa de Chile, situada al oeste de Santiago. Tiene playas hermosas, excelentes hoteles, casinos y buenos restaurantes. El poeta Pablo Neruda pasó muchos años allí.

¡LENGUA VIVA!

The term **quinceañera** refers to a girl who is celebrating her 15th birthday. The party is called **la fiesta de quince años**.

6 **Cambiar** En parejas, imaginen que son dos hermanos/as de diferentes edades. Cada vez que el/la hermano/a menor dice algo, se equivoca. El/La hermano/a mayor lo/la corrige (*corrects him/her*), cambiando las expresiones subrayadas (*underlined*). Túrnense para ser mayor y menor, decir algo equivocado y corregir.

modelo

Estudiante 1: La niñez es cuando trabajamos mucho.
Estudiante 2: No, te equivocas (*you're wrong*). La madurez es cuando trabajamos mucho.

1. El nacimiento es el fin de la vida.
2. La juventud es la etapa cuando nos jubilamos.
3. A los sesenta y cinco años, muchas personas comienzan a trabajar.
4. Julián y nuestra prima se divorcian mañana.
5. Mamá odia a su hermana.
6. El abuelo murió, por eso la abuela es separada.
7. Cuando te gradúas de la universidad, estás en la etapa de la adolescencia.
8. Mi tío nunca se casó; es viudo.

AYUDA

Other ways to contradict someone:
No es verdad. *It's not true.*
Creo que no. *I don't think so.*
¡Claro que no! *Of course not!*
¡Qué va! *No way!*

Practice more at vhlcentral.com.

Comunicación

7 **Una cena especial** Planea con un(a) compañero/a una cena para celebrar la graduación de tu hermano/a mayor de la escuela secundaria. Recuerda incluir la siguiente información.

1. ¿Qué tipo de cena es? ¿Dónde va a ser? ¿Cuándo va a ser?
2. ¿A cuántas personas piensan invitar? ¿A quiénes van a invitar?
3. ¿Van a pedir un menú especial? ¿Qué van a comer?
4. ¿Cuánto dinero piensan gastar? ¿Cómo van a compartir los gastos?
5. ¿Qué van a hacer todos durante la cena?
6. Después de la cena, ¿quiénes van a limpiar (*to clean*)?

recursos
vText
CPA
p. 130

8 **Encuesta** Tu profesor(a) va a darte una hoja. Haz las preguntas de la hoja a dos o tres compañeros/as de clase para saber qué actitudes tienen en sus relaciones personales. Luego comparte los resultados de la encuesta con la clase y comenta tus conclusiones.

Preguntas	Nombres	Actitudes
1. ¿Te importa la amistad? ¿Por qué?		
2. ¿Es mejor tener un(a) buen(a) amigo/a o muchos/as amigos/as?		
3. ¿Cuáles son las características que buscas en tus amigos/as?		
4. ¿A qué edad es posible enamorarse?		
5. ¿Deben las parejas hacer todo juntos? ¿Deben tener las mismas opiniones? ¿Por qué?		

¡LENGUA VIVA!

While a **buen(a) amigo/a** is a *good friend,* the term **amigo/a íntimo/a** refers to a *close friend,* or a very good friend, without any romantic overtones.

9 **Minidrama** En parejas, consulten la ilustración de la página 302 y luego, usando las palabras de la lista, preparen un minidrama para representar las etapas de la vida de Sergio. Pueden inventar más información sobre su vida.

amor	celebrar	enamorarse	romper
boda	comprometerse	graduarse	salir
cambiar	cumpleaños	jubilarse	separarse
casarse	divorciarse	nacer	tener una cita

El Día de Muertos

La familia Díaz conmemora el Día de Muertos.

PERSONAJES

MARISSA

JIMENA

FELIPE

JUAN CARLOS

Video: *Fotonovela*

MAITE FUENTES El Día de Muertos se celebra en México el primero y el segundo de noviembre. Como pueden ver, hay calaveras de azúcar, flores, música y comida por todas partes. Ésta es una fiesta única que todos deben ver por lo menos una vez en la vida.

MARISSA *Holy moley!* ¡Está delicioso!

TÍA ANA MARÍA Mi mamá me enseñó a prepararlo. El mole siempre fue el plato favorito de mi papá. Mi hijo Eduardo nació el día de su cumpleaños. Por eso le pusimos su nombre.

TÍO RAMÓN ¿Dónde están mis hermanos?

JIMENA Mi papá y Felipe están en el otro cuarto. Esos dos antipáticos no quieren decirnos qué están haciendo. Y la tía Ana María...

TÍO RAMÓN ... está en la cocina.

TÍA ANA MARÍA Ramón, ¿cómo estás?

TÍO RAMÓN Bien, gracias. ¿Y Mateo? ¿No vino contigo?

TÍA ANA MARÍA No. Ya sabes que me casé con un doctor y, pues, trabaja muchísimo.

SR. DÍAZ Familia Díaz, deben prepararse...

FELIPE ... ¡para la sorpresa de sus vidas!

JUAN CARLOS Gracias por invitarme.

SR. DÍAZ Juan Carlos, como eres nuestro amigo, ya eres parte de la familia.

SRA. DÍAZ

SR. DÍAZ

TÍA ANA MARÍA

TÍO RAMÓN

TÍA NAYELI

DON DIEGO

MARTA

VALENTINA

MAITE FUENTES

TÍA ANA MARÍA Marissa, ¿le puedes llevar esa foto que está ahí a Carolina? La necesita para el altar.

MARISSA Sí. ¿Son sus padres?

TÍA ANA MARÍA Sí, el día de su boda.

MARISSA ¿Cómo se conocieron?

TÍA ANA MARÍA En la fiesta de un amigo. Fue amor a primera vista.

MARISSA (*Señala la foto.*) La voy a llevar al altar.

(*En el cementerio*)

JIMENA Yo hice las galletas y el pastel. ¿Dónde los puse?

MARTA Postres... ¿Cuál prefiero? ¿Galletas? ¿Pastel? ¡Dulces!

VALENTINA Me gustan las galletas.

SR. DÍAZ Brindamos por ustedes, mamá y papá.

TÍO RAMÓN Todas las otras noches estamos separados. Pero esta noche estamos juntos.

TÍA ANA MARÍA Con gratitud y amor.

recursos

vText | CPA pp. 131–132 | vhlcentral

Expresiones útiles

Discussing family history

El mole siempre fue el plato favorito de mi papá.
Mole *was always my dad's favorite dish.*

Mi hijo Eduardo nació el día de su cumpleaños.
My son Eduardo was born on his birthday.

Por eso le pusimos su nombre.
That's why we named him after him (after my father).

¿Cómo se conocieron sus padres?
How did your parents meet?

En la fiesta de un amigo. Fue amor a primera vista.
At a friend's party. It was love at first sight.

Talking about a party/ celebration

Ésta es una fiesta única que todos deben ver por lo menos una vez.
This is a unique celebration that everyone should see at least once.

Gracias por invitarme.
Thanks for inviting me.

Brindamos por ustedes.
A toast to you.

Additional vocabulary

alma *soul*
altar *altar*
ángel *angel*
calavera de azúcar *skull made out of sugar*
cementerio *cemetery*
cocina *kitchen*
disfraz *costume*

¿Qué pasó?

1 **Completar** Completa las oraciones con la información correcta, según la **Fotonovela**.

1. El Día de Muertos es una _____ única que todos deben ver.
2. La tía Ana María preparó _____ para celebrar.
3. Marissa lleva la _____ al altar.
4. Jimena hizo las _____ y el _____.
5. Marta no sabe qué _____ prefiere.

2 **Identificar** Identifica quién puede decir estas oraciones. Vas a usar un nombre dos veces.

1. Mis padres se conocieron en la fiesta de un amigo.
2. El Día de Muertos se celebra con flores, calaveras de azúcar, música y comida.
3. Gracias por invitarme a celebrar este Día de Muertos.
4. Los de la foto son mis padres el día de su boda.
5. A mí me gustan mucho las galletas.
6. ¡Qué bueno que estás aquí, Juan Carlos! Eres uno más de la familia.

SR. DÍAZ

MAITE FUENTES

JUAN CARLOS

VALENTINA

TÍA ANA MARÍA

3 **Seleccionar** Selecciona algunas de las opciones de la lista para completar las oraciones.

amor	días de fiesta	pasarlo bien	salieron
el champán	divorciarse	postres	se enamoraron
cumpleaños	flan	la quinceañera	una sorpresa

1. El Sr. Díaz y Felipe prepararon _____ para la familia.
2. Los _____, como el Día de Muertos, se celebran con la familia.
3. Eduardo, el hijo de Ana María, nació el día del _____ de su abuelo.
4. La tía Ana María siente gratitud y _____ hacia (*toward*) sus padres.
5. Los días de fiesta también son para _____ con los amigos.
6. El Día de Muertos se hacen muchos _____.
7. Los padres de la tía Ana María _____ a primera vista.

4 **Una cena** Trabajen en grupos para representar una conversación en una cena de Año Nuevo.

- Una persona brinda por el año que está por comenzar y por estar con su familia y amigos.
- Cada persona del grupo habla de cuál es su comida favorita en año nuevo.
- Después de la cena, una persona del grupo dice que es hora de (*it's time to*) comer las uvas.
- Cada persona del grupo dice qué desea para el año que empieza.
- Después, cada persona del grupo debe desear Feliz Año Nuevo a las demás.

Practice more at vhlcentral.com.

NOTA CULTURAL

Comer doce uvas a las doce de la noche del 31 de diciembre de cada año es una costumbre que nació en España y que también se observa en varios países de Latinoamérica. Se debe comer una uva por cada una de las 12 campanadas (*strokes*) del reloj y se cree que (*it's believed that*) quien lo hace va a tener un año próspero.

Pronunciación

Audio

The letters h, j, and g

helado **hombre** **hola** **hermosa**

The Spanish **h** is always silent.

José **jubilarse** **dejar** **pareja**

The letter **j** is pronounced much like the English *h* in *his*.

agencia **general** **Gil** **Gisela**

The letter **g** can be pronounced three different ways. Before **e** or **i**, the letter **g** is pronounced much like the English *h*.

Gustavo, gracias por llamar el domingo.

At the beginning of a phrase or after the letter **n**, the Spanish **g** is pronounced like the English *g* in *girl*.

Me gradué en agosto.

In any other position, the Spanish **g** has a somewhat softer sound.

guerra **conseguir** **guantes** **agua**

In the combinations **gue** and **gui**, the **g** has a hard sound and the **u** is silent. In the combination **gua**, the **g** has a hard sound and the **u** is pronounced like the English *w*.

Práctica Lee las palabras en voz alta, prestando atención a la **h**, la **j** y la **g**.

1. hamburguesa
2. jugar
3. oreja
4. guapa
5. geografía
6. magnífico
7. espejo
8. hago
9. seguir
10. gracias
11. hijo
12. galleta
13. Jorge
14. tengo
15. ahora
16. guantes

Oraciones Lee las oraciones en voz alta, prestando atención a la **h**, la **j** y la **g**.

1. Hola. Me llamo Gustavo Hinojosa Lugones y vivo en Santiago de Chile.
2. Tengo una familia grande; somos tres hermanos y tres hermanas.
3. Voy a graduarme en mayo.
4. Para celebrar mi graduación, mis padres van a regalarme un viaje a Egipto.
5. ¡Qué generosos son!

Refranes Lee los refranes en voz alta, prestando atención a la **h**, la **j** y la **g**.

1 Too much of a good thing.
2 The clothes don't make the man.

recursos

vText CPA p. 133 CH p. 133 vhlcentral

EN DETALLE

Additional Reading

Semana Santa: vacaciones y tradición

¿Te imaginas pasar veinticuatro horas tocando un tambor° entre miles de personas? Así es como mucha gente celebra el Viernes Santo° en el pequeño pueblo de **Calanda,** España.

De todas las celebraciones hispanas, la Semana Santa° es una de las más espectaculares y únicas. Semana Santa es la semana antes de Pascua°, una celebración religiosa que conmemora la Pasión de Jesucristo. Generalmente, la gente tiene unos días de vacaciones en esta semana. Algunas personas aprovechan° estos días para viajar, pero otras prefieren participar en las tradicionales celebraciones religiosas en las calles. En **Antigua,** Guatemala, hacen alfombras° de flores° y altares; también organizan Vía Crucis° y danzas. En las famosas procesiones y desfiles° religiosos de **Sevilla,** España, los fieles° sacan a las calles imágenes religiosas. Las imágenes van encima de plataformas ricamente decoradas con abundantes flores y velas°. En la procesión, los penitentes llevan túnicas y unos sombreros cónicos que les cubren° la cara°. En sus manos llevan faroles° o velas encendidas.

Procesión en Sevilla, España

Alfombra de flores en Antigua, Guatemala

Si visitas algún país hispano durante la Semana Santa, debes asistir a un desfile. Las playas pueden esperar hasta la semana siguiente.

Otras celebraciones famosas

Ayacucho, Perú: Además de alfombras de flores y procesiones,aquí hay una antigua tradición llamada "quema de la chamiza"°.

Iztapalapa, Ciudad de México: Es famoso el Vía Crucis del cerro° de la Estrella. Es una representación del recorrido° de Jesucristo con la cruz°

Popayán, Colombia: En las procesiones "chiquitas" los niños llevan imágenes que son copias pequeñas de las que llevan los mayores.

tocando un tambor *playing a drum* Viernes Santo *Good Friday* Semana Santa *Holy Week* Pascua *Easter Sunday* aprovechan *take advantage of* alfombras *carpets* flores *flowers* Vía Crucis *Stations of the Cross* desfiles *parades* fieles *faithful* velas *candles* cubren *cover* cara *face* faroles *lamps* quema de la chamiza *burning of brushwood* cerro *hill* recorrido *route* cruz *cross*

ACTIVIDADES

1 **¿Cierto o falso?** Indica si lo que dicen las oraciones sobre Semana Santa en países hispanos es **cierto** o **falso.** Corrige las falsas.

1. La Semana Santa se celebra después de Pascua.
2. Las personas tienen días libres durante la Semana Santa.
3. Todas las personas asisten a las celebraciones religiosas.
4. En los países hispanos, las celebraciones se hacen en las calles.
5. En Antigua y en Ayacucho es típico hacer alfombras de flores.
6. En Sevilla, sacan imágenes religiosas a las calles.
7. En Sevilla, las túnicas cubren la cara.
8. En la procesión en Sevilla algunas personas llevan flores en sus manos.
9. El Vía Crucis de Iztapalapa es en el interior de una iglesia.
10. Las procesiones "chiquitas" son famosas en Sevilla, España.

ASÍ SE DICE

Fiestas y celebraciones

la despedida de soltero/a	*bachelor(ette) party*
el día feriado/festivo	**el día de fiesta**
disfrutar	*to enjoy*
festejar	**celebrar**
los fuegos artificiales	*fireworks*
pasarlo en grande	**divertirse mucho**
la vela	*candle*

EL MUNDO HISPANO

Celebraciones latinoamericanas

- **Oruro, Bolivia** Durante el carnaval de Oruro se realiza la famosa Diablada, una antigua danza° que muestra la lucha° entre el Bien y el Mal: ángeles contra° demonios.
- **Panchimalco, El Salvador** La primera semana de mayo, Panchimalco se cubre de flores y de color. También hacen el Desfile de las palmas° y bailan danzas antiguas.
- **Quito, Ecuador** El mes de agosto es el Mes de las Artes. Danza, teatro, música, cine, artesanías° y otros eventos culturales inundan la ciudad.
- **San Pedro Sula, Honduras** En junio se celebra la Feria Juniana. Hay comida típica, bailes, desfiles, conciertos, rodeos, exposiciones ganaderas° y eventos deportivos y culturales.

danza *dance* lucha *fight* contra *versus* palmas palm *leaves* artesanías *handcrafts* exposiciones ganaderas *cattle shows*

PERFIL

Festival de Viña del Mar

En 1959 unos estudiantes de **Viña del Mar**, Chile, celebraron una fiesta en una casa de campo conocida como la Quinta Vergara donde hubo° un espectáculo° musical. En 1960 repitieron el evento. Asistió tanta gente que muchos vieron el espectáculo parados° o sentados en el suelo°. Algunos se subieron a los árboles°.

Años después, se convirtió en el **Festival Internacional de la Canción.** Se celebra en febrero, en el mismo lugar donde empezó. ¡Pero ahora nadie necesita subirse a un árbol para verlo! Hay un anfiteatro con capacidad para quince mil personas y el evento se transmite por la televisión.

Nelly Furtado

En el festival hay concursos° musicales y conciertos de artistas famosos como Calle 13 y Nelly Furtado.

hubo *there was* espectáculo *show* parados *standing* suelo *floor* se subieron a los árboles *climbed trees* concursos *competitions*

Conexión Internet

¿Qué celebraciones hispanas hay en los Estados Unidos y Canadá?

Go to **vhlcentral.com** to find more cultural information related to this **Cultura** section.

ACTIVIDADES

2 **Comprensión** Responde a las preguntas.

1. ¿Cuántas personas por día pueden asistir al Festival de Viña del Mar?
2. ¿Qué es la Diablada?
3. ¿Qué celebran en Quito en agosto?
4. Nombra dos atracciones en la Feria Juniana de San Pedro Sula.
5. ¿Qué es la Quinta Vergara?

3 **¿Cuál es tu celebración favorita?** Escribe un pequeño párrafo sobre la celebración que más te gusta de tu comunidad. Explica cómo se llama, cuándo ocurre y cómo es.

Practice more at vhlcentral.com.

recursos

vText

CH p. 134

vhlcentral

9.1 Irregular preterites

Tutorial

ANTE TODO

You already know that the verbs **ir** and **ser** are irregular in the preterite. You will now learn other verbs whose preterite forms are also irregular.

Preterite of tener, venir, and decir

		tener (**u**-stem)	**venir** (**i**-stem)	**decir** (**j**-stem)
SINGULAR FORMS	yo	tuv**e**	vin**e**	dij**e**
	tú	tuv**iste**	vin**iste**	dij**iste**
	Ud./él/ella	tuv**o**	vin**o**	dij**o**
PLURAL FORMS	nosotros/as	tuv**imos**	vin**imos**	dij**imos**
	vosotros/as	tuv**isteis**	vin**isteis**	dij**isteis**
	Uds./ellos/ellas	tuv**ieron**	vin**ieron**	dij**eron**

▶ **¡Atención!** The endings of these verbs are the regular preterite endings of **-er/-ir** verbs, except for the **yo** and **usted/él/ella** forms. Note that these two endings are unaccented.

▶ These verbs observe similar stem changes to **tener, venir,** and **decir**.

INFINITIVE	U-STEM	PRETERITE FORMS
poder	pud-	pude, pudiste, pudo, pudimos, pudisteis, pudieron
poner	pus-	puse, pusiste, puso, pusimos, pusisteis, pusieron
saber	sup-	supe, supiste, supo, supimos, supisteis, supieron
estar	estuv-	estuve, estuviste, estuvo, estuvimos, estuvisteis, estuvieron

INFINITIVE	I-STEM	PRETERITE FORMS
querer	quis-	quise, quisiste, quiso, quisimos, quisisteis, quisieron
hacer	hic-	hice, hiciste, hizo, hicimos, hicisteis, hicieron

INFINITIVE	J-STEM	PRETERITE FORMS
traer	traj-	traje, trajiste, trajo, trajimos, trajisteis, trajeron
conducir	conduj-	conduje, condujiste, condujo, condujimos, condujisteis, condujeron
traducir	traduj-	traduje, tradujiste, tradujo, tradujimos, tradujisteis, tradujeron

¡ATENCIÓN!

Note the **c** → **z** spelling change in the third-person singular form of **hacer**: **hizo**.

▶ **¡Atención!** Most verbs that end in **-cir** are **j**-stem verbs in the preterite. For example, **producir** → **produje, produjiste,** etc.

Produjimos un documental sobre los accidentes en la casa.
We produced a documentary about accidents in the home.

▶ Notice that the preterites with **j**-stems omit the letter **i** in the **ustedes/ellos/ellas** form.

Mis amigos **trajeron** comida a la fiesta.
My friends brought food to the party.

Ellos **dijeron** la verdad.
They told the truth.

The preterite of dar

SINGULAR FORMS		PLURAL FORMS	
yo	d**i**	nosotros/as	d**imos**
tú	d**iste**	vosotros/as	d**isteis**
Ud./él/ella	d**io**	Uds./ellos/ellas	d**ieron**

- The endings for **dar** are the same as the regular preterite endings for **-er** and **-ir** verbs, except that there are no accent marks.

La camarera me **dio** el menú.
The waitress gave me the menu.

Le **di** a Juan algunos consejos.
I gave Juan some advice.

Los invitados le **dieron** un regalo.
The guests gave him/her a gift.

Nosotros **dimos** una gran fiesta.
We gave a great party.

- The preterite of **hay** (*inf.* **haber**) is **hubo** (*there was; there were*).

Marissa le dio la foto a la Sra. Díaz.

Hubo una celebración en casa de los Díaz.

¡INTÉNTALO! Escribe la forma correcta del pretérito de cada verbo que está entre paréntesis.

1. (querer) tú quisiste
2. (decir) usted _____
3. (hacer) nosotras _____
4. (traer) yo _____
5. (conducir) ellas _____
6. (estar) ella _____
7. (tener) tú _____
8. (dar) ella y yo _____
9. (traducir) yo _____
10. (haber) ayer _____
11. (saber) usted _____
12. (poner) ellos _____
13. (venir) yo _____
14. (poder) tú _____
15. (querer) ustedes _____
16. (estar) nosotros _____
17. (decir) tú _____
18. (saber) ellos _____
19. (hacer) él _____
20. (poner) yo _____
21. (traer) nosotras _____
22. (tener) yo _____
23. (dar) tú _____
24. (poder) ustedes _____

recursos
vText
CPA pp. 134–136
CH pp. 135–138
vhlcentral

Práctica

1 **Completar** Completa estas oraciones con el pretérito de los verbos entre paréntesis.

1. El sábado _____ (haber) una fiesta sorpresa para Elsa en mi casa.
2. Sofía _____ (hacer) un pastel para la fiesta y Miguel _____ (traer) un flan.
3. Los amigos y parientes de Elsa _____ (venir) y _____ (traer) regalos.
4. El hermano de Elsa no _____ (venir) porque _____ (tener) que trabajar.
5. Su tía María Dolores tampoco _____ (poder) venir.
6. Cuando Elsa abrió la puerta, todos gritaron: "¡Feliz cumpleaños!" y su esposo le _____ (dar) un beso.
7. Elsa no _____ (saber) cómo reaccionar (*to react*). _____ (Estar) un poco nerviosa al principio, pero pronto sus amigos _____ (poner) música y ella _____ (poder) relajarse bailando con su esposo.
8. Al final de la noche, todos _____ (decir) que se divirtieron mucho.

NOTA CULTURAL

El **flan** es un postre muy popular en los países de habla hispana. Se prepara con huevos, leche y azúcar y se sirve con salsa de caramelo. Existen variedades deliciosas como el flan de chocolate o el flan de coco.

2 **Describir** En parejas, usen verbos de la lista para describir lo que estas personas hicieron. Deben dar por lo menos dos oraciones por cada dibujo.

dar	estar	poner	traer
decir	hacer	tener	venir

1. el señor López

2. Norma

3. anoche nosotros

4. Roberto y Elena

Practice more at vhlcentral.com.

Comunicación

3 **Preguntas** En parejas, túrnense para hacerse y responder a estas preguntas.

1. ¿Fuiste a una fiesta de cumpleaños el año pasado? ¿De quién?
2. ¿Quiénes fueron a la fiesta?
3. ¿Quién condujo el auto?
4. ¿Cómo estuvo el ambiente de la fiesta?
5. ¿Quién llevó regalos, bebidas o comida? ¿Llevaste algo especial?
6. ¿Hubo comida? ¿Quién la hizo?
7. ¿Qué regalo hiciste tú? ¿Qué otros regalos trajeron los invitados?
8. ¿Cuántos invitados hubo en la fiesta?
9. ¿Qué tipo de música hubo?
10. ¿Qué te dijeron algunos invitados de la fiesta?

4 **Encuesta** Tu profesor(a) va a darte una hoja de actividades. Para cada una de las actividades de la lista, encuentra a alguien que hizo esa actividad.

modelo

traer dulces a clase

Estudiante 1: ¿Trajiste dulces a clase?

Estudiante 2: Sí, traje galletas y helado a la fiesta del fin del semestre.

Actividades	Nombres
1. ponerse un disfraz (*costume*) de Halloween	
2. traer dulces a clase	
3. llegar a la escuela en auto	
4. estar en la biblioteca ayer	
5. dar un regalo a alguien ayer	
6. poder levantarse temprano esta mañana	
7. hacer un viaje a un país hispano en el verano	
8. ver una película anoche	
9. ir a una fiesta el fin de semana pasado	
10. tener que estudiar el sábado pasado	

Síntesis

5 **Conversación** En parejas, preparen una conversación en la que uno/a de ustedes va a visitar a su hermano/a para explicarle por qué no fue a su fiesta de graduación y para saber cómo estuvo la fiesta. Incluyan esta información en la conversación:

- cuál fue el menú
- quiénes vinieron a la fiesta y quiénes no pudieron venir
- quiénes prepararon la comida o trajeron algo
- si él/ella tuvo que preparar algo
- lo que la gente hizo antes y después de comer
- cómo lo pasaron, bien o mal

9.2 Verbs that change meaning in the preterite

Tutorial

ANTE TODO The verbs **conocer, saber, poder,** and **querer** change meanings when used in the preterite. Because of this, each of them corresponds to more than one verb in English, depending on its tense.

Verbs that change meaning in the preterite

Present	Preterite
conocer	
to know; to be acquainted with **Conozco** a esa pareja. *I know that couple.*	*to meet* **Conocí** a esa pareja ayer. *I met that couple yesterday.*
saber	
to know information; to know how to do something **Sabemos** la verdad. *We know the truth.*	*to find out; to learn* **Supimos** la verdad anoche. *We found out (learned) the truth last night.*
poder	
to be able; can **Podemos** hacerlo. *We can do it.*	*to manage; to succeed (could and did)* **Pudimos** hacerlo ayer. *We managed to do it yesterday.*
querer	
to want; to love **Quiero** ir, pero tengo que trabajar. *I want to go, but I have to work.*	*to try* **Quise** evitarlo, pero fue imposible. *I tried to avoid it, but it was impossible.*

¡ATENCIÓN!

In the preterite, the verbs **poder** and **querer** have different meanings when they are used in affirmative or negative sentences.

pude *I succeeded*
no pude *I failed (to)*
quise *I tried (to)*
no quise *I refused (to)*

¡INTÉNTALO! Elige la respuesta más lógica.

1. Yo no hice lo que me pidieron mis padres. ¡Tengo mis principios!
   a. No quise hacerlo. b. No supe hacerlo.
2. Hablamos por primera vez con Nuria y Ana en la boda.
   a. Las conocimos en la boda. b. Les dijimos en la boda.
3. Por fin hablé con mi hermano después de llamarlo siete veces.
   a. No quise hablar con él. b. Pude hablar con él.
4. Josefina se acostó para relajarse. Se durmió inmediatamente.
   a. Pudo relajarse. b. No pudo relajarse.
5. Después de mucho buscar, encontraste la definición en el diccionario.
   a. No supiste la respuesta. b. Supiste la respuesta.
6. Las chicas fueron a la fiesta. Cantaron y bailaron mucho.
   a. Ellas pudieron divertirse. b. Ellas no supieron divertirse.

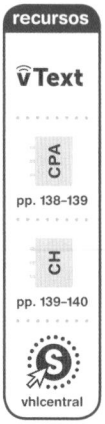

Práctica y Comunicación

1 **Carlos y Eva** Forma oraciones con los siguientes elementos. Usa el pretérito y haz todos los cambios necesarios. Al final, inventa la razón del divorcio de Carlos y Eva.

1. anoche / mi esposa y yo / saber / que / Carlos y Eva / divorciarse
2. los / conocer / viaje / isla de Pascua
3. no / poder / hablar / mucho / con / ellos / ese día
4. pero / ellos / ser / simpático / y / nosotros / hacer planes / vernos / con más / frecuencia
5. yo / poder / encontrar / su / número / teléfono / páginas / amarillo
6. (yo) querer / llamar / los / ese día / pero / no / tener / tiempo
7. cuando / los / llamar / nosotros / poder / hablar / Eva
8. nosotros / saber / razón / divorcio / después / hablar / ella
9. _____

NOTA CULTURAL

La isla de Pascua es un remoto territorio chileno situado en el océano Pacífico Sur. Sus inmensas estatuas son uno de los mayores misterios del mundo: nadie sabe cómo o por qué se crearon. Para más información, véase **Panorama**, p. 329.

2 **Completar** Completa estas frases de una manera lógica.

1. Ayer mi compañero/a de clase supo...
2. Esta mañana no pude...
3. Conocí a mi mejor amigo/a en...
4. Mis padres no quisieron...
5. Mi mejor amigo/a no pudo...
6. Mi novio/a y yo nos conocimos en...
7. La semana pasada supe...
8. Ayer mis amigos quisieron...

3 **Telenovela** En parejas, escriban el diálogo para una escena de una telenovela (*soap opera*). La escena trata de una situación amorosa entre tres personas: Mirta, Daniel y Raúl. Usen el pretérito de **conocer, poder, querer** y **saber** en su diálogo.

Practice more at vhlcentral.com.

Síntesis

4 **Conversación** En una hoja de papel, escribe dos listas: las cosas que hiciste durante el fin de semana y las cosas que quisiste hacer, pero no pudiste. Luego, compara tu lista con la de un(a) compañero/a, y expliquen ambos por qué no pudieron hacer esas cosas.

9.3 ¿Qué? and ¿cuál?

Tutorial

ANTE TODO You've already learned how to use interrogative words and phrases. As you know, **¿qué?** and **¿cuál?** or **¿cuáles?** mean *what?* or *which?* However, they are not interchangeable.

- **¿Qué?** is used to ask for a definition or an explanation.

  ¿**Qué** es el flan?
  What is flan?

  ¿**Qué** estudias?
  What do you study?

- **¿Cuál(es)?** is used when there is more than one possibility to choose from.

  ¿**Cuál** de los dos prefieres, las galletas o el helado?
  Which of these (two) do you prefer, cookies or ice cream?

  ¿**Cuáles** son tus medias, las negras o las blancas?
  Which ones are your socks, the black ones or the white ones?

- **¿Cuál?** should not be used before a noun; in this case, **¿qué?** is used.

  ¿**Qué** sorpresa te dieron tus amigos?
  What surprise did your friends give you?

  ¿**Qué** colores te gustan?
  What colors do you like?

- **¿Qué?** used before a noun has the same meaning as **¿cuál?**

  ¿**Qué regalo** te gusta?
  What (Which) gift do you like?

  ¿**Qué dulces** quieren ustedes?
  What (Which) sweets do you want?

Review of interrogative words and phrases

¿a qué hora?	*at what time?*	**¿cuántos/as?**	*how many?*
¿adónde?	*(to) where?*	**¿de dónde?**	*from where?*
¿cómo?	*how?*	**¿dónde?**	*where?*
¿cuál(es)?	*what?; which?*	**¿por qué?**	*why?*
¿cuándo?	*when?*	**¿qué?**	*what?; which?*
¿cuánto/a?	*how much?*	**¿quién(es)?**	*who?*

¡INTÉNTALO! Completa las preguntas con **¿qué?** o **¿cuál(es)?**, según el contexto.

1. ¿ Cuál de los dos te gusta más?
2. ¿ _____ es tu teléfono?
3. ¿ _____ tipo de pastel pediste?
4. ¿ _____ es una galleta?
5. ¿ _____ haces ahora?
6. ¿ _____ son tus platos favoritos?
7. ¿ _____ bebidas te gustan más?
8. ¿ _____ es esto?
9. ¿ _____ es el mejor?
10. ¿ _____ es tu opinión?
11. ¿ _____ fiestas celebras tú?
12. ¿ _____ regalo prefieres?
13. ¿ _____ es tu helado favorito?
14. ¿ _____ pones en la mesa?
15. ¿ _____ restaurante prefieres?
16. ¿ _____ estudiantes estudian más?
17. ¿ _____ quieres comer esta noche?
18. ¿ _____ es la sorpresa mañana?
19. ¿ _____ postre prefieres?
20. ¿ _____ opinas?

recursos
vText
CPA pp. 140–141
CH pp. 141–142
vhlcentral

Práctica y Comunicación

1 **Completar** Tu clase de español va a crear un sitio web. Completa estas preguntas con palabras interrogativas. Luego, con un(a) compañero/a, hagan y contesten las preguntas para obtener la información para el sitio web.

1. ¿_____ es la fecha de tu cumpleaños?
2. ¿_____ naciste?
3. ¿_____ es tu estado civil?
4. ¿_____ te relajas?
5. ¿_____ es tu mejor amigo/a?
6. ¿_____ cosas te hacen reír?
7. ¿_____ postres te gustan? ¿_____ te gusta más?
8. ¿_____ problemas tuviste el primer día en esta escuela?

2 **Una invitación** En parejas, lean esta invitación. Luego, túrnense para hacer y contestar preguntas con **qué** y **cuál** basadas en la información de la invitación.

modelo

Estudiante 1: ¿Cuál es el nombre del padre de la novia?
Estudiante 2: Su nombre es Fernando Sandoval Valera.

Fernando Sandoval Valera
Isabel Arzipe de Sandoval

Lorenzo Vásquez Amaral
Elena Soto de Vásquez

tienen el agrado de invitarlos
a la boda de sus hijos

María Luisa y José Antonio

La ceremonia religiosa tendrá lugar
el sábado 10 de junio a las dos de la tarde
en el Templo de Santo Domingo
(Calle Santo Domingo, 961).

Después de la ceremonia, sírvanse pasar a la recepción en el salón de baile del Hotel Metrópoli (Sotero del Río, 465).

¡LENGUA VIVA!

The word **invitar** is not always used exactly like *invite*. Sometimes, if you say **Te invito un café,** it means that you are offering to buy that person a coffee.

3 **Quinceañera** Trabaja con un(a) compañero/a. Uno/a de ustedes es el/la director(a) del salón de fiestas "Renacimiento". La otra persona es el padre/la madre de Sandra, quien quiere hacer la fiesta de quince años de su hija gastando menos de $25 por invitado. Su profesor(a) va a darles la información necesaria para confirmar la reservación.

modelo

Estudiante 1: ¿Cuánto cuestan los entremeses?
Estudiante 2: Depende. Puede escoger champiñones por 50 centavos o camarones por dos dólares.
Estudiante 1: ¡Uf! A mi hija le gustan los camarones, pero son muy caros.
Estudiante 2: Bueno, también puede escoger quesos por un dólar por invitado.

recursos
vText
CPA
pp. 142–143

Practice more at vhlcentral.com.

9.4 Pronouns after prepositions

Tutorial

ANTE TODO In Spanish, as in English, the object of a preposition is the noun or pronoun that follows the preposition. Observe the following diagram.

PREPOSITION	NOUN	PREPOSITION	PRONOUN
La sopa es para	Alicia	y para	él.

Prepositional pronouns

	Singular		Plural	
	mí	*me*	**nosotros/as**	*us*
	ti	*you (fam.)*	**vosotros/as**	*you (fam.)*
preposition +	**Ud.**	*you (form.)*	**Uds.**	*you (form.)*
	él	*him*	**ellos**	*them (m.)*
	ella	*her*	**ellas**	*them (f.)*

- Note that, except for **mí** and **ti,** these pronouns are the same as the subject pronouns. **¡Atención! Mí** (*me*) has an accent mark to distinguish it from the possessive adjective **mi** (*my*).
- The preposition **con** combines with **mí** and **ti** to form **conmigo** and **contigo,** respectively.

  —¿Quieres venir **conmigo** a Concepción?
  Do you want to come with me to Concepción?

  —Sí, gracias, me gustaría ir **contigo.**
  Yes, thanks, I would like to go with you.

- The preposition **entre** is followed by **tú** and **yo** instead of **ti** and **mí.**

  Papá va a sentarse **entre tú y yo**.
  Dad is going to sit between you and me.

¡INTÉNTALO! Completa estas oraciones con las preposiciones y los pronombres apropiados.

1. *(with him)* No quiero ir con él.
2. *(for her)* Las galletas son _____.
3. *(for me)* Los mariscos son _____.
4. *(with you,* pl. form.*)* Preferimos estar _____.
5. *(with you,* sing. fam.*)* Me gusta salir _____.
6. *(with me)* ¿Por qué no quieres tener una cita _____?
7. *(for her)* La cuenta es _____.
8. *(for them,* m.*)* La habitación es muy pequeña _____.
9. *(with them,* f.*)* Anoche celebré la Navidad _____.
10. *(for you,* sing. fam.*)* Este beso es _____.
11. *(with you,* sing. fam.*)* Nunca me aburro _____.
12. *(with you,* pl. form.*)* ¡Qué bien que vamos _____!
13. *(for you,* sing. fam.*)* _____ la vida es muy fácil.
14. *(for them,* f.*)* _____ no hay sorpresas.

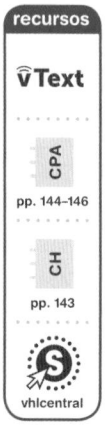

Práctica y Comunicación

1 **Completar** David sale con sus amigos a comer. Para saber quién come qué, lee el mensaje electrónico que David le envió (*sent*) a Cecilia dos días después y completa el diálogo en el restaurante con los pronombres apropiados.

modelo

Camarero: Los camarones en salsa verde, ¿para quién son?
David: Son para ___ella___.

Para: Cecilia | Asunto: El menú

Hola, Cecilia:
¿Recuerdas la comida del viernes? Quiero repetir el menú en mi casa el miércoles. Ahora voy a escribir lo que comimos, luego me dices si falta algún plato. Yo pedí el filete de pescado y Maribel camarones en salsa verde. Tatiana pidió un plato grandísimo de machas a la parmesana. Diana y Silvia pidieron langostas, ¿te acuerdas? Y tú, ¿qué pediste? Ah, sí, un bistec grande con papas. Héctor también pidió un bistec, pero más pequeño. Miguel pidió pollo y agua mineral para todos. Y la profesora comió ensalada verde porque está a dieta. ¿Falta algo? Espero tu mensaje. Hasta pronto. David.

NOTA CULTURAL

Las **machas a la parmesana** son un plato muy típico de Chile. Se prepara con machas, un tipo de almeja (*clam*) que se encuentra en Suramérica. Las machas a la parmesana se hacen con queso parmesano, limón, sal, pimienta y mantequilla, y luego se ponen en el horno (*oven*).

CAMARERO El filete de pescado, ¿para quién es?
DAVID Es para (1)_____.
CAMARERO Aquí está. ¿Y las machas a la parmesana y las langostas?
DAVID Las machas son para (2)_____.
SILVIA Y DIANA Las langostas son para (3)_____.
CAMARERO Tengo un bistec grande...
DAVID Cecilia, es para (4)_____, ¿no es cierto? Y el bistec más pequeño es para (5)_____.
CAMARERO ¿Y la botella de agua mineral?
MIGUEL Es para todos (6)_____, y el pollo es para (7)_____.
CAMARERO (*a la profesora*) Entonces la ensalada verde es para (8)_____.

recursos
vText
CPA
pp. 147–148

2 **Compartir** Tu profesor(a) va a darte una hoja de actividades en la que hay un dibujo. En parejas, hagan preguntas para saber dónde está cada una de las personas en el dibujo. Ustedes tienen dos versiones diferentes de la ilustración. Al final deben saber dónde está cada persona.

modelo

Estudiante 1: ¿Quién está al lado de Óscar?
Estudiante 2: Alfredo está al lado de él.

AYUDA

Here are some other useful prepositions: **al lado de, debajo de, a la derecha de, a la izquierda de, cerca de, lejos de, delante de, detrás de, entre.**

Alfredo	Dolores	Graciela	Raúl
Sra. Blanco	Enrique	Leonor	Rubén
Carlos	Sra. Gómez	Óscar	Yolanda

Practice more at vhlcentral.com.

SUBJECT Javier CONJUGATED FORM empiezo Main clause Dudan

Recapitulación

Diagnostics

Completa estas actividades para repasar los conceptos de gramática que aprendiste en esta lección.

1 **Completar** Completa la tabla con el pretérito de los verbos. 18 pts.

Infinitive	yo	ella	nosotros
conducir			
hacer			
saber			

2 **Mi fiesta** Completa este mensaje electrónico con el pretérito de los verbos de la lista. Vas a usar cada verbo sólo una vez. 20 pts.

dar	haber	tener
decir	hacer	traer
estar	poder	venir
	poner	

Hola, Omar:

Como tú no (1) _____ venir a mi fiesta de cumpleaños, quiero contarte cómo fue. El día de mi cumpleaños, muy temprano por la mañana, mis hermanos me (2) _____ una gran sorpresa: ellos (3) _____ un regalo delante de la puerta de mi habitación: ¡una bicicleta roja preciosa! Mi madre nos preparó un desayuno riquísimo. Después de desayunar, mis hermanos y yo (4) _____ que limpiar toda la casa, así que (*therefore*) no (5) _____ más celebración hasta la tarde. A las seis y media (nosotros) (6) _____ una barbacoa en el patio de la casa. Todos los invitados (7) _____ bebidas y regalos. (8) _____ todos mis amigos, excepto tú, ¡qué pena! :-(La fiesta (9) _____ muy animada hasta las diez de la noche, cuando mis padres (10) _____ que los vecinos (*neighbors*) iban a (*were going to*) protestar y entonces todos se fueron a sus casas.

Tu amigo,
Andrés

RESUMEN GRAMATICAL

9.1 Irregular preterites *pp. 310–311*

u-stem	estar poder poner saber tener	estuv- pud- pus- sup- tuv-	-e, -iste, -o, -imos, -isteis, -(i)eron
i-stem	hacer querer venir	hic- quis- vin-	
j-stem	conducir decir traducir traer	conduj- dij- traduj- traj-	

- Preterite of **dar**: **di, diste, dio, dimos, disteis, dieron**
- Preterite of **hay** (*inf.* **haber**): **hubo**

9.2 Verbs that change meaning in the preterite *p. 314*

Present	Preterite
conocer	
to know; to be acquainted with	*to meet*
saber	
to know info.; to know how to do something	*to find out; to learn*
poder	
to be able; can	*to manage; to succeed*
querer	
to want; to love	*to try*

9.3 ¿Qué? and ¿cuál? *p. 316*

- Use **¿qué?** to ask for a definition or an explanation.
- Use **¿cuál(es)?** when there is more than one possibility to choose from.
- **¿Cuál?** cannot be used before a noun; use **¿qué?** instead.
- **¿Qué?** used before a noun has the same meaning as **¿cuál?**

9.4 Pronouns after prepositions *p. 318*

Prepositional pronouns

	Singular	Plural
Preposition +	mí	nosotros/as
	ti	vosotros/as
	Ud.	Uds.
	él	ellos
	ella	ellas

► Exceptions: **conmigo, contigo, entre tú y yo**

3 **¿Presente o pretérito?** Escoge la forma correcta de los verbos entre paréntesis. 12 pts.

1. Después de muchos intentos (*tries*), (podemos/pudimos) hacer una piñata.
2. —¿Conoces a Pepe?
   —Sí, lo (conozco/conocí) en tu fiesta.
3. Como no es de aquí, Cristina no (sabe/supo) mucho de las celebraciones locales.
4. Yo no (quiero/quise) ir a un restaurante grande, pero tú decides.
5. Ellos (quieren/quisieron) darme una sorpresa, pero Nina me lo dijo todo.
6. Mañana se terminan las vacaciones; por fin (podemos/pudimos) volver a la escuela.

4 **Preguntas** Escribe una pregunta para cada respuesta con los elementos dados. Empieza con **qué**, **cuál** o **cuáles** de acuerdo con el contexto y haz los cambios necesarios. 8 pts.

1. —¿? / pastel / querer —Quiero el pastel de chocolate.
2. —¿? / ser / flan —El flan es un postre típico hispano.
3. —¿? / ser / restaurante favorito —Mis restaurantes favoritos son Dalí y Jaleo.
4. —¿? / ser / dirección electrónica —Mi dirección electrónica es paco@email.com.

5 **¿Dónde me siento?** Completa la conversación con los pronombres apropiados. 14 pts.

JUAN A ver, te voy a decir dónde te vas a sentar. Manuel, ¿ves esa silla? Es para _____. Y esa otra silla es para tu novia, que todavía no está aquí.

MANUEL Muy bien, yo la reservo para _____.

HUGO ¿Y esta silla es para _____?

JUAN No, Hugo. No es para _____. Es para Carmina, que viene con Julio.

HUGO No, Carmina y Julio no pueden venir. Hablé con _____ y me avisaron.

JUAN Pues ellos se lo pierden (*it's their loss*). ¡Más comida para _____ (*us*)!

CAMARERO Aquí tienen el menú. Les doy un minuto y enseguida estoy con _____.

6 **Cumpleaños feliz** Escribe cinco oraciones que describan cómo celebraste tu último cumpleaños. Usa el pretérito y los pronombres que aprendiste en esta lección. 28 pts.

7 **Adivinanza** Completa la adivinanza con la palabra que falta y adivina la respuesta.
¡4 puntos EXTRA!

"Sólo una vez al año
tú celebras ese día,
y conmemoras° la fecha
en que llegaste a la vida.
¿_____ es?"

(El _____)

conmemoras *commemorate*

recursos
vText
vhlcentral

Practice more at vhlcentral.com.

Lectura

Audio: Reading
Additional Reading

Antes de leer

Estrategia

Recognizing word families

Recognizing root words can help you guess the meaning of words in context, ensuring better comprehension of a reading selection. Using this strategy will enrich your Spanish vocabulary as you will see below.

Examinar el texto

Familiarízate con el texto usando las estrategias de lectura más efectivas para ti. ¿Qué tipo de documento es? ¿De qué tratan° las cuatro secciones del documento? Explica tus respuestas.

Raíces°

Completa el siguiente cuadro° para ampliar tu vocabulario. Usa palabras de la lectura de esta lección y vocabulario de las lecciones anteriores. ¿Qué significan las palabras que escribiste en el cuadro?

Verbo	Sustantivos	Otras formas
1. agradecer *to thank, to be grateful for*	agradecimiento/ gracias *gratitude/thanks*	agradecido *grateful, thankful*
2. estudiar	_____	_____
3. _____	_____	celebrado
4. _____	baile	_____
5. bautizar	_____	_____

¿De qué tratan...? *What are... about?* Raíces *Roots* cuadro *chart*

recursos
vText | CH pp. 144–145 | vhlcentral

VIDA SOCIAL

Matrimonio

Espinoza Álvarez–Reyes Salazar

El día sábado 17 de junio a las 19 horas, se celebró el matrimonio de Silvia Reyes y Carlos Espinoza en la catedral de Santiago. La ceremonia fue oficiada por el pastor Federico Salas y participaron los padres de los novios, el señor Jorge Espinoza y señora, y el señor José Alfredo Reyes y señora. Después de la ceremonia, los padres de los recién casados ofrecieron una fiesta bailable en el restaurante La Misión.

Bautismo

José María recibió el bautismo el 26 de junio.

Sus padres, don Roberto Lagos Moreno y doña María Angélica Sánchez, compartieron la alegría de la fiesta con todos sus parientes y amigos. La ceremonia religiosa tuvo lugar° en la catedral de Aguas Blancas. Después de la ceremonia, padres, parientes y amigos celebraron una fiesta en la residencia de la familia Lagos.

32B

Fiesta de quince años

El doctor don Amador Larenas Fernández y la señora Felisa Vera de Larenas celebraron los quince años de su hija Ana Ester junto a sus parientes y amigos. La quinceañera reside en la ciudad de Valparaíso y es estudiante del Colegio Francés. La fiesta de presentación en sociedad de la señorita Ana Ester fue el día viernes 2 de mayo a las 19 horas en el Club Español. Entre los invitados especiales asistieron el alcalde° de la ciudad, don Pedro Castedo, y su esposa. La música estuvo a cargo de la Orquesta Americana. ¡Feliz cumpleaños, le deseamos a la señorita Ana Ester en su fiesta bailable!

Expresión de gracias
Carmen Godoy Tapia

Agradecemos° sinceramente a todas las personas que nos acompañaron en el último adiós a nuestra apreciada esposa, madre, abuela y tía, la señora Carmen Godoy Tapia. El funeral tuvo lugar el día 28 de junio en la ciudad de Viña del Mar. La vida de Carmen Godoy fue un ejemplo de trabajo, amistad, alegría y amor para todos nosotros. Su esposo, hijos y familia agradecen de todo corazón° su asistencia° al funeral a todos los parientes y amigos.

tuvo lugar *took place* **alcalde** *mayor* **Agradecemos** *We thank* **de todo corazón** *sincerely* **asistencia** *attendance*

Después de leer

Corregir

Escribe estos comentarios otra vez para corregir la información errónea.

1. El alcalde y su esposa asistieron a la boda de Silvia y Carlos.
2. Todos los anuncios (*announcements*) describen eventos felices.
3. Felisa Vera de Larenas cumple quince años.
4. Roberto Lagos y María Angélica Sánchez son hermanos.
5. Carmen Godoy Tapia les dio las gracias a las personas que asistieron al funeral.

Identificar

Escribe los nombres de la(s) persona(s) descrita(s) (*described*).

1. Dejó viudo a su esposo el 28 de junio.
2. Sus padres y todos los invitados brindaron por él, pero él no entendió por qué.
3. El Club Español les presentó una cuenta considerable.
4. Unió a los novios en santo matrimonio.
5. Su fiesta de cumpleaños se celebró en Valparaíso.

Un anuncio

Trabajen en grupos pequeños para inventar un anuncio breve sobre una celebración importante. Puede ser una graduación, un cumpleaños o una gran fiesta en la que ustedes participan. Incluyan la siguiente información.

1. nombres de los participantes
2. la fecha, la hora y el lugar
3. qué se celebra
4. otros detalles de interés

Practice more at vhlcentral.com.

Escritura

Estrategia

Planning and writing a comparative analysis

Writing any kind of comparative analysis requires careful planning. Venn diagrams are useful for organizing your ideas visually before comparing and contrasting people, places, objects, events, or issues. To create a Venn diagram, draw two circles that overlap one another and label the top of each circle. List the differences between the two elements in the outer rings of the two circles, then list their similarities where the two circles overlap. Review the following example.

Diferencias y similitudes

La lista de palabras y expresiones a la derecha puede ayudarte a escribir este tipo de ensayo (*essay*).

recursos

vText | CPA pp. 149–150 | CH pp. 146–148 | vhlcentral

Tema

Escribir una composición

Compara una celebración familiar (como una boda, una fiesta de cumpleaños o una graduación) a la que tú asististe recientemente con otro tipo de celebración. Utiliza palabras y expresiones de esta lista.

Para expresar similitudes

además; también	*in addition; also*
al igual que	*the same as*
como	*as; like*
de la misma manera	*in the same manner (way)*
del mismo modo	*in the same manner (way)*
tan + [*adjetivo*] + como	*as* + [adjective] + *as*
tanto/a(s) + [*sustantivo*] + como	*as many/much* + [noun] + *as*

Para expresar diferencias

a diferencia de	*unlike*
a pesar de	*in spite of*
aunque	*although*
en cambio	*on the other hand*
más/menos... que	*more/less . . . than*
no obstante	*nevertheless; however*
por otro lado	*on the other hand*
por el contrario	*on the contrary*
sin embargo	*nevertheless; however*

Escuchar

Audio

Estrategia

Guessing the meaning of words through context

When you hear an unfamiliar word, you can often guess its meaning by listening to the words and phrases around it.

To practice this strategy, you will now listen to a paragraph. Jot down the unfamiliar words that you hear. Then listen to the paragraph again and jot down the word or words that give the most useful clues to the meaning of each unfamiliar word.

Preparación

Lee la invitación. ¿De qué crees que van a hablar Rosa y Josefina?

Margarita Robles de García
y Roberto García Olmos

Piden su presencia en la celebración
del décimo aniversario de bodas
el día 13 de marzo
con una misa en la Iglesia Virgen del Coromoto
a las 6:30

seguida por cena y baile
en el restaurante El Campanero,
Calle Principal, Las Mercedes
a las 8:30

Ahora escucha

Ahora escucha la conversación entre Josefina y Rosa. Cuando oigas una de las palabras de la columna A, usa el contexto para identificar el sinónimo o la definición en la columna B.

A	B
____ festejar	a. conmemoración religiosa de una muerte
____ dicha	b. tolera
____ bien parecido	c. suerte
____ finge (fingir)	d. celebrar
____ soporta (soportar)	e. me divertí
____ yo lo disfruté (disfrutar)	f. horror
	g. crea una ficción
	h. guapo

Comprensión

¿Cierto o falso?

Lee cada oración e indica si lo que dice es **cierto** o **falso**. Corrige las oraciones falsas.

1. No invitaron a mucha gente a la fiesta de Margarita y Roberto porque ellos no conocen a muchas personas.
2. Algunos fueron a la fiesta con pareja y otros fueron sin compañero/a.
3. Margarita y Roberto decidieron celebrar el décimo aniversario porque no hicieron una fiesta el día de su boda.
4. Rafael les parece interesante a Rosa y a Josefina.
5. Josefina se divirtió mucho en la fiesta porque bailó toda la noche con Rafael.

Preguntas

Responde a estas preguntas con oraciones completas.

1. ¿Son solteras Rosa y Josefina? ¿Cómo lo sabes?
2. ¿Tienen las chicas una amistad de mucho tiempo con la pareja que celebra su aniversario? ¿Cómo lo sabes?

recursos
vText
vhlcentral

en pantalla

Video: TV Clip

Fiestas Patrias: Chilevisión

Noviembre: disfraces, dulces...

Preparación

Contesta las siguientes preguntas y después comparte las respuestas con un grupo de compañeros/as.

1. ¿Por qué son importantes las celebraciones de una nación?
2. ¿Cuál es la fiesta más importante de tu país? ¿Cómo se celebra?
3. ¿Cómo celebra tu familia las fiestas más importantes del año?

Las Fiestas Patrias

El 18 de septiembre, Chile conmemora su independencia de España, y los chilenos celebran toda una semana. Durante las Fiestas Patrias°, casi todas las oficinas° y escuelas se cierran para que la gente se reúna° a festejar. Desfiles y rodeos representan la tradición de los vaqueros° del país, y la gente baila cueca, el baile nacional. Las familias y los amigos se reúnen para disfrutar platos tradicionales como las empanadas y los asados. Otra de las tradiciones de estas fiestas son las cometas°, llamadas volantines. En este video podrás ver cómo se celebran otras fiestas en Chile.

Fiestas Patrias *Independence Day celebrations* oficinas *offices* se reúna *would get together* vaqueros *cowboys* cometas/volantines *kites*

Vocabulario útil

conejo	*bunny*
disfraces	*costumes*
mariscal	*traditional Chilean soup with raw seafood*
sustos	*frights*
vieja (Chi.)	*mother*

Comprensión

Selecciona la palabra que no está relacionada con cada grupo.

1. disfraces • noviembre • arbolito • sustos
2. volantines • arbolito • regalos • diciembre
3. conejo • enero • huevitos • chocolates
4. septiembre • volantines • disfraces • asado

Conversación

Discute estas preguntas con un(a) compañero/a.

¿En tu país existen fiestas similares a las de Chile durante todo el año? ¿Cómo se celebran? ¿Y cómo se celebran las Fiestas Patrias de tu país?

Aplicación

En grupos pequeños, preparen una presentación sobre una fiesta o evento importante en la vida de sus familias o su comunidad. Incluyan imágenes en su presentación y describan estos aspectos: cuándo y dónde se celebra, quiénes la celebran, los elementos que identifican esta celebración y la diferencian de otras, los alimentos, la música y los regalos que forman parte del evento.

Practice more at vhlcentral.com.

recursos vText vhlcentral

Video: *Flash cultura*

El Día de los Reyes Magos* es una celebración muy popular en muchos países hispanos. No sólo es el día en que los reyes les traen regalos a los niños, también es una fiesta llena° de tradiciones. La tarde del 5 de enero, en muchas ciudades como Barcelona, España, se hace un desfile° en que los reyes regalan dulces a los niños y reciben sus cartas con peticiones. Esa noche, antes de irse a dormir, los niños deben dejar° un zapato junto a la ventana y un bocado° para los reyes. En Puerto Rico, por ejemplo, los niños ponen una caja con hierba° bajo su cama para alimentar a los camellos° de los reyes.

Vocabulario útil

los cabezudos	*carnival figures with large heads*
los carteles	*posters*
fiesta de pueblo	*popular celebration*
santos de palo	*wooden saints*

Preparación

¿Se celebra la Navidad en tu país? ¿Qué otras fiestas importantes se celebran? En cada caso, ¿cuántos días dura la fiesta? ¿Cuáles son las tradiciones y actividades típicas? ¿Hay alguna comida típica en esa celebración?

Elegir

Indica cuál de las dos opciones resume mejor este episodio.

a. Las Navidades puertorriqueñas son las más largas y terminan después de las fiestas de la calle San Sebastián. Esta fiesta de pueblo se celebra con baile, música y distintas expresiones artísticas típicas.

b. En la celebración de las Navidades puertorriqueñas, los cabezudos son una tradición de España y son el elemento más importante de la fiesta. A la gente le gusta bailar y hacer procesiones por la noche.

** According to the Christian tradition, the Three Wise Men were the three kings that traveled to Bethlehem after the birth of Baby Jesus, carrying with them gifts of gold, frankincense, and myrrh to pay him homage.*

llena *full* desfile *parade* dejar *leave* bocado *snack* hierba *grass* alimentar los camellos *feed the camels*

Las fiestas

Los cabezudos son una tradición [...] de España.

Hay mucha gente y mucho arte.

Es una fiesta de pueblo... una tradición. Vengo todos los años.

Practice more at vhlcentral.com.

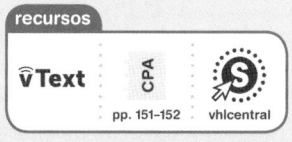

Chile

Video: *Panorama cultural*
Interactive Map

El país en cifras

- **Área:** 756.950 km² (292.259 millas²), *dos veces el área de Montana*
- **Población:** 17.363.000
  Aproximadamente el 80 por ciento de la población del país es urbana.
- **Capital:** Santiago de Chile—6.034.000
- **Ciudades principales:** Valparaíso—865.000, Concepción, Viña del Mar, Temuco
- **Moneda:** peso chileno
- **Idiomas:** español (oficial), mapuche

Bandera de Chile

Chilenos célebres

- **Bernardo O'Higgins,** militar° y héroe nacional (1778–1842)
- **Gabriela Mistral,** Premio Nobel de Literatura, 1945; poeta y diplomática (1889–1957)
- **Pablo Neruda,** Premio Nobel de Literatura, 1971; poeta (1904–1973)
- **Isabel Allende,** novelista (1942–)
- **Ana Tijoux,** cantante (1977–)

Pablo Neruda

militar *soldier* desierto *desert* más seco *driest* mundo *world*
han tenido *have had* ha sido usado *has been used* Marte *Mars*

recursos
vText
CPA pp. 153–156
vhlcentral

¡Increíble pero cierto!

El desierto° de Atacama, en el norte de Chile, es el más seco° del mundo°. Con más de cien mil km² de superficie, algunas zonas de este desierto nunca han tenido° lluvia. Atacama ha sido usado° como escenario para representar a Marte° en películas y series de televisión.

Lugares • **La isla de Pascua**

La isla de Pascua° recibió ese nombre porque los exploradores holandeses° llegaron a la isla por primera vez el día de Pascua de 1722. Ahora es parte del territorio de Chile. La isla de Pascua es famosa por los *moái,* estatuas enormes que representan personas con rasgos° muy exagerados. Estas estatuas las construyeron los *rapa nui,* los antiguos habitantes de la zona. Todavía no se sabe mucho sobre los *rapa nui,* ni tampoco se sabe por qué decidieron abandonar la isla.

Deportes • **Los deportes de invierno**

Hay muchos lugares para practicar deportes de invierno en Chile porque las montañas nevadas de los Andes ocupan gran parte del país. El Parque Nacional Villarrica, por ejemplo, situado al pie de un volcán y junto a° un lago, es un sitio popular para el esquí y el *snowboard.* Para los que prefieren deportes más extremos, el centro de esquí Valle Nevado organiza excursiones para practicar heliesquí.

Ciencias • **Astronomía**

Los observatorios chilenos, situados en los Andes, son lugares excelentes para las observaciones astronómicas. Científicos° de todo el mundo van a Chile para estudiar las estrellas° y otros cuerpos celestes°. Hoy día Chile está construyendo nuevos observatorios y telescopios para mejorar las imágenes del universo.

Economía • **El vino**

La producción de vino comenzó en Chile en el siglo° XVI. Ahora la industria del vino constituye una parte importante de la actividad agrícola del país y la exportación de sus productos está aumentando° cada vez más. Los vinos chilenos son muy apreciados internacionalmente por su gran variedad, sus ricos y complejos sabores° y su precio moderado. Los más conocidos son los vinos de Aconcagua y del valle del Maipo.

¿Qué aprendiste? Responde a cada pregunta con una oración completa.

1. ¿Qué porcentaje (*percentage*) de la población chilena es urbana?
2. ¿Qué son los *moái*? ¿Dónde están?
3. ¿Qué deporte extremo ofrece el centro de esquí Valle Nevado?
4. ¿Por qué van a Chile científicos de todo el mundo?
5. ¿Cuándo comenzó la producción de vino en Chile?
6. ¿Por qué son apreciados internacionalmente los vinos chilenos?

Conexión Internet Investiga estos temas en **vhlcentral.com.**

1. Busca información sobre Pablo Neruda e Isabel Allende. ¿Dónde y cuándo nacieron? ¿Cuáles son algunas de sus obras (*works*)? ¿Cuáles son algunos de los temas de sus obras?
2. Busca información sobre sitios donde los chilenos y los turistas practican deportes de invierno en Chile. Selecciona un sitio y descríbeselo a tu clase.

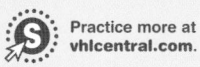

La isla de Pascua *Easter Island* holandeses *Dutch* rasgos *features* junto a *beside* Científicos *Scientists* estrellas *stars* cuerpos celestes *celestial bodies* siglo *century* aumentando *increasing* complejos sabores *complex flavors*

Las celebraciones

el aniversario (de bodas)	*(wedding) anniversary*
la boda	*wedding*
el cumpleaños	*birthday*
el día de fiesta	*holiday*
la fiesta	*party*
el/la invitado/a	*guest*
la Navidad	*Christmas*
la quinceañera	*young woman celebrating her fifteenth birthday*
la sorpresa	*surprise*
brindar	*to toast* (drink)
celebrar	*to celebrate*
divertirse (e:ie)	*to have fun*
invitar	*to invite*
pasarlo bien/mal	*to have a good/bad time*
regalar	*to give* (a gift)
reírse (e:i)	*to laugh*
relajarse	*to relax*
sonreír (e:i)	*to smile*
sorprender	*to surprise*

Los postres y otras comidas

la botella (de vino)	*bottle (of wine)*
el champán	*champagne*
los dulces	*sweets; candy*
el flan (de caramelo)	*baked (caramel) custard*
la galleta	*cookie*
el helado	*ice cream*
el pastel (de chocolate)	*(chocolate) cake; pie*
el postre	*dessert*

Las relaciones personales

la amistad	*friendship*
el amor	*love*
el divorcio	*divorce*
el estado civil	*marital status*
el matrimonio	*marriage*
la pareja	*(married) couple; partner*
el/la recién casado/a	*newlywed*
casarse (con)	*to get married (to)*
comprometerse (con)	*to get engaged (to)*
divorciarse (de)	*to get divorced (from)*
enamorarse (de)	*to fall in love (with)*
llevarse bien/mal (con)	*to get along well/ badly (with)*
odiar	*to hate*
romper (con)	*to break up (with)*
salir (con)	*to go out (with); to date*
separarse (de)	*to separate (from)*
tener una cita	*to have a date; to have an appointment*
casado/a	*married*
divorciado/a	*divorced*
juntos/as	*together*
separado/a	*separated*
soltero/a	*single*
viudo/a	*widower/widow*

Las etapas de la vida

la adolescencia	*adolescence*
la edad	*age*
el estado civil	*marital status*
las etapas de la vida	*the stages of life*
la juventud	*youth*
la madurez	*maturity; middle age*
la muerte	*death*
el nacimiento	*birth*
la niñez	*childhood*
la vejez	*old age*
cambiar (de)	*to change*
graduarse (de/en)	*to graduate (from/in)*
jubilarse	*to retire (from work)*
nacer	*to be born*

Palabras adicionales

la alegría	*happiness*
el beso	*kiss*
conmigo	*with me*
contigo	*with you*

Expresiones útiles	*See page 305.*

Apéndice A

Glossary of Grammatical Terms pages 332–335

Apéndice B

Verb Conjugation Tables pages 336–345

Vocabulario

Spanish–English pages 346–356
English–Spanish pages 357–367

References pages 368–379

Índice pages 380–381

Credits pages 382–383

Glossary of Grammatical Terms

ADJECTIVE A word that modifies, or describes, a noun or pronoun.

muchos libros
many books

un hombre **rico**
*a **rich** man*

las mujeres **altas**
*the **tall** women*

Demonstrative adjective An adjective that specifies which noun a speaker is referring to.

esta fiesta
this party

ese chico
that boy

aquellas flores
those flowers

Possessive adjective An adjective that indicates ownership or possession.

mi mejor vestido
my best dress

Éste es **mi** hermano.
*This is **my** brother.*

Stressed possessive adjective A possessive adjective that emphasizes the owner or possessor.

Es un libro **mío**.
*It's **my book**./It's a book **of mine**.*

Es amiga **tuya**; yo no la conozco.
*She's a friend **of yours**; I don't know her.*

ADVERB A word that modifies, or describes, a verb, adjective, or other adverb.

Pancho escribe **rápidamente**.
*Pancho writes **quickly**.*

Este cuadro es **muy** bonito.
*This picture is **very** pretty.*

ARTICLE A word that points out a noun in either a specific or a non-specific way.

Definite article An article that points out a noun in a specific way.

el libro
the book

la maleta
the suitcase

los diccionarios
the dictionaries

las palabras
the words

Indefinite article An article that points out a noun in a general, non-specific way.

un lápiz
a pencil

una computadora
a computer

unos pájaros
some birds

unas escuelas
some schools

CLAUSE A group of words that contains both a conjugated verb and a subject, either expressed or implied.

Main (or Independent) clause A clause that can stand alone as a complete sentence.

Pienso ir a cenar pronto.
I plan to go to dinner soon.

Subordinate (or Dependent) clause A clause that does not express a complete thought and therefore cannot stand alone as a sentence.

Trabajo en la cafetería **porque necesito dinero para la escuela.**
*I work in the cafeteria **because I need money for school.***

COMPARATIVE A construction used with an adjective or adverb to express a comparison between two people, places, or things.

Este programa es **más interesante que** el otro.
*This program is **more interesting than** the other one.*

Tomás no es **tan alto como** Alberto.
*Tomás is not **as tall as** Alberto.*

CONJUGATION A set of the forms of a verb for a specific tense or mood or the process by which these verb forms are presented.

Preterite conjugation of **cantar:**

canté	cant**amos**
cant**aste**	cant**asteis**
cantó	cant**aron**

CONJUNCTION A word used to connect words, clauses, or phrases.

Susana es de Cuba **y** Pedro es de España.
*Susana is from Cuba **and** Pedro is from Spain.*

No quiero estudiar **pero** tengo que hacerlo.
*I don't want to study, **but** I have to.*

CONTRACTION The joining of two words into one. The only contractions in Spanish are **al** and **del**.

Mi hermano fue **al** concierto ayer.
*My brother went **to the** concert yesterday.*

Saqué dinero **del** banco.
*I took money **from the** bank.*

DIRECT OBJECT A noun or pronoun that directly receives the action of the verb.

Tomás lee **el libro**. — **La** pagó ayer.
*Tomás reads **the book**.* — *She paid **it** yesterday.*

GENDER The grammatical categorizing of certain kinds of words, such as nouns and pronouns, as masculine, feminine, or neuter.

Masculine
articles **el, un**
pronouns **él, lo, mío, éste, ése, aquél**
adjective **simpático**

Feminine
articles **la, una**
pronouns **ella, la, mía, ésta, ésa, aquélla**
adjective **simpática**

IMPERSONAL EXPRESSION A third-person expression with no expressed or specific subject.

Es muy importante. — **Llueve** mucho.
It's very important. — ***It's raining** hard.*

Aquí **se habla** español.
*Spanish **is spoken** here.*

INDIRECT OBJECT A noun or pronoun that receives the action of the verb indirectly; the object, often a living being, to or for whom an action is performed.

Eduardo **le** dio un libro **a Linda**.
*Eduardo gave a book **to Linda**.*

La profesora **me** puso una C en el examen.
*The professor gave **me** a C on the test.*

INFINITIVE The basic form of a verb. Infinitives in Spanish end in **-ar**, **-er**, or **-ir**.

hablar	**correr**	**abrir**
to speak	*to run*	*to open*

INTERROGATIVE An adjective or pronoun used to ask a question.

¿Quién habla? — **¿Cuántos** compraste?
***Who** is speaking?* — ***How many** did you buy?*

¿Qué piensas hacer hoy?
***What** do you plan to do today?*

INVERSION Changing the word order of a sentence, often to form a question.

Statement: Elena pagó la cuenta del restaurante.

Inversion: ¿Pagó Elena la cuenta del restaurante?

MOOD A grammatical distinction of verbs that indicates whether the verb is intended to make a statement or command or to express a doubt, emotion, or condition contrary to fact.

Imperative mood Verb forms used to make commands.

Di la verdad. — **Caminen** ustedes conmigo.
***Tell** the truth.* — ***Walk** with me.*

¡Comamos ahora!
***Let's eat** now!*

Indicative mood Verb forms used to state facts, actions, and states considered to be real.

Sé que **tienes** el dinero.
***I know** that **you have** the money.*

Subjunctive mood Verb forms used principally in subordinate (dependent) clauses to express wishes, desires, emotions, doubts, and certain conditions, such as contrary-to-fact situations.

Prefieren que **hables** en español.
*They prefer that **you speak** in Spanish.*

Dudo que Luis **tenga** el dinero necesario.
*I doubt that Luis **has** the necessary money.*

NOUN A word that identifies people, animals, places, things, and ideas.

hombre	**gato**
man	*cat*
México	**casa**
Mexico	*house*
libertad	**libro**
freedom	*book*

NUMBER A grammatical term that refers to singular or plural. Nouns in Spanish and English have number. Other parts of a sentence, such as adjectives, articles, and verbs, can also have number.

Singular	Plural
una cosa *a thing*	**unas** cosas *some things*
el profesor *the professor*	**los** profesores *the professors*

NUMBERS Words that represent amounts.

Cardinal numbers Words that show specific amounts.

cinco minutos
five minutes

el año **dos mil veintitrés**
the year 2023

Ordinal numbers Words that indicate the order of a noun in a series.

el **cuarto** jugador *the **fourth** player*	la **décima** hora *the **tenth** hour*

PAST PARTICIPLE A past form of the verb used in compound tenses. The past participle may also be used as an adjective, but it must then agree in number and gender with the word it modifies.

Han **buscado** por todas partes.
*They have **searched** everywhere.*

Yo no había **estudiado** para el examen.
*I hadn't **studied** for the exam.*

Hay una **ventana abierta** en la sala.
*There is an **open window** in the living room.*

PERSON The form of the verb or pronoun that indicates the speaker, the one spoken to, or the one spoken about. In Spanish, as in English, there are three persons: first, second, and third.

Person	Singular	Plural
1st	**yo** *I*	**nosotros/as** *we*
2nd	**tú, Ud.** *you*	**vosotros/as, Uds.** *you*
3rd	**él, ella** *he, she*	**ellos, ellas** *they*

PREPOSITION A word or words that describe(s) the relationship, most often in time or space, between two other words.

Anita es **de** California.
*Anita is **from** California.*

La chaqueta está **en** el carro.
*The jacket is **in** the car.*

Marta se peinó **antes de** salir.
*Marta combed her hair **before** going out.*

PRESENT PARTICIPLE In English, a verb form that ends in *-ing*. In Spanish, the present participle ends in **-ndo**, and is often used with **estar** to form a progressive tense.

Mi hermana está **hablando** por teléfono ahora mismo.
*My sister is **talking** on the phone right now.*

PRONOUN A word that takes the place of a noun or nouns.

Demonstrative pronoun A pronoun that takes the place of a specific noun.

Quiero **ésta**.
*I want **this one**.*

¿Vas a comprar **ése**?
*Are you going to buy **that one**?*

Juan prefirió **aquéllos**.
*Juan preferred **those** (over there).*

Object pronoun A pronoun that functions as a direct or indirect object of the verb.

Te digo la verdad.
*I'm telling **you** the truth.*

Me lo trajo Juan.
*Juan brought **it** to **me**.*

Reflexive pronoun A pronoun that indicates that the action of a verb is performed by the subject on itself. These pronouns are often expressed in English with *-self: myself, yourself*, etc.

Yo **me bañé** antes de salir.
*I **bathed (myself)** before going out.*

Elena **se acostó** a las once y media.
*Elena **went to bed** at eleven-thirty.*

Relative pronoun A pronoun that connects a subordinate clause to a main clause.

El chico **que** nos escribió viene a visitar mañana.
*The boy **who** wrote us is coming to visit tomorrow.*

Ya sé **lo que** tenemos que hacer.
*I already know **what** we have to do.*

Subject pronoun A pronoun that replaces the name or title of a person or thing, and acts as the subject of a verb.

Tú debes estudiar más.
***You** should study more.*

Él llegó primero.
***He** arrived first.*

SUBJECT A noun or pronoun that performs the action of a verb and is often implied by the verb.

María va al supermercado.
***María** goes to the supermarket.*

(**Ellos**) Trabajan mucho.
***They** work hard.*

Esos **libros** son muy caros.
*Those **books** are very expensive.*

SUPERLATIVE A word or construction used with an adjective or adverb to express the highest or lowest degree of a specific quality among three or more people, places, or things.

De todas mis clases, ésta es la **más interesante**.
*Of all my classes, this is the **most interesting**.*

Raúl es el **menos simpático** de los chicos.
*Raúl is the **least pleasant** of the boys.*

TENSE A set of verb forms that indicates the time of an action or state: past, present, or future.

Compound tense A two-word tense made up of an auxiliary verb and a present or past participle. In Spanish, there are two auxiliary verbs: **estar** and **haber**.

En este momento, **estoy estudiando**.
*At this time, **I am studying**.*

El paquete no **ha llegado** todavía.
*The package **has** not **arrived** yet.*

Simple tense A tense expressed by a single verb form.

María **estaba** enferma anoche.
*María **was** sick last night.*

Juana **hablará** con su mamá mañana.
*Juana **will speak** with her mom tomorrow.*

VERB A word that expresses actions or states-of-being.

Auxiliary verb A verb used with a present or past participle to form a compound tense. **Haber** is the most commonly used auxiliary verb in Spanish.

Los chicos **han** visto los elefantes.
*The children **have** seen the elephants.*

Espero que **hayas** comido.
*I hope you **have** eaten.*

Reflexive verb A verb that describes an action performed by the subject on itself and is always used with a reflexive pronoun.

Me compré un carro nuevo.
*I **bought myself** a new car.*

Pedro y Adela **se levantan** muy temprano.
*Pedro and Adela **get (themselves) up** very early.*

Spelling-change verb A verb that undergoes a predictable change in spelling, in order to reflect its actual pronunciation in the various conjugations.

practicar	c→qu	practico	practiqué
dirigir	g→j	dirigí	dirijo
almorzar	z→c	almorzó	almorcé

Stem-changing verb A verb whose stem vowel undergoes one or more predictable changes in the various conjugations.

entender (i:ie)	entiendo
pedir (e:i)	piden
dormir (o:ue, u)	duermo, durmieron

Verb Conjugation Tables

The verb lists

The list of verbs below and the model verb tables that start on page 338 show you how to conjugate every verb taught in DESCUBRE. Each verb in the list is followed by a model verb conjugated according to the same pattern. The number in parentheses indicates where in the verb tables you can find the conjugated forms of the model verb. If you want to find out how to conjugate **divertirse**, for example, look up number 33, **sentir**, the model for verbs that follow the **e:ie** stem-change pattern.

How to use the verb tables

In the tables you will find the infinitive, present and past participles, and all the simple forms of each model verb. The formation of the compound tenses of any verb can be inferred from the table of compound tenses, pages 338–339, either by combining the past participle of the verb with a conjugated form of **haber** or by combining the present participle with a conjugated form of **estar**.

abrazar (z:c) like cruzar (37)
abrir like vivir (3) *except* past participle is abierto
aburrir(se) like vivir (3)
acabar de like hablar (1)
acampar like hablar (1)
acompañar like hablar (1)
aconsejar like hablar (1)
acordarse (o:ue) like contar (24)
acostarse (o:ue) like contar (24)
adelgazar (z:c) like cruzar (37)
afeitarse like hablar (1)
ahorrar like hablar (1)
alegrarse like hablar (1)
aliviar like hablar (1)
almorzar (o:ue) like contar (24) *except* (z:c)
alquilar like hablar (1)
andar like hablar (1) *except* preterite stem is anduv-
anunciar like hablar (1)
apagar (g:gu) like llegar (41)
aplaudir like vivir (3)
apreciar like hablar (1)
aprender like comer (2)
apurarse like hablar (1)
arrancar (c:qu) like tocar (43)
arreglar like hablar (1)
asistir like vivir (3)
aumentar like hablar (1)
ayudar(se) like hablar (1)
bailar like hablar (1)
bajar(se) like hablar (1)
bañarse like hablar (1)
barrer like comer (2)
beber like comer (2)
besar(se) like hablar (1)
borrar like hablar (1)
brindar like hablar (1)
bucear like hablar (1)
buscar (c:qu) like tocar (43)
caber (4)
caer(se) (5)
calentarse (e:ie) like pensar (30)
calzar (z:c) like cruzar (37)
cambiar like hablar (1)
caminar like hablar (1)
cantar like hablar (1)
casarse like hablar (1)
cazar (z:c) like cruzar (37)
celebrar like hablar (1)
cenar like hablar (1)
cepillarse like hablar (1)
cerrar (e:ie) like pensar (30)
cobrar like hablar (1)
cocinar like hablar (1)
comenzar (e:ie) (z:c) like empezar (26)
comer (2)
compartir like vivir (3)
comprar like hablar (1)
comprender like comer (2)
comprometerse like comer (2)
comunicarse (c:qu) like tocar (43)
conducir (c:zc) (6)
confirmar like hablar (1)
conocer (c:zc) (35)
conseguir (e:i) (gu:g) like seguir (32)
conservar like hablar (1)
consumir like vivir (3)
contaminar like hablar (1)
contar (o:ue) (24)
contestar like hablar (1))
contratar like hablar (1)
controlar like hablar (1)
conversar like hablar (1)
correr like comer (2)
costar (o:ue) like contar (24)
creer (y) (36)
cruzar (z:c) (37)
cuidar like hablar (1)
cumplir like vivir (3)
dañar like hablar (1)
dar (7)
deber like comer (2)
decidir like vivir (3)
decir (e:i) (8)
declarar like hablar (1)
dejar like hablar (1)
depositar like hablar (1)
desarrollar like hablar (1)
desayunar like hablar (1)
descansar like hablar (1)
descargar (g:gu) like llegar (41)
describir like vivir (3) *except* past participle is descrito
descubrir like vivir (3) *except* past participle is descubierto
desear like hablar (1)
despedirse (e:i) like pedir (29)
despertarse (e:ie) like pensar (30)
destruir (y) (38)
dibujar like hablar (1)
dirigir like vivir (3) *except* (g:j)
disfrutar like hablar (1)
divertirse (e:ie) like sentir (33)
divorciarse like hablar (1)
doblar like hablar (1)
doler (o:ue) like volver (34) *except* past participle is regular
dormir(se) (o:ue) (25)
ducharse like hablar (1)
dudar like hablar (1)
durar like hablar (1)
echar like hablar (1)
elegir (e:i) like pedir (29) *except* (g:j)
emitir like vivir (3)
empezar (e:ie) (z:c) (26)

enamorarse like hablar (1)
encantar like hablar (1)
encontrar(se) (o:ue) like contar (24)
enfermarse like hablar (1)
engordar like hablar (1)
enojarse like hablar (1)
enseñar like hablar (1)
ensuciar like hablar (1)
entender (e:ie) (27)
entrenarse like hablar (1)
entrevistar like hablar (1)
enviar (envío) (39)
escalar like hablar (1)
escanear like hablar (1)
escoger (g:j) like proteger (42)
escribir like vivir (3) *except* past participle is escrito
escuchar like hablar (1)
esculpir like vivir (3)
esperar like hablar (1)
esquiar (esquío) like enviar (39)
establecer (c:zc) like conocer (35)
estacionar like hablar (1)
estar (9)
estornudar like hablar (1)
estudiar like hablar (1)
evitar like hablar (1)
explicar (c:qu) like tocar (43)
faltar like hablar (1)
fascinar like hablar (1)
firmar like hablar (1)
fumar like hablar (1)
funcionar like hablar (1)
ganar like hablar (1)
gastar like hablar (1)
grabar like hablar (1)
graduarse (gradúo) (40)
guardar like hablar (1)
gustar like hablar (1)
haber (hay) (10)
hablar (1)
hacer (11)
importar like hablar (1)
imprimir like vivir (3)
indicar (c:qu) like tocar (43)
informar like hablar (1)
insistir like vivir (3)
interesar like hablar (1)
invertir (e:ie) like sentir (33)
invitar like hablar (1)
ir(se) (12)
jubilarse like hablar (1)
jugar (u:ue) (g:gu) (28)
lastimarse like hablar (1)
lavar(se) like hablar (1)
leer (y) like creer (36)
levantar(se) like hablar (1)
limpiar like hablar (1)
llamar(se) like hablar (1)
llegar (g:gu) (41)
llenar like hablar (1)
llevar(se) like hablar (1)
llover (o:ue) like volver (34) *except* past participle is regular
luchar like hablar (1)
mandar like hablar (1)
manejar like hablar (1)
mantener(se) like tener (20)
maquillarse like hablar (1)
mejorar like hablar (1)
merendar (e:ie) like pensar (30)
mirar like hablar (1)
molestar like hablar (1)
montar like hablar (1)
morir (o:ue) like dormir (25) *except* past participle is *muerto*
mostrar (o:ue) like contar (24)
mudarse like hablar (1)
nacer (c:zc) like conocer (35)
nadar like hablar (1)
navegar (g:gu) like llegar (41)
necesitar like hablar (1)
negar (e:ie) like pensar (30) *except* (g:gu)
nevar (e:ie) like pensar (30)
obedecer (c:zc) like conocer (35)
obtener like tener (20)
ocurrir like vivir (3)
odiar like hablar (1)
ofrecer (c:zc) like conocer (35)
oír (y) (13)
olvidar like hablar (1)
pagar (g:gu) like llegar (41)
parar like hablar (1)
parecer (c:zc) like conocer (35)
pasar like hablar (1)
pasear like hablar (1)
patinar like hablar (1)
pedir (e:i) (29)
peinarse like hablar (1)
pensar (e:ie) (30)
perder (e:ie) like entender (27)
pescar (c:qu) like tocar (43)
pintar like hablar (1)
planchar like hablar (1)
poder (o:ue) (14)
poner(se) (15)
practicar (c:qu) like tocar (43)
preferir (e:ie) like sentir (33)
preguntar like hablar (1)
prender like comer (2)
preocuparse like hablar (1)
preparar like hablar (1)
presentar like hablar (1)
prestar like hablar (1)
probar(se) (o:ue) like contar (24)
prohibir like vivir (3)
proteger (g:j) (42)
publicar (c:qu) like tocar (43)
quedar(se) like hablar (1)
querer (e:ie) (16)
quitar(se) like hablar (1)
recetar like hablar (1)
recibir like vivir (3)
reciclar like hablar (1)
recoger (g:j) like proteger (42)
recomendar (e:ie) like pensar (30)
recordar (o:ue) like contar (24)
reducir (c:zc) like conducir (6)
regalar like hablar (1)
regatear like hablar (1)
regresar like hablar (1)
reír(se) (e:i) (31)
relajarse like hablar (1)
renunciar like hablar (1)
repetir (e:i) like pedir (29)
resolver (o:ue) like volver (34)
respirar like hablar (1)
revisar like hablar (1)
rogar (o:ue) like contar (24) *except* (g:gu)
romper(se) like comer (2) *except* past participle is roto
saber (17)
sacar (c:qu) like tocar (43)
sacudir like vivir (3)
salir (18)
saludar(se) like hablar (1)
secar(se) (c:q) like tocar (43)
seguir (e:i) (32)
sentarse (e:ie) like pensar (30)
sentir(se) (e:ie) (33)
separarse like hablar (1)
ser (19)
servir (e:i) like pedir (29)
solicitar like hablar (1)
sonar (o:ue) like contar (24)
sonreír (e:i) like reír(se) (31)
sorprender like comer (2)
subir like vivir (3)
sudar like hablar (1)
sufrir like vivir (3)
sugerir (e:ie) like sentir (33)
suponer like poner (15)
temer like comer (2)
tener (20)
terminar like hablar (1)
tocar (c:qu) (43)
tomar like hablar (1)
torcerse (o:ue) like volver (34) *except* (c:z) and past participle is regular; e.g. yo tuerzo
toser like comer (2)
trabajar like hablar (1)
traducir (c:zc) like conducir (6)
traer (21)
transmitir like vivir (3)
tratar like hablar (1)
usar like hablar (1)
vencer (c:z) (44)
vender like comer (2)
venir (22)
ver (23)
vestirse (e:i) like pedir (29)
viajar like hablar (1)
visitar like hablar (1)
vivir (3)
volver (o:ue) (34)
votar like hablar (1)

Regular verbs: simple tenses

		INDICATIVE					SUBJUNCTIVE		IMPERATIVE
	Infinitive	Present	Imperfect	Preterite	Future	Conditional	Present	Past	
1	hablar	hablo	hablaba	hablé	hablaré	hablaría	hable	hablara	
		hablas	hablabas	hablaste	hablarás	hablarías	hables	hablaras	habla tú (no hables)
	Participles:	habla	hablaba	habló	hablará	hablaría	hable	hablara	hable Ud.
	hablando	hablamos	hablábamos	hablamos	hablaremos	hablaríamos	hablemos	habláramos	hablemos
	hablado	habláis	hablabais	hablasteis	hablaréis	hablaríais	habléis	hablarais	hablad (no habléis)
		hablan	hablaban	hablaron	hablarán	hablarían	hablen	hablaran	hablen Uds.
2	comer	como	comía	comí	comeré	comería	coma	comiera	
		comes	comías	comiste	comerás	comerías	comas	comieras	come tú (no comas)
	Participles:	come	comía	comió	comerá	comerían	coma	comiera	coma Ud.
	comiendo	comemos	comíamos	comimos	comeremos	comeríamos	comamos	comiéramos	comamos
	comido	coméis	comíais	comisteis	comeréis	comeríais	comáis	comierais	comed (no comáis)
		comen	comían	comieron	comerán	comerían	coman	comieran	coman Uds.
3	vivir	vivo	vivía	viví	viviré	viviría	viva	viviera	
		vives	vivías	viviste	vivirás	vivirías	vivas	vivieran	vive tú (no vivas)
	Participles:	vive	vivía	vivió	vivirá	viviría	viva	viviera	viva Ud.
	viviendo	vivimos	vivíamos	vivimos	viviremos	viviríamos	vivamos	viviéramos	vivamos
	vivido	vivís	vivíais	vivisteis	viviréis	viviríais	viváis	vivierais	vivid (no viváis)
		viven	vivían	vivieron	vivirán	vivirían	vivan	vivieran	vivan Uds.

All verbs: compound tenses

PERFECT TENSES											
INDICATIVE									SUBJUNCTIVE		
Present Perfect		Past Perfect		Future Perfect		Conditional Perfect			Present Perfect	Past Perfect	
he	hablado	había	hablado	habré	hablado	habría	hablado		haya	hubiera	hablado
has	comido	habías	comido	habrás	comido	habrías	comido		hayas	hubieras	comido
ha	vivido	había	vivido	habrá	vivido	habría	vivido		haya	hubiera	vivido
hemos		habíamos		habremos		habríamos			hayamos	hubiéramos	
habéis		habíais		habréis		habríais			hayáis	hubierais	
han		habían		habrán		habrían			hayan	hubieran	

PROGRESSIVE TENSES											
INDICATIVE									SUBJUNCTIVE		
Present Progressive		Past Progressive		Future Progressive		Conditional Progressive			Present Progressive		Past Progressive	
estoy	hablando	estaba	hablando	estaré	hablando	estaría	hablando		esté	hablando	estuviera	hablando
estás	comiendo	estabas	comiendo	estarás	comiendo	estarías	comiendo		estés	comiendo	estuvieras	comiendo
está	viviendo	estaba	viviendo	estará	viviendo	estaría	viviendo		esté	viviendo	estuviera	viviendo
estamos		estábamos		estaremos		estaríamos			estemos		estuviéramos	
estáis		estabais		estaréis		estaríais			estéis		estuvierais	
están		estaban		estarán		estarían			estén		estuvieran	

Irregular verbs

	INDICATIVE					SUBJUNCTIVE		IMPERATIVE
Infinitive	Present	Imperfect	Preterite	Future	Conditional	Present	Past	
4 caber	**quepo**	cabía	**cupe**	**cabré**	**cabría**	**quepa**	**cupiera**	
	cabes	cabías	**cupiste**	**cabrás**	**cabrías**	**quepas**	**cupieras**	cabe tú (no **quepas**)
Participles:	cabe	cabía	**cupo**	**cabrá**	**cabría**	**quepa**	**cupiera**	**quepa** Ud.
cabiendo	cabemos	cabíamos	**cupimos**	**cabremos**	**cabríamos**	**quepamos**	**cupiéramos**	**quepamos**
cabido	cabéis	cabíais	**cupisteis**	**cabréis**	**cabríais**	**quepáis**	**cupierais**	cabed (no **quepáis**)
	caben	cabían	**cupieron**	**cabrán**	**cabrían**	**quepan**	**cupieran**	**quepan** Uds.
5 caer(se)	**caigo**	caía	caí	caeré	caería	**caiga**	**cayera**	
	caes	caías	**caíste**	caerás	caerías	**caigas**	**cayeras**	cae tú (no **caigas**)
Participles:	cae	caía	**cayó**	caerá	caería	**caiga**	**cayera**	**caiga** Ud.
cayendo	caemos	caíamos	**caímos**	caeremos	caeríamos	**caigamos**	**cayéramos**	**caigamos**
caído	caéis	caíais	**caísteis**	caeréis	caeríais	**caigáis**	**cayerais**	caed (no **caigáis**)
	caen	caían	**cayeron**	caerán	caerían	**caigan**	**cayeran**	**caigan** Uds.
6 conducir	**conduzco**	conducía	**conduje**	conduciré	conduciría	**conduzca**	**condujera**	
(c:zc)	conduces	conducías	**condujiste**	conducirás	conducirías	**conduzcas**	**condujeras**	conduce tú (no **conduzcas**)
	conduce	conducía	**condujo**	conducirá	conduciría	**conduzca**	**condujera**	**conduzca** Ud.
Participles:	conducimos	conducíamos	**condujimos**	conduciremos	conduciríamos	**conduzcamos**	**condujéramos**	**conduzcamos**
conduciendo	conducís	conducíais	**condujisteis**	conduciréis	conduciríais	**conduzcáis**	**condujerais**	conducid (no **conduzcáis**)
conducido	conducen	conducían	**condujeron**	conducirán	conducirían	**conduzcan**	**condujeran**	**conduzcan** Uds.

		INDICATIVE					SUBJUNCTIVE		IMPERATIVE
	Infinitive	Present	Imperfect	Preterite	Future	Conditional	Present	Past	
7	dar	**doy**	daba	**di**	daré	daría	**dé**	**diera**	
		das	dabas	**diste**	darás	darías	des	**dieras**	da tú (no des)
	Participles:	da	daba	**dio**	dará	daría	**dé**	**diera**	**dé** Ud.
	dando	damos	dábamos	**dimos**	daremos	daríamos	demos	**diéramos**	demos
	dado	**dais**	dabais	**disteis**	daréis	daríais	**deis**	**dierais**	dad (no **deis**)
		dan	daban	**dieron**	darán	darían	den	**dieran**	den Uds.
8	decir (e:i)	**digo**	decía	**dije**	**diré**	**diría**	**diga**	**dijera**	
		dices	decías	**dijiste**	**dirás**	**dirías**	**digas**	**dijeras**	**di** tú (no **digas**)
	Participles:	**dice**	decía	**dijo**	**dirá**	**diría**	**diga**	**dijera**	**diga** Ud.
	diciendo	decimos	decíamos	**dijimos**	**diremos**	**diríamos**	**digamos**	**dijéramos**	**digamos**
	dicho	decís	decíais	**dijisteis**	**diréis**	**diríais**	**digáis**	**dijerais**	decid (no **digáis**)
		dicen	decían	**dijeron**	**dirán**	**dirían**	**digan**	**dijeran**	**digan** Uds.
9	estar	**estoy**	estaba	**estuve**	estaré	estaría	**esté**	**estuviera**	
		estás	estabas	**estuviste**	estarás	estarías	**estés**	**estuvieras**	**está** tú (no **estés**)
	Participles:	**está**	estaba	**estuvo**	estará	estaría	**esté**	**estuviera**	**esté** Ud.
	estando	estamos	estábamos	**estuvimos**	estaremos	estaríamos	estemos	**estuviéramos**	estemos
	estado	estáis	estabais	**estuvisteis**	estaréis	estaríais	estéis	**estuvierais**	estad (no estéis)
		están	estaban	**estuvieron**	estarán	estarían	**estén**	**estuvieran**	**estén** Uds.
10	haber	**he**	había	**hube**	**habré**	**habría**	**haya**	**hubiera**	
		has	habías	**hubiste**	**habrás**	**habrías**	**hayas**	**hubieras**	
	Participles:	**ha**	había	**hubo**	**habrá**	**habría**	**haya**	**hubiera**	
	habiendo	**hemos**	habíamos	**hubimos**	**habremos**	**habríamos**	**hayamos**	**hubiéramos**	
	habido	habéis	habíais	**hubisteis**	**habréis**	**habríais**	**hayáis**	**hubierais**	
		han	habían	**hubieron**	**habrán**	**habrían**	**hayan**	**hubieran**	
11	hacer	**hago**	hacía	**hice**	**haré**	**haría**	**haga**	**hiciera**	
		haces	hacías	**hiciste**	**harás**	**harías**	**hagas**	**hicieras**	**haz** tú (no **hagas**)
	Participles:	hace	hacía	**hizo**	**hará**	**haría**	**haga**	**hiciera**	**haga** Ud.
	haciendo	hacemos	hacíamos	**hicimos**	**haremos**	**haríamos**	**hagamos**	**hiciéramos**	**hagamos**
	hecho	hacéis	hacíais	**hicisteis**	**haréis**	**haríais**	**hagáis**	**hicierais**	haced (no **hagáis**)
		hacen	hacían	**hicieron**	**harán**	**harían**	**hagan**	**hicieran**	**hagan** Uds.
12	ir	**voy**	**iba**	**fui**	iré	iría	**vaya**	**fuera**	
		vas	**ibas**	**fuiste**	irás	irías	**vayas**	**fueras**	**ve** tú (no **vayas**)
	Participles:	**va**	**iba**	**fue**	irá	iría	**vaya**	**fuera**	**vaya** Ud.
	yendo	**vamos**	**íbamos**	**fuimos**	iremos	iríamos	**vayamos**	**fuéramos**	**vamos** (no **vayamos**)
	ido	**vais**	**ibais**	**fuisteis**	iréis	iríais	**vayáis**	**fuerais**	id (no **vayáis**)
		van	**iban**	**fueron**	irán	irían	**vayan**	**fueran**	**vayan** Uds.
13	oír (y)	**oigo**	oía	oí	oiré	oiría	**oiga**	**oyera**	
		oyes	oías	**oíste**	oirás	oirías	**oigas**	**oyeras**	**oye** tú (no **oigas**)
	Participles:	**oye**	oía	**oyó**	oirá	oiría	**oiga**	**oyera**	**oiga** Ud.
	oyendo	**oímos**	oíamos	**oímos**	oiremos	oiríamos	**oigamos**	**oyéramos**	**oigamos**
	oído	oís	oíais	**oísteis**	oiréis	oiríais	**oigáis**	**oyerais**	**oíd** (no **oigáis**)
		oyen	oían	**oyeron**	oirán	oirían	**oigan**	**oyeran**	**oigan** Uds.

		INDICATIVE					SUBJUNCTIVE		IMPERATIVE
	Infinitive	Present	Imperfect	Preterite	Future	Conditional	Present	Past	
14	poder (o:ue)	**puedo**	podía	**pude**	**podré**	**podría**	**pueda**	**pudiera**	
		puedes	podías	**pudiste**	**podrás**	**podrías**	**puedas**	**pudieras**	**puede** tú (no **puedas**)
	Participles:	**puede**	podía	**pudo**	**podrá**	**podría**	**pueda**	**pudiera**	**pueda** Ud.
	pudiendo	podemos	podíamos	**pudimos**	**podremos**	**podríamos**	podamos	**pudiéramos**	podamos
	podido	podéis	podíais	**pudisteis**	**podréis**	**podríais**	podáis	**pudierais**	poded (no podáis)
		pueden	podían	**pudieron**	**podrán**	**podrían**	**puedan**	**pudieran**	**puedan** Uds.
15	poner	**pongo**	ponía	**puse**	**pondré**	**pondría**	**ponga**	**pusiera**	
		pones	ponías	**pusiste**	**pondrás**	**pondrías**	**pongas**	**pusieras**	**pon** tú (no **pongas**)
	Participles:	pone	ponía	**puso**	**pondrá**	**pondría**	**ponga**	**pusiera**	**ponga** Ud.
	poniendo	ponemos	poníamos	**pusimos**	**pondremos**	**pondríamos**	**pongamos**	**pusiéramos**	**pongamos**
	puesto	ponéis	poníais	**pusisteis**	**pondréis**	**pondríais**	**pongáis**	**pusierais**	poned (no **pongáis**)
		ponen	ponían	**pusieron**	**pondrán**	**pondrían**	**pongan**	**pusieran**	**pongan** Uds.
16	querer (e:ie)	**quiero**	quería	**quise**	**querré**	**querría**	**quiera**	**quisiera**	
		quieres	querías	**quisiste**	**querrás**	**querrías**	**quieras**	**quisieras**	**quiere** tú (no **quieras**)
	Participles:	**quiere**	quería	**quiso**	**querrá**	**querría**	**quiera**	**quisiera**	**quiera** Ud.
	queriendo	queremos	queríamos	**quisimos**	**querremos**	**querríamos**	queramos	**quisiéramos**	queramos
	querido	queréis	queríais	**quisisteis**	**querréis**	**querríais**	queráis	**quisierais**	quered (no queráis)
		quieren	querían	**quisieron**	**querrán**	**querrían**	**quieran**	**quisieran**	**quieran** Uds.
17	saber	**sé**	sabía	**supe**	**sabré**	**sabría**	**sepa**	**supiera**	
		sabes	sabías	**supiste**	**sabrás**	**sabrías**	**sepas**	**supieras**	sabe tú (no **sepas**)
	Participles:	sabe	sabía	**supo**	**sabrá**	**sabría**	**sepa**	**supiera**	**sepa** Ud.
	sabiendo	sabemos	sabíamos	**supimos**	**sabremos**	**sabríamos**	**sepamos**	**supiéramos**	**sepamos**
	sabido	sabéis	sabíais	**supisteis**	**sabréis**	**sabríais**	**sepáis**	**supierais**	sabed (no **sepáis**)
		saben	sabían	**supieron**	**sabrán**	**sabrían**	**sepan**	**supieran**	**sepan** Uds.
18	salir	**salgo**	salía	salí	**saldré**	**saldría**	**salga**	saliera	
		sales	salías	saliste	**saldrás**	**saldrías**	**salgas**	salieras	**sal** tú (no **salgas**)
	Participles:	sale	salía	salió	**saldrá**	**saldría**	**salga**	saliera	**salga** Ud.
	saliendo	salimos	salíamos	salimos	**saldremos**	**saldríamos**	**salgamos**	saliéramos	**salgamos**
	salido	salís	salíais	salisteis	**saldréis**	**saldríais**	**salgáis**	salierais	salid (no **salgáis**)
		salen	salían	salieron	**saldrán**	**saldrían**	**salgan**	salieran	**salgan** Uds.
19	ser	**soy**	**era**	**fui**	seré	sería	**sea**	**fuera**	
		eres	**eras**	**fuiste**	serás	serías	**seas**	**fueras**	**sé** tú (no **seas**)
	Participles:	**es**	**era**	**fue**	será	sería	**sea**	**fuera**	**sea** Ud.
	siendo	**somos**	**éramos**	**fuimos**	seremos	seríamos	**seamos**	**fuéramos**	**seamos**
	sido	**sois**	**erais**	**fuisteis**	seréis	seríais	**seáis**	**fuerais**	sed (no **seáis**)
		son	**eran**	**fueron**	serán	serían	**sean**	**fueran**	**sean** Uds.
20	tener	**tengo**	tenía	**tuve**	**tendré**	**tendría**	**tenga**	**tuviera**	
		tienes	tenías	**tuviste**	**tendrás**	**tendrías**	**tengas**	**tuvieras**	**ten** tú (no **tengas**)
	Participles:	**tiene**	tenía	**tuvo**	**tendrá**	**tendría**	**tenga**	**tuviera**	**tenga** Ud.
	teniendo	tenemos	teníamos	**tuvimos**	**tendremos**	**tendríamos**	**tengamos**	**tuviéramos**	**tengamos**
	tenido	tenéis	teníais	**tuvisteis**	**tendréis**	**tendríais**	**tengáis**	**tuvierais**	tened (no **tengáis**)
		tienen	tenían	**tuvieron**	**tendrán**	**tendrían**	**tengan**	**tuvieran**	**tengan** Uds.

		INDICATIVE					SUBJUNCTIVE		IMPERATIVE
	Infinitive	Present	Imperfect	Preterite	Future	Conditional	Present	Past	
21	traer	**traigo**	traía	**traje**	traeré	traería	**traiga**	**trajera**	
		traes	traías	**trajiste**	traerás	traerías	**traigas**	**trajeras**	trae tú (no **traigas**)
	Participles:	trae	traía	**trajo**	traerá	traería	**traiga**	**trajera**	**traiga** Ud.
	trayendo	traemos	traíamos	**trajimos**	traeremos	traeríamos	**traigamos**	**trajéramos**	**traigamos**
	traído	traéis	traíais	**trajisteis**	traeréis	traeríais	**traigáis**	**trajerais**	traed (no **traigáis**)
		traen	traían	**trajeron**	traerán	traerían	**traigan**	**trajeran**	**traigan** Uds.
22	venir	**vengo**	venía	**vine**	**vendré**	**vendría**	**venga**	**viniera**	
		vienes	venías	**viniste**	**vendrás**	**vendrías**	**vengas**	**vinieras**	**ven** tú (no **vengas**)
	Participles:	**viene**	venía	**vino**	**vendrá**	**vendría**	**venga**	**viniera**	**venga** Ud.
	viniendo	venimos	veníamos	**vinimos**	**vendremos**	**vendríamos**	**vengamos**	**viniéramos**	**vengamos**
	venido	venís	veníais	**vinisteis**	**vendréis**	**vendríais**	**vengáis**	**vinierais**	venid (no **vengáis**)
		vienen	venían	**vinieron**	**vendrán**	**vendrían**	**vengan**	**vinieran**	**vengan** Uds.
23	ver	**veo**	**veía**	**vi**	veré	vería	**vea**	viera	
		ves	**veías**	viste	verás	verías	**veas**	vieras	ve tú (no **veas**)
	Participles:	ve	**veía**	**vio**	verá	vería	**vea**	viera	**vea** Ud.
	viendo	vemos	**veíamos**	vimos	veremos	veríamos	**veamos**	viéramos	**veamos**
	visto	**veis**	**veíais**	visteis	veréis	veríais	**veáis**	vierais	ved (no **veáis**)
		ven	**veían**	vieron	verán	verían	**vean**	vieran	**vean** Uds.

Stem-changing verbs

		INDICATIVE					SUBJUNCTIVE		IMPERATIVE
	Infinitive	Present	Imperfect	Preterite	Future	Conditional	Present	Past	
24	contar	**cuento**	contaba	conté	contaré	contaría	**cuente**	contara	
	(o:ue)	**cuentas**	contabas	contaste	contarás	contarías	**cuentes**	contaras	**cuenta** tú (no **cuentes**)
		cuenta	contaba	contó	contará	contaría	**cuente**	contara	**cuente** Ud.
	Participles:	contamos	contábamos	contamos	contaremos	contaríamos	contemos	contáramos	contemos
	contando	contáis	contabais	contasteis	contaréis	contaríais	contéis	contarais	contad (no contéis)
	contado	**cuentan**	contaban	contaron	contarán	contarían	**cuenten**	contaran	**cuenten** Uds.
25	dormir	**duermo**	dormía	dormí	dormiré	dormiría	**duerma**	**durmiera**	
	(o:ue)	**duermes**	dormías	dormiste	dormirás	dormirías	**duermas**	**durmieras**	**duerme** tú (no **duermas**)
		duerme	dormía	**durmió**	dormirá	dormiría	**duerma**	**durmiera**	**duerma** Ud.
	Participles:	dormimos	dormíamos	dormimos	dormiremos	dormiríamos	**durmamos**	**durmiéramos**	**durmamos**
	durmiendo	dormís	dormíais	dormisteis	dormiréis	dormiríais	**durmáis**	**durmierais**	dormid (no **durmáis**)
	dormido	**duermen**	dormían	**durmieron**	dormirán	dormirían	**duerman**	**durmieran**	**duerman** Uds.
26	empezar	**empiezo**	empezaba	**empecé**	empezaré	empezaría	**empiece**	empezara	
	(e:ie) (z:c)	**empiezas**	empezabas	empezaste	empezarás	empezarías	**empieces**	empezaras	**empieza** tú (no **empieces**)
		empieza	empezaba	empezó	empezará	empezaría	**empiece**	empezara	**empiece** Ud.
	Participles:	empezamos	empezábamos	empezamos	empezaremos	empezaríamos	**empecemos**	empezáramos	**empecemos**
	empezando	empezáis	empezabais	empezasteis	empezaréis	empezaríais	**empecéis**	empezarais	empezad (no **empecéis**)
	empezado	**empiezan**	empezaban	empezarán	empezarán	empezarían	**empiecen**	empezaran	**empiecen** Uds.

		INDICATIVE					SUBJUNCTIVE		IMPERATIVE
	Infinitive	Present	Imperfect	Preterite	Future	Conditional	Present	Past	
27	entender	**entiendo**	entendía	entendí	entenderé	entendería	**entienda**	entendiera	
	(e:ie)	**entiendes**	entendías	entendiste	entenderás	entenderías	**entiendas**	entendieras	**entiende** tú (no **entiendas**)
		entiende	entendía	entendió	entenderá	entendería	**entienda**	entendiera	**entienda** Ud.
	Participles:	entendemos	entendíamos	entendimos	entenderemos	entenderíamos	entendamos	entendiéramos	entendamos
	entendiendo	entendéis	entendíais	entendisteis	entenderéis	entenderíais	entendáis	entendierais	entended (no entendáis)
	entendido	**entienden**	entendían	entendieron	entenderán	entenderían	**entiendan**	entendieran	**entiendan** Uds.
28	jugar (u:ue)	**juego**	jugaba	**jugué**	jugaré	jugaría	**juegue**	jugara	
	(g:gu)	**juegas**	jugabas	jugaste	jugarás	jugarías	**juegues**	jugaras	**juega** tú (no **juegues**)
		juega	jugaba	jugó	jugará	jugaría	**juegue**	jugara	**juegue** Ud
	Participles:	jugamos	jugábamos	jugamos	jugaremos	jugaríamos	**juguemos**	jugáramos	**juguemos**
	jugando	jugáis	jugabais	jugasteis	jugaréis	jugaríais	**juguéis**	jugarais	jugad (no **juguéis**)
	jugado	**juegan**	jugaban	jugaron	jugarán	jugarían	**jueguen**	jugaran	**jueguen** Uds.
29	pedir (e:i)	**pido**	pedía	pedí	pediré	pediría	**pida**	**pidiera**	
		pides	pedías	pediste	pedirás	pedirías	**pidas**	**pidieras**	**pide** tú (no **pidas**)
	Participles:	**pide**	pedía	**pidió**	pedirá	pediría	**pida**	**pidiera**	**pida** Ud.
	pidiendo	pedimos	pedíamos	pedimos	pediremos	pediríamos	**pidamos**	**pidiéramos**	**pidamos**
	pedido	pedís	pedíais	pedisteis	pediréis	pediríais	**pidáis**	**pidierais**	pedid (no **pidáis**)
		piden	pedían	**pidieron**	pedirán	pedirían	**pidan**	**pidieran**	**pidan** Uds.
30	pensar	**pienso**	pensaba	pensé	pensaré	pensaría	**piense**	pensara	
	(e:ie)	**piensas**	pensabas	pensaste	pensarás	pensarías	**pienses**	pensaras	**piensa** tú (no **pienses**)
		piensa	pensaba	pensó	pensará	pensaría	**piense**	pensara	**piense** Ud.
	Participles:	pensamos	pensábamos	pensamos	pensaremos	pensaríamos	pensemos	pensáramos	pensemos
	pensando	pensáis	pensabais	pensasteis	pensaréis	pensaríais	penséis	pensarais	pensad (no penséis)
	pensado	**piensan**	pensaban	pensaron	pensarán	pensarían	**piensen**	pensaran	**piensen** Uds.
31	reír (e:i)	**río**	reía	reí	reiré	reiría	**ría**	**riera**	
		ríes	reías	**reíste**	reirás	reirías	**rías**	**rieras**	**ríe** tú (no **rías**)
	Participles:	**ríe**	reía	**rió**	reirá	reiría	**ría**	**riera**	**ría** Ud.
	riendo	**reímos**	reíamos	**reímos**	reiremos	reiríamos	**riamos**	**riéramos**	**riamos**
	reído	reís	reíais	**reísteis**	reiréis	reiríais	**riáis**	**rierais**	**reíd** (no **riáis**)
		ríen	reían	**rieron**	reirán	reirían	**rían**	**rieran**	**rían** Uds.
32	seguir (e:i)	**sigo**	seguía	seguí	seguiré	seguiría	**siga**	**siguiera**	
	(gu:g)	**sigues**	seguías	seguiste	seguirás	seguirías	**sigas**	**siguieras**	**sigue** tú (no **sigas**)
		sigue	seguía	**siguió**	seguirá	seguiría	**siga**	**siguiera**	**siga** Ud.
	Participles:	seguimos	seguíamos	seguimos	seguiremos	seguiríamos	**sigamos**	**siguiéramos**	**sigamos**
	siguiendo	seguís	seguíais	seguisteis	seguiréis	seguiríais	**sigáis**	**siguierais**	seguid (no **sigáis**)
	seguido	**siguen**	seguían	**siguieron**	seguirán	seguirían	**sigan**	**siguieran**	**sigan** Uds.
33	sentir (e:ie)	**siento**	sentía	sentí	sentiré	sentiría	**sienta**	**sintiera**	
		sientes	sentías	sentiste	sentirás	sentirías	**sientas**	**sintieras**	**siente** tú (no **sientas**)
		siente	sentía	**sintió**	sentirá	sentiría	**sienta**	**sintiera**	**sienta** Ud.
	Participles:	sentimos	sentíamos	sentimos	sentiremos	sentiríamos	**sintamos**	**sintiéramos**	**sintamos**
	sintiendo	sentís	sentíais	sentisteis	sentiréis	sentiríais	**sintáis**	**sintierais**	sentid (no **sintáis**)
	sentido	**sienten**	sentían	**sintieron**	sentirán	sentirían	**sientan**	**sintieran**	**sientan** Uds.

	INDICATIVE					SUBJUNCTIVE		IMPERATIVE
Infinitive	Present	Imperfect	Preterite	Future	Conditional	Present	Past	
34 volver	**vuelvo**	volvía	volví	volveré	volvería	**vuelva**	volviera	
(o:ue)	**vuelves**	volvías	volviste	volverás	volverías	**vuelvas**	volvieras	**vuelve** tú (no **vuelvas**)
	vuelve	volvía	volvió	volverá	volvería	**vuelva**	volviera	**vuelva** Ud.
Participles:	volvemos	volvíamos	volvimos	volveremos	volveríamos	volvamos	volviéramos	volvamos
volviendo	volvéis	volvíais	volvisteis	volveréis	volveríais	volváis	volvierais	volved (no volváis)
vuelto	**vuelven**	volvían	volvieron	volverán	volverían	**vuelvan**	volvieran	**vuelvan** Uds.

Verbs with spelling changes only

	INDICATIVE					SUBJUNCTIVE		IMPERATIVE
Infinitive	Present	Imperfect	Preterite	Future	Conditional	Present	Past	
35 conocer	**conozco**	conocía	conocí	conoceré	conocería	**conozca**	conociera	
(c:zc)	conoces	conocías	conociste	conocerás	conocerías	**conozcas**	conocieras	conoce tú (no **conozcas**)
	conoce	conocía	conoció	conocerá	conocería	**conozca**	conociera	**conozca** Ud.
Participles:	conocemos	conocíamos	conocimos	conoceremos	conoceríamos	**conozcamos**	conociéramos	**conozcamos**
conociendo	conocéis	conocíais	conocisteis	conoceréis	conoceríais	**conozcáis**	conocierais	conoced (no **conozcáis**)
conocido	conocen	conocían	conocieron	conocerán	conocerían	**conozcan**	conocieran	**conozcan** Uds.
36 creer (y)	creo	creía	creí	creeré	creería	crea	**creyera**	
	crees	creías	**creíste**	creerás	creerías	creas	**creyeras**	cree tú (no creas)
Participles:	cree	creía	**creyó**	creerá	creería	crea	**creyera**	crea Ud.
creyendo	creemos	creíamos	**creímos**	creeremos	creeríamos	creamos	**creyéramos**	creamos
creído	creéis	creíais	**creísteis**	creeréis	creeríais	creáis	**creyerais**	creed (no creáis)
	creen	creían	**creyeron**	creerán	creerían	crean	**creyeran**	crean Uds.
37 cruzar (z:c)	cruzo	cruzaba	**crucé**	cruzaré	cruzaría	**cruce**	cruzara	
	cruzas	cruzabas	cruzaste	cruzarás	cruzarías	**cruces**	cruzaras	cruza tú (no **cruces**)
Participles:	cruza	cruzaba	cruzó	cruzará	cruzaría	**cruce**	cruzara	**cruce** Ud.
cruzando	cruzamos	cruzábamos	cruzamos	cruzaremos	cruzaríamos	**crucemos**	cruzáramos	**crucemos**
cruzado	cruzáis	cruzabais	cruzasteis	cruzaréis	cruzaríais	**crucéis**	cruzarais	cruzad (no **crucéis**)
	cruzan	cruzaban	cruzaron	cruzarán	cruzarían	**crucen**	cruzaran	**crucen** Uds.
38 destruir (y)	**destruyo**	destruía	destruí	destruiré	destruiría	**destruya**	**destruyera**	
	destruyes	destruías	destruiste	destruirás	destruirías	**destruyas**	**destruyeras**	**destruye** tú (no **destruyas**)
Participles:	**destruye**	destruía	**destruyó**	destruirá	destruiría	**destruya**	**destruyera**	**destruya** Ud.
destruyendo	destruimos	destruíamos	destruimos	destruiremos	destruiríamos	**destruyamos**	**destruyéramos**	**destruyamos**
destruido	destruís	destruíais	destruisteis	destruiréis	destruiríais	**destruyáis**	**destruyerais**	destruid (no **destruyáis**)
	destruyen	destruían	**destruyeron**	destruirán	destruirían	**destruyan**	**destruyeran**	**destruyan** Uds.
39 enviar	**envío**	enviaba	envié	enviaré	enviaría	**envíe**	enviara	
(envío)	**envías**	enviabas	enviaste	enviarás	enviarías	**envíes**	enviaras	**envía** tú (no **envíes**)
	envía	enviaba	envió	enviará	enviaría	**envíe**	enviara	**envíe** Ud.
Participles:	enviamos	enviábamos	enviamos	enviaremos	enviaríamos	enviemos	enviáramos	enviemos
enviando	enviáis	enviabais	enviasteis	enviaréis	enviaríais	enviéis	enviarais	enviad (no enviéis)
enviado	**envían**	enviaban	enviaron	enviarán	enviarían	**envíen**	enviaran	**envíen** Uds.

		INDICATIVE					SUBJUNCTIVE		IMPERATIVE
	Infinitive	Present	Imperfect	Preterite	Future	Conditional	Present	Past	
40	graduarse	**gradúo**	graduaba	gradué	graduaré	graduaría	**gradúe**	graduara	
	(gradúo)	**gradúas**	graduabas	graduaste	graduarás	graduarías	**gradúes**	graduaras	**gradúa** tú (no **gradúes**)
		gradúa	graduaba	graduó	graduará	graduaría	**gradúe**	graduara	**gradúe** Ud.
	Participles:	graduamos	graduábamos	graduamos	graduaremos	graduaríamos	graduemos	graduáramos	graduemos
	graduando	graduáis	graduabais	graduasteis	graduaréis	graduaríais	graduéis	graduarais	graduad (no graduéis)
	graduado	**gradúan**	graduaban	graduaron	graduarán	graduarían	**gradúen**	graduaran	**gradúen** Uds.
41	llegar (g:gu)	llego	llegaba	**llegué**	llegaré	llegaría	**llegue**	llegara	
		llegas	llegabas	llegaste	llegarás	llegarías	**llegues**	llegaras	llega tú (no **llegues**)
	Participles:	llega	llegaba	llegó	llegará	llegaría	**llegue**	llegara	**llegue** Ud.
	llegando	llegamos	llegábamos	llegamos	llegaremos	llegaríamos	**lleguemos**	llegáramos	**lleguemos**
	llegado	llegáis	llegabais	llegasteis	llegaréis	llegaríais	**lleguéis**	llegarais	llegad (no **lleguéis**)
		llegan	llegaban	llegaron	llegarán	llegarían	**lleguen**	llegaran	**lleguen** Uds.
42	proteger	**protejo**	protegía	protegí	protegeré	protegería	**proteja**	protegiera	
	(g:j)	proteges	protegías	protegiste	protegerás	protegerías	**protejas**	protegieras	protege tú (no **protejas**)
		protege	protegía	protegió	protegerá	protegería	**proteja**	protegiera	**proteja** Ud.
	Participles:	protegemos	protegíamos	protegimos	protegeremos	protegeríamos	**protejamos**	protegiéramos	**protejamos**
	protegiendo	protegéis	protegíais	protegisteis	protegeréis	protegeríais	**protejáis**	protegierais	proteged (no **protejáis**)
	protegido	protegen	protegían	protegieron	protegerán	protegerían	**protejan**	protegieran	**protejan** Uds.
43	tocar (c:qu)	toco	tocaba	**toqué**	tocaré	tocaría	**toque**	tocara	
		tocas	tocabas	tocaste	tocarás	tocarías	**toques**	tocaras	toca tú (no **toques**)
	Participles:	toca	tocaba	tocó	tocará	tocaría	**toque**	tocara	**toque** Ud.
	tocando	tocamos	tocábamos	tocamos	tocaremos	tocaríamos	**toquemos**	tocáramos	**toquemos**
	tocado	tocáis	tocabais	tocasteis	tocaréis	tocaríais	**toquéis**	tocarais	tocad (no **toquéis**)
		tocan	tocaban	tocaron	tocarán	tocarían	**toquen**	tocaran	**toquen** Uds.
44	vencer (c:z)	**venzo**	vencía	vencí	venceré	vencería	**venza**	venciera	
		vences	vencías	venciste	vencerás	vencerías	**venzas**	vencieras	vence tú (no **venzas**)
	Participles:	vence	vencía	venció	vencerá	vencería	**venza**	venciera	**venza** Ud.
	venciendo	vencemos	vencíamos	vencimos	venceremos	venceríamos	**venzamos**	venciéramos	**venzamos**
	vencido	vencéis	vencíais	vencisteis	venceréis	venceríais	**venzáis**	vencierais	venced (no **venzáis**)
		vencen	vencían	vencieron	vencerán	vencerían	**venzan**	vencieran	**venzan** Uds.

Guide to Vocabulary

Contents of the glossary

This glossary contains the words and expressions listed on the **Vocabulario** page found at the end of each lesson in **DESCUBRE** as well as other useful vocabulary. The number following an entry indicates the **DESCUBRE** level and lesson where the word or expression was introduced. Check the **Estructura** sections of each lesson for words and expressions related to those grammar topics.

Abbreviations used in this glossary

adj.	adjective	*f.*	feminine	*m.*	masculine	*prep.*	preposition
adv.	adverb	*fam.*	familiar	*n.*	noun	*pron.*	pronoun
art.	article	*form.*	formal	*obj.*	object	*ref.*	reflexive
conj.	conjunction	*indef.*	indefinite	*p.p.*	past participle	*sing.*	singular
def.	definite	*interj.*	interjection	*pl.*	plural	*sub.*	subject
d.o.	direct object	*i.o.*	indirect object	*poss.*	possessive	*v.*	verb

Note on alphabetization

In current practice, for purposes of alphabetization, **ch** and **ll** are not treated as separate letters, but **ñ** still follows **n**. Therefore, in this glossary you will find that **año**, for example, appears after **anuncio**.

Spanish-English

A

a *prep.* at; to 1.1
  a bordo aboard 1.1
  a la derecha to the right 1.2
  a la izquierda to the left 1.2
  a la(s) + *time* at + *time* 1.1
  a nombre de in the name of 1.5
  ¿A qué hora...? At what time...? 1.1
  a ver let's see 1.2
abeja *f.* bee
abierto/a *adj.* open 1.5
abrazo *m.* hug
abrigo *m.* coat 1.6
abril *m.* April 1.5
abrir *v.* to open 1.3
abuelo/a *m., f.* grandfather; grandmother 1.3
abuelos *pl.* grandparents 1.3
aburrido/a *adj.* bored; boring 1.5
aburrir *v.* to bore 1.7
acabar de (+ *inf.*) *v.* to have just (*done something*) 1.6
acampar *v.* to camp 1.5
aceite *m.* oil 1.8
acordarse (de) (o:ue) *v.* to remember 1.7
acostarse (o:ue) *v.* to go to bed 1.7
acuático/a *adj.* aquatic 1.4
adicional *adj.* additional
adiós *m.* good-bye 1.1
adjetivo *m.* adjective
administración de empresas *f.* business administration 1.2
adolescencia *f.* adolescence 1.9
¿adónde? *adv.* where (to)? (*destination*) 1.2
aduana *f.* customs 1.5
aeropuerto *m.* airport 1.5
afeitarse *v.* to shave 1.7
aficionado/a *adj.* fan 1.4
afirmativo/a *adj.* affirmative
agencia de viajes *f.* travel agency 1.5
agente de viajes *m., f.* travel agent 1.5
agosto *m.* August 1.5
agradable *adj.* pleasant
agua *f.* water 1.8
  agua mineral mineral water 1.8
ahora *adv.* now 1.2
  ahora mismo right now 1.5
aire *m.* air 1.5
ajo *m.* garlic 1.8
al (*contraction of* **a + el**) 1.2
  al aire libre open-air 1.6
  al lado de beside 1.2
alegre *adj.* happy; joyful 1.5
alegría *f.* happiness 1.9
alemán, alemana *adj.* German 1.3
algo *pron.* something; anything 1.7
algodón *m.* cotton 1.6
alguien *pron.* someone; somebody; anyone 1.7
algún, alguno/a(s) *adj.* any; some 1.7
alimento *m.* food
alimentación *f.* diet
allá *adv.* over there 1.2
allí *adv.* there 1.2
almacén *m.* department store 1.6
almorzar (o:ue) *v.* to have lunch 1.4
almuerzo *m.* lunch 1.8
alto/a *adj.* tall 1.3
amable *adj.* nice; friendly 1.5
amarillo/a *adj.* yellow 1.3
amigo/a *m., f.* friend 1.3
amistad *f.* friendship 1.9
amor *m.* love 1.9
anaranjado/a *adj.* orange 1.6
andar *v.* **en patineta** to skateboard 1.4
aniversario (de bodas) *m.* (wedding) anniversary 1.9
anoche *adv.* last night 1.6
anteayer *adv.* the day before yesterday 1.6
antes *adv.* before 1.7
  antes de *prep.* before 1.7
antipático/a *adj.* unpleasant 1.3
año *m.* year 1.5
  año pasado last year 1.6
aparato *m.* appliance
apellido *m.* last name 1.3
aprender (a + *inf.*) *v.* to learn 1.3
aquel, aquella *adj.* that 1.6
aquél, aquélla *pron.* that 1.6
aquello *neuter pron.* that; that thing; that fact 1.6
aquellos/as *pl. adj.* those (over there) 1.6
aquéllos/as *pl. pron.* those (ones) (over there) 1.6
aquí *adv.* here 1.1
  Aquí está... Here it is... 1.5
  Aquí estamos en... Here we are at/in...
Argentina *f.* Argentina 1.1
argentino/a *adj.* Argentine 1.3

arqueología *f.* archaeology 1.2
arriba *adv.* up
arroz *m.* rice 1.8
arte *m.* art 1.2
artista *m., f.* artist 1.3
arveja *m.* pea 1.8
asado/a *adj.* roast 1.8
ascensor *m.* elevator 1.5
asistir (a) *v.* to attend 1.3
atún *m.* tuna 1.8
aunque *conj.* although
autobús *m.* bus 1.1
automático/a *adj.* automatic
auto(móvil) *m.* auto(mobile) 1.5
avenida *f.* avenue
avergonzado/a *adj.* embarrassed 1.5
avión *m.* airplane 1.5
¡Ay! *interj.* Oh!
¡Ay, qué dolor! Oh, what pain!
ayer *adv.* yesterday 1.6
azúcar *m.* sugar 1.8
azul *adj.* blue 1.3

B

bailar *v.* to dance 1.2
bajo/a *adj.* short (*in height*) 1.3
bajo control under control 1.7
baloncesto *m.* basketball 1.4
banana *f.* banana 1.8
bandera *f.* flag
bañarse *v.* to bathe; to take a bath 1.7
baño *m.* bathroom 1.7
barato/a *adj.* cheap 1.6
barco *m.* boat 1.5
beber *v.* to drink 1.3
bebida *f.* drink 1.8
béisbol *m.* baseball 1.4
beso *m.* kiss 1.9
biblioteca *f.* library 1.2
bicicleta *f.* bicycle 1.4
bien *adj., adv.* well 1.1
billete *m.* paper money; ticket
billón *m.* trillion
biología *f.* biology 1.2
bisabuelo/a *m.* great-grandfather; great-grandmother 1.3
bistec *m.* steak 1.8
bizcocho *m.* biscuit
blanco/a *adj.* white 1.3
(blue)jeans *m., pl.* jeans 1.6
blusa *f.* blouse 1.6
boda *f.* wedding 1.9
bolsa *f.* purse, bag 1.6
bonito/a *adj.* pretty 1.3
borrador *m.* eraser 1.2
bota *f.* boot 1.6
botella *f.* bottle 1.9
botella de vino bottle of wine 1.9
botones *m., f. sing* bellhop 1.5
brindar *v.* to toast (*drink*) 1.9
bucear *v.* to scuba dive 1.4
bueno *adv.* well 1.2
buen, bueno/a *adj.* good 1.3, 1.6
¡Buen viaje! Have a good trip! 1.1
Buena idea. Good idea. 1.4
Buenas noches. Good evening.; Good night. 1.1
Buenas tardes. Good afternoon. 1.1
buenísimo extremely good
¿Bueno? Hello. (*on telephone*)
Buenos días. Good morning. 1.1
bulevar *m.* boulevard
buscar *v.* to look for 1.2

C

caballo *m.* horse 1.5
cada *adj.* each 1.6
café *m.* café 1.4; *adj.* brown 1.6; *m.* coffee 1.8
cafetería *f.* cafeteria 1.2
caja *f.* cash register 1.6
calcetín (calcetines) *m.* sock(s) 1.6
calculadora *f.* calculator 1.2
caldo *m.* soup
calidad *f.* quality 1.6
calor *m.* heat 1.4
calzar *v.* to take size... shoes 1.6
cama *f.* bed 1.5
camarero/a *m., f.* waiter/waitress 1.8
camarón *m.* shrimp 1.8
cambiar (de) *v.* to change 1.9
cambio *m.* **de moneda** currency exchange
caminar *v.* to walk 1.2
camino *m.* road
camión *m* truck; bus
camisa *f.* shirt 1.6
camiseta *f.* t-shirt 1.6
campo *m.* countryside 1.5
canadiense *adj.* Canadian 1.3
cansado/a *adj.* tired 1.5
cantar *v.* to sing 1.2
capital *f.* capital city 1.1
cara *f.* face 1.7
caramelo *m.* caramel 1.9
carne *f.* meat 1.8
carne de res *f.* beef 1.8
caro/a *adj.* expensive 1.6
carta *f.* letter 1.4; (*playing*) card 1.5
cartera *f.* wallet 1.6
casa *f.* house; home 1.2
casado/a *adj.* married 1.9
casarse (con) *v.* to get married (to) 1.9
catorce *n., adj.* fourteen 1.1
cebolla *f.* onion 1.8
celebrar *v.* to celebrate 1.9
cena *f.* dinner 1.8
cenar *v.* to have dinner 1.2
centro *m.* downtown 1.4
centro comercial shopping mall 1.6
cepillarse los dientes/el pelo *v.* to brush one's teeth/one's hair 1.7
cerca de *prep.* near 1.2
cerdo *m.* pork 1.8
cereales *m., pl.* cereal; grains 1.8
cero *m.* zero 1.1
cerrado/a *adj.* closed 1.5
cerrar (e:ie) *v.* to close 1.4
cerveza *f.* beer 1.8
ceviche *m.* marinated fish dish 1.8
ceviche de camarón *m.* lemon-marinated shrimp 1.8
chaleco *m.* vest
champán *m.* champagne 1.9
champiñón *m.* mushroom 1.8
champú *m.* shampoo 1.7
chaqueta *f.* jacket 1.6
chau *fam. interj.* bye 1.1
chévere *adj., fam.* terrific
chico/a *m., f.* boy; girl 1.1
chino/a *adj.* Chinese 1.3
chocar (con) *v.* to run into
chocolate *m.* chocolate 1.9
chuleta *f.* chop (*food*) 1.8
chuleta de cerdo *f.* pork chop 1.8
cibercafé *m.* cybercafé
ciclismo *m.* cycling 1.4
cien(to) *n., adj.* one hundred 1.2
ciencia *f.* science 1.2
cinco *n., adj.* five 1.1
cincuenta *n., adj.* fifty 1.2
cine *m.* movie theater 1.4
cinta *f.* (audio)tape
cinturón *m.* belt 1.6
cita *f.* date; appointment 1.9
ciudad *f.* city 1.4
clase *f.* class 1.2
cliente/a *m., f.* customer 1.6
color *m.* color 1.3, 1.6
comenzar (e:ie) *v.* to begin 1.4
comer *v.* to eat 1.3
comida *f.* food; meal 1.8
como *prep., conj.* like; as 1.8
¿cómo? *adv.* what?; how? 1.1
¿Cómo es...? What's... like? 1.3
¿Cómo está usted? *form.* How are you? 1.1
¿Cómo estás? *fam.* How are you? 1.1
¿Cómo se llama (usted)? *form.* What's your name? 1.1
¿Cómo te llamas (tú)? *fam.* What's your name? 1.1
cómodo/a *adj.* comfortable 1.5
compañero/a de clase *m., f.* classmate 1.2
compañero/a de cuarto *m., f.* roommate 1.2

compartir *v.* to share 1.3
completamente *adv.* completely 1.5
comprar *v.* to buy 1.2
compras *f., pl.* purchases 1.5
  ir de compras to go shopping 1.5
comprender *v.* to understand 1.3
comprobar (o:ue) *v.* to check
comprometerse (con) *v.* to get engaged (to) 1.9
computación *f.* computer science 1.2
computadora *f.* computer 1.1
comunidad *f.* community 1.1
con *prep.* with 1.2
  Con permiso. Pardon me.; Excuse me. 1.1
concordar (o:ue) *v.* to agree
conducir *v.* to drive 1.6
conductor(a) *m., f.* driver 1.1
confirmar *v.* to confirm 1.5
  confirmar *v.* **una reservación** *f.* to confirm a reservation 1.5
confundido/a *adj.* confused 1.5
conmigo *pron.* with me 1.4, 1.9
conocer *v.* to know; to be acquainted with 1.6
conocido/a *adj.; p.p.* known
conseguir (e:i) *v.* to get; to obtain 1.4
consejo *m.* advice
construir *v.* to build
contabilidad *f.* accounting 1.2
contar (o:ue) *v.* to count; to tell 1.4
contento/a *adj.* happy; content 1.5
contestar *v.* to answer 1.2
contigo *fam. pron.* with you 1.9
control *m.* control 1.7
conversación *f.* conversation 1.1
conversar *v.* to converse, to chat 1.2
corbata *f.* tie 1.6
correo electrónico *m.* e-mail 1.4
correr *v.* to run 1.3
cortesía *f.* courtesy
corto/a *adj.* short (in length) 1.6
cosa *f.* thing 1.1
Costa Rica *f.* Costa Rica 1.1
costar (o:ue) *f.* to cost 1.6
costarricense *adj.* Costa Rican 1.3
creer (en) *v.* to believe (in) 1.3
crema de afeitar *f.* shaving cream 1.7
cuaderno *m.* notebook 1.1
¿cuál(es)? *pron.* which?; which one(s)? 1.2
  ¿Cuál es la fecha de hoy? What is today's date? 1.5
cuando *conj.* when 1.7
  ¿cuándo? *adv.* when? 1.2
¿cuánto(s)/a(s)? *adj.* how much/how many? 1.1
  ¿Cuánto cuesta...? How much does... cost? 1.6
  ¿Cuántos años tienes? How old are you? 1.3
cuarenta *n., adj.* forty 1.2
cuarto *m.* room 1.2; 1.7
  cuarto de baño *m.* bathroom 1.7
cuarto/a *n., adj.* fourth 1.5
  menos cuarto quarter to (*time*)
  y cuarto quarter after (*time*) 1.1
cuatro *n., adj.* four 1.1
cuatrocientos/as *n., adj.* four hundred 1.2
Cuba *f.* Cuba 1.1
cubano/a *adj.* Cuban 1.3
cubiertos *m., pl.* silverware
cubierto/a *p.p.* covered
cubrir *v.* to cover
cultura *f.* culture 1.2
cuenta *f.* bill 1.8
cuidado *m.* care 1.3
cumpleaños *m., sing.* birthday 1.9
cumplir años *v.* to have a birthday 1.9
cuñado/a *m., f.* brother-in-law; sister-in-law 1.3
curso *m.* course 1.2

D

dar *v.* to give 1.6, 1.9
  dar un consejo *v.* to give advice
de *prep.* of; from 1.1
  ¿De dónde eres? *fam.* Where are you from? 1.1
  ¿De dónde es usted? *form.* Where are you from? 1.1
  ¿de quién...? whose...? *sing.* 1.1
  ¿de quiénes...? whose...? *pl.* 1.1
  de algodón (made) of cotton 1.6
  de buen humor in a good mood 1.5
  de compras shopping 1.5
  de cuadros plaid 1.6
  de excursión hiking 1.4
  de hecho in fact
  de ida y vuelta roundtrip 1.5
  de la mañana in the morning; A.M. 1.1
  de la noche in the evening; at night; P.M. 1.1
  de la tarde in the afternoon; in the early evening; P.M. 1.1
  de lana (made) of wool 1.6
  de lunares polka-dotted 1.6
  de mal humor in a bad mood 1.5
  de moda in fashion 1.6
  De nada. You're welcome. 1.1
  de rayas striped 1.6
  de repente *adv.* suddenly 1.6
  de seda (made) of silk 1.6
debajo de *prep.* below; under 1.2
deber (+ *inf.*) *v.* should; must; ought to 1.3
  Debe ser... It must be... 1.6
decidir (+ *inf.*) *v.* to decide 1.3
décimo/a *adj.* tenth 1.5
decir (e:i) *v.* to say; to tell 1.4, 1.9
  decir la respuesta to say the answer 1.4
  decir la verdad to tell the truth 1.4
  decir mentiras to tell lies 1.4
dejar una propina *v.* to leave a tip 1.9
del (contraction of **de + el**) of the; from the
delante de *prep.* in front of 1.2
delgado/a *adj.* thin; slender 1.3
delicioso/a *adj.* delicious 1.8
demás *adj.* the rest
demasiado *adj., adv.* too much 1.6
dependiente/a *m., f.* clerk 1.6
deporte *m.* sport 1.4
deportista *m.* sports person
deportivo/a *adj.* sports-related 1.4
derecha *f.* right 1.2
  a la derecha de to the right of 1.2
derecho *adj.* straight (ahead)
desayunar *v.* to have breakfast 1.2
desayuno *m.* breakfast 1.8
descansar *v.* to rest 1.2
describir *v.* to describe 1.3
desde *prep.* from 1.6
desear *v.* to wish; to desire 1.2
desordenado/a *adj.* disorderly 1.5
despedida *f.* farewell; good-bye
despedirse (e:i) (de) *v.* to say good-bye (to)
despejado/a *adj.* clear (*weather*)
despertador *m.* alarm clock 1.7
despertarse (e:ie) *v.* to wake up 1.7
después *adv.* afterwards; then 1.7

después de *prep.* after 1.7
detrás de *prep.* behind 1.2
día *m.* day 1.1
día de fiesta holiday 1.9
diario/a *adj.* daily 1.7
diccionario *m.* dictionary 1.1
diciembre *m.* December 1.5
diecinueve *n., adj.* nineteen 1.1
dieciocho *n., adj.* eighteen 1.1
dieciséis *n., adj.* sixteen 1.1
diecisiete *n., adj.* seventeen 1.1
diente *m.* tooth 1.7
diez *n., adj.* ten 1.1
difícil *adj.* difficult; hard 1.3
dinero *m.* money 1.6
diseño *m.* design
diversión *f.* fun activity; entertainment; recreation 1.4
divertido/a *adj.* fun 1.7
divertirse (e:ie) *v.* to have fun 1.9
divorciado/a *adj.* divorced 1.9
divorciarse (de) *v.* to get divorced (from) 1.9
divorcio *m.* divorce 1.9
doble *adj.* double
doce *n., adj.* twelve 1.1
doctor(a) *m., f.* doctor 1.3
documentos de viaje *m., pl.* travel documents
domingo *m.* Sunday 1.2
don *m.* Mr.; sir 1.1
doña *m.* Mrs.; ma'am 1.1
donde *prep.* where
¿dónde? *adv.* where? 1.1
¿Dónde está...? Where is...? 1.2
dormir (o:ue) *v.* to sleep 1.4
dormirse (o:ue) *v.* to go to sleep; to fall asleep 1.7
dos *n., adj.* two 1.1
dos veces *f.* twice; two times 1.6
doscientos/as *n., adj.* two hundred 1.2
ducha *f.* shower 1.7
ducharse *v.* to shower; to take a shower 1.7
dueño/a *m., f.* owner; landlord 1.8
dulces *m., pl.* sweets; candy 1.9
durante *prep.* during 1.7

E

e *conj.* (used instead of ***y*** before words beginning with ***i*** and ***hi***) and 1.4
economía *f.* economics 1.2
Ecuador *m.* Ecuador 1.1
ecuatoriano/a *adj.* Ecuadorian 1.3
edad *f.* age 1.9
(en) efectivo *m.* cash 1.6
el *m., sing., def. art.* the 1.1
él *sub. pron.* he 1.1; *pron., obj. of prep.* him 1.9
elegante *adj.* elegant 1.6
ella *sub. pron.* she 1.1; *pron., obj. of prep.* her 1.9
ellos/as *sub. pron.* they 1.1; *pron., obj. of prep.* them 1.9
emocionante *adj.* exciting
empezar (e:ie) *v.* to begin 1.4
empleado/a *m., f.* employee 1.5
en *prep.* in; on; at 1.2
en casa at home 1.7
en línea inline 1.4
en mi nombre in my name
en punto on the dot; exactly; sharp (*time*) 1.1
en qué in what; how 1.2
¿En qué puedo servirles? How can I help you? 1.5
enamorado/a (de) *adj.* in love (with) 1.5
enamorarse (de) *v.* to fall in love (with) 1.9
encantado/a *adj.* delighted; pleased to meet you 1.1
encantar *v.* to like very much; to love (*inanimate objects*) 1.7
encima de *prep.* on top of 1.2
encontrar (o:ue) *v.* to find 1.4
enero *m.* January 1.5
enojado/a *adj.* mad; angry 1.5
enojarse (con) *v.* to get angry (with) 1.7
ensalada *f.* salad 1.8
enseguida *adv.* right away 1.8
enseñar *v.* to teach 1.2
entender (e:ie) *v.* to understand 1.4
entonces *adv.* then 1.7
entre *prep.* between; among 1.2
entremeses *m., pl.* hors d'oeuvres; appetizers 1.8
equipaje *m.* luggage 1.5
equipo *m.* team 1.4
equivocado/a *adj.* wrong 1.5
eres *fam.* you are 1.1
es he/she/it is 1.1
Es de... He/She is from... 1.1
Es la una. It's one o'clock. 1.1
esa(s) *f., adj.* that; those 1.6
ésa(s) *f., pron.* those (ones) 1.6
escalar *v.* to climb 1.4
escalar montañas *v.* to climb mountains 1.4
escoger *v.* to choose 1.8
escribir *v.* to write 1.3
escribir un mensaje electrónico to write an e-mail message 1.4
escribir una carta to write a letter 1.4
escribir una postal to write a postcard
escritorio *m.* desk 1.2
escuchar *v.* to listen (to) 1.2
escuchar la radio to listen to the radio 1.2
escuchar música to listen to music 1.2
escuela *f.* school 1.1
ese *m., sing., adj.* that 1.6
ése *m., sing., pron.* that (one) 1.6
eso *neuter pron.* that; that thing 1.6
esos *m., pl., adj.* those 1.6
ésos *m., pl., pron.* those (ones) 1.6
España *f.* Spain 1.1
español *m.* Spanish (language) 1.2
español(a) *adj.* Spanish 1.3
espárragos *m., pl.* asparagus 1.8
especialización *f.* major 1.2
espejo *m.* mirror 1.7
esperar (+ *inf.*) *v.* to wait (for); to hope 1.2
esposo/a *m., f.* husband; wife; spouse 1.3
esquí (acuático) *m.* (water) skiing 1.4
esquiar *v.* to ski 1.4
está he/she/it is, you are 1.2
Está (muy) despejado. It's (very) clear. (*weather*)
Está lloviendo. It's raining. 1.5
Está nevando. It's snowing. 1.5
Está (muy) nublado. It's (very) cloudy. (*weather*) 1.5
esta(s) *f., adj.* this; these 1.6
esta noche tonight 1.4
ésta(s) *f., pron.* this (one); these (ones) 1.6
Ésta es... *f.* This is... (*introducing someone*) 1.1
estación *f.* station; season 1.5
estación de autobuses bus station 1.5
estación del metro subway station 1.5
estación de tren train station 1.5
estadio *m.* stadium 1.2
estado civil *m.* marital status 1.9
Estados Unidos *m.* (EE.UU.; E.U.) United States 1.1
estadounidense *adj.* from the United States 1.3
estampado/a *adj.* print
estar *v.* to be 1.2
estar aburrido/a to be bored 1.5
estar bajo control to be under control 1.7
estar de moda to be in fashion 1.6

estar de vacaciones to be on vacation 1.5
estar seguro/a to be sure 1.5
No está nada mal. It's not bad at all. 1.5
este *m., sing., adj.* this 1.6
éste *m., sing., pron.* this (one) 1.6
Éste es... *m.* This is... (*introducing someone*) 1.1
estilo *m.* style
esto *neuter pron.* this; this thing 1.6
estos *m., pl., adj.* these 1.6
éstos *m., pl., pron.* these (ones) 1.6
estudiante *m., f.* student 1.1, 1.2
estudiantil *adj.* student 1.2
estudiar *v.* to study 1.2
estupendo/a *adj.* stupendous 1.5
etapa *f.* stage 1.9
examen *m.* test; exam 1.2
excelente *adj.* excellent 1.5
excursión *f.* hike; tour; excursion 1.4
excursionista *m., f.* hiker
explicar *v.* to explain 1.2
explorar *v.* to explore
expresión *f.* expression

F

fabuloso/a *adj.* fabulous 1.5
fácil *adj.* easy 1.3
falda *f.* skirt 1.6
faltar *v.* to lack; to need 1.7
familia *f.* family 1.3
fascinar *v.* to fascinate 1.7
favorito/a *adj.* favorite 1.4
febrero *m.* February 1.5
fecha *f.* date 1.5
feliz *adj.* happy 1.5
¡Feliz cumpleaños! Happy birthday! 1.9
¡Felicidades! Congratulations! 1.9
¡Felicitaciones! Congratulations! 1.9
fenomenal *adj.* great, phenomenal 1.5
feo/a *adj.* ugly 1.3
fiesta *f.* party 1.9
fijo/a *adj.* fixed, set 1.6
fin *m.* end 1.4
fin de semana weekend 1.4
física *f.* physics 1.2
flan (de caramelo) *m.* baked (caramel) custard 1.9
folleto *m.* brochure
foto(grafía) *f.* photograph 1.1
francés, francesa *adj.* French 1.3
frenos *m., pl.* brakes
fresco/a *adj.* cool 1.5
frijoles *m., pl.* beans 1.8
frío/a *adj.* cold 1.5
frito/a *adj.* fried 1.8
fruta *f.* fruit 1.8
frutilla *f.* strawberry
fuera *adv.* outside
fútbol *m.* soccer 1.4
fútbol americano *m.* football 1.4

G

gafas (de sol) *f., pl.* (sun)glasses 1.6
gafas (oscuras) *f., pl.* (sun)glasses
galleta *f.* cookie 1.9
ganar *v.* to win 1.4
ganga *f.* bargain 1.6
gastar *v.* to spend (*money*) 1.6
gemelo/a *m., f.* twin 1.3
gente *f.* people 1.3
geografía *f.* geography 1.2
gimnasio *m.* gymnasium 1.4
golf *m.* golf 1.4
gordo/a *adj.* fat 1.3
gracias *f., pl.* thank you; thanks 1.1
Gracias por todo. Thanks for everything. 1.9
Gracias una vez más. Thanks again. 1.9
graduarse (de/en) *v.* to graduate (from/in) 1.9
gran, grande *adj.* big; large 1.3
grillo *m.* cricket
gris *adj.* gray 1.6
gritar *v.* to scream 1.7
guantes *m., pl.* gloves 1.6
guapo/a *adj.* handsome; good-looking 1.3
guía *m., f.* guide
gustar *v.* to be pleasing to; to like 1.2
Me gustaría... I would like...
gusto *m.* pleasure 1.1
El gusto es mío. The pleasure is mine. 1.1
Mucho gusto. Pleased to meet you. 1.1

H

habitación *f.* room 1.5
habitación doble double room 1.5
habitación individual single room 1.5
hablar *v.* to talk; to speak 1.2
hacer *v.* to do; to make 1.4
Hace buen tiempo. The weather is good. 1.5
Hace (mucho) calor. It's (very) hot. (*weather*) 1.5
Hace fresco. It's cool. (*weather*) 1.5
Hace (mucho) frío. It's very cold. (*weather*) 1.5
Hace mal tiempo. The weather is bad. 1.5
Hace (mucho) sol. It's (very) sunny. (*weather*) 1.5
Hace (mucho) viento. It's (very) windy. (*weather*) 1.5
hacer juego (con) to match (with) 1.6
hacer las maletas to pack (one's) suitcases 1.5
hacer (wind)surf to (wind) surf 1.5
hacer turismo to go sightseeing
hacer un viaje to take a trip 1.5
hacer una excursión to go on a hike; to go on a tour
hambre *f.* hunger 1.3
hamburguesa *f.* hamburger 1.8
hasta *prep.* until 1.6; toward
Hasta la vista. See you later. 1.1
Hasta luego. See you later. 1.1
Hasta mañana. See you tomorrow. 1.1
Hasta pronto. See you soon. 1.1
hay *v.* there is; there are 1.1
Hay (mucha) contaminación. It's (very) smoggy.
Hay (mucha) niebla. It's (very) foggy.
No hay de qué. You're welcome. 1.1
helado/a *adj.* iced 1.8
helado *m.* ice cream 1.9
hermanastro/a *m., f.* stepbrother; stepsister 1.3
hermano/a *m., f.* brother; sister 1.3
hermano/a mayor/menor *m., f.* older/younger brother/sister 1.3
hermanos *m., pl.* siblings (brothers and sisters) 1.3
hermoso/a *adj.* beautiful 1.6
hijastro/a *m., f.* stepson; stepdaughter 1.3
hijo/a *m., f.* son; daughter 1.3
hijo/a único/a *m., f.* only child 1.3
hijos *m., pl.* children 1.3
historia *f.* history 1.2
hockey *m.* hockey 1.4
hola *interj.* hello; hi 1.1
hombre *m.* man 1.1

hora *f.* hour 1.1; the time
horario *m.* schedule 1.2
hotel *m.* hotel 1.5
hoy *adv.* today 1.2
  hoy día *adv.* nowadays
  Hoy es... Today is... 1.2
huésped *m., f.* guest 1.5
huevo *m.* egg 1.8
humanidades *f., pl.* humanities 1.2

I

ida *f.* one way (*travel*)
idea *f.* idea 1.4
iglesia *f.* church 1.4
igualmente *adv.* likewise 1.1
impermeable *m.* raincoat 1.6
importante *adj.* important 1.3
importar *v.* to be important to; to matter 1.7
increíble *adj.* incredible 1.5
individual *adj.* private (*room*) 1.5
ingeniero/a *m., f.* engineer 1.3
inglés *m.* English (*language*) 1.2
inglés, inglesa *adj.* English 1.3
inodoro *m.* toilet 1.7
inspector(a) de aduanas *m., f.* customs inspector 1.5
inteligente *adj.* intelligent 1.3
intercambiar *v.* to exchange
interesante *adj.* interesting 1.3
interesar *v.* to be interesting to; to interest 1.7
invierno *m.* winter 1.5
invitado/a *m., f.* guest 1.9
invitar *v.* to invite 1.9
ir *v.* to go 1.4
  ir a (+ *inf.*) to be going to *do something* 1.4
  ir de compras to go shopping 1.5
  ir de excursión (a las montañas) to go on a hike (in the mountains) 1.4
  ir de pesca to go fishing
  ir de vacaciones to go on vacation 1.5
  ir en autobús to go by bus 1.5
  ir en auto(móvil) to go by car 1.5
  ir en avión to go by plane 1.5
  ir en barco to go by boat 1.5
  ir en metro to go by subway
  ir en motocicleta to go by motorcycle 1.5
  ir en taxi to go by taxi 1.5
  ir en tren to go by train
irse *v.* to go away; to leave 1.7
italiano/a *adj.* Italian 1.3
izquierdo/a *adj.* left 1.2
  a la izquierda de to the left of 1.2

J

jabón *m.* soap 1.7
jamás *adv.* never; not ever 1.7
jamón *m.* ham 1.8
japonés, japonesa *adj.* Japanese 1.3
joven *adj. m., f., sing.* (**jóvenes** *pl.*) young 1.3
joven *m., f., sing.* (**jóvenes** *pl.*) youth; young person 1.1
jubilarse *v.* to retire (*from work*) 1.9
juego *m.* game
jueves *m., sing.* Thursday 1.2
jugador(a) *m., f.* player 1.4
jugar (u:ue) *v.* to play 1.4
  jugar a las cartas to play cards 1.5
jugo *m.* juice 1.8
  jugo de fruta *m.* fruit juice 1.8
julio *m.* July 1.5
junio *m.* June 1.5
juntos/as *adj.* together 1.9
juventud *f.* youth 1.9

L

la *f., sing., def. art.* the 1.1
la *f., sing., d.o. pron.* her, it; *form.* you 1.5
laboratorio *m.* laboratory 1.2
lana *f.* wool 1.6
langosta *f.* lobster 1.8
lápiz *m.* pencil 1.1
largo/a *adj.* long 1.6
las *f., pl., def. art.* the 1.1
las *f., pl., d.o. pron.* them; *form.* you 1.5
lavabo *m.* sink 1.7
lavarse *v.* to wash oneself 1.7
  lavarse la cara to wash one's face 1.7
  lavarse las manos to wash one's hands 1.7
le *sing., i.o. pron.* to/for him, her; *form.* you 1.6
  Le presento a... *form.* I would like to introduce you to (name). 1.1
lección *f.* lesson 1.1
leche *f.* milk 1.8
lechuga *f.* lettuce 1.8
leer *v.* to read 1.3
  leer correo electrónico to read e-mail 1.4
  leer un periódico to read a newspaper 1.4
  leer una revista to read a magazine 1.4
lejos de *prep.* far from 1.2
lengua *f.* language 1.2
  lenguas extranjeras *f., pl.* foreign languages 1.2
lentes (de sol) (sun)glasses
lentes de contacto *m., pl.* contact lenses
les *pl., i.o. pron.* to/for them; *form.* you 1.6
levantarse *v.* to get up 1.7
libre *adj.* free 1.4
librería *f.* bookstore 1.2
libro *m.* book 1.2
limón *m.* lemon 1.8
limpio/a *adj.* clean 1.5
línea *f.* line
listo/a *adj.* ready; smart 1.5
literatura *f.* literature 1.2
llamarse *v.* to be called; to be named 1.7
llave *f.* key 1.5
llegada *f.* arrival 1.5
llegar *v.* to arrive 1.2
llevar *v.* to carry 1.2; to wear; to take 1.6
  llevarse bien/mal (con) to get along well/badly (with) 1.9
llover (o:ue) *v.* to rain 1.5
  Llueve. It's raining. 1.5
lo *m., sing., d.o. pron.* him, it; *form.* you 1.5
  Lo siento. I'm sorry. 1.1
  Lo siento muchísimo. I'm so sorry. 1.4
loco/a *adj.* crazy 1.6
los *m., pl., def. art.* the 1.1
los *m., pl., d.o. pron.* them; *form.* you 1.5
luego *adv.* then 1.7; *adv.* later 1.1
lugar *m.* place 1.4
lunares *m.* polka dots 1.6
lunes *m., sing.* Monday 1.2

M

madrastra *f.* stepmother 1.3
madre *f.* mother 1.3
madurez *f.* maturity; middle age 1.9
magnífico/a *adj.* magnificent 1.5
maíz *m.* corn 1.8
mal, malo/a *adj.* bad 1.3
maleta *f.* suitcase 1.1
mamá *f.* mom 1.3
mano *f.* hand 1.1
  ¡Manos arriba! Hands up!
mantequilla *f.* butter 1.8
manzana *f.* apple 1.8
mañana *f.* morning, A.M. 1.1; tomorrow 1.1

mapa *m.* map 1.2
maquillaje *m.* makeup 1.7
maquillarse *v.* to put on makeup 1.7
mar *m.* sea 1.5
maravilloso/a *adj.* marvelous 1.5
margarina *f.* margarine 1.8
mariscos *m., pl.* shellfish 1.8
marrón *adj.* brown 1.6
martes *m., sing.* Tuesday 1.2
marzo *m.* March 1.5
más *pron.* more 1.2
  más de (+ *number*) more than 1.8
  más tarde later (on) 1.7
  más... que more... than 1.8
matemáticas *f., pl.* mathematics 1.2
materia *f.* course 1.2
matrimonio *m.* marriage 1.9
mayo *m.* May 1.5
mayonesa *f.* mayonnaise 1.8
mayor *adj.* older 1.3
  el/la mayor *adj.* the eldest 1.8; the oldest
me *sing., d.o. pron.* me 1.5; *sing. i.o. pron.* to/for me 1.6
  Me gusta... I like... 1.2
  No me gustan nada. I don't like them at all. 1.2
  Me llamo... My name is... 1.1
  Me muero por... I'm dying to (for)...
mediano/a *adj.* medium
medianoche *f.* midnight 1.1
medias *f., pl.* pantyhose, stockings 1.6
médico/a *m., f.* doctor 1.3
medio/a *adj.* half 1.3
  medio/a hermano/a *m., f.* half-brother; half-sister 1.3
  mediodía *m.* noon 1.1
  y media thirty minutes past the hour (*time*) 1.1
mejor *adj.* better 1.8
  el/la mejor *adj.* the best 1.8
melocotón *m.* peach 1.8
menor *adj.* younger 1.3
  el/la menor *adj.* the youngest 1.8
menos *adv.* less
  menos cuarto..., menos quince... quarter to... (*time*) 1.1
  menos de (+ *number*) fewer than 1.8
  menos... que less... than 1.8
mensaje electrónico *m.* e-mail message 1.4
mentira *f.* lie 1.4
menú *m.* menu 1.8
mercado *m.* market 1.6
  mercado al aire libre *m.* open-air market 1.6
merendar (e:ie) *v.* to snack 1.8; to have an afternoon snack
mes *m.* month 1.5
mesa *f.* table 1.2
metro *m.* subway 1.5
mexicano/a *adj.* Mexican 1.3
México *m.* Mexico 1.1
mí *pron., obj. of prep.* me 1.9
mi(s) *poss. adj.* my 1.3
miedo *m.* fear 1.3
miércoles *m., sing.* Wednesday 1.2
mil *m.* one thousand 1.2
  Mil perdones. I'm so sorry. (*lit. A thousand pardons.*) 1.4
mil millones *m.* billion
millón *m.* million 1.2
millones (de) *m.* millions (of)
minuto *m.* minute 1.1
mirar *v.* to look (at); to watch 1.2
  mirar (la) televisión to watch television 1.2
mismo/a *adj.* same 1.3
mochila *f.* backpack 1.2
moda *f.* fashion 1.6
módem *m.* modem
molestar *v.* to bother; to annoy 1.7
montaña *f.* mountain 1.4
montar a caballo *v.* to ride a horse 1.5
monumento *m.* monument 1.4
mora *f.* blackberry 1.8
morado/a *adj.* purple 1.6
moreno/a *adj.* brunet(te) 1.3
morir (o:ue) *v.* to die 1.8
mostrar (o:ue) *v.* to show 1.4
motocicleta *f.* motorcycle 1.5
motor *m.* motor
muchacho/a *m., f.* boy; girl 1.3
mucho/a *adj., adv.* a lot of; much 1.2; many 1.3
  (Muchas) gracias. Thank you (very much).; Thanks (a lot). 1.1
  Muchísimas gracias. Thank you very, very much. 1.9
  Mucho gusto. Pleased to meet you. 1.1
muchísimo very much 1.2
muela *f.* tooth; molar
muerte *f.* death 1.9
mujer *f.* woman 1.1
  mujer policía *f.* female police officer
multa *f.* fine
mundial *adj.* worldwide
municipal *adj.* municipal
museo *m.* museum 1.4
música *f.* music 1.2
muy *adv.* very 1.1
  Muy amable. That's very kind of you. 1.5
  (Muy) bien, gracias. (Very) well, thanks. 1.1

N

nacer *v.* to be born 1.9
nacimiento *m.* birth 1.9
nacionalidad *f.* nationality 1.1
nada *pron., adv.* nothing 1.1; not anything 1.7
  nada mal not bad at all 1.5
nadar *v.* to swim 1.4
nadie *pron.* no one, nobody, not anyone 1.7
naranja *f.* orange 1.8
natación *f.* swimming 1.4
Navidad *f.* Christmas 1.9
necesitar (+ *inf.*) *v.* to need 1.2
negativo/a *adj.* negative
negro/a *adj.* black 1.3
nervioso/a *adj.* nervous 1.5
nevar (e:ie) *v.* to snow 1.5
  Nieva. It's snowing. 1.5
ni... ni neither... nor 1.7
niebla *f.* fog
nieto/a *m., f.* grandson; granddaughter 1.3
nieve *f.* snow
ningún, ninguno/a(s) *adj., pron.* no; none; not any 1.7
  ningún problema no problem
niñez *f.* childhood 1.9
niño/a *m., f.* child 1.3
no *adv. no; not* 1.1
  ¿no? right? 1.1
  No está nada mal. It's not bad at all. 1.5
  no estar de acuerdo to disagree
  No estoy seguro. I'm not sure.
  no hay there is not; there are not 1.1
  No hay de qué. You're welcome. 1.1
  No hay problema. No problem. 1.7
  No me gustan nada. I don't like them at all. 1.2
  no muy bien not very well 1.1
  No quiero. I don't want to. 1.4
  No sé. I don't know.
  No se preocupe. *(form.)* Don't worry. 1.7
  No te preocupes. *(fam.)* Don't worry. 1.7
  no tener razón to be wrong 1.3

noche *f.* night 1.1
nombre *m.* name 1.1
norteamericano/a *adj.* (North) American 1.3
nos *pl., d.o. pron.* us 1.5; *pl., i.o. pron.* to/for us 1.6
Nos vemos. See you. 1.1
nosotros/as *sub. pron.* we 1.1; *pron., obj. of prep.* us 1.9
novecientos/as *n., adj.* nine hundred 1.2
noveno/a *n., adj.* ninth 1.5
noventa *n., adj.* ninety 1.2
noviembre *m.* November 1.5
novio/a *m., f.* boyfriend/girlfriend 1.3
nublado/a *adj.* cloudy 1.5
Está (muy) nublado. It's very cloudy. 1.5
nuera *f.* daughter-in-law 1.3
nuestro(s)/a(s) *poss. adj.* our 1.3
nueve *n., adj.* nine 1.1
nuevo/a *adj.* new 1.6
número *m.* number 1.1; (shoe) size 1.6
nunca *adv.* never; not ever 1.7

O

o *conj.* or 1.7
o... o; either... or 1.7
océano *m.* ocean
ochenta *n., adj.* eighty 1.2
ocho *n., adj.* eight 1.1
ochocientos/as *n., adj.* eight hundred 1.2
octavo/a *n., adj.* eighth 1.5
octubre *m.* October 1.5
ocupado/a *adj.* busy 1.5
odiar *v.* to hate 1.9
ofrecer *v.* to offer 1.6
oír *v.* to hear 1.4
Oiga./Oigan. *form., sing./pl.* Listen. (*in conversation*) 1.1
Oye. *fam., sing.* Listen. (*in conversation*) 1.1
once *n., adj.* eleven 1.1
ordenado/a *adj.* orderly 1.5
ordinal *adj.* ordinal (number)
ortografía *f.* spelling
ortográfico/a *adj.* spelling
os *fam., pl., d.o. pron.* you 1.5; *fam., pl., i.o. pron.* to/for you 1.6
otoño *m.* autumn 1.5
otro/a *adj.* other; another 1.6
otra vez *adv.* again

P

padrastro *m.* stepfather 1.3
padre *m.* father 1.3
padres *m., pl.* parents 1.3
pagar *v.* to pay 1.6, 1.9
pagar la cuenta to pay the bill 1.9
país *m.* country 1.1
paisaje *m.* landscape 1.5
palabra *f.* word 1.1
pan *m.* bread 1.8
pan tostado *m.* toasted bread 1.8
pantalones *m., pl.* pants 1.6
pantalones cortos *m., pl. shorts* 1.6
pantuflas *f., pl.* slippers 1.7
papa *f.* potato 1.8
papas fritas *f., pl.* fried potatoes; French fries 1.8
papá *m.* dad 1.3
papás *m., pl.* parents 1.3
papel *m.* paper 1.2
papelera *f.* wastebasket 1.2
par *m.* pair 1.6
par de zapatos *m.* pair of shoes 1.6
parecer *v.* to seem 1.6
pareja *f.* (married) couple; partner 1.9
parientes *m., pl.* relatives 1.3
parque *m.* park 1.4
párrafo *m.* paragraph
partido *m.* game; match (*sports*) 1.4
pasado/a *adj.* last; past 1.6
pasado *p.p.* passed
pasaje *m.* ticket 1.5
pasaje de ida y vuelta *m.* roundtrip ticket 1.5
pasajero/a *m., f.* passenger 1.1
pasaporte *m.* passport 1.5
pasar *v.* to go through 1.5
pasar por la aduana to go through customs
pasar tiempo to spend time
pasarlo bien/mal to have a good/bad time 1.9
pasatiempo *m.* pastime; hobby 1.4
pasear *v.* to take a walk; to stroll 1.4
pasear en bicicleta to ride a bicycle 1.4
pasear por to walk around 1.4
pasta *f.* **de dientes** toothpaste 1.7
pastel *m.* cake; pie 1.9
pastel de chocolate *m.* chocolate cake 1.9
pastel de cumpleaños *m.* birthday cake
patata *f.* potato 1.8
patatas fritas *f., pl.* fried potatoes; French fries 1.8
patinar (en línea) *v.* to (inline) skate 1.4
patineta *f.* skateboard 1.4
pavo *m.* turkey 1.8
pedir (e:i) *v.* to ask for; to request 1.4; to order (*food*) 1.8
peinarse *v.* to comb one's hair 1.7
película *f.* movie 1.4
pelirrojo/a *adj.* red-haired 1.3
pelo *m.* hair 1.7
pelota *f.* ball 1.4
pensar (e:ie) *v.* to think 1.4
pensar (+ *inf.*) *v.* to intend to; to plan to (*do something*) 1.4
pensar en *v.* to think about 1.4
pensión *f.* boardinghouse
peor *adj.* worse 1.8
el/la peor *adj.* the worst 1.8
pequeño/a *adj.* small 1.3
pera *f.* pear 1.8
perder (e:ie) *v.* to lose; to miss 1.4
Perdón. Pardon me.; Excuse me. 1.1
perezoso/a *adj.* lazy
perfecto/a *adj.* perfect 1.5
periódico *m.* newspaper 1.4
periodismo *m.* journalism 1.2
periodista *m., f.* journalist 1.3
permiso *m.* permission
pero *conj.* but 1.2
persona *f.* person 1.3
pesca *f.* fishing
pescado *m.* fish (*cooked*) 1.8
pescador(a) *m., f.* fisherman/fisherwoman
pescar *v.* to fish 1.5
pimienta *f.* black pepper 1.8
piña *f.* pineapple 1.8
piscina *f.* swimming pool 1.4
piso *m.* floor (*of a building*) 1.5
pizarra *f.* blackboard 1.2
planes *m., pl.* plans
planta baja *f.* ground floor 1.5
plato *m.* dish (*in a meal*) 1.8
plato principal *m.* main dish 1.8
playa *f.* beach 1.5
plaza *f.* city or town square 1.4
pluma *f.* pen 1.2
pobre *adj.* poor 1.6
pobreza *f.* poverty
poco/a *adj.* little; few 1.5
poder (o:ue) *v.* to be able to; can 1.4
pollo *m.* chicken 1.8
pollo asado *m.* roast chicken 1.8
ponchar *v.* to go flat
poner *v.* to put; to place 1.4
ponerse (+ *adj.*) *v.* to become (+ *adj.*) 1.7; to put on 1.7

por *prep.* in exchange for; for; by; in; through; around; along; during; because of; on account of; on behalf of; in search of; by way of
por avión by plane
por favor please 1.1
por la mañana in the morning 1.7
por la noche at night 1.7
por la tarde in the afternoon 1.7
¿por qué? why? 1.2
por teléfono by phone; on the phone
por último finally 1.7
porque *conj.* because 1.2
posesivo/a *adj.* possessive 1.3
postal *f.* postcard
postre *m.* dessert 1.9
practicar *v.* to practice 1.2
practicar deportes *m., pl.* to play sports 1.4
precio (fijo) *m.* (fixed; set) price 1.6
preferir (e:ie) *v.* to prefer 1.4
pregunta *f.* question
preguntar *v.* to ask (*a question*) 1.2
preocupado/a (por) *adj.* worried (about) 1.5
preocuparse (por) *v.* to worry (about) 1.7
preparar *v.* to prepare 1.2
preposición *f.* preposition
presentación *f.* introduction
presentar *v.* to introduce
Le presento a... I would like to introduce you to (name). 1.1
Te presento a... I would like to introduce you to (name). *(fam.)* 1.1
prestado/a *adj.* borrowed
prestar *v.* to lend; to loan 1.6
primavera *f.* spring 1.5
primer, primero/a *n., adj.* first 1.5
primo/a *m., f.* cousin 1.3
principal *adj.* main 1.8
prisa *f.* haste 1.3
probar (o:ue) *v.* to taste; to try 1.8
probarse (o:ue) *v.* to try on 1.7
problema *m.* problem 1.1
profesión *f.* profession 1.3
profesor(a) *m., f.* teacher 1.1, 1.2
programa *m.* 1.1
programador(a) *m., f.* computer programmer 1.3
pronombre *m.* pronoun
propina *f.* tip 1.8
prueba *f.* test; quiz 1.2
psicología *f.* psychology 1.2
pueblo *m.* town 1.4
puerta *f.* door 1.2
Puerto Rico *m.* Puerto Rico 1.1
puertorriqueño/a *adj.* Puerto Rican 1.3
pues *conj.* well 1.2

Q

que *conj.* that; which
¡Qué...! How...! 1.3
¡Qué dolor! What pain!
¡Qué ropa más bonita! What pretty clothes! 1.6
¡Qué sorpresa! What a surprise!
¿qué? *pron.* what? 1.1
¿Qué día es hoy? What day is it? 1.2
¿Qué hay de nuevo? What's new? 1.1
¿Qué hora es? What time is it? 1.1
¿Qué les parece? What do you (*pl.*) think?
¿Qué pasa? What's happening?; What's going on? 1.1
¿Qué precio tiene? What is the price?
¿Qué tal...? How are you?; How is it going? 1.1; How is/are...? 1.2
¿Qué talla lleva/usa? What size do you wear? (*form.*) 1.6
¿Qué tiempo hace? How's the weather? 1.5
¿En qué...? In which...? 1.2
quedar *v.* to be left over; to fit (*clothing*) 1.7
quedarse *v.* to stay; to remain 1.7
querer (e:ie) *v.* to want; to love 1.4
queso *m.* cheese 1.8
quien(es) *pron.* who; whom
¿Quién es...? Who is...? 1.1
¿quién(es)? *pron.* who?; whom? 1.1
química *f.* chemistry 1.2
quince *n., adj.* fifteen 1.1
menos quince quarter to (*time*) 1.1
y quince quarter after (*time*) 1.1
quinceañera *f.* young woman celebrating her fifteenth birthday 1.9
quinientos/as *n., adj.* five hundred 1.2
quinto/a *n., adj.* fifth 1.5
quitarse *v.* to take off 1.7
quizás *adv.* maybe 1.5

R

radio *f.* radio (*medium*) 1.2
radio *m.* radio (*set*) 1.2
ratos libres *m., pl.* spare (*free*) time 1.4
raya *f.* stripe 1.6
razón *f.* reason 1.3
rebaja *f.* sale 1.6
recibir *v.* to receive 1.3
recién casado/a *m., f.* newlywed 1.9
recomendar (e:ie) *v.* to recommend 1.8
recordar (o:ue) *v.* to remember 1.4
recorrer *v.* to tour an area
refresco *m.* soft drink 1.8
regalar *v.* to give (a gift) 1.9
regalo *m.* gift 1.6
regatear *v.* to bargain 1.6
regresar *v.* to return 1.2
regular *adj.* so-so; OK 1.1
reírse (e:i) *v.* to laugh 1.9
relaciones *f., pl.* relationships
relajarse *v.* to relax 1.9
reloj *m.* clock; watch 1.2
repetir (e:i) *v.* to repeat 1.4
residencia estudiantil *f.* dormitory 1.2
respuesta *f.* answer
restaurante *m.* restaurant 1.4
revista *f.* magazine 1.4
rico/a *adj.* rich 1.6; tasty; delicious 1.8
riquísimo/a *adj.* extremely delicious 1.8
rojo/a *adj.* red 1.3
romper (con) *v.* to break up (with) 1.9
ropa *f.* clothing; clothes 1.6
ropa interior *f.* underwear 1.6
rosado/a *adj.* pink 1.6
rubio/a *adj.* blond(e) 1.3
ruso/a *adj.* Russian 1.3
rutina *f.* routine 1.7
rutina diaria *f.* daily routine 1.7

S

sábado *m.* Saturday 1.2
saber *v.* to know; to know how 1.6; to taste 1.8
saber (a) to taste (like) 1.8
sabrosísimo/a *adj.* extremely delicious 1.8
sabroso/a *adj.* tasty; delicious 1.8
sacar *v.* to take out
sacar fotos to take photos 1.5
sal *f.* salt 1.8
salchicha *f.* sausage 1.8

salida *f.* departure; exit 1.5
salir *v.* to leave 1.4; to go out
  salir (con) to go out (with); to date 1.9
  salir de to leave from
  salir para to leave for (*a place*)
salmón *m.* salmon 1.8
saludo *m.* greeting 1.1
  saludos a... greetings to... 1.1
sandalia *f.* sandal 1.6
sandía *f.* watermelon
sándwich *m.* sandwich 1.8
se *ref. pron.* himself, herself, itself; *form.* yourself, themselves, yourselves 1.7
secarse *v.* to dry oneself 1.7
sección de (no) fumar *f.* (non) smoking section 1.8
secuencia *f.* sequence
sed *f.* thirst 1.3
seda *f.* silk 1.6
seguir (e:i) *v.* to follow; to continue 1.4
según *prep.* according to
segundo/a *n., adj.* second 1.5
seguro/a *adj.* sure; safe 1.5
seis *n., adj.* six 1.1
seiscientos/as *n., adj.* six hundred 1.2
semana *f.* week 1.2
  fin *m.* **de semana** weekend 1.4
  semana *f.* **pasada** last week 1.6
semestre *m.* semester 1.2
sentarse (e:ie) *v.* to sit down 1.7
sentir(se) (e:ie) *v.* to feel 1.7
señor (Sr.) *m.* Mr.; sir 1.1
señora (Sra.) *f.* Mrs.; ma'am 1.1
señorita (Srta.) *f.* Miss 1.1
separado/a *adj.* separated 1.9
separarse (de) *v.* to separate (from) 1.9
septiembre *m.* September 1.5
séptimo/a *adj.* seventh 1.5
ser *v.* to be 1.1
  ser aficionado/a (a) to be a fan (of) 1.4
serio/a *adj.* serious
servir (e:i) *v.* to serve 1.8; to help 1.5
sesenta *n., adj.* sixty 1.2
setecientos/as *n., adj.* seven hundred 1.2
setenta *n., adj.* seventy 1.2
sexto/a *n., adj.* sixth 1.5
sí *adv.* yes 1.1
si *conj.* if 1.4
siempre *adv.* always 1.7
siete *n., adj.* seven 1.1
silla *f.* seat 1.2
similar *adj.* similar
simpático/a *adj.* nice; likeable 1.3
sin *prep.* without 1.2
  sin duda without a doubt
  sin embargo however
sino *conj.* but (rather) 1.7
situado/a *adj., p.p.* located
sobre *prep.* on; over 1.2
sobrino/a *m., f.* nephew; niece 1.3
sociología *f.* sociology 1.2
sol *m.* sun 1.4; 1.5
soleado/a *adj.* sunny
sólo *adv.* only 1.3
solo *adj.* alone
soltero/a *adj.* single 1.9
sombrero *m.* hat 1.6
Son las dos. It's two o'clock. 1.1
sonreír (e:i) *v.* to smile 1.9
sopa *f.* soup 1.8
sorprender *v.* to surprise 1.9
sorpresa *f.* surprise 1.9
soy I am 1.1
  Soy yo. That's me. 1.1
  Soy de... I'm from... 1.1
su(s) *poss. adj.* his, her, its; *form.* your, their 1.3
sucio/a *adj.* dirty 1.5
suegro/a *m., f.* father-in-law; mother-in-law 1.3
sueño *m.* sleep 1.3
suerte *f.* luck 1.3
suéter *m.* sweater 1.6
suponer *v.* to suppose 1.4
sustantivo *m.* noun

T

tabla de (wind)surf *f.* surf board/sailboard 1.5
tal vez *adv.* maybe 1.5
talla *f.* size 1.6
  talla grande *f.* large
también *adv.* also; too 1.2; 1.7
tampoco *adv.* neither; not either 1.7
tan *adv.* so 1.5
  tan... como as... as 1.8
tanto *adv.* so much
  tanto... como as much... as 1.8
  tantos/as... como as many... as 1.8
tarde *adv.* late 1.7
tarde *f.* afternoon; evening; P.M. 1.1
tarea *f.* homework 1.2
tarjeta *f.* card
  tarjeta de crédito *f.* credit card 1.6
  tarjeta postal *f.* postcard
taxi *m.* taxi 1.5
te *sing., fam., d.o. pron.* you 1.5; *sing., fam., i.o. pron.* to/for you 1.6
  Te presento a... *fam.* I would like to introduce you to (name). 1.1
  ¿Te gusta(n)...? Do you like...? 1.2
té *m.* tea 1.8
  té helado *m.* iced tea 1.8
televisión *f.* television 1.2
temprano *adv.* early 1.7
tener *v.* to have 1.3
  tener... años to be... years old 1.3
  Tengo... años. I'm... years old. 1.3
  tener (mucho) calor to be (very) hot 1.3
  tener (mucho) cuidado to be (very) careful 1.3
  tener (mucho) frío to be (very) cold 1.3
  tener ganas de (+ *inf.***)** to feel like (*doing something*) 1.3
  tener (mucha) hambre to be (very) hungry 1.3
  tener (mucho) miedo (de) to be (very) afraid (of); to be (very) scared (of) 1.3
  tener miedo (de) que to be afraid that
  tener planes to have plans
  tener (mucha) prisa to be in a (big) hurry 1.3
  tener que (+ *inf.***)** *v.* to have to (*do something*) 1.3
  tener razón to be right 1.3
  tener (mucha) sed to be (very) thirsty 1.3
  tener (mucho) sueño to be (very) sleepy 1.3
  tener (mucha) suerte *f.* to be (very) lucky 1.3
  tener tiempo to have time 1.4
  tener una cita to have a date; to have an appointment 1.9
tenis *m.* tennis 1.4
tercer, tercero/a *n., adj.* third 1.5
terminar *v.* to end; to finish 1.2
  terminar de (+ *inf.***)** *v.* to finish (*doing something*) 1.4
ti *pron., obj. of prep., fam.* you 1.9
tiempo *m.* time 1.4; weather 1.5
  tiempo libre free time
tienda *f.* shop; store 1.6
  tienda de campaña tent
tinto/a *adj.* red (wine) 1.8
tío/a *m., f.* uncle; aunt 1.3
tíos *m.* aunts and uncles 1.3
título *m.* title
tiza *f.* chalk 1.2
toalla *f.* towel 1.7
todavía *adv.* yet; still 1.5

todo *m.* everything 1.5
Todo está bajo control. Everything is under control. 1.7
todo(s)/a(s) *adj.* all; whole 1.4
todos *m., pl.* all of us; everybody; everyone
tomar *v.* to take; to drink 1.2
tomar clases to take classes 1.2
tomar el sol to sunbathe 1.4
tomar en cuenta to take into account
tomar fotos to take photos 1.5
tomate *m.* tomato 1.8
tonto/a *adj.* silly; foolish 1.3
tortilla *f.* tortilla 1.8
tortilla de maíz corn tortilla 1.8
tostado/a *adj.* toasted 1.8
trabajador(a) *adj.* hard-working 1.3
trabajar *v.* to work 1.2
traducir *v.* to translate 1.6
traer *v.* to bring 1.4
traje *m.* suit 1.6
traje de baño *m.* bathing suit 1.6
tranquilo/a *adj.* calm
Tranquilo. Relax. 1.7
trece *n., adj.* thirteen 1.1
treinta *n., adj.* thirty 1.1, 1.2
y treinta thirty minutes past the hour (*time*) 1.1
tren *m.* train 1.5
tres *n., adj.* three 1.1
trescientos/as *n., adj.* three hundred 1.2
trimestre *m.* trimester; quarter 1.2
triste *adj.* sad 1.5
tú *fam. sub. pron.* you 1.1
Tú eres... You are... 1.1
tu(s) *fam. poss. adj.* your 1.3
turismo *m.* tourism 1.5
turista *m., f.* tourist 1.1
turístico/a *adj.* touristic

U

Ud. *form. sing.* you 1.1
Uds. *form., pl.* you 1.1
último/a *adj.* last
un, uno/a *indef. art.* a, an; one 1.1
uno/a *m., f., sing. pron.* one 1.1
a la una at one o'clock 1.1
una vez *adv.* once; one time 1.6
una vez más one more time 1.9
unos/as *m., f., pl. indef. art.* some; *pron.* some 1.1
único/a *adj.* only 1.3
universidad *f.* university; college 1.2
usar *v.* to wear; to use 1.6
usted (Ud.) *form. sing.* you 1.1
ustedes (Uds.) *form., pl.* you 1.1
útil *adj.* useful
uva *f.* grape 1.8

V

vacaciones *f. pl.* vacation 1.5
vamos let's go 1.4
varios/as *adj., pl.* various; several 1.8
veces *f., pl.* times 1.6
veinte *n., adj.* twenty 1.1
veinticinco *n., adj.* twenty-five 1.1
veinticuatro *n., adj.* twenty-four 1.1
veintidós *n., adj.* twenty-two 1.1
veintinueve *n., adj.* twenty-nine 1.1
veintiocho *n., adj.* twenty-eight 1.1
veintiséis *n., adj.* twenty-six 1.1
veintisiete *n., adj.* twenty-seven 1.1
veintitrés *n., adj.* twenty-three 1.1
veintiún, veintiuno/a *n., adj.* twenty-one 1.1
vejez *f.* old age 1.9
vendedor(a) *m., f.* salesperson 1.6
vender *v.* to sell 1.6
venir *v.* to come 1.3
ventana *f.* window 1.2
ver *v.* to see 1.4
a ver let's see 1.2
ver películas to see movies 1.4
verano *m.* summer 1.5
verbo *m.* verb
verdad *f.* truth
¿verdad? right? 1.1
verde *adj.* green 1.3
verduras *f., pl.* vegetables 1.8
vestido *m.* dress 1.6
vestirse (e:i) *v.* to get dressed 1.7
vez *f.* time 1.6
viajar *v.* to travel 1.2
viaje *m.* trip 1.5
viajero/a *m., f.* traveler 1.5
vida *f.* life 1.9
video *m.* video 1.1
videojuego *m.* video game 1.4
viejo/a *adj.* old 1.3
viento *m.* wind 1.5
viernes *m., sing.* Friday 1.2
vinagre *m.* vinegar 1.8
vino *m.* wine 1.8
vino blanco *m.* white wine 1.8
vino tinto *m.* red wine 1.8
visitar *v.* to visit 1.4
visitar monumentos to visit monuments 1.4
viudo/a *adj.* widower; widow 1.9
vivir *v.* to live 1.3
vivo/a *adj.* bright; lively; living
vóleibol *m.* volleyball 1.4
volver (o:ue) *v.* to return 1.4
vos *pron.* you
vosotros/as *pron., form., pl.* you 1.1
vuelta *f.* return trip
vuestro(s)/a(s) *form., poss. adj.* your 1.3

W

walkman *m.* walkman

Y

y *conj.* and 1.1
y cuarto quarter after (*time*) 1.1
y media half-past (*time*) 1.1
y quince quarter after (*time*) 1.1
y treinta thirty (minutes past the hour) 1.1
¿Y tú? *fam.* And you? 1.1
¿Y usted? *form.* And you? 1.1
ya *adv.* already 1.6
yerno *m.* son-in-law 1.3
yo *sub. pron.* I 1.1
Yo soy... I'm... 1.1
yogur *m.* yogurt 1.8

Z

zanahoria *f.* carrot 1.8
zapatos *m., pl.* shoes
zapatos de tenis tennis shoes, sneakers 1.6

English-Spanish

A

a **un, uno/a** *m., f., sing.; indef. art.* 1.1
A.M. **mañana** *f.* 1.1
able: be able to **poder (o:ue)** *v.* 1.4
aboard **a bordo** 1.1
accounting **contabilidad** *f.* 1.2
acquainted: be acquainted with **conocer** *v.* 1.6
additional **adicional** *adj.*
adjective **adjetivo** *m.*
adolescence **adolescencia** *f.* 1.9
advice **consejo** *m.* 1.6
  give advice **dar consejos** 1.6
affirmative **afirmativo/a** *adj.*
afraid: be (very) afraid (of) **tener (mucho) miedo (de)** 1.3
  be afraid that **tener miedo (de) que**
after **después de** *prep.* 1.7
afternoon **tarde** *f.* 1.1
afterward **después** *adv.* 1.7
again *adv.* **otra vez**
age **edad** *f.* 1.9
agree **concordar (o:ue)** *v.*
airplane **avión** *m.* 1.5
airport **aeropuerto** *m.* 1.5
alarm clock **despertador** *m.* 1.7
all **todo(s)/a(s)** *adj.* 1.4
  all of us **todos** 1.1
  all over the world **en todo el mundo**
alleviate **aliviar** *v.*
alone **solo/a** *adj.*
already **ya** *adv.* 1.6
also **también** *adv.* 1.2; 1.7
although *conj.* **aunque**
always **siempre** *adv.* 1.7
American (North) **norteamericano/a** *adj.* 1.3
among **entre** *prep.* 1.2
amusement **diversión** *f.*
and **y** 1.1, **e** (before words beginning with ***i*** or ***hi***) 1.4
  And you? **¿Y tú?** *fam.* 1.1; **¿Y usted?** *form.* 1.1
angry **enojado/a** *adj.* 1.5
  get angry (with) **enojarse** *v.* **(con)** 1.7
anniversary **aniversario** *m.* 1.9
  (wedding) anniversary **aniversario** *m.* (de bodas) 1.9
annoy **molestar** *v.* 1.7
another **otro/a** *adj.* 1.6
answer **contestar** *v.* 1.2; **respuesta** *f.*
any **algún, alguno/a(s)** *adj.* 1.7
anyone **alguien** *pron.* 1.7
anything **algo** *pron.* 1.7
appear **parecer** *v.*
appetizers **entremeses** *m., pl.* 1.8
apple **manzana** *f.* 1.8
appointment **cita** *f.* 1.9
  have an appointment **tener** *v.* **una cita** 1.9
April **abril** *m.* 1.5
aquatic **acuático/a** *adj.* 1.4
archaeology **arqueología** *f.* 1.2
Argentina **Argentina** *f.* 1.1
Argentine **argentino/a** *adj.* 1.3
arrival **llegada** *f.* 1.5
arrive **llegar** *v.* 1.2
art **arte** *m.* 1.2
artist **artista** *m., f.* 1.3
as **como** 1.8
  as... as **tan... como** 1.8
  as many... as **tantos/as... como** 1.8
  as much... as **tanto... como** 1.8
ask (a question) **preguntar** *v.* 1.2
  ask for **pedir (e:i)** *v.* 1.4
asparagus **espárragos** *m., pl.* 1.8
at **a** *prep.* 1.1; **en** *prep.* 1.2
  at + *time* **a la(s)** + *time* 1.1
  at home **en casa** 1.7
  at night **por la noche** 1.7
  At what time...? **¿A qué hora...?** 1.1
attend **asistir (a)** *v.* 1.3
attract **atraer** *v.* 1.4
August **agosto** *m.* 1.5
aunt **tía** *f.* 1.3
  aunts and uncles **tíos** *m., pl.* 1.3
automatic **automático/a** *adj.*
automobile **automóvil** *m.* 1.5
autumn **otoño** *m.* 1.5
avenue **avenida** *f.*

B

backpack **mochila** *f.* 1.2
bad **mal, malo/a** *adj.* 1.3
  It's not at all bad. **No está nada mal.** 1.5
bag **bolsa** *f.* 1.6
ball **pelota** *f.* 1.4
banana **banana** *f.* 1.8
bargain **ganga** *f.* 1.6; **regatear** *v.* 1.6
baseball (*game*) **béisbol** *m.* 1.4
basketball (*game*) **baloncesto** *m.* 1.4
bathe **bañarse** *v.* 1.7
bathing suit **traje** *m.* **de baño** 1.6
bathroom **baño** *m.* 1.7; **cuarto de baño** *m.* 1.7
be **ser** *v.* 1.1; **estar** *v.* 1.2
  be... years old **tener... años** 1.3
beach **playa** *f.* 1.5
beans **frijoles** *m., pl.* 1.8
beautiful **hermoso/a** *adj.* 1.6
because **porque** *conj.* 1.2
become (+ *adj.*) **ponerse (+** *adj.***)** 1.7; **convertirse (e:ie)** *v.*
bed **cama** *f.* 1.5
  go to bed **acostarse (o:ue)** *v.* 1.7
beef **carne de res** *f.* 1.8
before **antes** *adv.* 1.7; **antes de** *prep.* 1.7
begin **comenzar (e:ie)** *v.* 1.4; **empezar (e:ie)** *v.* 1.4
behind **detrás de** *prep.* 1.2
believe (in) **creer** *v.* **(en)** 1.3
bellhop **botones** *m., f. sing.* 1.5
below **debajo de** *prep.* 1.2
belt **cinturón** *m.* 1.6
beside **al lado de** *prep.* 1.2
best **mejor** *adj.*
  the best **el/la mejor** *adj.* 1.8
better **mejor** *adj.* 1.8
between **entre** *prep.* 1.2
bicycle **bicicleta** *f.* 1.4
big **gran, grande** *adj.* 1.3
bill **cuenta** *f.* 1.9
billion *m.* **mil millones**
biology **biología** *f.* 1.2
birth **nacimiento** *m.* 1.9
birthday **cumpleaños** *m., sing.* 1.9
  have a birthday **cumplir** *v.* **años** 1.9
biscuit **bizcocho** *m.*
black **negro/a** *adj.* 1.3
blackberry **mora** *f.* 1.8
blackboard **pizarra** *f.* 1.2
blond(e) **rubio/a** *adj.* 1.3
blouse **blusa** *f.* 1.6
blue **azul** *adj.* 1.3
boardinghouse **pensión** *f.*
boat **barco** *m.* 1.5
book **libro** *m.* 1.2
bookstore **librería** *f.* 1.2
boot **bota** *f.* 1.6
bore **aburrir** *v.* 1.7
bored **aburrido/a** *adj.* 1.5
  be bored **estar** *v.* **aburrido/a** 1.5
boring **aburrido/a** *adj.* 1.5
born: be born **nacer** *v.* 1.9
borrowed **prestado/a** *adj.*
bother **molestar** *v.* 1.7
bottle **botella** *f.* 1.9
bottom **fondo** *m.*
boulevard **bulevar** *m.*
boy **chico** *m.* 1.1; **muchacho** *m.* 1.3
boyfriend **novio** *m.* 1.3
brakes **frenos** *m., pl.*
bread **pan** *m.* 1.8
break up (with) **romper** *v.* **(con)** 1.9
breakfast **desayuno** *m.* 1.2, 1.8
  have breakfast **desayunar** *v.* 1.2
bring **traer** *v.* 1.4

brochure **folleto** *m.*
brother **hermano** *m.* 1.3
brothers and sisters **hermanos** *m., pl.* 1.3
brother-in-law **cuñado** *m.* 1.3
brown **café** *adj.* 1.6; **marrón** *adj.* 1.6
brunet(te) **moreno/a** *adj.* 1.3
brush **cepillar** *v.* 1.7
brush one's hair **cepillarse el pelo** 1.7
brush one's teeth **cepillarse los dientes** 1.7
build **construir** *v.* 1.4
bus **autobús** *m.* 1.1
bus station **estación** *f.* **de autobuses** 1.5
business administration **administración** *f.* **de empresas** 1.2
busy **ocupado/a** *adj.* 1.5
but **pero** *conj.* 1.2; (*rather*) **sino** *conj.* (*in negative sentences*) 1.7
butter **mantequilla** *f.* 1.8
buy **comprar** *v.* 1.2
by plane **en avión** 1.5
bye **chau** *interj. fam.* 1.1

C

café **café** *m.* 1.4
cafeteria **cafetería** *f.* 1.2
cake **pastel** *m.* 1.9
chocolate cake **pastel de chocolate** *m.* 1.9
calculator **calculadora** *f.* 1.2
call **llamar** *v.*
call on the phone **llamar por teléfono**
be called **llamarse** *v.* 1.7
camp **acampar** *v.* 1.5
can **poder (o:ue)** *v.* 1.4
Canadian **canadiense** *adj.* 1.3
candy **dulces** *m., pl.* 1.9
capital city **capital** *f.* 1.1
car **auto(móvil)** *m.* 1.5
caramel **caramelo** *m.* 1.9
card **tarjeta** *f.*; (*playing*) **carta** *f.* 1.5
care **cuidado** *m.* 1.3
careful: be (very) careful **tener** *v.* (mucho) **cuidado** 1.3
carrot **zanahoria** *f.* 1.8
carry **llevar** *v.* 1.2
cash **(en) efectivo** 1.6
cash register **caja** *f.* 1.6
cashier **cajero/a** *m., f.*
celebrate **celebrar** *v.* 1.9
celebration **celebración** *f.*
young woman's fifteenth birthday celebration **quinceañera** *f.* 1.9
cereal **cereales** *m., pl.* 1.8
chalk **tiza** *f.* 1.2
champagne **champán** *m.* 1.9
change **cambiar** *v.* **(de)** 1.9
chat **conversar** *v.* 1.2
chauffeur **conductor(a)** *m., f.* 1.1
cheap **barato/a** *adj.* 1.6
cheese **queso** *m.* 1.8
chemistry **química** *f.* 1.2
chicken **pollo** *m.* 1.8
child **niño/a** *m., f.* 1.3
childhood **niñez** *f.* 1.9
children **hijos** *m., pl.* 1.3
Chinese **chino/a** *adj.* 1.3
chocolate **chocolate** *m.* 1.9
chocolate cake **pastel** *m.* **de chocolate** 1.9
choose **escoger** *v.* 1.8
chop (*food*) **chuleta** *f.* 1.8
Christmas **Navidad** *f.* 1.9
church **iglesia** *f.* 1.4
city **ciudad** *f.* 1.4
class **clase** *f.* 1.2
take classes **tomar clases** 1.2
classmate **compañero/a** *m., f.* **de clase** 1.2
clean **limpio/a** *adj.* 1.5
clear (*weather*) **despejado/a** *adj.*
It's (very) clear. (*weather*) **Está (muy) despejado.**
clerk **dependiente/a** *m., f.* 1.6
climb **escalar** *v.* 1.4
climb mountains **escalar montañas** 1.4
clock **reloj** *m.* 1.2
close **cerrar (e:ie)** *v.* 1.4
closed **cerrado/a** *adj.* 1.5
clothes **ropa** *f.* 1.6
clothing **ropa** *f.* 1.6
cloudy **nublado/a** *adj.* 1.5
It's (very) cloudy. **Está (muy) nublado.** 1.5
coat **abrigo** *m.* 1.6
coffee **café** *m.* 1.8
cold **frío** *m.* 1.5;
be (feel) (very) cold **tener (mucho) frío** 1.3
It's (very) cold. (*weather*) **Hace (mucho) frío.** 1.5
college **universidad** *f.* 1.2
color **color** *m.* 1.3, 1.6
comb one's hair **peinarse** *v.* 1.7
come **venir** *v.* 1.3
comfortable **cómodo/a** *adj.* 1.5
community **comunidad** *f.* 1.1
comparison **comparación** *f.*
computer **computadora** *f.* 1.1
computer disc **disco** *m.*
computer programmer **programador(a)** *m., f.* 1.3
computer science **computación** *f.* 1.2
confirm **confirmar** *v.* 1.5
confirm a reservation **confirmar una reservación** 1.5
confused **confundido/a** *adj.* 1.5
Congratulations! **¡Felicidades!; ¡Felicitaciones!** *f. pl.* 1.9
contamination **contaminación** *f.*
content **contento/a** *adj.* 1.5
continue **seguir (e:i)** *v.* 1.4
control **control** *m.*
be under control **estar bajo control** 1.7
conversation **conversación** *f.* 1.1
converse **conversar** *v.* 1.2
cookie **galleta** *f.* 1.9
cool **fresco/a** *adj.* 1.5
Be cool. **Tranquilo/a.**
It's cool. (*weather*) **Hace fresco.** 1.5
corn **maíz** *m.* 1.8
cost **costar (o:ue)** *v.* 1.6
Costa Rica **Costa Rica** *f.* **1.1**
Costa Rican **costarricense** *adj.* 1.3
cotton **algodón** *f.* 1.6
(made of) cotton **de algodón** 1.6
count (on) **contar (o:ue)** *v.* **(con)** 1.4
country (*nation*) **país** *m.* 1.1
countryside **campo** *m.* 1.5
couple (married) **pareja** *f.* 1.9
course **curso** *m.* 1.2; **materia** *f.* 1.2
courtesy **cortesía** *f.*
cousin **primo/a** *m., f.* 1.3
cover **cubrir** *v.*
covered **cubierto** *p.p.*
crazy **loco/a** *adj.* 1.6
create **crear** *v.*
credit **crédito** *m.* 1.6
credit card **tarjeta** *f.* **de crédito** 1.6
Cuba **Cuba** *f.* **1.1**
Cuban **cubano/a** *adj.* **1.3**
culture **cultura** *f.* **1.2**
currency exchange **cambio** *m.* **de moneda**
custard (*baked*) **flan** *m.* 1.9
custom **costumbre** *f.* 1.1
customer **cliente/a** *m., f.* 1.6
customs **aduana** *f.* 1.5
customs inspector **inspector(a)** *m., f.* **de aduanas** 1.5
cycling **ciclismo** *m.* 1.4

D

dad **papá** *m.* 1.3
daily **diario/a** *adj.* 1.7
daily routine **rutina** *f.* **diaria** 1.7
dance **bailar** *v.* 1.2
date (*appointment*) **cita** *f.* 1.9; (*calendar*) **fecha** *f.* 1.5; (*someone*) **salir** *v.* **con (alguien)** 1.9
have a date **tener una cita** 1.9
daughter **hija** *f.* 1.3
daughter-in-law **nuera** *f.* 1.3
day **día** *m.* 1.1

day before yesterday **anteayer** *adv.* 1.6
death **muerte** *f.* 1.9
December **diciembre** *m.* 1.5
decide **decidir** *v.* **(+** *inf.***)** 1.3
delicious **delicioso/a** *adj.* 1.8; **rico/a** *adj.* 1.8; **sabroso/a** *adj.* 1.8
delighted **encantado/a** *adj.* 1.1
department store **almacén** *m.* 1.6
departure **salida** *f.* 1.5
describe **describir** *v.* 1.3
design **diseño** *m.*
desire **desear** *v.* 1.2
desk **escritorio** *m.* 1.2
dessert **postre** *m.* 1.9
diary **diario** *m.* 1.1
dictionary **diccionario** *m.* 1.1
die **morir (o:ue)** *v.* 1.8
difficult **difícil** *adj.* 1.3
dinner **cena** *f.* 1.2, 1.8
have dinner **cenar** *v.* 1.2
dirty **ensuciar** *v.*; **sucio/a** *adj.* 1.5
disagree **no estar de acuerdo**
dish **plato** *m.* 1.8
main dish *m.* **plato principal** 1.8
disk **disco** *m.*
disorderly **desordenado/a** *adj.* 1.5
dive **bucear** *v.* 1.4
divorce **divorcio** *m.* 1.9
divorced **divorciado/a** *adj.* 1.9
get divorced (from) **divorciarse** *v.* **(de)** 1.9
do **hacer** *v.* 1.4
(I) don't want to. **No quiero.** 1.4
doctor **doctor(a)** *m., f.* 1.3; **médico/a** *m., f.* 1.3
domestic **doméstico/a** *adj.*
domestic appliance **electrodoméstico** *m.*
door **puerta** *f.* 1.2
dormitory **residencia** *f.* **estudiantil** 1.2
double **doble** *adj.* 1.5
double room **habitación** *f.* **doble** 1.5
downtown **centro** *m.* 1.4
draw **dibujar** *v.* 1.2
dress **vestido** *m.* 1.6
get dressed **vestirse (e:i)** *v.* 1.7
drink **beber** *v.* 1.3; **tomar** *v.* 1.2
bebida *f.* 1.8
drive **conducir** *v.* 1.6
driver **conductor(a)** *m., f.* 1.1
dry oneself **secarse** *v.* 1.7
during **durante** *prep.* 1.7

E

each **cada** *adj.* 1.6
eagle **águila** *f.*
early **temprano** *adv.* 1.7
ease **aliviar** *v.*
easy **fácil** *adj.* 1.3
eat **comer** *v.* 1.3
economics **economía** *f.* 1.2
Ecuador **Ecuador** *m.* 1.1
Ecuadorian **ecuatoriano/a** *adj.* 1.3
effective **eficaz** *adj.*
egg **huevo** *m.* 1.8
eight **ocho** *n., adj.* 1.1
eight hundred **ochocientos/as** *n., adj.* 1.2
eighteen **dieciocho** *n., adj.* 1.1
eighth **octavo/a** *adj.* 1.5
eighty **ochenta** *n., adj.* 1.2
either... or **o... o** *conj.* 1.7
eldest **el/la mayor** *adj.* 1.8
elegant **elegante** *adj.* 1.6
elevator **ascensor** *m.* 1.5
eleven **once** *n., adj.* 1.1
e-mail **correo** *m.* **electrónico** 1.4
e-mail message **mensaje** *m.* **electrónico** 1.4
read e-mail **leer** *v.* **el correo electrónico** 1.4
embarrassed **avergonzado/a** *adj.* 1.5
employee **empleado/a** *m., f.* 1.5
end **fin** *m.* 1.4; **terminar** *v.* 1.2
engaged: get engaged (to) **comprometerse** *v.* **(con)** 1.9
engineer **ingeniero/a** *m., f.* 1.3
English (*language*) **inglés** *m.* 1.2; **inglés, inglesa** *adj.* 1.3
entertainment **diversión** *f.* 1.4
eraser **borrador** *m.* 1.2
establish **establecer** *v.*
evening **tarde** *f.* 1.1
everybody **todos** *m., pl.*
everything **todo** *m.* 1.5
Everything is under control. **Todo está bajo control.** 1.7
exactly **en punto** 1.1
exam **examen** *m.* 1.2
excellent **excelente** *adj.* 1.5
exciting **emocionante** *adj.*
excursion **excursión** *f.*
excuse **disculpar** *v.*
Excuse me. (*May I?*) **Con permiso.** 1.1; (*I beg your pardon.*) **Perdón.** 1.1
exit **salida** *f.* 1.5
expensive **caro/a** *adj.* 1.6
explain **explicar** *v.* 1.2
explore **explorar** *v.*
expression **expresión** *f.*
extremely delicious **riquísimo/a** *adj.* 1.8

F

fabulous **fabuloso/a** *adj.* 1.5
face **cara** *f.* 1.7
fact: in fact **de hecho**
fall (*season*) **otoño** *m.* 1.5
fall: fall asleep **dormirse (o:ue)** *v.* 1.7
fall in love (with) **enamorarse** *v.* **(de)** 1.9
family **familia** *f.* 1.3
fan **aficionado/a** *adj.* 1.4
be a fan (of) **ser aficionado/a (a)** 1.4
far from **lejos de** *prep.* 1.2
farewell **despedida** *f.* 1.1
fascinate **fascinar** *v.* 1.7
fashion **moda** *f.* 1.6
be in fashion **estar de moda** 1.6
fast **rápido/a** *adj.*
fat **gordo/a** *adj.* 1.3
father **padre** *m.* 1.3
father-in-law **suegro** *m.* 1.3
favorite **favorito/a** *adj.* 1.4
fear **miedo** *m.* 1.3
February **febrero** *m.* 1.5
feel **sentir(se) (e:ie)** *v.* 1.7
feel like (*doing something*) **tener ganas de (+** *inf.***)** 1.3
few **pocos/as** *adj., pl.*
fewer than **menos de** *(+ number)* 1.8
field: major field of study **especialización** *f.*
fifteen *n., adj.* **quince** 1.1
fifteen-year-old girl **quinceañera** *f.* 1.9
young woman celebrating her fifteenth birthday **quinceañera** *f.* 1.9
fifth **quinto/a** *n., adj.* 1.5
fifty **cincuenta** *n., adj.* 1.2
figure (*number*) **cifra** *f.*
finally **por último** 1.7
find **encontrar (o:ue)** *v.* 1.4
find (each other) **encontrar(se)** *v.*
fine **multa** *f.*
finish **terminar** *v.* 1.2
finish (*doing something*) **terminar** *v.* **de (+ *inf.*)** 1.4
first **primer, primero/a** *n., adj.* 1.5
fish (*food*) **pescado** *m.* 1.8
fisherman **pescador** *m.*
fisherwoman **pescadora** *f.*
fishing **pesca** *f.* 1.5
fit (*clothing*) **quedar** *v.* 1.7
five **cinco** *n., adj.* 1.1
five hundred **quinientos/as** *n., adj.* 1.2
fixed **fijo/a** *adj.* 1.6
flag **bandera** *f.*
flank steak **lomo** *m.* 1.8

floor (*of a building*) **piso** *m.* 1.5
ground floor **planta** *f.* **baja** 1.5
top floor **planta** *f.* **alta**
fog **niebla** *f.*
follow **seguir (e:i)** *v.* 1.4
food **comida** *f.* 1.8; **alimento** *m.*
foolish **tonto/a** *adj.* 1.3
football **fútbol** *m.* **americano** 1.4
for me **para mí** 1.8
forbid **prohibir** *v.*
foreign languages **lenguas** *f. pl.* **extranjeras** 1.2
forty **cuarenta** *n., adj.* 1.2
four **cuatro** *n., adj.* 1.1
four hundred **cuatrocientos/as** *n., adj.* 1.2
fourteen **catorce** *n., adj.* 1.1
fourth **cuarto/a** *n., adj.* 1.5
free **libre** *adj.* 1.4
free time **tiempo libre; ratos libres** 1.4
French **francés, francesa** *adj.* 1.3
French fries **papas** *f., pl.* **fritas** 1.8; **patatas** *f., pl.* **fritas** 1.8
Friday **viernes** *m., sing.* 1.2
fried **frito/a** *adj.* 1.8
fried potatoes **papas** *f., pl.* **fritas** 1.8; **patatas** *f., pl.* **fritas** 1.8
friend **amigo/a** *m., f.* 1.3
friendly **amable** *adj.* 1.5
friendship **amistad** *f.* 1.9
from **de** *prep.* 1.1; **desde** *prep.* 1.6
from the United States **estadounidense** *adj.* 1.3
He/She/It is from... **Es de....** 1.1
I'm from... **Soy de...** 1.1
fruit **fruta** *f.* 1.8
fruit juice **jugo** *m.* **de fruta** 1.8
fun **divertido/a** *adj.* 1.7
fun activity **diversión** *f.* 1.4
have fun **divertirse (e:ie)** *v.* 1.9
function **funcionar** *v.*

G

game **juego** *m.*; *(match)* **partido** *m.* 1.4
garlic **ajo** *m.* 1.8
geography **geografía** *f.* 1.2
German **alemán, alemana** *adj.* 1.3
get **conseguir (e:i)** *v.* 1.4
get along well/badly (with) **llevarse bien/mal (con)** 1.9
get up **levantarse** *v.* 1.7
gift **regalo** *m.* 1.6
girl **chica** *f.* 1.1; **muchacha** *f.* 1.3
girlfriend **novia** *f.* 1.3
give **dar** *v.* 1.6, 1.9; (*as a gift*) **regalar** 1.9
glasses **gafas** *f., pl.* 1.6
sunglasses **gafas** *f., pl.* **de sol** 1.6
gloves **guantes** *m., pl.* 1.6
go **ir** *v.* 1.4
go away **irse** 1.7
go by boat **ir en barco** 1.5
go by bus **ir en autobús** 1.5
go by car **ir en auto(móvil)** 1.5
go by motorcycle **ir en motocicleta** 1.5
go by taxi **ir en taxi** 1.5
go down **bajar(se)** *v.*
go on a hike (in the mountains) **ir de excursión (a las montañas)** 1.4
go out **salir** *v.* 1.9
go out (with) **salir** *v.* **(con)** 1.9
go up **subir** *v.*
Let's go. **Vamos.** 1.4
be going to (*do something*) **ir a (+** *inf.***)** 1.4
golf **golf** *m.* 1.4
good **buen, bueno/a** *adj.* 1.3, 1.6
Good afternoon. **Buenas tardes.** 1.1
Good evening. **Buenas noches.** 1.1
Good idea. **Buena idea.** 1.4
Good morning. **Buenos días.** 1.1
Good night. **Buenas noches.** 1.1
good-bye **adiós** *m.* 1.1
say good-bye (to) **despedirse (e:i) (de)** *v.*
good-looking **guapo/a** *adj.* 1.3
graduate (from/in) **graduarse** *v.* **(de/en)** 1.9
grains **cereales** *m., pl.* 1.8
granddaughter **nieta** *f.* 1.3
grandfather **abuelo** *m.* 1.3
grandmother **abuela** *f.* 1.3
grandparents **abuelos** *m. pl.* 1.3
grandson **nieto** *m.* 1.3
grape **uva** *f.* 1.8
gray **gris** *adj.* 1.6
great **fenomenal** *adj.* 1.5
great-grandfather **bisabuelo** *m.* 1.3
great-grandmother **bisabuela** *f.* 1.3
green **verde** *adj.* 1.3
greeting **saludo** *m.* 1.1
Greetings to... **Saludos a...** 1.1
grilled flank steak **lomo** *m.* **a la plancha** 1.8
ground floor **planta baja** *f.* 1.5
guest (at a house/hotel) **huésped** *m., f.* 1.5; (*invited to a function*) **invitado/a** *m., f.* 1.9
gymnasium **gimnasio** *m.* 1.4

H

hair **pelo** *m.* 1.7
half **medio/a** *adj.* 1.3
half-past... (*time*) **...y media** 1.1
half-brother **medio hermano** 1.3
half-sister **media hermana** 1.3
ham **jamón** *m.* 1.8
hamburger **hamburguesa** *f.* 1.8
hand **mano** *f.* 1.1
Hands up! **¡Manos arriba!**
handsome **guapo/a** *adj.* 1.3
happiness **alegría** *v.* 1.9
happy **alegre** *adj.* 1.5; **contento/a** *adj.* 1.5; **feliz** *adj.* 1.5
Happy birthday! **¡Feliz cumpleaños!** 1.9
hard **difícil** *adj.* 1.3
hard-working **trabajador(a)** *adj.* 1.3
haste **prisa** *f.* 1.3
hat **sombrero** *m.* 1.6
hate **odiar** *v.* 1.9
have **tener** *v.* 1.3
Have a good trip! **¡Buen viaje!** 1.1
have time **tener tiempo** 1.4
have to (*do something*) **tener que (+** *inf.***)** 1.3; **deber** (*+ inf.*)
he **él** *sub. pron.* 1.1
hear **oír** *v.* 1.4
heat **calor** *m.* 1.5
Hello. **Hola.** 1.1
help **servir (e:i)** *v.* 1.5
her **su(s)** *poss. adj.* 1.3; **la** *f., sing., d.o. pron.* 1.5
to/for her **le** *f., sing., i.o. pron.* 1.6
here **aquí** *adv.* 1.1
Here it is. **Aquí está.** 1.5
Here we are at/in... **Aquí estamos en...**
Hi. **Hola.** 1.1
hike **excursión** *f.* 1.4
go on a hike **hacer una excursión; ir de excursión** 1.4
hiker **excursionista** *m., f.*
hiking **de excursión** 1.4
him **lo** *m., sing., d.o. pron.* 1.5
to/for him **le** *m., sing., i.o. pron.* 1.6
his **su(s)** *poss. adj.* 1.3
history **historia** *f.* 1.2
hobby **pasatiempo** *m.* 1.4

hockey **hockey** *m.* 1.4
holiday **día** *m.* **de fiesta** 1.9
home **casa** *f.* 1.2
homework **tarea** *f.* 1.2
hope **esperar** *v.* **(+** *inf.***)** 1.2
hors d'oeuvres **entremeses** *m., pl.* 1.8
horse **caballo** *m.* 1.5
hot: be *(feel)* (very) hot **tener (mucho) calor** 1.3
It's (very) hot **Hace (mucho) calor** 1.5
hotel **hotel** *m.* 1.5
hour **hora** *f.* 1.1
house **casa** *f.* 1.2
How...! **¡Qué...!** 1.3
how? **¿cómo?** *adv.* 1.1
How are you? **¿Qué tal?** 1.1
How are you? **¿Cómo estás?** *fam.* 1.1
How are you? **¿Cómo está usted?** *form.* 1.1
How can I help you? **¿En qué puedo servirles?** 1.5
How is it going? **¿Qué tal?** 1.1
How is/are...? **¿Qué tal...?** 1.2
How much/many? **¿Cuánto(s)/a(s)?** 1.1
How much does... cost? **¿Cuánto cuesta...?** 1.6
How old are you? **¿Cuántos años tienes?** *fam.* 1.3
however **sin embargo**
humanities **humanidades** *f., pl.* 1.2
hundred **cien, ciento** *n., adj.* 1.2
hunger **hambre** *f.* 1.3
hungry: be (very) hungry **tener** *v.* **(mucha) hambre** 1.3
hurry
be in a (big) hurry **tener** *v.* **(mucha) prisa** 1.3
husband **esposo** *m.* 1.3

I

I **Yo** *sub. pron.* 1.1
I am... **Yo soy...** 1.1
ice cream **helado** *m.* 1.9
iced **helado/a** *adj.* 1.8
iced tea **té** *m.* **helado** 1.8
idea **idea** *f.* 1.4
if **si** *conj.* 1.4
important **importante** *adj.* 1.3
be important to **importar** *v.* 1.7
in **en** *prep.* 1.2
in a bad mood **de mal humor** 1.5
in a good mood **de buen humor** 1.5
in front of **delante de** *prep.* 1.2
in love (with) **enamorado/a (de)** 1.5
in the afternoon **de la tarde** 1.1; **por la tarde** 1.7
in the direction of **para** *prep.* 1.1
in the early evening **de la tarde** 1.1
in the evening **de la noche** 1.1; **por la tarde** 1.7
in the morning **de la mañana** 1.1; **por la mañana** 1.7
incredible **increíble** *adj.* 1.5
inside **dentro** *adv.*
intelligent **inteligente** *adj.* 1.3
intend to **pensar** *v.* **(+** *inf.***)** 1.4
interest **interesar** *v.* 1.7
interesting **interesante** *adj.* 1.3
be interesting to **interesar** *v.* 1.7
introduction **presentación** *f.*
I would like to introduce you to (name). **Le presento a...** *form.* 1.1; **Te presento a...** *fam.* 1.1
invite **invitar** *v.* 1.9
it **lo/la** *sing., d.o., pron.* 1.5
It's me. **Soy yo.** 1.1
Italian **italiano/a** *adj.* 1.3
its **su(s)** *poss. adj.* 1.3

J

jacket **chaqueta** *f.* 1.6
January **enero** *m.* 1.5
Japanese **japonés, japonesa** *adj.* 1.3
jeans **(blue)jeans** *m., pl.* 1.6
jog **correr** *v.*
journalism **periodismo** *m.* 1.2
journalist **periodista** *m., f.* 1.3
joy **alegría** *f.* 1.9
give joy **dar** *v.* **alegría** 1.9
joyful **alegre** *adj.* 1.5
juice **jugo** *m.* 1.8
July **julio** *m.* 1.5
June **junio** *m.* 1.5
just **apenas** *adv.*
have just *(done something)* **acabar de** *(+ inf.)* 1.6

K

key **llave** *f.* 1.5
kind: That's very kind of you. **Muy amable.** 1.5
kiss **beso** *m.* 1.9
know **saber** *v.* 1.6; **conocer** *v.* 1.6
know how **saber** *v.* 1.6

L

laboratory **laboratorio** *m.* 1.2
lack **faltar** *v.* 1.7
landlord **dueño/a** *m., f.* 1.8
landscape **paisaje** *m.* 1.5
language **lengua** *f.* 1.2
large **grande** *adj.* 1.3; *(clothing size)* **talla grande**
last **pasado/a** *adj.* 1.6; **último/a** *adj.*
last name **apellido** *m.* 1.3
last night **anoche** *adv.* 1.6
last week **semana** *f.* **pasada** 1.6
last year **año** *m.* **pasado** 1.6
late **tarde** *adv.* 1.7
later (on) **más tarde** 1.7
See you later. **Hasta la vista.** 1.1; **Hasta luego.** 1.1
laugh **reírse (e:i)** *v.* 1.9
lazy **perezoso/a** *adj.*
learn **aprender** *v.* **(a +** *inf.***)** 1.3
leave **salir** *v.* 1.4; **irse** *v.* 1.7
leave a tip **dejar una propina** 1.9
leave for *(a place)* **salir para**
leave from **salir de**
left **izquierdo/a** *adj.* 1.2
be left over **quedar** *v.* 1.7
to the left of **a la izquierda de** 1.2
lemon **limón** *m.* 1.8
lend **prestar** *v.* 1.6
less **menos** *adv.*
less... than **menos... que** 1.8
less than **menos de** *(+ number)* 1.8
lesson **lección** *f.* 1.1
let's see **a ver** 1.2
letter **carta** *f.* 1.4
lettuce **lechuga** *f.* 1.8
library **biblioteca** *f.* 1.2
lie **mentira** *f.* 1.4
life **vida** *f.* 1.9
like **como** *prep.* 1.8; **gustar** *v.* 1.2
Do you like...? **¿Te gusta(n)...?** 1.2
I don't like them at all. **No me gustan nada.** 1.2
I like... **Me gusta(n)...** 1.2
like very much **encantar** *v.*; **fascinar** *v.* 1.7
likeable **simpático/a** *adj.* 1.3
likewise **igualmente** *adv.* 1.1
line **línea** *f.*
listen (to) **escuchar** *v.* 1.2
Listen! *(command)* **¡Oye!** *fam., sing.* 1.1; **¡Oiga/Oigan!** *form., sing./pl.* 1.1
listen to music **escuchar música** 1.2
listen (to) the radio **escuchar la radio** 1.2
literature **literatura** *f.* 1.2
little *(quantity)* **poco/a** *adj.* 1.5
live **vivir** *v.* 1.3
loan **prestar** *v.* 1.6
lobster **langosta** *f.* 1.8

long **largo/a** *adj.* 1.6
look (at) **mirar** *v.* 1.2
look for **buscar** *v.* 1.2
lose **perder (e:ie)** *v.* 1.4
lot of, a **mucho/a** *adj.* 1.2, 1.3
love (*another person*) **querer (e:ie)** *v.* 1.4; (*inanimate objects*) **encantar** *v.* 1.7; **amor** *m.* 1.9
in love **enamorado/a** *adj.* 1.5
luck **suerte** *f.* 1.3
lucky: be (very) lucky **tener (mucha) suerte** 1.3
luggage **equipaje** *m.* 1.5
lunch **almuerzo** *m.* 1.8
have lunch **almorzar (o:ue)** *v.* 1.4

M

ma'am **señora (Sra.)** *f.* 1.1
mad **enojado/a** *adj.* 1.5
magazine **revista** *f.* 1.4
magnificent **magnífico/a** *adj.* 1.5
main **principal** *adj.* 1.8
major **especialización** *f.* 1.2
make **hacer** *v.* 1.4
makeup **maquillaje** *m.* 1.7
put on makeup **maquillarse** *v.* 1.7
man **hombre** *m.* 1.1
many **mucho/a** *adj.* 1.3
map **mapa** *m.* 1.2
March **marzo** *m.* 1.5
margarine **margarina** *f.* 1.8
marinated fish **ceviche** *m.* 1.8
lemon-marinated shrimp **ceviche** *m.* **de camarón** 1.8
marital status **estado** *m.* **civil** 1.9
market **mercado** *m.* 1.6
open-air market **mercado al aire libre** 1.6
marriage **matrimonio** *m.* 1.9
married **casado/a** *adj.* 1.9
get married (to) **casarse** *v.* **(con)** 1.9
marvelous **maravilloso/a** *adj.* 1.5
match (*sports*) **partido** *m.* 1.4
match (with) **hacer** *v.* **juego (con)** 1.6
mathematics **matemáticas** *f., pl.* 1.2
matter **importar** *v.* 1.7
maturity **madurez** *f.* 1.9
May **mayo** *m.* 1.5
maybe **tal vez** *adv.* 1.5; **quizás** *adv.* 1.5
mayonnaise **mayonesa** *f.* 1.8
me **me** *sing., d.o. pron.* 1.5; *mí pron., obj. of prep.* 1.9
to/for me **me** *sing., i.o. pron.* 1.6
meal **comida** *f.* 1.8
meat **carne** *f.* 1.8
medium **mediano/a** *adj.*
meet (*each other*) **conocer(se)** *v.* 1.8
menu **menú** *m.* 1.8
message **mensaje** *m.*
Mexican **mexicano/a** *adj.* 1.3
Mexico **México** *m.* 1.1
middle age **madurez** *f.* 1.9
midnight **medianoche** *f.* 1.1
milk **leche** *f.* 1.8
million **millón** *m.* 1.2
million of **millón de** *m.* 1.2
mineral water **agua** *f.* **mineral** 1.8
minute **minuto** *m.* 1.1
mirror **espejo** *m.* 1.7
Miss **señorita (Srta.)** *f.* 1.1
miss **perder (e:ie)** *v.* 1.4
mistaken **equivocado/a** *adj.*
modem **módem** *m.*
mom **mamá** *f.* 1.3
Monday **lunes** *m., sing.* 1.2
money **dinero** *m.* 1.6
month **mes** *m.* 1.5
monument **monumento** *m.* 1.4
more **más** 1.2
more... than **más... que** 1.8
more than **más de (+ *number*)** 1.8
morning **mañana** *f.* 1.1
mother **madre** *f.* 1.3
mother-in-law **suegra** *f.* 1.3
motor **motor** *m.*
motorcycle **motocicleta** *f.* 1.5
mountain **montaña** *f.* 1.4
movie **película** *f.* 1.4
movie theater **cine** *m.* 1.4
Mr. **señor (Sr.); don** *m.* 1.1
Mrs. **señora (Sra.); doña** *f.* 1.1
much **mucho/a** *adj.* 1.2, 1.3
very much **muchísimo/a** *adj.* 1.2
municipal **municipal** *adj. m., f.*
museum **museo** *m.* 1.4
mushroom **champiñón** *m.* 1.8
music **música** *f.* 1.2
must **deber** *v.* **(+ *inf.*)** 1.3
It must be... **Debe ser...** 1.6
my **mi(s)** *poss. adj.* 1.3

N

name **nombre** *m.* 1.1
be named **llamarse** *v.* 1.7
in the name of **a nombre de** 1.5
last name *m.* **apellido**
My name is... **Me llamo...** 1.1
nationality **nacionalidad** *f.* 1.1
near **cerca de** *prep.* 1.2
need **faltar** *v.* 1.7; **necesitar** *v.* **(+ *inf.*)** 1.2
negative **negativo/a** *adj.*
neither **tampoco** *adv.* 1.7
neither... nor **ni... ni** *conj.* 1.7
nephew **sobrino** *m.* 1.3
nervous **nervioso/a** *adj.* 1.5
never **nunca** *adv.* 1.7; **jamás** *adv.* 1.7
new **nuevo/a** *adj.* 1.6
newlywed **recién casado/a** *m., f.* 1.9
newspaper **periódico** *m.* 1.4
next to **al lado de** *prep.* 1.2
nice **simpático/a** *adj.* 1.3; **amable** *adj.* 1.5
niece **sobrina** *f.* 1.3
night **noche** *f.* 1.1
nine **nueve** *n., adj.* 1.1
nine hundred **novecientos/as** *n., adj.* 1.2
nineteen **diecinueve** *n., adj.* 1.1
ninety **noventa** *n., adj.* 1.2
ninth **noveno/a** *n., adj.* 1.5
no **no** *adv.* 1.1; **ningún, ninguno/a(s)** *adj.* 1.7
no one **nadie** *pron.* 1.7
No problem. **No hay problema.** 1.7
nobody **nadie** *pron.* 1.7
none **ningún, ninguno/a(s)** *pron.* 1.7
noon **mediodía** *m.* 1.1
nor **ni** *conj.* 1.7
not **no** 1.1
not any **ningún, ninguno/a(s)** *adj.* 1.7
not anyone **nadie** *pron.* 1.7
not anything **nada** *pron.* 1.7
not bad at all **nada mal** 1.5
not either **tampoco** *adv.* 1.7
not ever **nunca** *adv.* 1.7; **jamás** *adv.* 1.7
Not very well. **No muy bien.** 1.1
notebook **cuaderno** *m.* 1.1
nothing **nada** *pron.* 1.1; 1.7
noun **sustantivo** *m.*
November **noviembre** *m.* 1.5
now **ahora** *adv.* 1.2
nowadays **hoy día** *adv.*
number **número** *m.* 1.1

O

obtain **conseguir (e:i)** *v.* 1.4
o'clock: It's... o'clock. **Son las...** 1.1
It's one o'clock. **Es la una.** 1.1
October **octubre** *m.* 1.5
of **de** *prep.* 1.1
offer **ofrecer** *v.* 1.6
Oh! **¡Ay!**
oil **aceite** *m.* 1.8
OK **regular** *adj.* 1.1
It's okay. **Está bien.**
old **viejo/a** *adj.* 1.3

old age **vejez** *f.* 1.9
older **mayor** *adj.* 1.3
  older brother/sister **hermano/a mayor** *m., f.* 1.3
oldest **el/la mayor** *adj.* 1.8
on **en** *prep.* 1.2; **sobre** *prep.* 1.2
  on the dot **en punto** 1.1
  on top of **encima de** 1.2
once **una vez** 1.6
one **un, uno/a** *m., f., sing. pron.* 1.1
  one hundred **cien(to)** *n., adj.* 1.2
  one million **un millón** *m.* 1.2
  one more time **una vez más** 1.9
  one thousand **mil** *n., adj.* 1.2
  one time **una vez** 1.6
onion **cebolla** *f.* 1.8
only **sólo** *adv.* 1.3; **único/a** *adj.* 1.3
  only child **hijo/a único/a** *m., f.* 1.3
open **abierto/a** *adj.* 1.5; **abrir** *v.* 1.3
open-air **al aire libre** 1.6
or **o** *conj.* 1.7
orange **anaranjado/a** *adj.* 1.6; **naranja** *f.* 1.8
order (*food*) **pedir (e:i)** *v.* 1.8
orderly **ordenado/a** *adj.* 1.5
ordinal (*numbers*) **ordinal** *adj.*
other **otro/a** *adj.* 1.6
ought to **deber** *v.* **(+** *inf.***)** 1.3
our **nuestro(s)/a(s)** *poss. adj.* 1.3
over **sobre** *prep.* 1.2
over there **allá** *adv.* 1.2
owner **dueño/a** *m., f.* 1.8

P

P.M. **tarde** *f.* 1.1
pack (one's suitcases) **hacer** *v.* **las maletas** 1.5
pair **par** *m.* 1.6
  pair of shoes **par de zapatos** *m.* 1.6
pants **pantalones** *m., pl.* 1.6
pantyhose **medias** *f., pl.* 1.6
paper **papel** *m.* 1.2
Pardon me. (*May I?*) **Con permiso.** 1.1; (*Excuse me.*) Pardon me. **Perdón.** 1.1
parents **padres** *m., pl.* 1.3; **papás** *m., pl.* 1.3
park **parque** *m.* 1.4
partner (*one of a married couple*) **pareja** *f.* 1.9
party **fiesta** *f.* 1.9
passed **pasado/a** *adj., p.p.*
passenger **pasajero/a** *m., f.* 1.1
passport **pasaporte** *m.* 1.5
past **pasado/a** *adj.* 1.6
pastime **pasatiempo** *m.* 1.4
pay **pagar** *v.* 1.6
  pay the bill **pagar la cuenta** 1.9
pea **arveja** *m.* 1.8
peach **melocotón** *m.* 1.8
pear **pera** *f.* 1.8
pen **pluma** *f.* 1.2
pencil **lápiz** *m.* 1.1
people **gente** *f.* 1.3
pepper (*black*) **pimienta** *f.* 1.8
perfect **perfecto/a** *adj.* 1.5
perhaps **quizás** *adv.*; **tal vez** *adv.*
permission **permiso** *m.*
person **persona** *f.* 1.3
phenomenal **fenomenal** *adj.* 1.5
photograph **foto(grafía)** *f.* 1.1
physician **doctor(a)** *m., f.*, **médico/a** *m., f.* 1.3
physics **física** *f. sing.* 1.2
pie **pastel** *m.* 1.9
pineapple **piña** *f.* 1.8
pink **rosado/a** *adj.* 1.6
place **lugar** *m.* 1.4; **poner** *v.* 1.4
plaid **de cuadros** 1.6
plans **planes** *m., pl.*
  have plans **tener planes**
play **jugar (u:ue)** *v.* 1.4; (cards) **jugar a (las cartas)** 1.5
  play sports **practicar deportes** 1.4
player **jugador(a)** *m., f.* 1.4
pleasant **agradable** *adj.*
please **por favor** 1.1
  Pleased to meet you. **Mucho gusto.** 1.1; **Encantado/a.** *adj.* 1.1
pleasing: be pleasing to **gustar** *v.* 1.2, 1.7
pleasure **gusto** *m.* 1.1
  The pleasure is mine. **El gusto es mío.** 1.1
polka-dotted **de lunares** 1.6
pool **piscina** *f.* 1.4
poor **pobre** *adj.* 1.6
pork **cerdo** *m.* 1.8
  pork chop **chuleta** *f.* **de cerdo** 1.8
possessive **posesivo/a** *adj.* 1.3
postcard **postal** *f.*
potato **papa** *f.* 1.8; **patata** *f.* 1.8
practice **practicar** *v.* 1.2
prefer **preferir (e:ie)** *v.* 1.4
prepare **preparar** *v.* 1.2
preposition **preposición** *f.*
pretty **bonito/a** *adj.* 1.3
price **precio** *m.* 1.6
  (fixed, set) price **precio** *m.* **fijo** 1.6
print **estampado/a** *adj*
private (*room*) **individual** *adj.*
problem **problema** *m.* 1.1
profession **profesión** *f.* 1.3
professor **profesor(a)** *m., f.*
program **programa** *m.* 1.1
programmer **programador(a)** *m., f.* 1.3
pronoun **pronombre** *m.*
psychology **psicología** *f.* 1.2
Puerto Rican **puertorriqueño/a** *adj.* 1.3
Puerto Rico **Puerto Rico** *m.* 1.1
pull a tooth **sacar una muela**
purchases **compras** *f., pl.* 1.5
purple **morado/a** *adj.* 1.6
purse **bolsa** *f.* 1.6
put **poner** *v.* 1.4
  put on (*clothing*) **ponerse** *v.* 1.7
  put on makeup **maquillarse** *v.* 1.7

Q

quality **calidad** *f.* 1.6
quarter **trimestre** *m.* 1.2
  quarter after (*time*) **y cuarto** 1.1; **y quince** 1.1
  quarter to (*time*) **menos cuarto** 1.1; **menos quince** 1.1
question **pregunta** *f.* 1.2
quiz **prueba** *f.* 1.2

R

radio (*medium*) **radio** *f.* 1.2
rain **llover (o:ue)** *v.* 1.5
  It's raining. **Llueve.** 1.5; **Está lloviendo.** 1.5
raincoat **impermeable** *m.* 1.6
read **leer** *v.* 1.3.
  read e-mail **leer correo electrónico** 1.4
  read a magazine **leer una revista** 1.4
  read a newspaper **leer un periódico** 1.4
ready **listo/a** *adj.* 1.5
receive **recibir** *v.* 1.3
recommend **recomendar (e:ie)** *v.* 1.8
recreation **diversión** *f.* 1.4
red **rojo/a** *adj.* 1.3
red-haired **pelirrojo/a** *adj.* 1.3
relatives **parientes** *m., pl.* 1.3
relax **relajarse** *v.* 1.9; **Tranquilo/a.** 1.7
remain **quedarse** *v.* 1.7
remember **acordarse (o:ue)** *v.* **(de)** 1.7; **recordar (o:ue)** *v.* 1.4
repeat **repetir (e:i)** *v.* 1.4
request **pedir (e:i)** *v.* 1.4
reservation **reservación** *f.* 1.5
rest **descansar** *v.* 1.2
restaurant **restaurante** *m.* 1.4
retire (*from work*) **jubilarse** *v.* 1.9
return **regresar** *v.* 1.2; **volver (o:ue)** *v.* 1.4

return trip **vuelta** *f.*
rice **arroz** *m.* 1.8
rich **rico/a** *adj.* 1.6
ride: ride a bicycle **pasear** *v.* **en bicicleta** 1.4
ride a horse **montar** *v.* **a caballo** 1.5
right **derecha** *f.* 1.2
be right **tener razón** 1.3
right away **enseguida** *adv.* 1.9
right now **ahora mismo** 1.5
to the right of **a la derecha de** 1.2
right? (*question tag*) **¿no?** 1.1; **¿verdad?** 1.1
road **camino** *m.*
roast **asado/a** *adj.* 1.8
roast chicken **pollo** *m.* **asado** 1.8
rollerblade **patinar en línea** *v.*
room **habitación** *f.* 1.5; **cuarto** *m.* 1.2; 1.7
roommate **compañero/a** *m., f.* **de cuarto** 1.2
roundtrip **de ida y vuelta** 1.5
roundtrip ticket **pasaje** *m.* **de ida y vuelta** 1.5
routine **rutina** *f.* 1.7
run **correr** *v.* 1.3
Russian **ruso/a** *adj.* 1.3

S

sad **triste** *adj.* 1.5
safe **seguro/a** *adj.* 1.5
sailboard **tabla de windsurf** *f.* 1.5
salad **ensalada** *f.* 1.8
sale **rebaja** *f.* 1.6
salesperson **vendedor(a)** *m., f.* 1.6
salmon **salmón** *m.* 1.8
salt **sal** *f.* 1.8
same **mismo/a** *adj.* 1.3
sandal **sandalia** *f.* 1.6
sandwich **sándwich** *m.* 1.8
Saturday **sábado** *m.* 1.2
sausage **salchicha** *f.* 1.8
say **decir** *v.* 1.4
say (that) **decir (que)** *v.* 1.4, 1.9
say the answer **decir la respuesta** 1.4
scared: be (very) scared (of) **tener (mucho) miedo (de)** 1.3
schedule **horario** *m.* 1.2
school **escuela** *f.* 1.1
science *f.* **ciencia** 1.2
scuba dive **bucear** *v.* 1.4
sea **mar** *m.* 1.5
season **estación** *f.* 1.5
seat **silla** *f.* 1.2
second **segundo/a** *n., adj.* 1.5
see **ver** *v.* 1.4
see movies **ver películas** 1.4
See you. **Nos vemos.** 1.1
See you later. **Hasta la vista.** 1.1; **Hasta luego.** 1.1
See you soon. **Hasta pronto.** 1.1
See you tomorrow. **Hasta mañana.** 1.1
seem **parecer** *v.* 1.6
sell **vender** *v.* 1.6
semester **semestre** *m.* 1.2
separate (from) **separarse** *v.* **(de)** 1.9
separated **separado/a** *adj.* 1.9
September **septiembre** *m.* 1.5
sequence **secuencia** *f.*
serve **servir (e:i)** *v.* 1.8
set (*fixed*) **fijo/a** *adj.* 1.6
seven **siete** *n., adj.* 1.1
seven hundred **setecientos/as** *n., adj.* 1.2
seventeen **diecisiete** *n., adj.* 1.1
seventh **séptimo/a** *n., adj.* 1.5
seventy **setenta** *n., adj.* 1.2
several **varios/as** *adj. pl.* 1.8
shampoo **champú** *m.* 1.7
share **compartir** *v.* 1.3
sharp (*time*) **en punto** 1.1
shave **afeitarse** *v.* 1.7
shaving cream **crema** *f.* **de afeitar** 1.7
she **ella** *sub. pron.* 1.1
shellfish **mariscos** *m., pl.* 1.8
ship **barco** *m.*
shirt **camisa** *f.* 1.6
shoe **zapato** *m.* 1.6
shoe size **número** *m.* 1.6
tennis shoes **zapatos** *m., pl.* **de tenis** 1.6
shop **tienda** *f.* 1.6
shopping: to go shopping **ir de compras** 1.5
shopping mall **centro comercial** *m.* 1.6
short (*in height*) **bajo/a** *adj.* 1.3; (*in length*) **corto/a** *adj.* 1.6
shorts **pantalones cortos** *m., pl.* 1.6
should (*do something*) **deber** *v.* **(+** *inf.***)** 1.3
show **mostrar (o:ue)** *v.* 1.4
shower **ducha** *f.* 1.7; **ducharse** *v.* 1.7
shrimp **camarón** *m.* 1.8
siblings **hermanos/as** *m., f. pl.* 1.3
silk **seda** *f.* 1.6
(made of) silk **de seda** 1.6
silly **tonto/a** *adj.* 1.3
since **desde** *prep.*
sing **cantar** *v.* 1.2
single **soltero/a** *adj.* 1.9
single room **habitación** *f.* **individual** 1.5
sink **lavabo** *m.* 1.7
sir **señor (Sr.)** *m.* 1.1
sister **hermana** *f.* 1.3
sister-in-law **cuñada** *f.* 1.3
sit down **sentarse (e:ie)** *v.* 1.7
six **seis** *n., adj.* 1.1
six hundred **seiscientos/as** *n., adj.* 1.2
sixteen **dieciséis** *n., adj.* 1.1
sixth **sexto/a** *n., adj.* 1.5
sixty **sesenta** *n., adj.* 1.2
size **talla** *f.* 1.6
shoe size **número** *m.* 1.6
skate (in-line) **patinar** *v.* **(en línea)** 1.4
skateboard **andar en patineta** *v.* 1.4
ski **esquiar** *v.* 1.4
skiing **esquí** *m.* 1.4
waterskiing **esquí** *m.* **acuático** 1.4
skirt **falda** *f.* 1.6
sleep **dormir (o:ue)** *v.* 1.4; **sueño** *m.* 1.3
go to sleep **dormirse (o:ue)** *v.* 1.7
sleepy: be (very) sleepy **tener (mucho) sueño** 1.3
slender **delgado/a** *adj.* 1.3
slippers **pantuflas** *f.* 1.7
small **pequeño/a** *adj.* 1.3
smart **listo/a** *adj.* 1.5
smile **sonreír (e:i)** *v.* 1.9
smoggy: It's (very) smoggy. **Hay (mucha) contaminación.**
smoke **fumar** *v.* 1.8
smoking section **sección** *f.* **de fumar** 1.8
nonsmoking section *f.* **sección de no fumar** 1.8
snack **merendar** *v.* 1.8
sneakers **los zapatos de tenis** 1.6
snow **nevar (e:ie)** *v.* 1.5; **nieve** *f.*
snowing: It's snowing. **Nieva.** 1.5; **Está nevando.** 1.5
so **tan** *adv.* 1.5
so much **tanto** *adv.*
so-so **regular** 1.1
soap **jabón** *m.* 1.7
soccer **fútbol** *m.* 1.4
sociology **sociología** *f.* 1.2
sock(s) **calcetín (calcetines)** *m.* 1.6
soft drink **refresco** *m.* 1.8
some **algún, alguno/a(s)** *adj.* 1.7; **unos/as** *pron. m., f. pl.; indef. art.* 1.1
somebody **alguien** *pron.* 1.7
someone **alguien** *pron.* 1.7
something **algo** *pron.* 1.7
son **hijo** *m.* 1.3
son-in-law **yerno** *m.* 1.3
soon **pronto** *adv.*
See you soon. **Hasta pronto.** 1.1

sorry
I'm sorry. **Lo siento.** 1.4
I'm so sorry. **Mil perdones.** 1.4; **Lo siento muchísimo.** 1.4
soup **sopa** *f.* 1.8
Spain **España** *f.* 1.1
Spanish (*language*) **español** *m.* 1.2; **español(a)** *adj.* 1.3
spare time **ratos libres** 1.4
speak **hablar** *v.* 1.2
spelling **ortografía** *f.*; **ortográfico/a** *adj.*
spend (*money*) **gastar** *v.* 1.6
sport **deporte** *m.* 1.4
sports-related **deportivo/a** *adj.* 1.4
spouse **esposo/a** *m., f.* 1.3
spring **primavera** *f.* 1.5
square (city or town) **plaza** *f.* 1.4
stadium **estadio** *m.* 1.2
stage **etapa** *f.* 1.9
station **estación** *f.* 1.5
status: marital status **estado** *m.* **civil** 1.9
stay **quedarse** *v.* 1.7
steak **bistec** *m.* 1.8
step **etapa** *f.*
stepbrother **hermanastro** *m.* 1.3
stepdaughter **hijastra** *f.* 1.3
stepfather **padrastro** *m.* 1.3
stepmother **madrastra** *f.* 1.3
stepsister **hermanastra** *f.* 1.3
stepson **hijastro** *m.* 1.3
still **todavía** *adv.* 1.5
stockings **medias** *f., pl.* 1.6
store **tienda** *f.* 1.6
strawberry **frutilla** *f.*; **fresa** *f.*
stripe **raya** *f.* 1.6
striped **de rayas** 1.6
stroll **pasear** *v.* 1.4
student **estudiante** *m., f.* 1.1, 1.2; **estudiantil** *adj.* 1.2
study **estudiar** *v.* 1.2
stupendous **estupendo/a** *adj.* 1.5
style **estilo** *m.*
subway **metro** *m.* 1.5
subway station **estación** *f.* **del metro** 1.5
such as **tales como**
suddenly **de repente** *adv.* 1.6
sugar **azúcar** *m.* 1.8
suit **traje** *m.* 1.6
suitcase **maleta** *f.* 1.1
summer **verano** *m.* 1.5
sun **sol** *m.* 1.5
sunbathe **tomar** *v.* **el sol** 1.4
Sunday **domingo** *m.* 1.2
sunglasses **gafas** *f., pl.* **de sol** 1.6
sunny: It's (very) sunny. **Hace (mucho) sol.** 1.5
suppose **suponer** *v.* 1.4
sure **seguro/a** *adj.* 1.5
be sure **estar seguro/a** 1.5
surfboard **tabla de surf** *f.* 1.5
surprise **sorprender** *v.* 1.9; **sorpresa** *f.* 1.9
sweater **suéter** *m.* 1.6
sweets **dulces** *m., pl.* 1.9
swim **nadar** *v.* 1.4
swimming **natación** *f.* 1.4
swimming pool **piscina** *f.* 1.4

T

table **mesa** *f.* 1.2
take **tomar** *v.* 1.2; **llevar** *v.* 1.6
take a bath **bañarse** *v.* 1.7
take (*wear*) a shoe size *v.* **calzar** 1.6
take a shower **ducharse** *v.* 1.7
take off **quitarse** *v.* 1.7
take photos **tomar fotos** 1.5; **sacar fotos** 1.5
talk *v.* **hablar** 1.2
tall **alto/a** *adj.* 1.3
tape (*audio*) **cinta** *f.*
taste **probar (o:ue)** *v.* 1.8; **saber** *v.* 1.8
taste (like) **saber (a)** 1.8
tasty **rico/a** *adj.* 1.8; **sabroso/a** *adj.* 1.8
taxi **taxi** *m.* 1.5
tea **té** *m.* 1.8
teach **enseñar** *v.* 1.2
teacher **profesor(a)** *m., f.* 1.1, 1.2
team **equipo** *m.* 1.4
television **televisión** *f.* 1.2
tell **contar (o:ue)** *v.* 1.4; **decir** *v.* 1.4
tell (that) **decir** *v.* **(que)** 1.4, 1.9
tell lies **decir mentiras** 1.4
tell the truth **decir la verdad** 1.4
ten **diez** *n., adj.* 1.1
tennis **tenis** *m.* 1.4
tennis shoes **zapatos** *m., pl.* **de tenis** 1.6
tent **tienda** *f.* **de campaña**
tenth **décimo/a** *n., adj.* 1.5
terrific **chévere** *adj.*
test **prueba** *f.* 1.2; **examen** *m.* 1.2
Thank you. **Gracias.** 1.1
Thank you (very much). **(Muchas) gracias.** 1.1
Thank you very, very much. **Muchísimas gracias.** 1.9
Thanks (a lot). **(Muchas) gracias.** 1.1
Thanks again. (*lit. Thanks one more time.*) **Gracias una vez más.** 1.9
Thanks for everything. **Gracias por todo.** 1.9
that (one) **ése, ésa, eso** *pron.* 1.6; **ese, esa** *adj.* 1.6
that (*over there*) **aquél, aquélla, aquello** *pron.* 1.6; **aquel, aquella** *adj.* 1.6
that's me **soy yo** 1.1
the **el** *m., sing.* **la** *f. sing.*, **los** *m., pl.* **las** *f., pl.*
their **su(s)** *poss. adj.* 1.3
them **los/las** *pl., d.o. pron.* 1.5; **ellos/as** *pron., obj. of prep.* 1.9
to/for them **les** *pl., i.o. pron.* 1.6
then **después** (*afterward*) *adv.* 1.7; **entonces** (*as a result*) *adv.* 1.7; **luego** (*next*) *adv.* 1.7
there **allí** *adv.* 1.2
There is/are... **Hay...** 1.1
There is/are not... **No hay...** 1.1
these **éstos, éstas** *pron.* 1.6; **estos, estas** *adj.* 1.6
they **ellos** *m., pron.* **ellas** *f., pron.*
thin **delgado/a** *adj.* 1.3
thing **cosa** *f.* 1.1
think **pensar (e:ie)** *v.* 1.4; (*believe*) **creer** *v.*
think about **pensar en** *v.* 1.4
third **tercero/a** *n., adj.* 1.5
thirst **sed** *f.* 1.3
thirsty: be (very) thirsty **tener (mucha) sed** 1.3
thirteen **trece** *n., adj.* 1.1
thirty **treinta** *n., adj.* 1.1; 1.2
thirty minutes past the hour **y treinta; y media** 1.1
this **este, esta** *adj.*; **éste, ésta, esto** *pron.* 1.6
This is... (*introduction*) **Éste/a es...** 1.1
those **ésos, ésas** *pron.* 1.6; **esos, esas** *adj.* 1.6
those (*over there*) **aquéllos, aquéllas** *pron.* 1.6; **aquellos, aquellas** *adj.* 1.6
thousand **mil** *n., adj.* 1.6
three **tres** *n., adj.* 1.1
three hundred **trescientos/as** *n., adj.* 1.2
Thursday **jueves** *m., sing.* 1.2
thus (*in such a way*) **así** *adj.*
ticket **pasaje** *m.* 1.5
tie **corbata** *f.* 1.6
time **vez** *f.* 1.6; **tiempo** *m.* 1.4
have a good/bad time **pasarlo bien/mal** 1.9
What time is it? **¿Qué hora es?** 1.1
(At) What time...? **¿A qué hora...?** 1.1
times **veces** *f., pl.* 1.6
two times **dos veces** 1.6
tip **propina** *f.* 1.9
tired **cansado/a** *adj.* 1.5
be tired **estar cansado/a** 1.5

to **a** *prep.* 1.1
toast (*drink*) **brindar** *v.* 1.9
toasted **tostado/a** *adj.* 1.8
  toasted bread **pan tostado** *m.* 1.8
today **hoy** *adv.* 1.2
  Today is... **Hoy es...** 1.2
together **juntos/as** *adj.* 1.9
toilet **inodoro** *m.* 1.7
tomato **tomate** *m.* 1.8
tomorrow **mañana** *f.* 1.1
  See you tomorrow. **Hasta mañana.** 1.1
tonight **esta noche** *adv.* 1.4
too **también** *adv.* 1.2; 1.7
  too much **demasiado** *adv.* 1.6
tooth **diente** *m.* 1.7
toothpaste **pasta** *f.* **de dientes** 1.7
tortilla **tortilla** *f.* 1.8
tour **excursión** *f.* 1.4
  tour an area **recorrer** *v.*
tourism **turismo** *m.* 1.5
tourist **turista** *m., f.* 1.1; **turístico/a** *adj.*
towel **toalla** *f.* 1.7
town **pueblo** *m.* 1.4
train **tren** *m.* 1.5
  train station **estación** *f.* **(de) tren** *m.* 1.5
translate **traducir** *v.* 1.6
travel **viajar** *v.* 1.2
travel agent **agente** *m., f.* **de viajes** 1.5
traveler **viajero/a** *m., f.* 1.5
trillion **billón** *m.*
trimester **trimestre** *m.* 1.2
trip **viaje** *m.* 1.5
  take a trip **hacer un viaje** 1.5
truth **verdad** *f.*
try **intentar** *v.*; **probar (o:ue)** *v.* 1.8
  try on **probarse (o:ue)** *v.* 1.7
t-shirt **camiseta** *f.* 1.6
Tuesday **martes** *m., sing.* 1.2
tuna **atún** *m.* 1.8
turkey **pavo** *m.* 1.8
twelve **doce** *n., adj.* 1.1
twenty **veinte** *n., adj.* 1.1
twenty-eight **veintiocho** *n., adj.* 1.1
twenty-five **veinticinco** *n., adj.* 1.1
twenty-four **veinticuatro** *n., adj.* 1.1
twenty-nine **veintinueve** *n., adj.* 1.1
twenty-one **veintiún, veintiuno/a** *n., adj.* 1.1
twenty-seven **veintisiete** *n., adj.* 1.1
twenty-six **veintiséis** *n., adj.* 1.1
twenty-three **veintitrés** *n., adj.* 1.1
twenty-two **veintidós** *n., adj.* 1.1
twice **dos veces** *adv.* 1.6
twin **gemelo/a** *m., f.* 1.3
two **dos** *n., adj.* 1.1
  two hundred **doscientos/as** *n., adj.* 1.2
  two times **dos veces** *adv.* 1.6

U

ugly **feo/a** *adj.* 1.3
uncle **tío** *m.* 1.3
under **bajo** *adv.* 1.7; **debajo de** *prep.* 1.2
understand **comprender** *v.* 1.3; **entender (e:ie)** *v.* 1.4
underwear **ropa interior** *f.* 1.6
United States **Estados Unidos (EE.UU.)** *m. pl.* 1.1
university **universidad** *f.* 1.2
unmarried **soltero/a** *adj.*
unpleasant **antipático/a** *adj.* 1.3
until **hasta** *prep.* 1.6
us **nos** *pl., d.o. pron.* 1.5
  to/for us **nos** *pl., i.o. pron.* 1.6
use **usar** *v.* 1.6
useful **útil** *adj.*

V

vacation **vacaciones** *f. pl.* 1.5
  be on vacation **estar de vacaciones** 1.5
  go on vacation **ir de vacaciones** 1.5
various **varios/as** *adj., pl.* 1.8
vegetables **verduras** *pl., f.* 1.8
verb **verbo** *m.*
very **muy** *adv.* 1.1
  very much **muchísimo** *adv.* 1.2
  (Very) well, thank you. **(Muy) bien gracias.** 1.1
video **video** *m.* 1.1
video game **videojuego** *m.* 1.4
vinegar **vinagre** *m.* 1.8
visit **visitar** *v.* 1.4
  visit monuments **visitar monumentos** 1.4
volleyball **vóleibol** *m.* 1.4

W

wait (for) **esperar** *v.* (+ *inf.*) 1.2
waiter/waitress **camarero/a** *m., f.* 1.8
wake up **despertarse (e:ie)** *v.* 1.7
walk **caminar** *v.* 1.2
  take a walk **pasear** *v.* 1.4
  walk around **pasear por** 1.4
walkman **walkman** *m.*
wallet **cartera** *f.* 1.6
want **querer (e:ie)** *v.* 1.4
wash **lavar** *v.*
  wash one's face/hands **lavarse la cara/las manos** 1.7
  wash oneself **lavarse** *v.* 1.7
wastebasket **papelera** *f.* 1.2
watch **mirar** *v.* 1.2; **reloj** *m.* 1.2
  watch television **mirar (la) televisión** 1.2
water **agua** *f.* 1.8
waterskiing *m.* **esquí acuático** 1.4
we **nosotros(as)** *m., f. sub. pron.* 1.1
wear **llevar** *v.* 1.6; **usar** *v.* 1.6
weather **tiempo** *m.*
  The weather is bad. **Hace mal tiempo.** 1.5
  The weather is good. **Hace buen tiempo.** 1.5
wedding **boda** *f.* 1.9
Wednesday **miércoles** *m., sing.* 1.2
week **semana** *f.* 1.2
weekend **fin** *m.* **de semana** 1.4
well **pues** *adv.* 1.2; **bueno** *adv.* 1.2
  (Very) well, thanks. **(Muy) bien, gracias.** 1.1
  well organized **ordenado/a** *adj.*
what? **¿qué?** *pron.* 1.1
  At what time...? **¿A qué hora...?** 1.1
  What day is it? **¿Qué día es hoy?** 1.2
  What do you guys think? **¿Qué les parece?** 1.9
  What is today's date? **¿Cuál es la fecha de hoy?** 1.5
  What nice clothes! **¡Qué ropa más bonita!** 1.6
  What size do you take? **¿Qué talla lleva (usa)?** 1.6
  What time is it? **¿Qué hora es?** 1.1
  What's going on? **¿Qué pasa?** 1.1
  What's happening? **¿Qué pasa?** 1.1
  What's... like? **¿Cómo es...?** 1.3
  What's new? **¿Qué hay de nuevo?** 1.1
  What's the weather like? **¿Qué tiempo hace?** 1.5
  What's your name? **¿Cómo se llama usted?** *form.* 1.1
  What's your name? **¿Cómo te llamas (tú)?** *fam.* 1.1
when **cuando** *conj.* 1.7
  When? **¿Cuándo?** *adv.* 1.2
where **donde** *prep.*
  where (to)? (*destination*)

¿adónde? *adv.* 1.2; (*location*) **¿dónde?** *adv.* 1.1
Where are you from? **¿De dónde eres (tú)?** *fam.* 1.1; **¿De dónde es (usted)?** *form.* 1.1
Where is...? **¿Dónde está...?** 1.2
which? **¿cuál?** *pron.* 1.2; **¿qué?** *adj.* 1.2
In which...? **¿En qué...?** 1.2
which one(s)? **¿cuál(es)?** *pron.* 1.2
white **blanco/a** *adj.* 1.3
white wine **vino blanco** 1.8
who? **¿quién(es)?** *pron.* 1.1
Who is...? **¿Quién es...?** 1.1
whole **todo/a** *adj.*
whose **¿de quién(es)?** *pron., adj.* 1.1
why? **¿por qué?** *adv.* 1.2
widower/widow **viudo/a** *adj.* 1.9
wife **esposa** *f.* 1.3
win **ganar** *v.* 1.4
wind **viento** *m.* 1.5
window **ventana** *f.* 1.2
windy: It's (very) windy. **Hace (mucho) viento.** 1.5
wine **vino** *m.* 1.8
red wine **vino tinto** 1.8
white wine **vino blanco** 1.8
winter **invierno** *m.* 1.5
wish **desear** *v.* 1.2
with **con** *prep.* 1.2
with me **conmigo** 1.4; 1.9
with you **contigo** *fam.* 1.9
without **sin** *prep.* 1.2
woman **mujer** *f.* 1.1
wool **lana** *f.* 1.6
(made of) wool **de lana** 1.6
word **palabra** *f.* 1.1
work **trabajar** *v.* 1.2
worldwide **mundial** *adj.*
worried (about) **preocupado/a (por)** *adj.* 1.5
worry (about) **preocuparse** *v.* **(por)** 1.7
Don't worry. **No se preocupe.** *form.* 1.7; **No te preocupes.** *fam.* 1.7; **Tranquilo.** *adj.*
worse **peor** *adj.* 1.8
worst **el/la peor** *adj.* **lo peor** *n.* 1.8
Would you like to...? **¿Te gustaría...?** *fam.* 1.4
write **escribir** *v.* 1.3
write a letter/e-mail message **escribir una carta/un mensaje electrónico** 1.4
wrong **equivocado/a** *adj.* 1.5
be wrong **no tener razón** 1.3

X

x-ray **radiografía** *f.*

Y

year **año** *m.* 1.5
be... years old **tener... años** 1.3
yellow **amarillo/a** *adj.* 1.3
yes **sí** *interj.* 1.1
yesterday **ayer** *adv.* 1.6
yet **todavía** *adv.* 1.5
yogurt **yogur** *m.* 1.8
you *sub pron.* **tú** *fam. sing.*, **usted (Ud.)** *form. sing.*, **vosotros/as** *fam. pl.*, **ustedes (Uds.)** *form. pl.* 1.1; *d. o. pron.* **te** *fam. sing.*, **lo/la** *form. sing.*, **os** *fam. pl.*, **los/las** *form. pl.* 1.5; *obj. of prep.* **ti** *fam. sing.*, **usted (Ud.)** *form. sing.*, **vosotros/as** *fam. pl.*, **ustedes (Uds.)** *form. pl.* 1.9
(to, for) you *i.o. pron.* **te** *fam. sing.*, **le** *form. sing.*, **os** *fam. pl.*, **les** *form. pl.* 1.6
You are... **Tú eres...** 1.1
You're welcome. **De nada.** 1.1; **No hay de qué.** 1.1
young **joven** *adj., sing.* (**jóvenes** *pl.*) 1.3
young person **joven** *m., f., sing.* (**jóvenes** *pl.*) 1.1
young woman **señorita (Srta.)** *f.*
younger **menor** *adj.* 1.3
younger brother/sister *m., f.* **hermano/a menor** 1.3
youngest **el/la menor** *m., f.* 1.8
your **su(s)** *poss. adj. form.* 1.3; **tu(s)** *poss. adj. fam. sing.* 1.3; **vuestro/a(s)** *poss. adj. form. pl.* 1.3
youth *f.* **juventud** 1.9

Z

zero **cero** *m.* 1.1

MATERIAS	ACADEMIC SUBJECTS
la administración de empresas	business administration
la agronomía	agriculture
el alemán	German
el álgebra	algebra
la antropología	anthropology
la arqueología	archaeology
la arquitectura	architecture
el arte	art
la astronomía	astronomy
la biología	biology
la bioquímica	biochemistry
la botánica	botany
el cálculo	calculus
el chino	Chinese
las ciencias políticas	political science
la computación	computer science
las comunicaciones	communications
la contabilidad	accounting
la danza	dance
el derecho	law
la economía	economics
la educación	education
la educación física	physical education
la enfermería	nursing
el español	Spanish
la filosofía	philosophy
la física	physics
el francés	French
la geografía	geography
la geología	geology
el griego	Greek
el hebreo	Hebrew
la historia	history
la informática	computer science
la ingeniería	engineering
el inglés	English
el italiano	Italian
el japonés	Japanese
el latín	Latin
las lenguas clásicas	classical languages
las lenguas romances	Romance languages
la lingüística	linguistics
la literatura	literature
las matemáticas	mathematics
la medicina	medicine
el mercadeo/ la mercadotecnia	marketing
la música	music
los negocios	business
el periodismo	journalism
el portugués	Portuguese
la psicología	psychology
la química	chemistry
el ruso	Russian
los servicios sociales	social services
la sociología	sociology
el teatro	theater
la trigonometría	trigonometry

LOS ANIMALES	ANIMALS
la abeja	bee
la araña	spider
la ardilla	squirrel
el ave (*f.*), el pájaro	bird
la ballena	whale
el burro	donkey
la cabra	goat
el caimán	alligator
el camello	camel
la cebra	zebra
el ciervo, el venado	deer
el cochino, el cerdo, el puerco	pig
el cocodrilo	crocodile
el conejo	rabbit
el coyote	coyote
la culebra, la serpiente, la víbora	snake
el elefante	elephant
la foca	seal
la gallina	hen
el gallo	rooster
el gato	cat
el gorila	gorilla
el hipopótamo	hippopotamus
la hormiga	ant
el insecto	insect
la jirafa	giraffe
el lagarto	lizard
el león	lion
el lobo	wolf
el loro, la cotorra, el papagayo, el perico	parrot
la mariposa	butterfly
el mono	monkey
la mosca	fly
el mosquito	mosquito
el oso	bear
la oveja	sheep
el pato	duck
el perro	dog
el pez	fish
la rana	frog
el ratón	mouse
el rinoceronte	rhinoceros
el saltamontes, el chapulín	grasshopper
el tiburón	shark
el tigre	tiger
el toro	bull
la tortuga	turtle
la vaca	cow
el zorro	fox

EL CUERPO HUMANO Y LA SALUD — THE HUMAN BODY AND HEALTH

El cuerpo humano — The human body

la barba	beard
el bigote	mustache
la boca	mouth
el brazo	arm
la cabeza	head
la cadera	hip
la ceja	eyebrow
el cerebro	brain
la cintura	waist
el codo	elbow
el corazón	heart
la costilla	rib
el cráneo	skull
el cuello	neck
el dedo	finger
el dedo del pie	toe
la espalda	back
el estómago	stomach
la frente	forehead
la garganta	throat
el hombro	shoulder
el hueso	bone
el labio	lip
la lengua	tongue
la mandíbula	jaw
la mejilla	cheek
el mentón, la barba, la barbilla	chin
la muñeca	wrist
el músculo	muscle
el muslo	thigh
las nalgas, el trasero, las asentaderas	buttocks
la nariz	nose
el nervio	nerve
el oído	(inner) ear
el ojo	eye
el ombligo	navel, belly button
la oreja	(outer) ear
la pantorrilla	calf
el párpado	eyelid
el pecho	chest
la pestaña	eyelash
el pie	foot
la piel	skin
la pierna	leg
el pulgar	thumb
el pulmón	lung
la rodilla	knee
la sangre	blood
el talón	heel
el tobillo	ankle
el tronco	torso, trunk
la uña	fingernail
la uña del dedo del pie	toenail
la vena	vein

Los cinco sentidos — The five senses

el gusto	taste
el oído	hearing
el olfato	smell
el tacto	touch
la vista	sight

La salud — Health

el accidente	accident
alérgico/a	allergic
el antibiótico	antibiotic
la aspirina	aspirin
el ataque cardiaco, el ataque al corazón	heart attack
el cáncer	cancer
la cápsula	capsule
la clínica	clinic
congestionado/a	congested
el consultorio	doctor's office
la curita	adhesive bandage
el/la dentista	dentist
el/la doctor(a), el/la médico/a	doctor
el dolor (de cabeza)	(head)ache, pain
embarazada	pregnant
la enfermedad	illness, disease
el/la enfermero/a	nurse
enfermo/a	ill, sick
la erupción	rash
el examen médico	physical exam
la farmacia	pharmacy
la fiebre	fever
la fractura	fracture
la gripe	flu
la herida	wound
el hospital	hospital
la infección	infection
el insomnio	insomnia
la inyección	injection
el jarabe	(cough) syrup
mareado/a	dizzy, nauseated
el medicamento	medication
la medicina	medicine
las muletas	crutches
la operación	operation
el/la paciente	patient
el/la paramédico/a	paramedic
la pastilla, la píldora	pill, tablet
los primeros auxilios	first aid
la pulmonía	pneumonia
los puntos	stitches
la quemadura	burn
el quirófano	operating room
la radiografía	x-ray
la receta	prescription
el resfriado	cold (illness)
la sala de emergencia(s)	emergency room
saludable	healthy, healthful
sano/a	healthy
el seguro médico	medical insurance
la silla de ruedas	wheelchair
el síntoma	symptom
el termómetro	thermometer
la tos	cough
la transfusión	transfusion

la vacuna	vaccination
la venda	bandage
el virus	virus

---

cortar(se)	to cut (oneself)
curar	to cure, to treat
desmayar(se)	to faint
enfermarse	to get sick
enyesar	to put in a cast
estornudar	to sneeze
guardar cama	to stay in bed
hinchar(se)	to swell
internar(se) en el hospital	to check into the hospital
lastimarse (el pie)	to hurt (one's foot)
mejorar(se)	to get better; to improve
operar	to operate
quemar(se)	to burn
respirar (hondo)	to breathe (deeply)
romperse (la pierna)	to break (one's leg)
sangrar	to bleed
sufrir	to suffer
tomarle la presión a alguien	to take someone's blood pressure
tomarle el pulso a alguien	to take someone's pulse
torcerse (el tobillo)	to sprain (one's ankle)
vendar	to bandage

EXPRESIONES ÚTILES PARA LA CLASE / USEFUL CLASSROOM EXPRESSIONS

Palabras útiles / Useful words

ausente	absent
el departamento	department
el dictado	dictation
la conversación, las conversaciones	conversation(s)
la expresión, las expresiones	expression(s)
el examen, los exámenes	test(s), exam(s)
la frase	sentence
la hoja de actividades	activity sheet
el horario de clases	class schedule
la oración, las oraciones	sentence(s)
el párrafo	paragraph
la persona	person
presente	present
la prueba	test, quiz
siguiente	following
la tarea	homework

Expresiones útiles / Useful expressions

Abra(n) su(s) libro(s).	Open your book(s).
Cambien de papel.	Change roles.
Cierre(n) su(s) libro(s).	Close your book(s).
¿Cómo se dice ___ en español?	How do you say ___ in Spanish?
¿Cómo se escribe ___ en español?	How do you write ___ in Spanish?
¿Comprende(n)?	Do you understand?
(No) comprendo.	I (don't) understand.
Conteste(n) las preguntas.	Answer the questions.
Continúe(n), por favor.	Continue, please.
Escriba(n) su nombre.	Write your name.
Escuche(n) el audio.	Listen to the audio.
Estudie(n) la Lección tres.	Study Lesson three.
Haga(n) la actividad (el ejercicio) número cuatro.	Do activity (exercise) number four.
Lea(n) la oración en voz alta.	Read the sentence aloud.
Levante(n) la mano.	Raise your hand(s).
Más despacio, por favor.	Slower, please.
No sé.	I don't know.
Páse(n)me los exámenes.	Pass me the tests.
¿Qué significa ___?	What does ___ mean?
Repita(n), por favor.	Repeat, please.
Siénte(n)se, por favor.	Sit down, please.
Siga(n) las instrucciones.	Follow the instructions.
¿Tiene(n) alguna pregunta?	Do you have any questions?
Vaya(n) a la página dos.	Go to page two.

COUNTRIES & NATIONALITIES / PAÍSES Y NACIONALIDADES

North America	Norteamérica	
Canada	**Canadá**	***canadiense***
Mexico	**México**	***mexicano/a***
United States	**Estados Unidos**	***estadounidense***
Central America	**Centroamérica**	
Belize	**Belice**	***beliceño/a***
Costa Rica	**Costa Rica**	***costarricense***
El Salvador	**El Salvador**	***salvadoreño/a***
Guatemala	**Guatemala**	***guatemalteco/a***
Honduras	**Honduras**	***hondureño/a***
Nicaragua	**Nicaragua**	***nicaragüense***
Panama	**Panamá**	***panameño/a***

The Caribbean	**El Caribe**	
Cuba	**Cuba**	***cubano/a***
Dominican Republic	**República Dominicana**	***dominicano/a***
Haiti	**Haití**	***haitiano/a***
Puerto Rico	**Puerto Rico**	***puertorriqueño/a***
South America	**Suramérica**	
Argentina	**Argentina**	***argentino/a***
Bolivia	**Bolivia**	***boliviano/a***
Brazil	**Brasil**	***brasileño/a***
Chile	**Chile**	***chileno/a***
Colombia	**Colombia**	***colombiano/a***
Ecuador	**Ecuador**	***ecuatoriano/a***
Paraguay	**Paraguay**	***paraguayo/a***
Peru	**Perú**	***peruano/a***
Uruguay	**Uruguay**	***uruguayo/a***
Venezuela	**Venezuela**	***venezolano/a***
Europe	**Europa**	
Armenia	**Armenia**	***armenio/a***
Austria	**Austria**	***austríaco/a***
Belgium	**Bélgica**	***belga***
Bosnia	**Bosnia**	***bosnio/a***
Bulgaria	**Bulgaria**	***búlgaro/a***
Croatia	**Croacia**	***croata***
Czech Republic	**República Checa**	***checo/a***
Denmark	**Dinamarca**	***danés, danesa***
England	**Inglaterra**	***inglés, inglesa***
Estonia	**Estonia**	***estonio/a***
Finland	**Finlandia**	***finlandés, finlandesa***
France	**Francia**	***francés, francesa***
Germany	**Alemania**	***alemán, alemana***
Great Britain (United Kingdom)	**Gran Bretaña (Reino Unido)**	***británico/a***
Greece	**Grecia**	***griego/a***
Hungary	**Hungría**	***húngaro/a***
Iceland	**Islandia**	***islandés, islandesa***
Ireland	**Irlanda**	***irlandés, irlandesa***
Italy	**Italia**	***italiano/a***
Latvia	**Letonia**	***letón, letona***
Lithuania	**Lituania**	***lituano/a***
Netherlands (Holland)	**Países Bajos (Holanda)**	***holandés, holandesa***
Norway	**Noruega**	***noruego/a***
Poland	**Polonia**	***polaco/a***
Portugal	**Portugal**	***portugués, portuguesa***
Romania	**Rumania**	***rumano/a***
Russia	**Rusia**	***ruso/a***
Scotland	**Escocia**	***escocés, escocesa***
Serbia	**Serbia**	***serbio/a***
Slovakia	**Eslovaquia**	***eslovaco/a***
Slovenia	**Eslovenia**	***esloveno/a***
Spain	**España**	***español(a)***
Sweden	**Suecia**	***sueco/a***
Switzerland	**Suiza**	***suizo/a***
Ukraine	**Ucrania**	***ucraniano/a***
Wales	**Gales**	***galés, galesa***
Asia	**Asia**	
Bangladesh	**Bangladés**	***bangladesí***
Cambodia	**Camboya**	***camboyano/a***
China	**China**	***chino/a***
India	**India**	***indio/a***
Indonesia	**Indonesia**	***indonesio/a***
Iran	**Irán**	***iraní***
Iraq	**Iraq, Irak**	***iraquí***

Israel	**Israel**	***israelí***
Japan	**Japón**	***japonés, japonesa***
Jordan	**Jordania**	***jordano/a***
Korea	**Corea**	***coreano/a***
Kuwait	**Kuwait**	***kuwaití***
Lebanon	**Líbano**	***libanés, libanesa***
Malaysia	**Malasia**	***malasio/a***
Pakistan	**Pakistán**	***pakistaní***
Russia	**Rusia**	***ruso/a***
Saudi Arabia	**Arabia Saudí**	***saudí***
Singapore	**Singapur**	***singapurés, singapuresa***
Syria	**Siria**	***sirio/a***
Taiwan	**Taiwán**	***taiwanés, taiwanesa***
Thailand	**Tailandia**	***tailandés, tailandesa***
Turkey	**Turquía**	***turco/a***
Vietnam	**Vietnam**	***vietnamita***
Africa	**África**	
Algeria	**Argelia**	***argelino/a***
Angola	**Angola**	***angoleño/a***
Cameroon	**Camerún**	***camerunés, camerunesa***
Congo	**Congo**	***congolés, congolesa***
Egypt	**Egipto**	***egipcio/a***
Equatorial Guinea	**Guinea Ecuatorial**	***ecuatoguineano/a***
Ethiopia	**Etiopía**	***etíope***
Ivory Coast	**Costa de Marfil**	***marfileño/a***
Kenya	**Kenia, Kenya**	***keniano/a, keniata***
Libya	**Libia**	***libio/a***
Mali	**Malí**	***maliense***
Morocco	**Marruecos**	***marroquí***
Mozambique	**Mozambique**	***mozambiqueño/a***
Nigeria	**Nigeria**	***nigeriano/a***
Rwanda	**Ruanda**	***ruandés, ruandesa***
Somalia	**Somalia**	***somalí***
South Africa	**Sudáfrica**	***sudafricano/a***
Sudan	**Sudán**	***sudanés, sudanesa***
Tunisia	**Tunicia, Túnez**	***tunecino/a***
Uganda	**Uganda**	***ugandés, ugandesa***
Zambia	**Zambia**	***zambiano/a***
Zimbabwe	**Zimbabue**	***zimbabuense***
Australia and the Pacific	**Australia y el Pacífico**	
Australia	**Australia**	***australiano/a***
New Zealand	**Nueva Zelanda**	***neozelandés, neozelandesa***
Philippines	**Filipinas**	***filipino/a***

MONEDAS DE LOS PAÍSES HISPANOS

CURRENCIES OF HISPANIC COUNTRIES

País Country	Moneda Currency
Argentina	el peso
Bolivia	el boliviano
Chile	el peso
Colombia	el peso
Costa Rica	el colón
Cuba	el peso
Ecuador	el dólar estadounidense
El Salvador	el dólar estadounidense
España	el euro
Guatemala	el quetzal
Guinea Ecuatorial	el franco
Honduras	el lempira
México	el peso
Nicaragua	el córdoba
Panamá	el balboa, el dólar estadounidense
Paraguay	el guaraní
Perú	el nuevo sol
Puerto Rico	el dólar estadounidense
República Dominicana	el peso
Uruguay	el peso
Venezuela	el bolívar

EXPRESIONES Y REFRANES

EXPRESSIONS AND SAYINGS

Expresiones y refranes con partes del cuerpo

Expressions and sayings with parts of the body

A cara o cruz	Heads or tails
A corazón abierto	Open heart
A ojos vistas	Clearly, visibly
Al dedillo	Like the back of one's hand
¡Choca/Vengan esos cinco!	Put it there!/Give me five!
Codo con codo	Side by side
Con las manos en la masa	Red-handed
Costar un ojo de la cara	To cost an arm and a leg
Darle a la lengua	To chatter/To gab
De rodillas	On one's knees
Duro de oído	Hard of hearing
En cuerpo y alma	In body and soul
En la punta de la lengua	On the tip of one's tongue
En un abrir y cerrar de ojos	In a blink of the eye
Entrar por un oído y salir por otro	In one ear and out the other
Estar con el agua al cuello	To be up to one's neck with/in
Estar para chuparse los dedos	To be delicious/To be finger-licking good
Hablar entre dientes	To mutter/To speak under one's breath
Hablar por los codos	To talk a lot/To be a chatterbox
Hacer la vista gorda	To turn a blind eye on something
Hombro con hombro	Shoulder to shoulder
Llorar a lágrima viva	To sob/To cry one's eyes out
Metérsele (a alguien) algo entre ceja y ceja	To get an idea in your head
No pegar ojo	Not to sleep a wink
No tener corazón	Not to have a heart
No tener dos dedos de frente	Not to have an ounce of common sense
Ojos que no ven, corazón que no siente	Out of sight, out of mind
Perder la cabeza	To lose one's head
Quedarse con la boca abierta	To be thunderstruck
Romper el corazón	To break someone's heart
Tener buen/mal corazón	Have a good/bad heart
Tener un nudo en la garganta	Have a knot in your throat
Tomarse algo a pecho	To take something too seriously
Venir como anillo al dedo	To fit like a charm/To suit perfectly

Expresiones y refranes con animales

Expressions and sayings with animals

A caballo regalado no le mires el diente.	Don't look a gift horse in the mouth.
Comer como un cerdo	To eat like a pig
Cuando menos se piensa, salta la liebre.	Things happen when you least expect it.
Llevarse como el perro y el gato	To fight like cats and dogs
Perro ladrador, poco mordedor./Perro que ladra no muerde.	His/her bark is worse than his/her bite.
Por la boca muere el pez.	Talking too much can be dangerous.
Poner el cascabel al gato	To stick one's neck out
Ser una tortuga	To be a slowpoke

Expresiones y refranes con alimentos

Expressions and sayings with food

Agua que no has de beber, déjala correr.	If you're not interested, don't ruin it for everybody else.
Con pan y vino se anda el camino.	Things never seem as bad after a good meal.
Contigo pan y cebolla.	You are all I need.
Dame pan y dime tonto.	I don't care what you say, as long as I get what I want.
Descubrir el pastel	To let the cat out of the bag
Dulce como la miel	Sweet as honey
Estar como agua para chocolate	To furious/To be at the boiling point
Estar en el ajo	To be in the know
Estar en la higuera	To have one's head in the clouds
Estar más claro que el agua	To be clear as a bell
Ganarse el pan	To earn a living/To earn one's daily bread
Llamar al pan, pan y al vino, vino.	Not to mince words.
No hay miel sin hiel.	Every rose has its thorn./ There's always a catch.
No sólo de pan vive el hombre.	Man doesn't live by bread alone.
Pan con pan, comida de tontos.	Variety is the spice of life.
Ser agua pasada	To be water under the bridge
Ser más bueno que el pan	To be kindness itself
Temblar como un flan	To shake/tremble like a leaf

Expresiones y refranes con colores

Expressions and sayings with colors

Estar verde	To be inexperienced/wet behind the ears
Poner los ojos en blanco	To roll one's eyes
Ponerle a alguien un ojo morado	To give someone a black eye
Ponerse rojo	To turn red/To blush
Ponerse rojo de ira	To turn red with anger
Ponerse verde de envidia	To be green with envy
Quedarse en blanco	To go blank
Verlo todo de color de rosa	To see the world through rose-colored glasses

Refranes	Sayings
A buen entendedor, pocas palabras bastan.	A word to the wise is enough.
Ande o no ande, caballo grande.	Bigger is always better.
A quien madruga, Dios le ayuda.	The early bird catches the worm.
Cuídate, que te cuidaré.	Take care of yourself, and then I'll take care of you.
De tal palo tal astilla.	A chip off the old block.
Del dicho al hecho hay mucho trecho.	Easier said than done.
Dime con quién andas y te diré quién eres.	A man is known by the company he keeps.
El saber no ocupa lugar.	One never knows too much.
Lo que es moda no incomoda.	You have to suffer in the name of fashion.
Más vale maña que fuerza.	Brains are better than brawn.
Más vale prevenir que curar.	Prevention is better than cure.
Más vale solo que mal acompañado.	Better alone than with people you don't like.
Más vale tarde que nunca.	Better late than never.
No es oro todo lo que reluce.	All that glitters is not gold.
Poderoso caballero es don Dinero.	Money talks.

COMMON FALSE FRIENDS

False friends are Spanish words that look similar to English words but have very different meanings. While recognizing the English relatives of unfamiliar Spanish words you encounter is an important way of constructing meaning, there are some Spanish words whose similarity to English words is deceptive. Here is a list of some of the most common Spanish false friends.

actualmente ≠ actually
actualmente = nowadays, currently
actually = **de hecho, en realidad, en efecto**

argumento ≠ argument
argumento = plot
argument = **discusión, pelea**

armada ≠ army
armada = navy
army = **ejército**

balde ≠ bald
balde = pail, bucket
bald = **calvo/a**

batería ≠ battery
batería = drum set
battery = **pila**

bravo ≠ brave
bravo = wild; fierce
brave = **valiente**

cándido/a ≠ candid
cándido/a = innocent
candid = **sincero/a**

carbón ≠ carbon
carbón = coal
carbon = **carbono**

casual ≠ casual
casual = accidental, chance
casual = **informal, despreocupado/a**

casualidad ≠ casualty
casualidad = chance, coincidence
casualty = **víctima**

colegio ≠ college
colegio = school
college = **universidad**

collar ≠ collar (of a shirt)
collar = necklace
collar = **cuello (de camisa)**

comprensivo/a ≠ comprehensive
comprensivo/a = understanding
comprehensive = **completo, extensivo**

constipado ≠ constipated
estar constipado/a = to have a cold
to be constipated = **estar estreñido/a**

crudo/a ≠ crude
crudo/a = raw, undercooked
crude = **burdo/a, grosero/a**

divertir ≠ to divert
divertirse = to enjoy oneself
to divert = **desviar**

educado/a ≠ educated
educado/a = well-mannered
educated = **culto/a, instruido/a**

embarazada ≠ embarrassed
estar embarazada = to be pregnant
to be embarrassed = **estar avergonzado/a; dar/tener vergüenza**

eventualmente ≠ eventually
eventualmente = possibly
eventually = **finalmente, al final**

éxito ≠ exit
éxito = success
exit = **salida**

físico/a ≠ physician
físico/a = physicist
physician = **médico/a**

fútbol ≠ football
fútbol = soccer
football = **fútbol americano**

lectura ≠ lecture
lectura = reading
lecture = **conferencia**

librería ≠ library
librería = bookstore
library = **biblioteca**

máscara ≠ mascara
máscara = mask
mascara = **rímel**

molestar ≠ to molest
molestar = to bother, to annoy
to molest = **abusar**

oficio ≠ office
oficio = trade, occupation
office = **oficina**

rato ≠ rat
rato = while, time
rat = **rata**

realizar ≠ to realize
realizar = to carry out; to fulfill
to realize = **darse cuenta de**

red ≠ red
red = net
red = **rojo/a**

revolver ≠ revolver
revolver = to stir, to rummage through
revolver = **revólver**

sensible ≠ sensible
sensible = sensitive
sensible = **sensato/a, razonable**

suceso ≠ success
suceso = event
success = **éxito**

sujeto ≠ subject (topic)
sujeto = fellow; individual
subject = **tema, asunto**

LOS ALIMENTOS — FOODS

Frutas — Fruits

la aceituna	olive
el aguacate	avocado
el albaricoque, el damasco	apricot
la banana, el plátano	banana
la cereza	cherry
la ciruela	plum
el dátil	date
la frambuesa	raspberry
la fresa, la frutilla	strawberry
el higo	fig
el limón	lemon; lime
el melocotón, el durazno	peach
la mandarina	tangerine
el mango	mango
la manzana	apple
la naranja	orange
la papaya	papaya
la pera	pear
la piña	pineapple
el pomelo, la toronja	grapefruit
la sandía	watermelon
las uvas	grapes

Vegetales — Vegetables

la alcachofa	artichoke
el apio	celery
la arveja, el guisante	pea
la berenjena	eggplant
el brócoli	broccoli
la calabaza	squash; pumpkin
la cebolla	onion
el champiñón, la seta	mushroom
la col, el repollo	cabbage
la coliflor	cauliflower
los espárragos	asparagus
las espinacas	spinach
los frijoles, las habichuelas	beans
las habas	fava beans
las judías verdes, los ejotes	string beans, green beans
la lechuga	lettuce
el maíz, el choclo, el elote	corn
la papa, la patata	potato
el pepino	cucumber
el pimentón	bell pepper
el rábano	radish
la remolacha	beet
el tomate, el jitomate	tomato
la zanahoria	carrot

El pescado y los mariscos — Fish and shellfish

la almeja	clam
el atún	tuna
el bacalao	cod
el calamar	squid
el cangrejo	crab
el camarón, la gamba	shrimp
la langosta	lobster
el langostino	prawn
el lenguado	sole; flounder
el mejillón	mussel
la ostra	oyster
el pulpo	octopus
el salmón	salmon
la sardina	sardine
la vieira	scallop

La carne — Meat

la albóndiga	meatball
el bistec	steak
la carne de res	beef
el chorizo	hard pork sausage
la chuleta de cerdo	pork chop
el cordero	lamb
los fiambres	cold cuts, food served cold
el filete	fillet
la hamburguesa	hamburger
el hígado	liver
el jamón	ham
el lechón	suckling pig, roasted pig
el pavo	turkey
el pollo	chicken
el cerdo	pork
la salchicha	sausage
la ternera	veal
el tocino	bacon

Otras comidas — Other foods

el ajo	garlic
el arroz	rice
el azúcar	sugar
el batido	milkshake
el budín	pudding
el cacahuete, el maní	peanut
el café	coffee
los fideos	noodles, pasta
la harina	flour
el huevo	egg
el jugo, el zumo	juice
la leche	milk
la mermelada	marmalade, jam
la miel	honey
el pan	bread
el queso	cheese
la sal	salt
la sopa	soup
el té	tea
la tortilla	omelet (Spain), tortilla (Mexico)
el yogur	yogurt

Cómo describir la comida — Ways to describe food

a la plancha, a la parrilla	grilled
ácido/a	sour
al horno	baked
amargo/a	bitter
caliente	hot
dulce	sweet
duro/a	tough
frío/a	cold
frito/a	fried
fuerte	strong, heavy
ligero/a	light
picante	spicy
sabroso/a	tasty
salado/a	salty

DÍAS FESTIVOS	HOLIDAYS
enero	January
Año Nuevo (1)	New Year's Day
Día de los Reyes Magos (6)	Three Kings Day (Epiphany)
Día de Martin Luther King, Jr.	Martin Luther King, Jr. Day
febrero	February
Día de San Blas (Paraguay) (3)	St. Blas Day (Paraguay)
Día de San Valentín, Día de los Enamorados (14)	Valentine's Day
Día de los Presidentes	Presidents' Day
Carnaval	Carnival (Mardi Gras)
marzo	March
Día de San Patricio (17)	St. Patrick's Day
Nacimiento de Benito Juárez (México) (21)	Benito Juárez's Birthday (Mexico)
abril	April
Semana Santa	Holy Week
Pésaj	Passover
Pascua	Easter
Declaración de la Independencia de Venezuela (19)	Declaration of Independence of Venezuela
Día de la Tierra (22)	Earth Day
mayo	May
Día del Trabajo (1)	Labor Day
Cinco de Mayo (5) (México)	Cinco de Mayo (May 5th) (Mexico)
Día de las Madres	Mother's Day
Independencia Patria (Paraguay) (15)	Independence Day (Paraguay)
Día Conmemorativo	Memorial Day
junio	June
Día de los Padres	Father's Day
Día de la Bandera (14)	Flag Day
Día del Indio (Perú) (24)	Native People's Day (Peru)
julio	July
Día de la Independencia de los Estados Unidos (4)	Independence Day (United States)
Día de la Independencia de Venezuela (5)	Independence Day (Venezuela)
Día de la Independencia de la Argentina (9)	Independence Day (Argentina)
Día de la Independencia de Colombia (20)	Independence Day (Colombia)
Nacimiento de Simón Bolívar (24)	Simón Bolívar's Birthday
Día de la Revolución (Cuba) (26)	Revolution Day (Cuba)
Día de la Independencia del Perú (28)	Independence Day (Peru)
agosto	August
Día de la Independencia de Bolivia (6)	Independence Day (Bolivia)
Día de la Independencia del Ecuador (10)	Independence Day (Ecuador)
Día de San Martín (Argentina) (17)	San Martín Day (anniversary of his death) (Argentina)
Día de la Independencia del Uruguay (25)	Independence Day (Uruguay)
septiembre	September
Día del Trabajo (EE. UU.)	Labor Day (U.S.)
Día de la Independencia de Costa Rica, El Salvador, Guatemala, Honduras y Nicaragua (15)	Independence Day (Costa Rica, El Salvador, Guatemala, Honduras, Nicaragua)
Día de la Independencia de México (16)	Independence Day (Mexico)
Día de la Independencia de Chile (18)	Independence Day (Chile)
Año Nuevo Judío	Jewish New Year
Día de la Virgen de las Mercedes (Perú) (24)	Day of the Virgin of Mercedes (Peru)
octubre	October
Día de la Raza (12)	Columbus Day
Noche de Brujas (31)	Halloween
noviembre	November
Día de los Muertos (2)	All Souls Day
Día de los Veteranos (11)	Veterans' Day
Día de la Revolución Mexicana (20)	Mexican Revolution Day
Día de Acción de Gracias	Thanksgiving
Día de la Independencia de Panamá (28)	Independence Day (Panama)
diciembre	December
Día de la Virgen (8)	Day of the Virgin
Día de la Virgen de Guadalupe (México) (12)	Day of the Virgin of Guadalupe (Mexico)
Januká	Chanukah
Nochebuena (24)	Christmas Eve
Navidad (25)	Christmas
Año Viejo (31)	New Year's Eve

NOTE: In Spanish, dates are written with the day first, then the month. Christmas Day is **el 25 de diciembre**. In Latin America and in Europe, abbreviated dates also follow this pattern. Halloween, for example, falls on 31/10. You may also see the numbers in dates separated by periods: 27.4.16. When referring to centuries, roman numerals are always used. The 16th century, therefore, is **el siglo XVI**.

PESOS Y MEDIDAS

WEIGHTS AND MEASURES

Longitud

Length

El sistema métrico Metric system	El equivalente estadounidense U.S. equivalent
milímetro = 0,001 metro millimeter = 0.001 meter	= 0.039 inch
centímetro = 0,01 metro centimeter = 0.01 meter	= 0.39 inch
decímetro = 0,1 metro decimeter = 0.1 meter	= 3.94 inches
metro meter	= 39.4 inches
decámetro = 10 metros dekameter = 10 meters	= 32.8 feet
hectómetro = 100 metros hectometer = 100 meters	= 328 feet
kilómetro = 1.000 metros kilometer = 1,000 meters	= .62 mile
U.S. system **El sistema estadounidense**	Metric equivalent **El equivalente métrico**
inch	= 2.54 centimeters
pulgada	**= 2,54 centímetros**
foot = 12 inches	= 30.48 centimeters
pie = 12 pulgadas	**= 30,48 centímetros**
yard = 3 feet	= 0.914 meter
yarda = 3 pies	**= 0,914 metro**
mile = 5,280 feet	= 1.609 kilometers
milla = 5.280 pies	**= 1,609 kilómetros**

Superficie

Surface Area

El sistema métrico Metric system	El equivalente estadounidense U.S. equivalent
metro cuadrado square meter	= 10.764 square feet
área = 100 metros cuadrados area = 100 square meters	= 0.025 acre
hectárea = 100 áreas hectare = 100 ares	= 2.471 acres
U.S. system **El sistema estadounidense**	Metric equivalent **El equivalente métrico**

yarda cuadrada = 9 pies cuadrados = 0,836 metros cuadrados
square yard = 9 square feet = 0.836 square meters
acre = 4.840 yardas cuadradas = 0,405 hectáreas
acre = 4,840 square yards = 0.405 hectares

Capacidad

Capacity

El sistema métrico Metric system	El equivalente estadounidense U.S. equivalent
mililitro = 0,001 litro milliliter = 0.001 liter	= 0.034 ounces
centilitro = 0,01 litro centiliter = 0.01 liter	= 0.34 ounces
decilitro = 0,1 litro deciliter = 0.1 liter	= 3.4 ounces
litro liter	= 1.06 quarts
decalitro = 10 litros dekaliter = 10 liters	= 2.64 gallons
hectolitro = 100 litros hectoliter = 100 liters	= 26.4 gallons
kilolitro = 1.000 litros kiloliter = 1,000 liters	= 264 gallons
U.S. system **El sistema estadounidense**	Metric equivalent **El equivalente métrico**
ounce	= 29.6 milliliters
onza	**= 29,6 mililitros**
cup = 8 ounces	= 236 milliliters
taza = 8 onzas	**= 236 mililitros**
pint = 2 cups	= 0.47 liters
pinta = 2 tazas	**= 0,47 litros**
quart = 2 pints	= 0.95 liters
cuarto = 2 pintas	**= 0,95 litros**
gallon = 4 quarts	= 3.79 liters
galón = 4 cuartos	**= 3,79 litros**

Peso

Weight

El sistema métrico Metric system	El equivalente estadounidense U.S. equivalent
miligramo = 0,001 gramo milligram = 0.001 gram	
gramo gram	= 0.035 ounce
decagramo = 10 gramos dekagram = 10 grams	= 0.35 ounces
hectogramo = 100 gramos hectogram = 100 grams	= 3.5 ounces
kilogramo = 1.000 gramos kilogram = 1,000 grams	= 2.2 pounds
tonelada (métrica) = 1.000 kilogramos metric ton = 1,000 kilograms	= 1.1 tons
U.S. system **El sistema estadounidense**	Metric equivalent **El equivalente métrico**
ounce	= 28.35 grams
onza	**= 28,35 gramos**
pound = 16 ounces	= 0.45 kilograms
libra = 16 onzas	**= 0,45 kilogramos**
ton = 2,000 pounds	= 0.9 metric tons
tonelada = 2.000 libras	**= 0,9 toneladas métricas**

Temperatura

Grados centígrados
Degrees Celsius
To convert from Celsius to Fahrenheit, multiply by $\frac{9}{5}$ and add 32.

Temperature

Grados Fahrenheit
Degrees Fahrenheit
To convert from Fahrenheit to Celsius, subtract 32 and multiply by $\frac{5}{9}$.

NÚMEROS

Números ordinales

primer, primero/a	**1º/1ª**	first	1st
segundo/a	**2º/2ª**	second	2nd
tercer, tercero/a	**3º/3ª**	third	3rd
cuarto/a	**4º/4ª**	fourth	4th
quinto/a	**5º/5ª**	fifth	5th
sexto/a	**6º/6ª**	sixth	6th
séptimo/a	**7º/7ª**	seventh	7th
octavo/a	**8º/8ª**	eighth	8th
noveno/a	**9º/9ª**	ninth	9th
décimo/a	**10º/10ª**	tenth	10th

Fracciones

$\frac{1}{2}$	**un medio, la mitad**	one half
$\frac{1}{3}$	**un tercio**	one third
$\frac{1}{4}$	**un cuarto**	one fourth (quarter)
$\frac{1}{5}$	**un quinto**	one fifth
$\frac{1}{6}$	**un sexto**	one sixth
$\frac{1}{7}$	**un séptimo**	one seventh
$\frac{1}{8}$	**un octavo**	one eighth
$\frac{1}{9}$	**un noveno**	one ninth
$\frac{1}{10}$	**un décimo**	one tenth
$\frac{2}{3}$	**dos tercios**	two thirds
$\frac{3}{4}$	**tres cuartos**	three fourths (quarters)
$\frac{5}{8}$	**cinco octavos**	five eighths

Decimales

un décimo	**0,1**	one tenth	0.1
un centésimo	**0,01**	one hundredth	0.01
un milésimo	**0,001**	one thousandth	0.001

NUMBERS

Ordinal numbers

Fractions

Decimals

OCUPACIONES	OCCUPATIONS
el/la abogado/a	lawyer
el actor, la actriz	actor
el/la administrador(a) de empresas	business administrator
el/la agente de bienes raíces	real estate agent
el/la agente de seguros	insurance agent
el/la agricultor(a)	farmer
el/la arqueólogo/a	archaeologist
el/la arquitecto/a	architect
el/la artesano/a	artisan
el/la auxiliar de vuelo	flight attendant
el/la basurero/a	garbage collector
el/la bibliotecario/a	librarian
el/la bombero/a	firefighter
el/la cajero/a	bank teller, cashier
el/la camionero/a	truck driver
el/la cantinero/a	bartender
el/la carnicero/a	butcher
el/la carpintero/a	carpenter
el/la científico/a	scientist
el/la cirujano/a	surgeon
el/la cobrador(a)	bill collector
el/la cocinero/a	cook, chef
el/la comprador(a)	buyer
el/la consejero/a	counselor, advisor
el/la contador(a)	accountant
el/la corredor(a) de bolsa	stockbroker
el/la diplomático/a	diplomat
el/la diseñador(a) (gráfico/a)	(graphic) designer
el/la electricista	electrician
el/la empresario/a de pompas fúnebres	funeral director
el/la especialista en dietética	dietician
el/la fisioterapeuta	physical therapist
el/la fotógrafo/a	photographer
el/la higienista dental	dental hygienist
el hombre/la mujer de negocios	businessperson
el/la ingeniero/a en computación	computer engineer
el/la intérprete	interpreter
el/la juez(a)	judge
el/la maestro/a	elementary school teacher
el/la marinero/a	sailor
el/la obrero/a	manual laborer
el/la obrero/a de la construcción	construction worker
el/la oficial de prisión	prision guard
el/la optometrista	optometrist
el/la panadero/a	baker
el/la paramédico/a	paramedic
el/la peluquero/a	hairdresser
el/la piloto	pilot
el/la pintor(a)	painter
el/la plomero/a	plumber
el/la político/a	politician
el/la programador(a)	computer programer
el/la psicólogo/a	psychologist
el/la quiropráctico/a	chiropractor
el/la redactor(a)	editor
el/la reportero/a	reporter
el/la sastre	tailor
el/la secretario/a	secretary
el/la supervisor(a)	supervisor
el/la técnico/a (en computación)	(computer) technician
el/la vendedor(a)	sales representative
el/la veterinario/a	veterinarian

A

absolute superlatives (8) **286**
acabar de + *infinitive* (6) **207**
academic courses (2) **40, 41, 76**
accents (4) **123**
adjectives
  demonstrative (6) **210**
  descriptive (3), (6) **88, 114, 192, 224**
  nationality (3) **89, 114**
  position (3) **90**
  possessive (3) **93**
  ser with adjectives (3) **88**
age questions (3) **83, 101**
al (contraction) (4) **126**
alphabet, Spanish (1) **9**
articles, definite and indefinite (1) **14**

B

b (5) **161**
bathroom objects (7) **226, 260**
birthdays (9) **300, 330**
body parts (7) **226, 260**
buildings
  campus (2) **40, 76**
  general (4) **118, 150**

C

c (8) **271**
campus buildings (2) **40, 76**
celebrations (9) **300, 330**
classroom objects and people (2) **40, 76**
clothing (6) **190, 224**
colors (3), (6) **89, 114, 192, 224**
comparisons (8) **281**
conducir
  present tense (6) **200**
  preterite tense (9) **310**
conocer and **saber** (6) **200**
courses (academic) (2) **40, 76**
courtesy expressions (1) **2, 7, 38**
Cultura
  Carolina Herrera (6) **199**
  Las cataratas del Iguazú (5) **162**
  ¿Cómo te llamas? (3) **86**
  La escuela secundaria (2) **48**
  La familia real española (3) **87**
  Ferran Adrià: arte en la cocina (8) **273**
  Festival de Viña del Mar (9) **309**
  Frutas y verduras de América (8) **272**
  El INFRAMEN (2) **49**
  El mate (7) **235**
  Los mercados al aire libre (6) **198**
  Miguel Cabrera y Paola Espinosa (4) **125**
  La plaza principal (1) **11**
  Punta del Este (5) **163**
  Real Madrid y Barça: rivalidad total (4) **124**
  Saludos y besos en los países hispanos (1) **10**
  Semana Santa: vacaciones y tradición (9) **308**
  La siesta (7) **234**

D

d (6) **197**
daily schedules (7) **226, 260**
dar
  expressions (6) **203**
  present tense (6) **203**
  preterite tense (9) **311**
dates (months) (5) **154**
days of the week (2) **42, 76**
decir
  expressions (4) **136**
  present tense (4) **133**
  preterite tense (9) **310**
definite articles (1) **14**
del (contraction) (1) **20**
demonstrative adjectives and pronouns (6) **210**
describing clothes (6) **190, 195, 224**
describing routines (7) **226, 260**
descriptive adjectives (3), (6) **88, 114, 192, 224**
diphthongs and linking (3) **85**
direct objects: nouns and pronouns (5) **174**
diversions, related verbs (9) **300, 330**
double object pronouns (8) **277**

E

entertainment, related verbs (9) **300, 330**
estar
  comparing **ser** and **estar** (5) **170**
  present tense (2) **59**
  preterite tense (9) **310**
  with conditions (5) **164**
  with emotions (5) **164**
  with health conditions (2) **59**
  with location (2) **59**

F

family members and relatives (3) **78, 114**
farewells (1) **2, 38**
food and drink (8) **262, 264, 298**
  parties, related foods (9) **300, 330**
forming questions (2) **55**

G

g (9) **307**
greetings and introductions (1) **2, 38**
grooming, personal (7) **226, 260**
gusta(n), me/te (2) **45, 52**
gustar (2) **52**
  verbs like **gustar** (7) **246**

H

h (9) **307**
hacer
  present tense (4) **136**
  preterite tense (9) **310**
hay (1) **16**
health
  conditions with **estar** (5) **164**
  questions (1) **2, 38**
hotels (5) **152, 188**
hygiene, personal (7) **226, 260**

I

indefinite articles (1) **14**
indefinite words (7) **240**
indirect object pronouns (6) **202**
information questions (2) **55**
interrogative words (2) **56**
intonation, question (2) **55**
introductions (1) **2, 38**
ir
  present tense (4) **126**
  preterite tense (7) **244**
  ir a + *infinitive* (4) **126**
irregular verbs
  preterite tense (9) **310**

J

j (9) **307**

L

life's stages (9) **302, 330**
linking (3) **85**
ll (8) **271**
location with **estar** (2) **59**

M

meals (8) **264, 298**
months of the year (5) **154**

N

names of Spanish-speaking countries (1) **38**
negation with **no** (2) **51**
negative words (7) **240**
nouns (1) **12**
numbers
  0–30 (1) **16**

31 and higher (2) **63**
ordinal (5) **155, 188**

Ñ

ñ (8) **271**

O

object pronouns
direct (5) **174**
double (8) **277**
indirect (6) **202**
prepositional (9) **318**
reflexive (7) **236**
occupations (3) **78, 114**
ofrecer, present tense (6) **200**
oír, present tense (4) **137**
ordinal numbers (5) **155, 188**

P

Panorama
Canadá (1) **36**
Chile (9) **328**
Cuba (6) **222**
Ecuador (3) **112**
España (2) **74**
Estados Unidos (1) **36**
Guatemala (8) **296**
México (4) **148**
Perú (7) **258**
Puerto Rico (5) **186**
participles
present with progressive tenses (5) **166**
parties, related people, items, foods (9) **300, 330**
parts of the body (7) **226, 260**
pastimes (4) **116, 150**
pero vs. **sino** (7) **241**
personal **a** (5) **174**
pluralization of nouns (1) **13**
poder
present tense (4) **130**
preterite tense (9) **310**
poner
present tense (4) **136**
preterite tense (9) **310**
position of adjectives (3) **90**
possessive adjectives (3) **93**
prepositions often used with **estar** (2) **60**
prepositional object pronouns (9) **318**
preterite tense
regular verbs (6) **206**
irregular verbs (9) **310**
verbs that change meaning (9) **314**
professions (3) **78, 114**
progressive tense
present (5) **166**
pronouns
demonstratives (6) **210**
direct object (5) **174**
double object (8) **277**
indirect object (6) **202**
prepositional object (9) **318**
reflexive (7) **236**
subject (1) **19**
use and omission of subject pronouns (2) **52**

Q

querer, preterite tense (9) **310**
questions, forming (2) **55**
age (3) **83**
information questions (2) **55**
intonation for questions (2) **55, 56**
¿qué? and **¿cuál?** (9) **316**
question words (2) **56**
tag questions (2) **55**

R

r and **rr** (7) **233**
reflexive verbs (7) **236**
regular verbs
present tense
-ar verbs (2) **50**
-er and **-ir** verbs (3) **96**
preterite (6) **206**
restaurants (8) **269**
routines (7) **226, 260**

S

saber
and **conocer** (6) **200**
preterite tense (9) **310**
salir, present tense (4) **136**
school vocabulary (2) **40, 76**
se constructions
reflexive verbs (7) **236**
seasons of the year (5) **154**
sequencing actions, words for (7) **226, 260**
ser
comparing **ser** and **estar** (5) **170**
present tense (1) **20**
preterite tense (7) **244**
to show identification (1) **20**
to show origin (1) **21**
to show possession (1) **20**
with adjectives (3) **88**
with nationalities (3) **89**
with professions (1) **21**
shopping (6) **190, 224**
Spanish alphabet (1) **9**
Spanish-speaking countries, names of (1) **38**
sports and leisure activities (4) **116, 150**
stages of life (9) **302, 330**
stem-changing verbs
present tense (4) **129, 133**
preterite tense (8) **274**
stress and accent marks (4) **123**
subject pronouns (1) **19**
use and omission (2) **52**
superlatives (8) **286**
absolute superlatives (8) **286**

T

t (6) **197**
tag questions (2) **55**
tener
expressions with (3) **101**
present tense (3) **100**
preterite tense (9) **310**
telling time (1) **24**
town places (4) **118, 150**
traducir
present tense (6) **200**
preterite tense (9) **310**
traer
present tense (4) **136**
preterite tense (9) **310**
travel terms (5) **152, 188**

V

v (5) **161**
vacation vocabulary (5) **152, 188**
venir
present tense (3) **100**
preterite tense (9) **310**
ver
present tense (4) **137**
verbs describing routines and personal grooming (7) **226, 260**
verbs like **gustar** (7) **246**
verbs that change meaning in the preterite (9) **314**
verbs with irregular **yo** forms (**hacer, oír, poner, salir, traer,** and **ver**) (4) **136, 137**
vowels (2) **47**

W

weather expressions (5) **154**
work-related terms (3) **78, 114**

Y

years (e.g. 2007) (2) **64**

Z

z (8) **271**

Every effort has been made to trace the copyright holders of the works published herein. If proper copyright acknowledgment has not been made, please contact the publisher and we will correct the information in future printings.

Photography and Art Credits

All images © Vista Higher Learning unless otherwise noted.

Cover: Robert Hamm/Alamy.

Front Matter (SE): xviii: (l) Bettmann/Corbis; (r) Florian Biamm/123RF; **xix:** (l) Lawrence Manning/Corbis; (r) Design Pics Inc/Alamy; **xx:** José Blanco; **xxi:** (l) Digital Vision/Getty Images; (r) Andres/Big Stock Photo; **xxii:** Fotolia IV/Fotolia; **xxiii:** (l) Goodshoot/Corbis; (r) Tyler Olson/Shutterstock; **xxiv:** Shelly Wall/Shutterstock; **xxv:** (t) Colorblind/Corbis; (b) Moodboard/Fotolia; **xxvi:** (t) Digital Vision/Getty Images; (b) Purestock/Getty Images.

Front Matter (TE): T15: Mike Flippo/Shutterstock; **T16:** Jean Glueck/Media Bakery; **T35:** SimmiSimons/iStockphoto; **T39:** Monkeybusinessimages/Big Stock Photo.

Lección preliminar: 1: Somos/Media Bakery; **8:** *The Encounter between Hernando Cortes (1485-1547) and Montezuma II (1466-1520), from Le Costume Ancien et Moderne, Volume I,* plate 63, by Jules Ferrario, published c.1820s-30s (colour engraving), Gallina, Gallo (1796-1874)/Private Collection/The Stapleton Collection/Bridgeman Images; **9:** Craig Lovell/Eagle Visions Photography/Alamy; **16:** Agan/Shutterstock.

Lesson 5: 151: DreamPictures/Media Bakery; **162:** Gary Cook/Alamy; **163:** (t) AFP/Getty Images; (b) Pierre-Yves Babelon/123RF; **167:** Iofoto/Fotolia; **180:** Steven Gaertner/123RF; **181:** (tl) Corel/Corbis; (tr) Reed Kaestner/Corbis; (m) Juice Images/Alamy; (b) Gabriela Medina/Blend Images/Getty Images; **182:** Carolina Zapata; **186:** (tl) Miguel A. Alvarez/Shutterstock; (tr) José Blanco; (ml) Teresa Canino Rivera/Nuevo Dia de Meta/Newscom; (mr) Capricornis Photographic Inc/Shutterstock; (b) Dave G. Houser/Corbis; **187:** (tl) José Blanco; (tr) Anton Gvozdikov/Shutterstock; (br) PhotoDisc/Getty Images; (bl) Chris Parypa Photography/Shutterstock.

Lesson 6: 189: Asiapix Royalty-Free/Inmagine; **198:** (l) Jose Caballero Digital Press Photos/Newscom; (r) Janet Dracksdorf; **199:** (t) Carlos Alvarez/Getty Images; (bl) Guiseppe Carace/Getty Images; (br) Mark Mainz/Getty Images; **201:** Jack Hollingsworth/Corbis; **204:** (all) Pascal Pernix; **209:** (all) Martín Bernetti; **210:** (all) Paula Díez; **211:** Paula Díez; **216:** Paula Díez; **217:** Paula Díez; **218:** Chris Schmidt/iStockphoto; **219:** Martín Bernetti; **222:** (t, mtl, mtr, mb) Pascal Pernix; (b) PhotoDisc/Getty Images; **223:** (tl) Drew A. Kelley/ZUMA Press/Newscom; (tr, bl) Pascal Pernix; (br) Road Movie Prods/The Kobal Collection.

Lesson 7: 225: Karen Montoya Betancur; **234:** Stewart Cohen/Blend Images/Corbis; **235:** (t) Ali Burafi; (b) Janet Dracksdorf; **237:** (l) Blend Images/Alamy; (r) Arek Malang/Shutterstock; **239:** (l) Martín Bernetti; (r) MediaBakery; **242:** José Blanco; **243:** Monkey Business Images/Shutterstock; **252-253:** Didem Hizar/Fotolia; **254:** Traveler/Shutterstock; **255:** Blend Images/Alamy; **258:** (t, mtr) Martín Bernetti; (ml) Daniel Ferreia-Leites/123RF; (mbl) Joao Relvas/EPA/Newscom; (mbr) Kobby Dagan /123RF; (b) Yann Arthus-Bertrand/Corbis; **259:** (tl) Elzbieta Sekowska/Shutterstock; (tr) Mick Roessler/Corbis; (bl) Andrey Gontarev/Shutterstock; (br) Marshall Bruce/iStockphoto.

Lesson 8: 261: Liliana P. Bobadilla; **267:** (l) Somos Images/Alamy; (r) Monkeybusinessimages/Big Stock Photo; **272:** (t) Rachel Distler; (b) MediaBakery; **273:** (t) Carlos Cazalis/Corbis; (bl) Foodio/Shutterstock; (br) Carlos Cazalis/Corbis; **276:** Paula Díez; **278:** (l) Pixtal/AGE Fotostock; (r) José Blanco; **282:** (l) Pascal Pernix; (r) José Blanco; **283:** (l) José Blanco; (r) Monkey Business Images/Shutterstock; **292:** Vanessa Bertozzi; **293:** Jack Hollingsworth/Getty Images; **296:** (t) Henryk Sadura/Shutterstock; (mt) Michael DeFreitas/Media Bakery; (mb) Henryk Sadura/Shutterstock; (b) Dave G. Houser/Corbis; **297:** (tl) Jenkedco/Shutterstock; (tr) Michael Fischer/Media Bakery; (bl) Vladimir Korostyshevskiy/Shutterstock; (br) Bill Bachmann/Danita Delimont Photography/Newscom.

Lesson 9: 299: Hill Street Studios/Blend Images RM/AGE Fotostock; **303:** Image Source/AGE Fotostock; **308:** (l) Silvia B. Jakiello/Shutterstock; (r) PictureNet/Corbis; **309:** (t) Simon Cruz/AP Images; (b) Rune Hellestad/Corbis; **322:** (t) Katrina Brown/123RF; (b) Esteban Corbo; **323:** Armando Brito; **324:** Monkeybusinessimages/Big Stock Photo; **328:** (tl, tr, mtr) Lauren Krolick; (mtl) Kathryn Alena Korf; (mbl) Bettmann/Corbis; (mbr) Macarena Minguell/AFP/Getty Images; (b) Bruce R. Korf; **329:** (tl) Lars Rosen Gunnilstam; (tr, br) Lauren Krolick; (bl) Nikolay Starchenko/Shutterstock.

Television Credits

184 © Santander Chile.
220 Courtesy of Cinematheque Jean Marie Boursicot.
256 Courtesy of Asepxia, Genommalab and Kepel & Mata.
294 Courtesy of Arroz Roa.
326 Courtesy of Javier Ugarte, Chilevision Network. Santiago, Chile.